THE EMOTIONALLY RESILIENT EXPAT

ENGAGE, ADAPT AND THRIVE ACROSS CULTURES

Linda A. Janssen

"The original premise of this book, even the need for this book, comes from our time in history. We are today a world which is indeed global and wanting to be resilient, happy, and engaged. Linda A. Janssen reminds us we can maintain, enhance, restore and renew our levels of resiliency. It may take time, effort, energy, persistence and mindful attention, but it is possible. We can only look forward to more from her."

Julia Simens Author, *Emotional Resilience and the Expat Child*. www.jsimens.com

"The topic of emotional resiliency is near and dear to my own heart, and in *The Emotionally Resilient Expat: Engage, Adapt and Thrive Across Cultures,* Janssen has written a comprehensive guide to help expats navigate the multiple challenges and stresses that come with living overseas. Reading this will help parents to become more aware of the experiences their children and adolescents might face, and find tools that will help their families to become more resilient. School personnel and therapists who work with Third Culture Kids will also benefit from reading this book if they want to truly understand the joys, as well as the tribulations, of life outside one's home culture and country."

Rebecca Grappo, Med. http://rnginternational.com

"Have you ever tried to explain something to your children in the hope they would just listen and take your word for it? That they wouldn't have to find it out the hard way by actually experiencing it? Welcome to a parental treasure trove. In writing this book, Linda Janssen takes us under her parental wing and invites us to do just that: listen. Browse this book before you move. Flip through its pages while unpacking boxes. Open it randomly in the fall, winter, and spring. When you reach the end, start all over again.

These pages contain a well-written harvest of wisdom, both Janssen's own and that of many wise others, gleaned from many fields of human experience. As with any food rich in nutrition, this book is best sampled regularly and digested slowly. If Janssen had had a book like this at her disposal, she might not have had to write this herself, meaning we wouldn't be able to read it. Go figure. That must be the power of emotional resilience."

Drs. Douglas W. Ota
NIP Psychologist, NMI Mediator, Family Therapist. www.dougota.nl

"Janssen skillfully weaves her own thoughts and experiences with those who have lived, loved and studied all facets of the expatriate life. With this book, which should be packed in the suitcase of anyone heading to that vast unknown, Expatland, the chances of becoming The Emotionally Resilient Expat will be significantly increased."

Apple Gidley
Author, *Expat Life Slice by Slice*. http://my.telegraph.co.uk/applegidley

"Linda A. Janssen provides the modern day expat with a roadmap of emotional resilience. A rich smorgasbord of tools and techniques, including a diverse selection of personal vignettes, current research/ theory and her own experience, invaluable help is at hand for those facing the challenges encountered in a new culture."

Laura J. Stephens, MBACP
Author, *An Inconvenient Posting: An Expat Wife's Memoir of Lost Identity*.
http://laurajstephens.com

"What's it like down your neck of the expat woods? Exhilarating? Challenging? Tough? Isolating? Life-enhancing? Alienating? All these things wrapped up in a bow? You are not alone. We live in a global village where it has never been easier to pitch a tent in a foreign field. But it's a sprawling village of brain-aching complexity and diversity, which can stump even the most adventurous and resilient. Janssen has managed to capture the very essence of what it means to try a different culture on for size, assembling an exhaustive toolkit to help the expat explorer adapt and prosper. It's quite a coup."

Jack Scott
Author, *Perking the Pansies*. www.perkingthepansies.com

"*The Emotionally Resilient Expat* is a siren call for establishing resilience as a key function of successful expat life. Linda Janssen presents the research you need, and an intellectually responsible guide for a great workout in the mind-gym of emotional resilience. A true guide is someone who has taken the path and knows her ways around the gym. Janssen lives on the path and shows how she and others have grown fully fit for the ups and downs of global living.

She rightly cites identity as a core issue, especially for those of us who live overseas. Looking at what is meant by cultural congruence, she tackles the challenge of how we can keep that identity in spite of where we live. The highlight of this wonderful book is, for me, the fact Janssen sees accompanying spouses as an answer to the challenge of cross cultural adjustment, and not the problem.* HR professionals, take note!"

Kathleen McAnear Smith
Author, *Parents on the Move!* and *Beyond Broken Families* www.parentsonthemove.com

*Based in part on the Report of the *Career Choice and the Accompanying Partner Survey* Evelyn Simpson & Louise Wiles

The Emotionally Resilient Expat: Engage, Adapt and Thrive Across Cultures
by Linda A. Janssen

First published Great Britain 2013

© Copyright Linda A. Janssen

ISBN 978-1-909193-33-8

Design by Lemonberry
www.lemonberry.com

DEDICATION

To Son and Daughter, who have grown immeasurably while exploring the world, embracing the opportunities and overcoming the challenges of living across cultures.

To Husband, my partner in marriage, parenting, international living and life. Your unwavering support is such a gift, encouraging me to dream big, tackle new challenges and enjoy the journey along the way.

ACKNOWLEDGEMENTS

The list of people who have helped shape, contribute to and support this project is exhaustive, and to thank each and every one threatens unintended oversight. There are, however, a small number whose participation and guidance have been so instrumental, that without their input this book wouldn't exist.

Ruth Van Reken has been, and remains, a driving force in bringing people together to share their collective experience and wisdom, to help those who come after. Beginning a dialogue back in 2011, seeing how positively you responded to my hope that this book would 'continue the conversation', the back-and-forth discussions which have challenged and reaffirmed my thoughts – these are the special moments from which this book emerged. You are an inspiration to many.

I wish to heartily thank the authors of the foreword, Tina Quick, and the afterword, Julia Simens, for continuing to share their insights in a manner that reinforces the experiences and stories of so many. I thank them and fellow luminaries including Robin Pascoe, Barbara Schaetti, Anne Copeland, Janet Bennett, Duncan Westwood, Doug Ota and the late David Pollock, among others, for their collective body of work. I am deeply appreciative of how they have researched and expanded on prior topics and introduced new insights.

The many contributors who responded to my queries have my immense gratitude for opening their souls and sharing their stories.

Thank you to all authors quoted throughout the book. I value the knowledge shared in their books and articles, and have made every effort to accurately reflect and fully attribute their work.

A special thank you to Jo Parfitt of Summertime Publishing, my publisher and writing mentor, as her ongoing support helped bring this book to fruition.

Thank you also to Lisa Hall of Lemonberry for design of the covers and layout. You made physical my vision of the look and feel of this book, always a delight to work with.

Above all, I am firmly indebted to Jane Dean, my trusted advisor, editor and dear friend. From the very beginning you had a clear understanding of my intent and my writing voice, and always ensured I stayed true to both. Despite innumerable delays on my part, in your patient, professional hands, I never feared or waivered.

Finally, deepest gratitude and love for my family's interest, patience and support. You are the reason this book was written.

TABLE OF CONTENTS

PART I: UNDERSTANDING EXPATRIATE, CROSS-CULTURAL LIFE

GATHERING STORM

PART II: PIECES OF THE EMOTIONAL RESILIENCE PUZZLE

HOWLING WINDS

PART III: PUTTING IT ALL TOGETHER

LIGHTNING UNLEASHED

PART IV: THE EMOTIONALLY RESILIENT EXPAT

STORM'S AFTERMATH

FOREWORD

Peshawar, Pakistan in 1989 was a dusty, unsanitary, over-populated city in the Frontier Province, reminiscent in many ways of the US Wild West. A reconnaissance visit six months earlier convinced me this was no place for a family with two toddlers in tow, but my charming husband was too persuasive to refuse. I gave in to the rationalization that this overseas posting would mean less work travel on his part. I decided to treat this complete upheaval in our lives as an adventure.

Despite all the thrills of having house help for the first time in my adult life and thriving in the daily routines of meeting up with friends and playing tennis at the American Club, three months into our relocation I hit rock bottom. I experienced a deep and continued sadness I could not explain or shake off. It brought back a flood of childhood memories of frequent losses and separations. (The dictates of my father's military career had forced 15 family moves by the time I hit the sixth grade.)

Suddenly, and mercifully, I remembered the unsolicited advice offered from a complete stranger I had bumped into months earlier, at our farewell party hosted by my husband's organization. He told me that after I had been in Pakistan for three months I would hate it there, get depressed and want to go home. The next piece of advice he offered most likely saved me and my marriage. He said, "Don't worry. It will go away and you will be fine." His serendipitous words normalized for me what I now understand to be culture shock.

This is exactly what *The Emotionally Resilient Expat* offers the reader. Linda Janssen's book is the one resource that has been missing from the expat stockpile for years. Emotional resilience is a relatively new notion to me and I was deeply interested to learn, as she puts it: *'We all have a level of emotional resilience. We all have the ability to increase these reserves, and draw upon and restore our emotional resilience baseline.'*

This statement made me think – learning emotional resilience is a lot like learning a new skill, such as playing the piano or tennis. We typically take lessons and put in a lot of practice. Some people are naturally talented, will take to it more easily than others, and build on their inherent abilities to become better. How affirming it is to know we are all naturally talented in emotional resilience. We already possess the baseline, the natural talent. I believe through the experience of processing the shock and dealing with the negative emotions of this move as a young mother, coupled with all my childhood transitions, I had begun my own journey with building emotional resilience. I just didn't know it. The thoughtfully constructed chapters of this book will guide readers in building on what they already own.

Janssen does a stellar job of laying out the fundamentals of cross-cultural life and the key challenges which accompany it. It struck me instantly that the models of emotional, social and cultural intelligence – converging to build emotional resilience – are relevant to everyone, and the life changes we all encounter, whether it be at home or abroad. It is **especially** pertinent to expatriates whose international relocation entails not only having to deal with a major life transition, but also with the heaping dose of cultural changes that come along with it.

A seasoned expatriate herself, Janssen speaks directly from the heart and the head. She offers insights learned from her own family's transition struggles, and peppers the book with personal anecdotes, advice and words of self-taught wisdom other expert expats and cross-culturals openly share to help bring the subject material to life.

A personal nerve was struck as I read through Janssen's book. I was pleasantly surprised to learn that, apparently, throughout all of my family's transitions, I had intuitively employed some of the factors which help build emotional resilience. However, I had several 'Aha!' moments throughout these pages when I realized how much I had missed that could have contributed to my own and my family's reserves of resilience.

I came to understand that the time it took me to complete my cycle of transitional stages was directly proportional to the number of moves I had made. On life relocation number 26 I remember clearly telling family back home in the US, "I can't wait for it to be three months from now." What I was trying to articulate – but didn't understand – was I inherently knew it would take me that long to know how to get around my new surroundings and start establishing relationships. In other words, the time it took for me to get past the chaos of the 'transition' stage and be completely embedded in the 'entering' stage of the transition cycle.

I now recognize how, after having lived a total of 19 years abroad, I feel my TCKness more than at any other point in my life. I have come to appreciate I was perhaps doubly impacted by my search for identity as a global nomad child, and the loss of identity my adult relocations have brought about.

I received a wake-up call when I also realized how, upon repatriation, I had put my own transitional needs behind those of my husband and children. I was so busy making sure they settled in well and made strong friendships, I had not managed to build my own connections in this new place. Janssen's and other contributors' advice reminded me of the importance of community and how it is never too late to seek it and build it, even if takes a bit of effort.

And I was powerfully reminded of how we all need and are able to sustain ourselves through any life transition by being gentle with, and genuinely caring for, our 'self'.

The helpful examples, advice and strategies liberally sprinkled throughout the book have given me a packed tool kit, not only for dealing with my repatriation experience, but for all future life transitions that will undoubtedly unfold. This is true for all of us, regardless of the transition stage we are currently in, the number of moves we have made, or if we have finished with relocating altogether. The reflections in these chapters are poignant for any situation and any person – the globally mobile as well as the eternally domestic – because life is a constant journey of transitions great and small.

Wherever your baseline of emotional resilience rests, my hope is that this book will launch you into a life-long quest to build your reserves. Enjoy the journey.

Tina L. Quick

Author, *The Global Nomad's Guide to University Transition*

PREFACE

Until the second half of the twentieth century the body of literature on expatriate life has tended toward memoir – individuals sharing tales of either privilege and opulence, or hardship and deprivation, of exotic places filled with colorful characters and observable cultural distinctions. In recent years we have seen the emergence of books and articles going beyond the descriptive to analyzing the impact on individuals and families of living outside one's country or culture.

As a newly arrived expat to the Netherlands several years ago, I was fortunate enough to attend a lecture on culture shock early on. It was there I was introduced to the late David C. Pollock and the very lively Ruth Van Reken's groundbreaking book, *Third Culture Kids: Growing Up Among Worlds*. Eager to glean insights into the benefits and repercussions of living overseas, I sought answers to the nagging questions which arose, as my family and I rode the roller coaster of emotions and reactions while settling into life away from our home country and culture. I took in all Pollock and Van Reken had to offer and came away wanting to learn more.

In the intervening years I've read many books and articles and scoured websites, each pointing the way to still others. Initially all of the disparate information seemed overwhelming and confusing. The more I read, the more questions I asked and the more conversations I had with current and former expats. I struggled to make sense of what the words and theories imparted, seeking a framework in which to catalogue and convey the essence of what I, and other expats, needed to know.

As I began to take in the nuances of points made, warnings raised and recommendations offered, I started to better understand a number of key issues – identity, belonging, home, continual transitions, loss and unexpressed grief, ever present change – affecting not only expats, but all those *living across cultures*. I began thinking about the import and impact of emotional resilience, emotional and social intelligence, cultural intelligence, intercultural competence, the newer psychological field of positive psychology (also referred to as 'optimism') and mind-body connections, and what developments in these areas could bring to bear on enhancing the benefits and mitigating the challenges of expat life.

I am not a psychologist or therapist, nor an expat coach. However, I *am* an expat/cross-cultural. I'm married to an adult Third Culture Kid, and the mother of two Third Culture Kids who each envision themselves living and working abroad during their lifetime (more about these labels in *CHAPTER 1: EXPATRIATE CROSS-CULTURAL LIFE*). We live in a world in which technological developments and increased mobility have converged to fuel the exponential growth of global connectivity and human migratory patterns.

I've spent almost my entire adult life studying, traveling, working or living in the international arena. My policy-making background has taught me to studiously research, analyze and present complicated topics and issues in a clear, concise manner, and to relish the dialogue among constituencies and interested parties. I'm a firm believer in the value of bringing fresh eyes to any subject, and the benefit of listening to many voices and varying viewpoints.

In my personal quest for answers, which led to this book project, the guiding questions that have driven me have always remained the same: *What does this all mean for expats/those living across cultures? What does it mean for **my** family and for me?*

I've come to believe that emotional resilience – the psychological ability to adapt to the significant challenges, misfortunes and set-backs life throws our way, while maintaining or returning to a positive view of oneself during or after such turmoil – is absolutely essential for everyone, but *especially* for those living a mobile, cross-cultural, global life.

As I wrote this book over the last twelve months, my family and I were bombarded with a number of highly personal, extremely difficult developments which turned our lives upside down. These trials came one upon the other – Bam! Bam! Bam! – and were emotionally exhausting and physically draining at the very moments we needed to be alert, engaged and taking decisive action.

I already held a deep appreciation for both the need to maintain and renew our stores of emotional resilience and how to go about doing so. The events of this past year presented me with my own opportunities to field-test the tips and suggestions included in this book. I had already incorporated many of them into my life. As things worsened, I found myself employing more, and then more, and still more. These practices have been essential to maintaining a sense of well-being throughout this difficult period, and I believe they will work for you too. The turmoil in our family life is far from over, but even if it were, I would still continue to employ many of the recommended actions in the pages that follow.

All of us have our own level of emotional resilience, a personal baseline of resiliency, if you will. This baseline may be naturally higher or lower for some than for others. That said, I firmly believe the ability exists within each of us to develop, increase, and enhance our own emotional resilience reserves. In doing so we are not only able to raise our emotional resilience baseline, but also to draw upon it in times of difficulty and stress. We can recognize immediate benefits by improving our current – and potentially future – quality of life, resulting in the most rewarding and enriching experiences afforded by expatriate, cross-cultural life.

I know, because I've *lived* this book.

Linda A. Janssen

INTRODUCTION

Writing this book began as a journey to learn more about the challenges of expatriate life. It grew to embrace emotional resilience as integral to dealing with difficulties and change. Eventually it led to ways to increase my own reserves of resilience, those of my family and of close friends going through tough times.

I realized technological developments, increased globalization and significant growth in connectivity have all contributed to what we're seeing today – myriad permutations on people's international lives, where they've lived and how they identify themselves. The literature, research and experiences of expats can be extrapolated in great part to a much wider, cross-cultural group. I believe expats are indeed a subset of this broader group of cross-culturals – anyone who lives in, has lived in, or meaningfully interacts with two or more cultures, regardless of when in their lives this occurs or where the different cultures may be located (i.e., beyond borders or not).

At some point what began as an exercise in gaining knowledge to help loved ones became a book-in-the-making. I feel compelled to share what I've learned, especially how implementing many of the suggestions within these pages has made a difference. As life threw more and more our way, I've been grateful for stockpiling the emotional resilience reserves I have and conscientious about restoring those I've depleted.

When the going has been toughest, I have appreciated knowing if I keep doing certain things I will not only *feel* better but will *be* better, more advantageously positioned to deal with the challenges before me. What began as something I wanted to share with others has become a gift to myself.

As expats/ cross-culturals/ global nomads/ TCKs, we are the *Who*, and our intercultural, mobile life; contributing to the turmoil and upheaval we face, is the *What* in the overall schematic. Healthy identity development and congruence represent the *Why* we need emotional resilience. The transitional phases tell us *Where* we are in the transition process, and by their order, approximately *When*. Kübler-Ross's change model helps inform us *Which* stage we're in as we navigate the transition process. Emotional, social and cultural intelligence, intercultural competence, positive psychology (optimism), mindfulness and other practices, offer us tools contributing to our emotional resilience – they help us with *How* we can increase our resilience reserves to help prepare for, respond to, and ultimately bounce back from, whatever we experience.

This book is comprised of four sections, *PARTS I* through *IV*. If you wish to understand the challenges driving the need for emotional resilience, new developments that help inform ways to build resilience, practical tips and sound suggestions to implement strengthened resiliency, followed by a summary wrap-up, I suggest you read this book from start to finish. If you want to 'cut to the chase' of what to do to maintain or build up your emotional resilience, feel free to jump to *PART III*, but then do go back and fill in the blanks, as there are great recommendations and techniques throughout the book. Do you enjoy reading about the experiences of others first? Rifle through, going from story to story, and then circle back to read the accompanying text.

At the beginning of each *PART*, I share a personal snapshot of a point in my own family's experience over the last year in which we were struggling with, and severely tested by, a variety of emerging developments – either stemming directly from, or exacerbated by, expatriate life. Our story is *not* unique. If anything, talking to and hearing the stories of dozens of expats and cross-culturals from around the world has taught me just how commonplace the difficulties we experienced have been. Details and specifics may differ, but we are all dealing not only with the amazing opportunities afforded by expat life, but also with deeply challenging issues and situations, too.

PART I: UNDERSTANDING EXPATRIATE, CROSS-CULTURAL LIFE looks at the expat scene, challenges of a highly mobile, global lifestyle, key terms, phases of the transition process, stages of the change model, culture shock, identity and other issues which make intercultural life more difficult than a sedentary, monocultural one.

PART II: PIECES OF THE EMOTIONAL RESILIENCE PUZZLE looks at scientific research, social science concepts and developments in the primary areas of emotional resilience, emotional and social intelligence, cultural intelligence and intercultural competence, brain-body connections and positive psychology.

I believe wholeheartedly that everyone – every single person – who has lived, is living or aspires to live cross-culturally, can benefit greatly from enhancing and maintaining their reserves of emotional resilience. Others have championed emotional resilience in dealing with expatriate life, but I wish to draw in a much wider range of thought areas such as emotional and social intelligence, positive psychology/ optimism, visualization, mindfulness, cultural intelligence, intercultural competence, physical and emotional self-care, empathy, gratitude and more, for a more holistic approach.

How important is emotional resilience? Tiny, focused efforts to build emotional resilience through a variety of tools and techniques help us:

- Reduce stress, discomfort and emotional discord
- Avoid negative behaviors and calm self-defeating thoughts
- Pick up on signals that we, or someone we care about, are unhappy or struggling with transitions and change
- Increase positivity and humor
- Reflect gratitude, empathy and compassion
- Gain a sense of context, perspective, and connectedness
- Find greater meaning and purpose in a global life lived fully

PART III: PUTTING IT ALL TOGETHER explains how to enhance emotional resilience through tested and recommended tips, techniques and practices that help us develop much-needed connections, communication, visualization and optimism.

Above all, if it is to demonstrate its true value, this precious information has to be presented in simple terms everyone can understand and to which they can relate. This is the reason I developed **FACTORS**™ – **Family, Awareness, Communication, Transitions, Optimism, Rituals and Significance/ Something Bigger Than Ourselves** – as a framework in which the various tools, techniques, tips and practices can be sorted and more easily remembered. You can find the full accounting of FACTORS™ in *PART IV: THE EMOTIONALLY RESILIENT EXPAT*, which also concludes with a call to 'continue the conversation' of aiding and encouraging expats and cross-culturals to live healthier, more positive, emotionally engaged, culturally connected global lives.

While I have written this book in American English, the insights and stories contributed by the many expats/ cross-culturals involved in this undertaking have been left in the version of English in which they were submitted.

Finally, for their privacy, I refer to my husband and children as I have lovingly done for several years on my blog, *Adventures in Expat Land:* Husband, Son and Daughter.

Linda A. Janssen

PART I:

UNDERSTANDING EXPATRIATE, CROSS-CULTURAL LIFE

'Travel is fatal to prejudice, bigotry and narrow-mindedness, and many of our people need it sorely on these accounts. Broad, wholesome, charitable views of men and things cannot be acquired by vegetating in one little corner of the earth all one's lifetime.'

Mark Twain

GATHERING STORM

I heard the key turning in the lock of the heavy oak front door, and glanced up at the clock.

He's home early tonight, I thought to myself, pulling the baby spinach from the refrigerator and setting it on the counter. *Must have made an effort to tie up loose ends and get out early.*

A light smile played at the corners of my mouth. Pleased my husband had arrived home earlier than usual in honor of my birthday, I nudged the refrigerator door shut with my hip. I pivoted around, leaning my head back to call out my welcome down the long hallway, connecting the front hall to the kitchen of our classic Dutch *rijtjeshuis*, a narrow, three-story brick town house, "I'm in here, pulling things together for dinner."

I moved to the sink, deftly reaching up above the kitchen cabinet to pull down the wooden salad bowl before turning on the water. Grabbing the spinach from the counter, I began rinsing off the greens.

"You're home early," I said, pausing to turn my face upwards for the kiss coming my way.

"Of course," Husband said. He leaned in and gave me a quick kiss, squeezing my arm as he turned away. "It's your birthday. Time to celebrate."

He moved over toward one of the kitchen stools and perched on it, carefully transferring the folded suit jacket from his arm to the remaining empty stool. He settled in, loosened his tie and removed it.

"Where are the kids?" he asked.

"Son's upstairs, he got home a few minutes before you. I dropped off Daughter at Kaiya's house an hour ago. They're meeting up with the rest of their friends for the barbecue on the beach, remember?"

He nodded absentmindedly as he recalled the end-of-year party Daughter had been talking about for weeks. I turned off the faucet, grabbed the clean towel and began patting dry the damp spinach.

"Last night was Jennifer's birthday party. Tomorrow afternoon is Lara's farewell get together. Tonight is the beach blast," I said, throwing the spinach into the salad bowl. "I don't remember having such a full social schedule after final exams when I was in high school, do you?" I set a red pepper and some celery stalks, rinsed earlier, on the cutting board. Taking a knife from the drawer, I began dicing.

Not hearing a response, I glanced over my shoulder. Husband was gazing intently out the kitchen window into the small enclosed garden. He slowly twirled the blue silk tie around his forefinger, unwinding it gently before twirling it around again.

"I said, did you ever have such a full social..." I managed to get out before he interrupted.

"Remember that job in Geneva, the one I didn't get?"

I froze, hands poised above the last slice of pepper. Turning around slowly, I leaned back against the counter and looked up into Husband's face.

"I got a call this afternoon. There's another Senior Director position open and they want me to apply for it."

Time seemed to stand still. I could hear the soft ticking of the second hand as it swept around the Parisian-style clock face. Our cairn terrier, Oli, circled my feet, impatiently awaiting his dinner. I struggled to get my brain in gear before I engaged my mouth.

"Uh huh," I whispered. "And...?"

"I know we said the window had closed on making a move this summer, but they're looking to fill this position quickly. They want to fly me to Geneva on Tuesday for an interview. They're promising a decision within two weeks, three weeks at the most."

Slowly nodding as I took in my husband's eager face, I read the glimmer of excitement that he might finally get the promotion he deserved, in a city and country we had been thrilled to consider moving to only six months before.

"I know this is sudden, but they seem to really want me to apply."

I noted his barely concealed enthusiasm, the expectant look in his eyes. Earlier in the year Husband had just missed getting the original position, edged out at the wire by a French candidate. He had taken the news in stride, well aware that sometimes the difference between getting a job and getting passed over is political – one in which geographical representation and all manners of diversity might be in play. Still, I knew underneath he'd been disappointed.

Never mind that when the job had fallen through we'd confidently told Daughter we'd be staying put in the Netherlands for her last two years of high school. She'd bravely insisted she was game for a move when the issue was broached six months ago, but had since put it out of her mind when assured we wouldn't be moving after all. She loved her friends, her classes and her activities for the coming year, and looked forward to her junior year.

And Son? He was home with us for the summer, working at an internship after his freshman year of university back in the States. Granted, he'd already started the process of leaving the nest, but he loved The Hague and would be disappointed to leave his remaining friends and the place he'd graduated high school.

Daughter and I were getting on a plane in a week for an extended trip back to the US, which meant if he were to get the job, Husband would have to handle the logistics of househunting by himself, with me relegated to the role of an observer updated via Skype and email.

What about Oli and our cat, Ava? How would they handle the move almost five hundred miles away? We'd have to give notice to our landlord with whom we'd just extended our lease another year. Myriad details began to crowd my mind.

My thoughts turned to my elderly father's recent health scare. Diagnosed with cancer two months earlier, during tests for an upcoming surgery his doctors had discovered a pulmonary embolism. While the prognosis was good, his situation – and by extension, that of my mother – was tenuous at the moment.

What about my friends, and my writing? I was in the midst of writing my first book. Both my editor and publisher were in located in The Hague. I'd worked hard to build a fulfilling life here, and now...

"I can make it clear that accepting would have to be contingent on getting Daughter a place in the local international school," he said. "Look, I think I have a decent shot at this. I'd like to do the interview and see how it goes. If it doesn't work out, fine, we're happy to stay here. And if it does... well, it would mean altering some plans and a hectic summer, but we all agreed it would be a great place to live. Either way, we'll know in a couple weeks. What do you think?"

Our eyes met.

"Why... why that's t-terrific, honey," I managed to stammer, a grin pasted on my face. "Geneva? Huh. Wow. How great would *that* be?"

CHAPTER 1: EXPATRIATE, CROSS-CULTURAL LIFE

Living abroad can be an enriching experience of growth, broadened perspectives and enhanced cultural understanding. Yet its transition-rich, change-driven, cross-cultural nature can place considerable demands leaving us stressed, disconnected, adrift, with our identity in flux. Cultural adaptation and integration can often feel superficial, leaving us wondering whether we will ever feel involved, rooted, at home again. Building on existing expat/ global nomad/ Third Culture Kid literature, and benefitting from recent developments in psychology and brain-body connections, I believe the key to successful transitions and beyond lies in enhancing our emotional resilience. Resilience provides us significant ways to adapt, adjust or simply accept. In easily accessible layman's terms, shared in *CHAPTER 8: ENHANCING EMOTIONAL RESILIENCE*, we can get to the heart of the matter by identifying the *Who, What, When, Where, Why, Which* and *How* of emotional resilience.

While enhancing emotional resilience for a healthier, deeper, more positive expat experience, we can draw on the simple device of FACTORS™ as a reminder to focus on what are most important – Family, Awareness, Communication, Transitions, Optimism, Rituals and Significance/ Something Bigger Than Ourselves. Through FACTORS™ (more in *PART IV's CHAPTER 14: FACTORS™ IN EMOTIONAL RESILIENCE*), I capture a wide array of practical tools, techniques and best practices – emotional and social intelligence, cultural intelligence, intercultural competence, positive psychology (optimism), brain-body connections, mindfulness, stress management and relaxation, visualization, empathy, gratitude, physical and emotional self-care and related areas – to live an involved, emotionally engaged, culturally connected life.

Throughout this book I draw from the deeply personal stories shared by dozens of seasoned expats and cross-culturals, research insights, practical information, and my own experience to help others enhance emotional resilience so we all can engage, adapt and thrive across cultures.

THE EVOLVING EXPAT SCENE

According to Ernst & Young's Globalization Report, *Looking Beyond the Obvious: Globalization and New Opportunities for Growth*, released in January 2013 and based on its annual Globalization Study, Globalization Index and interviews with corporate senior executives and high-level subject matter experts, the trend is clear: *'globalization continues to define our business landscape, increasing the levels of cross-border trade, capital and labor integration.'*

Despite the international financial crisis and subsequent recessions having contributed to an overall slowdown in globalization the last few years, the rampant growth in technology and inter-connectedness continues to affect markets worldwide. The need for getting the right employees with the right skill sets in the right places at the right times will only continue to grow, boding well for those interested in working internationally: *'The overall rate of globalization is slowing, and its character is different. Although trade in goods and services is returning to pre-financial crisis levels and the flow of capital shows a stable increase, the game changer today is technology and the flow of ideas.'*

'Technology is the foundation of today's increasingly digital and connected world and it is having a profound impact on every market. By contrast, the globalization of talent is still at an early stage: businesses worldwide struggle to find workers with the right skills and experience, and pools of top talent cluster in some locations but are scarce in others.'

Several factors are contributing to this growth in mobile, global employment:

- **Intersection of technology and mobility leading to shifts in employment locales:** Cheaper, faster, more wide-reaching transportation means more people traveling and living outside their countries of birth. Jobs can go to where people are, while people can go to where jobs currently exist or are predicted to grow.

- **Technological advances fostering explosive growth of the Internet and, by extension, how we work:** Information at our fingertips allows for adjustments in where, how and what we do for work. Hardware is smaller, lighter, transportable, more durable. Advancements in software, cloud storage and social media venues allow for content creation, sharing and working more efficiently and effectively, whether collaboratively or alone, at home, in the office, or around the world. As the tools we use become more sophisticated and mobile, we are shifting toward consolidation and use of fewer devices.

- **Untethered employment as well as geographic independence:** For a growing number of occupations – writers, editors, artists and other creative types, marketers, salespeople, communications specialists, content developers, consultants, coaches, therapists – it no longer matters where you are physically located when doing your work. Since it goes wherever you go, you are free to decide where that should be.

As changes ripple through the business landscape, fewer people are working for one organization their entire career. Today younger workers (i.e., those born in the late 1970s onward), fully expect their careers will likely be spent working a series of different jobs for multiple employers. Recent and continued worldwide recession may have slowed globalization somewhat, but not the aforementioned growth in workers moving across borders for employment opportunities. At the same time, more organizations are instituting cost-cutting measures such as reducing the number of traditional expatriate employees on payroll (i.e., those whose assignments are centrally managed from headquarters).

Some workers may accept a one-time transfer assignment for a set period hoping to burnish their résumé with additional experience and skills, expecting to return or move on to something else when their time is up. Other employees are being transitioned to local contract status, or replaced altogether with 'local' hires in which employees are recruited directly for jobs in global locations as needed. The former may be undecided as to the length and scope of their life and career abroad, and the latter may not even see themselves as expats but rather as immigrants, who expect to remain indefinitely or even permanently. Some would argue growth in the number of candidates in these categories is leading to subtle changes in the nature of the profile of expatriate employment itself.

SHIFT IN CANDIDATES SEEKING EXPATRIATE JOBS

"A big impact over the past five years has been a variation in expat philosophies. As economies are changing, organisations are looking at different compensation structures and policies of sending people abroad to cut costs. This means fewer people are sent abroad on secondments. Yet more and more people are applying directly, especially to organisations based in regions such as Africa and the Middle East. This means those people originally sent by their organisations are now less likely to be travelling – and those applying directly to organisations may have a different mentality and philosophy, one perhaps focused more on earning money and less on the ambition to develop an expatriate career.

Attitudes might be more individualistic, a little more close-minded, and perhaps even less helpful. I remember many times whereby new arrivals were adopted by expatriates to assist them during their first months – nowadays this is almost nonexistent. For single individuals it is therefore more difficult to adapt and thrive in these environments. Joining groups or other events may not bring the networking and social life it used to. It can become a lonely adventure, especially if you do not have the core strength of being able to entertain yourself and keep reminding yourself of your own goals."

Nicole Le Maire, Dutch serial expat (Germany, Italy, UK, Belgium, US, Kuwait, Saudi Arabia, Jordan)

While the nature of people's expatriate experiences and the manner in which they arrive at them may be changing, the underlying need for emotional resilience does not. Living in a culture or country other than the one you are used to still brings culture shock, significant change during and after the transition, and the emergence of issues directly pertinent to the cross-cultural lifestyle. We will take a look at these developments in more depth in *CHAPTER 2: IDENTITY ISSUES IN EXPAT LIFE.*

FUNDAMENTAL EXPAT TERMS

What we mean precisely by the words and labels we use is integral to our common understanding. Before we get too far along, I think it worthwhile to define the word *expatriate* and other related terms.

AN EXPAT DEFINED

For the purposes of this book, I am using the simplest definition possible for an expat: *'one who is living outside their country.'* Merriam-Webster's dictionary adds the word native to the definition, based on the Latin *ex-* (outside of) and *patria* (one's native country). Qualifying words such as 'birth', 'home' or 'passport' are often added in the interest of clarity, they may hold heartfelt significance to the individual, but in terms of the overarching definition these modifiers tend to muddy the waters.

As an American currently living in the Netherlands, it's easy enough for me to explain that my native/ birth/ passport country is the United States, and my country of residence is the Netherlands. Ask me where home is in the context of a specific place and I'll tell you it's wherever my family and I are living. If you're talking about affinity to a country, home for me is the US.

Yet when I go to the US for a vacation or to visit family and friends, I don't say 'I'm going home', although when I'm back in the American culture I often (but not always) feel 'at home'. I usually say, 'I'm going back to the US'. When the plane lands upon my return to the Netherlands, my thought is, 'I'm home', even though I don't foresee living here beyond a few years. I may go on to live in another country, and I can also see myself repatriating (i.e., returning to my country) at least to establish a home base of sorts.

For others, it is more complicated. The world is full of people who are born in one country, have citizenship in another, maintain a passport from still another, and consider home to be one or none of the above or yet another country (or countries) in which they've lived. The borders of many countries have changed over the years, often multiple times, and entire countries have emerged or disappeared over the course of time.

I am also not making a distinction between expats and immigrants. While the former generally don't arrive expecting to stay permanently and the latter usually do, the difference can often only be made in hindsight. People immigrate with the intention of staying forever and yet return or move on. Some expats assume they will return and never do. Both are certainly cross-culturals. For those who self-identify as refugees, they, too, can fit within my use of the terms 'expats' and 'cross-culturals'.

Simply put, I am using the word expat to mean 'living outside one's country'. I leave it to the individual to determine which country or countries that might be and for whatever reason(s). Why? To each of us, *this matters.*

GLOBAL NOMADS

For many of us, the term 'global nomad' brings to mind someone with an international lifestyle, perhaps drawn by employment, love of travel or cultural interests. However, dig a little deeper and you will find the term, as originally expressed by Norma McCaig in the 1980s and later in her 1996 essay, *Understanding Global Nomads,* referred to: *'someone who has lived abroad as a child as a consequence of a parent's job.'*

The daughter of an international business executive, McCaig grew up in the Philippines, Sri Lanka and India. She went on to become a cross-cultural consultant, trainer, writer and founder of Global Nomads International, a non-profit membership organization associated with the United Nations. McCaig felt that 'global nomad' accurately reflected not only the lifestyle lived growing up around the world as the children of expats, but also the way of life many of them embraced as adults. As an adult, she also didn't like the word 'kid' as part of a label explaining her global background.

Despite McCaig's reservations, the meaning has broadened considerably, due in large part to a changing world. Most now see the term as encompassing anyone traveling the globe, and not limited to adults who grew up abroad. Additionally, for an increasing number of expats, the decision to go abroad is now separate from their – or their parents' – location-independent jobs.

I particularly like the attitude behind this quote by Apple Gidley, veteran of 26 moves in 12 countries on five continents, from her memoir, *Expat Life: Slice by Slice:'I do not claim real citizenship of any country, though I am eligible to vote in two. I claim kinship with many. I have extraordinary memories from all those I have lived in, and some from others merely visited. I love a few. I am the epitome of a global nomad. I am happy wherever I am, though naturally happier in some places than others. There are a few I have no yen to return to. There are a couple I would leap on a plane for at a moment's notice, and some unknown for which I would do the same.'*

Nowadays, the term global nomad is more often used to identify anyone who enjoys living or traveling extensively throughout our highly mobile, culturally diverse, interconnected world. Similarly, the terms 'serial wanderers', 'global citizens', 'global adventurers' or 'location independents' have gained in favor to reflect the kindred spirits whose focus is living across cultures or roaming the world, seeing and experiencing as much of this great planet as possible.

THIRD CULTURE AND THIRD CULTURE KIDS

In their book, *Third Culture Kids: Growing Up Among Worlds*, David C. Pollock and Ruth Van Reken made popular their label for children growing up internationally. It was based on the definition of a 'third culture' developed in the 1950s by noted social scientists John Useem and Ruth Hill Useem. While researching Americans living and working in India, the Useems noticed the expats living there from all over the world seemed closely affiliated with each other in a shared international expat community. The Useems identified the first culture as the home culture of the expats, the second culture as the host culture in which they found themselves living. The third culture was interstitial, that is, filling in the spaces between the two (i.e.,

> 'A Third Culture Kid (TCK) is a person who has spent a significant part of his or her developmental years outside the parents' culture. The TCK frequently builds relationships to all of the cultures, while not having full ownership in any. Although elements from each culture may be assimilated into the TCK's life experiences, the sense of belonging is in relationship to others of similar backgrounds.'

not the intersection or overlapping elements of the first and second cultures).

When Pollock and Van Reken used this definition in their book 40 years later, some readers mistook them to mean a mixing of the home and host cultures to create a blended third. I still hear people mistakenly use this 'blended' definition when trying to explain it to others. But it's much more than that. What the Useems identified, and what Pollock and Van Reken have reiterated when referring to the third culture, is one of: '*shared commonalities of those living an internationally mobile lifestyle.*'

Pollock and Van Reken chose to focus on the children of this international, cross-cultural lifestyle, with their full definition of a Third Culture Kid: *'A Third Culture Kid (TCK) is a person who has spent a significant part of his or her developmental years outside the parents' culture. The TCK frequently builds relationships to all of the cultures, while not having full ownership in any. Although elements from each culture may be assimilated into the TCK's life experiences, the sense of belonging is in relationship to others of similar backgrounds.'*

The last phrase of the definition is crucial. Children who have grown up or are growing up in mobile, global situations tend to feel kinship with others like themselves, even if the others are from different countries/ cultures and have lived in entirely different places throughout the world. Many details of their lives may be different (tropical climate or polar, temperate or dry, Muslim or Christian, Buddhist or Jewish, open versus closed cultures, and so on), but the similarities exist by virtue of their having experienced diverse countries/ cultures as they move from place to place.

In a recent discussion with Ruth Van Reken, she summed it up like this, "The place of relationship is that TCKs understand what it feels like to live a life where they are not only interacting with many different cultural worlds, but are also living a life of high mobility – one where either they or their best friends are always coming or going."

TCKs who have reached adulthood, such as my own dear Husband (born in the US to American parents, childhood years spent living in Italy and England, now residing in the Netherlands), are often referred to as Adult TCKs or ATCKs.

DUTCH, YET NOT EXACTLY

"Let me take you back some years to a remote mission in Eastern Zambia near the Great East road, which is between Lusaka and the Malawian border. Halfway through the month of February a 'foreign' baby was born there in the African bush. The mother was assisted by Polish nuns and presented with a chicken to celebrate the birth. The news of the birth travelled slowly. The father had to drive to the capital and send a telegram to their family in the Netherlands – our firstborn daughter has been born and her second name will be a local African name. Well, I was that baby and during the following 19 years of life I grew to love the continent I was born on. My dad's work took us to Malawi and Zimbabwe. Every couple of years we went on leave to my passport country, the Netherlands. I have good memories of these holidays. After finishing secondary school I decided to go to university there. Nothing had prepared me for what was ahead.

My whole life I had said I was Dutch. I spoke Dutch, I had a Dutch passport, nearly all my family lived in the Netherlands, I even look Dutch and yet suddenly I did not feel Dutch. I discovered there were many things about normal Dutch life I did not know. It is so hard to explain, it is not only about knowing things but also about feeling different. I only just survived the culture shock at the time. It certainly was an emotional roller coaster, but the worst part of it was that I did not know what was wrong with me.

Looking back I realize I really missed my parents and brothers and sister, I missed home, I missed my friends, I missed the warmth of the African sun, I missed everything. I tried to fit in, observe and do as the other students did. I was the hidden immigrant and I did not know it. I had not heard of the term Third Culture Kid. When I read the book, Third Culture Kids, Growing up Among Worlds, *by David Pollock and Ruth Van Reken, it was such a relief to discover I was not strange, but that my strange feelings had everything to do with my growing up globally.*

I think having a <u>sense of cultural identity</u> adds to your emotional resilience. There are real challenges for Third Culture Kids, children growing up in multiple countries, continents, and communities. There is an 'identity issue'. Where do I belong? Where's home? Who am I? Where do I fit in? When I was growing up in Africa I cannot remember having any real identity issues. During primary school I attended an international school so there were kids from many different nationalities. We were all different, there was no problem there. The community was constantly changing. We were saying 'hello' and 'goodbye' regularly. It was a way of life. To me it was normal. During secondary school in Zimbabwe I remember being called 'the foreigner', but even that I could accept.

Apparently it helps to have access to some information before returning to your passport culture. This can be through a debriefing, from books, online or by talking to people who have walked that path before. Looking back, I had none of these. No debriefing, no books on the subject and nobody I knew who had walked the path before me. Sometimes we TCKs wander down lonely roads.

Being prepared, being informed, knowing what is ahead helps you to face the new challenges. I think it is very important that parents, teachers, therapists and even doctors know what Third Culture Kids are and the challenges they face. Please teach your expat children about these things. Tell them what TCKs are, tell them what culture shock is and that going to their passport culture might be the greatest difficulty they will face. Make sure they have access to good books on this topic. By informing and preparing them you are increasing their emotional resilience, their inner strength. They will be better able to cope with the transition stress and the challenges ahead. Instead of slowing sliding into a depression they will live life to the full and enjoy the best of all the different cultures and countries they grew up in. They can be the emotionally resilient global citizens of this age."

Janneke Jellema,
Dutch ATCK (Zambia, Malawi, Zimbabwe) living in the Netherlands

Today there are several informative websites run by and for young and adult Third/ Cross Culture Kids (and those who care about them). They include:

- Steph Yiu – <u>www.DenizenMag.com</u>
- Heidi Sand-Hart – <u>www.HomeKeepsMoving.blogspot.com</u>

ia, MD. – www.DrieCulturen.blogspot.nl (Three Cultures, in Dutch

lobal Transitions (FIGT) – www.figt.org
nan and Diana Smit – www.expatteenstalk.blogspot.com
nd – www.interchangeinstitute.org
- Tina Quick – www.internationalfamilytransitions.com
- Julia Simens – www.jsimens.com
- Kate Berger, MSc. – www.expatkidsclub.com

All are excellent sites focusing on the range of issues affecting expat/ cross-cultural individuals and families. Similarly, there are several wonderful short videos available online made by and for Third/ Cross-Cultural Kids. Here are three:

- I Am Home: Thoughts of a Nomad – http://vimeo.com/39100216
- Third Culture Kids – http://vimeo.com/42644304
- (Military) BRATS: Our Journey Home – http://youtu.be/qCFZyG06zfY

CROSS-CULTURALS

Speaking to audiences around the world, Pollock and Van Reken found their descriptions, stories and experiences resonated with others who did not fit the stereotypical TCK description. They struck up conversation after conversation with others who saw much of themselves in the TCK model, by virtue of having grown up cross-culturally. The authors began to envision a broader framework to be included in a revised edition of their international bestseller, *Third Culture Kids: Growing Up Among Worlds*. Sadly David Pollock died while their work was underway, but Ruth Van Reken carried on with their revisions and in 2009 the latest edition was published.

In her introduction to the new volume, Van Reken cited Pollock's own words from the original edition as the basis for updating and broadening their scope from TCKs to the wider cross-cultural audience: ' ... *since we are dealing with people, we are writing about process and progress, not a fixed entity. In the past two decades alone, dramatic changes related to the care of children and adults have occurred in the global nomad community, and undoubtedly new theories and practices will continue to evolve.*'

In the two decades since Pollock wrote those words, the rate of change within the international, intercultural, mobile community has shown no signs of slowing. While TCKs and their unique experiences remain the primary focus – and indeed the title – of their book, Van Reken rolled out a framework in which TCKs are seen as one type of Cross-Cultural Kids (CCKs). She defined a cross-cultural kid as: '*a person who is living or has lived in, or has meaningfully interacted with two or more cultural environments for a significant period of time during childhood.*' Similarly, CCKs grow up to become adult CCKs (or ACCKs).

CCKs include the following sub-groups:

- 'Traditional' expatriate TCKs
- Bi-cultural or/ multicultural children
- Bi-racial or/ multiracial children
- Educational CCKs (children attending an international school with a cultural base and student mix different than the home country)
- Domestic CCKs (moving in or among various subcultures within their home country)
- International adoptees
- Children of refugees
- Children of immigrants
- Borderlanders (those living and/ or working near and continually crossing national borders into difference cultures)
- Cultural minorities within a given country

I had the pleasure of first meeting Ruth Van Reken in the spring of 2011, when she spent a day at the international school my children were attending, The American School of The Hague (ASH). She spoke to students, parents, teachers, administrators, and the local community about TCKs, culture shock, transitions, loss, belonging and home.

I offered to drive her to the ASH campus in Wassenaar for her first speaking engagement, and looked forward to asking a few questions and hearing her insights. I arrived where she was staying to find she'd severely twisted her ankle (we later learned it was broken). Despite considerable pain, Ruth insisted on persevering with her crowded itinerary – she couldn't bear to miss the chance to meet everyone and discuss these topics she holds so dear.

Later that morning I found her discussion with a group of parents so energizing, I rearranged my schedule to attend her public presentation the same evening; I could also give her a ride back to her friends' home after an exhausting day. I have fond memories of her passionately explaining the importance of examining TCK issues in the broader

> *'I am using the term 'cross-culturals' in the broadest possible sense – anyone who lives in, has lived in, or meaningfully interacts with two or more cultures, regardless of when in their lives this occurs or where those different cultures may be located (i.e., beyond borders or not).'*

context of the cross-cultural experience, as we made our way through traffic. She was excited about where the growing research and literature in the field was going, and it was sitting beside Ruth in my car that the idea of 'continuing the conversation' was born.

Given technological developments, increased globalization, and significant growth in connectivity brought on by the advent of the Internet, what we're seeing today are myriad permutations on people's experiences, who comes from where, and how they identify themselves. Intentions of staying put or moving on aren't always realized. Life intervenes and plans change.

Therefore, I believe it is important to state unequivocally: I am using the term 'cross-culturals' in the broadest possible sense – anyone who lives in, has lived in, or meaningfully interacts with two or more cultures, regardless of when in their lives this occurs or where those different cultures may be located (i.e., beyond borders or not). Thus, cross-culturals not only include CCKs, ACCKs, TCKs and ATCKs, but also those who become expats as adults and those who move to, in and out of, or otherwise join another culture.

In essence, I am drawing the line of separation between monoculturals and cross-culturals, of whom expats are a large subset. Cross-culturals can include 'stereotypical' expat families moving every three years for one or both of the parents' work, and retirees leaving one country to live in another (and who may or may not end up eventually repatriating or moving on to yet another country/ culture). They are also the eager, location-independent twenty- and thirty-somethings who can take their work to whatever countries/ cultures they choose, and the individuals, couples or families who leave one country/ culture for another and may or may not spend significant time traveling back and forth or among two or more.

Someone who grows up in one stable culture and/ or country, and then crosses cultures either as an expat or through marriage and interaction with in-laws/ extended family, may not necessarily share the same level of mobility-induced transitions, or have the same identity development issues, as TCKs/ CCKs. However, these cross-culturals will still find the body of literature and experience informative – either as a parent of children who become TCKs/ CCKs, or simply in dealing with their own identity congruence issues. They, too, go through transition phases and change stages, experience culture shock and loss of people and places that matter to them, and grapple with questions of identity, belonging, and home. (More on these issues in *CHAPTER 2: IDENTITY ISSUES IN EXPAT LIFE* and *CHAPTER 3: OTHER KEY ISSUES IN EXPAT LIFE*.)

If expats are a subset of cross-culturals, why don't I use the latter as a catchall term throughout this book? Changes in terms take time, as we've seen over the years with labels such as *expatriate, global nomad, Third Culture Kids*, and *Cross-Cultural Kids*. Many expats don't see themselves in the term *cross-culturals* and vice versa – I will use them together (*expats/ cross-culturals*) so the broadest possible audience can see themselves included, while also reinforcing the connection between the two terms.

CHALLENGES OF EXPATRIATE, CROSS-CULTURAL LIFE

Different is as different does, and cross-cultural expat life is simply that – *different*. It's no surprise the term 'alien' begins to take on an entirely new meaning. Seemingly simple questions – *Who am I? Where is home? Where do I belong?* – become complicated treatises as we are shaped and affected by the different worlds we inhabit.

That's where emotional resilience comes in. The psychological ability to adapt to or deal with significant challenges, crises or misfortunes which come our way, is invaluable in cross-cultural life. Possessing emotional resilience doesn't mean we always remain upbeat or we don't suffer when bad things occur. What it *does* mean is we do our best to maintain or find our way back to a positive mindset – and view of ourselves – as quickly as possible. And by quickly I mean as long as it takes. It depends on what we're dealing with.

Maintaining a healthy sense of identity and self in a mobile, cross-cultural life is why we need emotional resilience. In addition to many positive attributes and benefits, living such a life comes with its own challenges. Whether a first-timer, a seasoned veteran of several international moves or even a third or fourth generation expat, we tend to face continual change and ongoing adjustments in our personal and cultural identity.

For expats, emotional resilience may be tested in the form of experiencing a sudden job transfer or loss due to the weakened state of the global economy. They draw upon emotional resilience when handling the transition into a new culture and language

> *'Possessing emotional resilience doesn't mean we always remain upbeat or we don't suffer when bad things occur. What it does mean is we do our best to maintain or find our way back to a positive mindset – and view of ourselves – as quickly as possible. And by quickly I mean as long as it takes.'*

vastly different than one's own, and dealing with our own or a loved one's difficulty in making that transition. They need it when facing a medical crisis while overseas.

Life has its ups and downs, and we will all experience our share of adversity. Emotional resilience helps us accept this, and allows us to understand we are not being singled out, that we aren't somehow 'deserving' of difficulties or unfairly saddled with misfortune – such events happen in the course of life and we can get through them, albeit some more easily than others.

There is often an implicit – and in certain instances an explicit – expectation for many expats that they are representing their country, corporation or organization. As such they must conduct themselves appropriately at all times, so as not to discredit the institution which employs them or their family members.

A few years ago a story hit the local Dutch papers of a small group of intoxicated TCKs relieving themselves on what they didn't realize were the wooded grounds of Queen Beatrix's residential palace here in The Hague. They were taken into custody until their parents could retrieve them. At a writing group I attended shortly afterwards, some of us were glad the fact the teens attended a local international school favored by expats hadn't made the press. However, two of the attendees of the same nationality as the perpetrators – which had been pointedly noted in the article – were overheard muttering, "Oh great, we're not going to live *this* down anytime soon..."

UNSTATED EXPECTATIONS PLACED ON SPOUSES/ SIGNIFICANT OTHERS

"My family and I recently began our latest Foreign Service assignment in Bolivia. Speaking as a foreign-born spouse, who is currently raising three Third-Culture children, moving every couple of years has become more intriguing than challenging. As a 'trailing-spouse', you are expected to be supportive, having an around-the-clock positive attitude, and try your best to perform well, as a mom-wife-friend. And why? No working spouse/ partner wants to come home to a not-so-happy counterpart. It may sound funny, but it's quite true.

How hard is that? Pretty hard, I'd say. Not all days are great. Not all evenings are surrounded by glamorous cocktails. Life is difficult for everyone, in different ways. Adjustment to your new posting, your new life in a different country, every so often requires a great deal of emotional resilience, lots of acceptance, understanding, and, why not say, some resignation, when one realizes it's simply impossible to change all things, all the time. Lack of these points would be a sure recipe for a disastrous life as an expatriate family."

Raquel L. Miranda, US Foreign Service spouse in Bolivia after Mozambique and Brazil

When we move to a different part of the same country there may be many new aspects we need to learn – becoming familiar with a faster (or slower) pace, how to procure groceries and the payment method involved, how pleasantries are exchanged (or not), a slightly different accent or dialect, and so on. This is challenging enough, but consider the expat or global nomad who must also navigate changes in the very processes of shopping, speaking (another language altogether), preparing food, banking practices, making payments and whether haggling is involved, identifying and maintaining personal space, using various modes of transportation, observing religious and cultural differences, among many, many more.

Expats/ cross-culturals know well the challenges of arriving in an unfamiliar place, of having to build a new life from the ground up. You may find yourself dropped into a society where others don't necessarily speak, think, believe or act in the same way as the society you've come from, or to which you are accustomed. While you're trying to wrap your head around these bigger concepts, you're also scrambling to learn new protocols for relatively simple things like doing laundry, using basic household appliances, queuing up in line, finding a hardware store and all-purpose department store, and other basic tasks you never thought twice about previously.

FIVE KILOMETERS FOR A SCREWDRIVER

"One thing that I wish I had known before we came over to the Netherlands – leave electrical appliances behind. When we were packing up to move everything over, I remember thinking to myself that so many people had made the trek ahead of us,

surely someone had a solution to making all of our appliances work. Wrong. We ended up blowing the circuit board on our 6-month-old dryer, and had to purchase a dryer locally. We also had to buy a couple of pretty big transformers and a signal converter to get a few of our other appliances to work. Our remaining appliances are in storage. We have purchased replacements for the necessary smaller appliances.

When we first moved into our apartment, I needed a screwdriver to assemble some of our new furniture (I don't know what we would have done without IKEA those first months). I made the mistake of asking a cashier at the Albert Heijn where I could find a screwdriver (pantomiming turning a screw while I asked the question). She shrugged and directed me to Praxis or Gamma. I walked the way I thought she said to go, missed the Praxis entirely. I finally came upon Gamma, where I scored a rather expensive screwdriver. I think I ended up walking 5km that day for a screwdriver. Of course, the very next week while shopping in AH, what did I spy? You guessed it – a whole rack of inexpensive screwdrivers."

Patti Tito, American expat living in the Netherlands

When I think back to when we arrived that first July in the Netherlands, I recall brilliant sun, bright blue sky and comfortably warm temperatures. Foliage was lush and full, the summer pace was slower, people looked healthy and relaxed, and it seemed people either walked or rode their bicycles everywhere. I remember feeling dazzled by it all.

And then we needed to arrange cable and Internet connectivity and it all came crashing down. What was, back in the States, usually a one-day operation at most to turn on connectivity – two or three if your house or apartment wasn't connected or you requested an upgrade to Wi-Fi and a technician needed to be dispatched – became a long, drawn out, four-week ordeal hampered in part by the fact that August was 'vacation month'.

I also remember being flabbergasted by the tedious process and copious paperwork required to acquire a simple cell phone. Gone was 'the more the merrier' approach of US cell phone providers falling over themselves to offer low-rate family plans. We became intimately familiar with a multi-step, carefully controlled system designed to thwart rampant fraud of more costly, yet less capable cell phones, by teams of thieves signing up for, and then skipping out on, lucratively exorbitant contracts by disappearing over porous borders.

The process by which I had to replace my expiring American driver's license with a Dutch one was equally confusing and time-consuming. Banking was a bit easier thanks in part to Husband setting up our accounts when he arrived ahead of us and to expedited service arranged through his employer. Believe me, I harbor no illusions that a Dutch person moving to the US (or frankly anyone moving from one country to another) would find various bureaucratic requirements any less annoying. Some things are easier, others more difficult. Getting frustrated by the situation won't change the manner in which each society sets up the processes and procedures by which it operates. At some point we need to chalk it up to the differences which make life interesting, and get on with it.

EXPAT TRANSITION PHASES

In their book on TCKs, Pollock and Van Reken applied the phases of a general transition model to expats (and not only their children). These five phases are:

- Involvement
- Leaving
- Transition
- Entry
- Re-involvement

Each of us experiences the expat transition cycle phases in our own way, moving through or remaining in the various phases for different periods of time as needed. But as we move from country to country, one culture to the next, we generally find ourselves in one of these five phases. Think of this cycle as the *where* and *when* of the mobile, cross-cultural experience –where we are in the process of moving and living abroad, and when these phases occur as we transition from one place to another.

Why is the transition cycle so critical to understanding expatriate/ cross-cultural life? Pollock and Van Reken said it best with this very telling observation: '*For most TCKs the collection of significant losses and separations before the end of adolescence is often more than most people experience in a lifetime.*' The impact of this on those children during their formative years of identity development is profound. But we should also remember that accompanying them during all those transitions were other family members also experiencing the painful losses and disconcerting separations from people, places, pets and possessions for which they also cared deeply.

> '*Life is full of transitions, with expatriate/ cross-cultural existence having more than its share. We would be well-served to learn how to deal with them, and in doing so, we dip into – and therefore need to resupply – the reserves of emotional resilience within us.*'

In her book, *The Global Nomad's Guide to University Transition*, Tina L. Quick built on the framework of Pollock and Van Reken's insights and five-phase transition cycle. Quick focuses on the experiences of TCKs/ global nomads as they leave their current culture/ country, transition to and enter into university life, often to a home country/ culture with which they are not familiar, or another one altogether. So important is the transition process during such milestone moments as heading off to university (or into the workforce), that she includes it as one of her 'Four Pearls' every TCK should learn and understand if they are to successfully adapt and eventually thrive. Quick's other three 'Pearls' are TCK identity development, unresolved grief and TCK relationships.

Quick invited Barbara Schaetti, Ph.D., interculturalist and second generation TCK/ global nomad, to write an addendum to her book. In the section entitled Final Reflections, Schaetti notes the maturation in the field of TCK/ global nomad literature. She also makes this important point – while Quick's book focuses on transition to university, it also teaches and reinforces thinking about: '*transitions as a process, a life experience that can be purposefully managed.*' In understanding the five-phase transition process when moving between cultures, you can: '*learn more broadly how to effectively engage all the transitions you encounter, throughout your life.*'

Schaetti's point about learning to manage transitions throughout life captured my attention. It goes to the heart of why I wrote this book: life is full of transitions, with expatriate/ cross-cultural existence having more than its share. We would be well-served to learn how to deal with them, and in doing so, we dip into – and therefore need to resupply – the reserves of emotional resilience within us.

INVOLVEMENT

The transition phases begin with our being settled and integrated into our culture. We have a home, work, routines, family and friends, favored activities. Days go by without reminders that we aren't 'from' the country/ culture in which we reside. We know what we're doing and how to do it. We feel comfortable and *a part* of society, not *apart* from it. Life is more than getting by from day to day – it includes looking forward to events, future thinking, planning ahead. The thought of leaving someday may cross our minds, but if it does, we're reminded of all the little things we would miss. In a word, we are engaged with the world around us.

LEAVING

Whether suddenly or over a period of time, we become aware of the need to leave. This may be the result of a change in employment such as a new government, military, or missionary posting, corporate restructuring or job reassignment. Leaving a place can be self-initiated or thrust upon us – we may welcome the opportunity for change, or desperately desire to remain where we are. We may have months to plan and execute an orderly move, or we may get word we need to go quickly, sending us into a frenzied dash to pack, tie up loose ends, and say hasty goodbyes.

LEAVING CREATES A HOLE, A GAP IN OUR LIVES

"Changing friendships is the one certainty of expatriate living. However stable our individual lives may seem at any one point in time, due to the nature of the international lifestyle change is always around us. New people come and old friends go. Saying goodbye to friends has been one of the toughest aspects of expatriate living. Watching my children say goodbye to friends who are traveling to the other side of the world has been particularly emotional for me. Their leaving creates a hole, a gap in our lives that will take time to fill.

How I have coped in these situations doesn't seem very emotionally resilient to me. I have cried, felt sad and wanted to remove myself from the international environment as a way of protecting myself and my children. What the process has shown me though, is that we are all emotionally resilient over the longer term. My children have handled goodbyes in very different ways – one howls and cries for 24 hours as though her heart is breaking. The other is calm and does not cry for days. She is poised and can talk rationally about the change and seems to be coping. Then something will happen that upsets her, it could be a bump on the head, a few unkind words from someone and she cracks and the emotions come flooding out. I am more like my second daughter. My way of coping is to bottle it up, to look outwardly calm and in control whilst inside I am a wreck. But the body's and mind's abilities to heal themselves are incredible and part of emotional resilience to me is to simply have faith in our ability to cope."

Louise Wiles, British expat living in Portugal after Spain

Here in the northern hemisphere, when it gets to be February, March and April, 'the season' begins. You would be forgiven for thinking I'm referring to the blossoming of springtime, but in fact it's time for what I refer to as The Clash Roulette – the latest round of 'Should I Stay or Should I Go?' Expats of all stripes begin the dance, circling tenuously around the question of whether they (or their friends and colleagues) will be moving on, repatriating or staying put.

Those of us who work for our governments (e.g., diplomatic corps or military) are usually on set orders – x years here, followed by x years there, and so on. Occasionally there is a one-year extension or abrupt change in plans, but for the most part we know when we're scheduled to leave. For those of us who work in international organizations, non-profits, religious-affiliated missionary groups or the private sector, it can be more of a roll of the dice. The decision to stay or go (and to where) may or may not rest in our hands, so a careful set of calculations ensues.

We find ourselves asking all sorts of hypothetical questions, trying to 'read the tea leaves' and consider various options:

- Is my job safe or should we strongly consider taking that opening in 'fill-in-the-blank'?
- Should we try to leave this year to avoid moving our child in their last year of school?
- Now our last child has left the nest, is it time to head back home?
- I've always wanted to live in that country/ region, what about now?
- Can I find a job in this economy if we decide to move home due to family considerations?
- Another round of layoffs is coming, what's our best course of action?
- Time to try something (or someplace) new – what are our options?
- What if I accept a lateral move in my organization – could we then stay a couple more years?

Even when you think the issue is settled, things can change in a heartbeat – falling in love, having a(nother) child, career change, job transfer, unexpected reassignment, divorce, serious illness, accident, even death. Or job opportunities you weren't expecting. We went through that scenario last year as Husband was approached to apply for positions in two very different countries, with diverse cultures, on opposite sides of the globe.

He's quite happy with his current position and we enjoy living here. Yet both opportunities were good career moves for him, and with Daughter facing her last two years of high school, they represented now-or-never (or more accurately, now-or-not-for-at-least-two-years) possibilities. But things aren't always what they seem (as in the case of the first job) and being asked to apply is not the same as being offered the job (as with the second). After a relatively tense few weeks we were able to step out of our own version of The Clash Roulette.

Often you don't get a choice in the matter. All you need do is check out the world news – behind the stories of natural disasters, uprisings or outbreaks of civil war, there are countless examples of rushed leave-taking as expats/ cross-culturals scramble to get out. Daughter's school soccer team attended the end-of-season tournament in Cairo in November 2011 – within three months the host school there had closed and families were fleeing the country during the demonstrations of Tahrir Square. Throughout the Arab Spring of 2012, the American School of The Hague took in many new students – some temporarily as they waited for their parents' new assignments, others for the remainder of the school year – from various countries in the Middle East whose families had been evacuated due to violence and civil unrest.

Two of the more poignant examples of a rushed leave-taking happened when the fathers in expat families died suddenly. In the case of the first, the death occurred while the parent was on a job assignment in another country. This contributed additional layers of emotional and bureaucratic complication into what was already an incredibly difficult time. As her husband died relatively young, the widow was left to arrange finances, housing, schooling and myriad other decisions she hadn't expected, all while mourning the loss of her life partner and father of her children.

In the second instance, the father died in the country in which the family was living, but the grieving wife and child's visa status required they leave the country within two weeks. Not surprisingly, they chose to leave sooner to take his body back to their home country for burial. It was summertime, so neither had the time or opportunity to say goodbye to many of their close friends, teachers or fellow students. A small group of friends, neighbors and parents from the son's school took charge and helped arrange for the packing up of the family's household contents, and handled the countless details that arise when taking leave of a country. I'd like to say that at some point the mother and son had an opportunity to return and say goodbye in a more orderly, personal way, but I've never heard whether this was the case.

Regardless of the circumstances under which we are leaving, we subconsciously begin to pull away physically and emotionally as we prepare ourselves to transition to our new intended 'home'. As we will see later, in the section on Handling Transitions in *CHAPTER 8: ENHANCING EMOTIONAL RESILIENCE*, we need to be careful not to take our leave too abruptly as this coping mechanism, while part of our nature, has its downside.

Transition

Once we've physically taken leave of the place we previously lived, we enter the transition phase. This period can be of varying length and stress depending on how quickly we move to our new country/ culture. For some, we finish up our tour of duty, pack up the household, head 'back home' or elsewhere for a visit with family/ friends or to undertake additional training. Weeks or months later we touch down in what will be our new host country. For others, we may wake up in our new home the day after leaving our former life. There are benefits and negatives associated with both options, but either way, transitions bring upheaval and change.

Overwhelm when leaving and moving on

"'Overwhelm' is something I have experienced firsthand and observed a number of times professionally and with friends. The feeling that people associate with overwhelm is almost like a brain fog. They know they have so much to do but can't seem to organize themselves to get the smallest task done. Their focus goes and even though there are clearly priority tasks, these are ignored and minor tasks are completed in their place – the knowledge of this feeds the sense of overwhelm even more.

But overwhelm isn't just about tasks and getting things done, it can also be a reaction to emotional overload. When I have observed people in overwhelm it is often at the point where emotional overload coincides with physical overload, often at the time of leaving and moving on. People are having to cope with the goodbyes, the sense of doubt often linked to big changes, and at the same time having to facilitate the packing and goodbye process. The sense of not quite wanting to face and accept the change that is about to occur can feed the inability to act. At a time when so many things need to be done, very few things are actually being done and so overwhelm feeds overwhelm.

Or overwhelm can occur after the event. The whole relocation process may be managed smoothly and seemingly calmly, but once the physical move has been made there may be a sense of emptiness and inability and unwillingness to set to and start to rebuild one's life.

In these cases, overwhelm needs to be recognized, the person needs to give themselves some space – space to relax, to regain a sense of inner calm. Then they need to focus on the things that need to be done in a logical and progressive way. I often suggest, start small and then work to build up."

Louise Wiles, British expat living in Portugal after Spain

Regardless of the duration or difficulty of the actual transition period, to ensure our physical and emotional resilience reserves remain at reasonable levels, we need to make every effort to maintain whatever routines or activities we are able. We can help ourselves immensely if we allow more down time to rest and rejuvenate, maintain a healthy diet, get sufficient exercise and employ other tips and techniques covered in *PARTS II* and *III*.

ENTRY

Entry into a new country/ region presents its own form of culture shock (more about that in *CHAPTER 2: IDENTITY ISSUES IN EXPAT LIFE*). We struggle to understand how our new culture operates at the same time we are processing the emotions of leaving our previous culture. We may experience the honeymoon phase of culture shock in which we are infatuated with our new surroundings – or not. We can feel torn between two (or more) realities, finding it difficult to embrace the new while we mourn the old. Sometimes it can feel as though we are literally aliens in a new land.

We long to belong, but often can't see how we're going to get there. Generally, the only way through the emotional and physical upheaval of this phase is directly through it. We have to wake up each day, put one foot in front of the other and keep going. Over time we find ourselves learning what we need to know – this gives us confidence and helps us begin to feel better.

This is true for our children, too. Tina Quick offers: '*The learning curve is steep when internationals first enter or global nomads re-enter. There are so many things coming at you at once that it feels overwhelming and even the slightest mishap or obstacle suddenly becomes an enormous problem. It is normal to feel this way. It will eventually settle down and you will be able to laugh at your experiences.*'

Recently I came across something I'd written early on about the blur of activity the first month after joining Husband here in The Hague. I suppose I wrote it to remind myself of all I had accomplished, but it still gives me chills remembering how new and different everything was, how I often felt the smallest activities required gargantuan effort, and the rush of learning how to do so many things so quickly. This was the result of moving from one westernized country to another. Imagine transitioning across an even greater cultural divide.

"Arrive at Schiphol with two teenagers, two cats, one dog and plenty of baggage – mental and physical – in tow. Finally get to see house Husband decided to rent, albeit in a neighborhood we had seen in our earlier visit. Movers had hastily unpacked household goods with much ending up in wrong rooms so unpacking, moving around furniture, clothes and household items. More unpacking. Putting things away is challenging with limited closet and storage space. Figure out how to do laundry. Grocery shopping. Hardware store, drug stores and finding a store equivalent to Target (note – I'm still looking) to pick up incidentals, restock or replace missing items, have keys made.

Figure out where/ how to buy strippenkaarts *for transportation. Learn to use the tram and bus, get to train station for transfer to a bus or to take the train. Picking up a rental car takes two tram rides and walking four blocks either way. Take short vacation to France, bringing Oli as it seems dog kennels book up months in advance. Glad it is France where everyone takes their dog along. Yet instead of feeling very European about this, I feel like the newbie making a rookie mistake. Vow to make kennel reservations far earlier next time.*

One week of school orientation with Son and Daughter, requiring tram and transfer at train station to bus each way. Kudos to the school for offering a separate, in-depth orientation for parents. Son and Daughter glad they will take school-arranged transportation when school starts.

Figure out where to have additional passport photos taken. School begins, with requisite paperwork. No landline phone or Internet connectivity despite regular assurances. Sign up for intensive Dutch language course to begin shortly. Cannot come quickly enough.

Look into high-level Dutch soccer club possibilities for Daughter. Call and arrange for immediate tryout as season is starting. Evening tryout in town 25km away requires taking a tram and two buses to get to the club. All goes well, Daughter happy to make top team while playing up in age. Return trip late evening requires bus, train and tram. (End up doing this three times a week for a month until finally get our car.) Must learn to call it voetbal.*"*

The names and details may differ but I know most of you can relate to this. Many of you have had it far worse. In the end, we muddle through and survive. Eventually we even begin to thrive, the last phase in the transition process.

RE-INVOLVEMENT

Re-involvement is the final phase in the transition process, the one in which we (hopefully) find ourselves settled into our new lives. There is no timeline with this phase because it differs from one person to another. Some of us dive in, create the sanctuary which becomes our home, learn the ropes, make friends and become part of the local community. Others of us take months, even longer, to reach the point where we feel settled, that we belong.

Eventually most of us integrate ourselves into the new culture (re-involvement), although sometimes at great emotional expense. As we gain experience moving back and forth between and among countries and cultures, we may get better at navigating the disconcerting feelings of change, but this can also lead to feeling caught between cultures, in limbo. This continual moving, shifting and changing may make re-involvement more demanding with each subsequent relocation. That's why some expats/ cross-culturals find, after a certain number of moves, they've hit a wall – they've experienced too much change, too much loss. They may know how to successfully become integrated in a new place, but they don't feel up to doing it yet again.

FINDING THE STRENGTH TO RETURN

"As all expats know well, there is a time when neither your country of origin nor the new one feels like home. After finishing my MPhil in Marketing at Tilburg University (the reason I came to the Netherlands in the first place), I decided to found my own company, IamExpat.nl. However, I had to return to Greece for personal reasons, and as we all know the situation in Greece is not ideal at the moment. Going back is not that difficult, especially if you know that your 'duties' won't last more than a year or so.

Besides, you have done this before; the decision to leave (your new home) is another exciting adventure, a déjà vu if you will, at least in the beginning. I had lived in three countries (Greece, Scotland, the Netherlands) in the previous three years and now I had to go back to Greece for one year, and find the courage to come back once again to the

Netherlands where I had started building my dreams. So, the tricky part is to find the strength to return. And this is where emotional resilience kicks in.

If you empty your mind for a second and try to see the big picture, it all comes down to this: 'what will make you happy?' If you know the answer then you are free, ready to decompose the problem and see how to overcome all issues. So, I sat down, evaluated my options and it turned out that the decision to go to Greece was easy. I accepted it and 14 months later I said goodbye to friends and family in Greece once again and returned to the Netherlands. Now, almost three years later, I can't say I regret my choice."

Charalampos Sergios, Greek expat living in the Netherlands, after Scotland

In the end, whatever transition process phase you find yourself in and how you handle it will differ among individuals. Awareness of what occurs in each phase helps us prepare to move through each of them, drawing on and rebuilding our stores of emotional resilience during the process can help us immensely.

CHANGE MODEL STAGES

In 1969, Elisabeth Kübler-Ross wrote the seminal book, *On Death and Dying*, in which she outlined the five stages of grief in dealing with one's own mortality or the death of a loved one. Over time, it became clear that Kübler-Ross' grief stages were actually a *change* model. In addition to death and dying, the stages could be applied to other personal transitions and events characterized by emotional turmoil. The five stages of the change model are:

- Denial
- Anger
- Bargaining
- Depression
- Acceptance

For those of us living across cultures, a major event triggering the change model can include job loss, accident, major illness, the transition phases of leaving one country and arriving in another, a child leaving the family nest, or death of a loved one.

Upon hearing 'the news', we may respond with disbelief, confusion or overwhelm. We can't believe this is happening, and it may feel surreal. Moving to a stage of frustration, irritation or anger, our feelings tend to turn decidedly negative. Our foul mood continues, and we feel as if a dark cloud hovers overhead. When denial and anger fail to work, we start to panic, desperately trying to make deals with God or some spiritual being, the source of our frustration, or ourselves. The depression stage can range from mild to moderate to severe as we are overwhelmed by sadness and mourn for what we've lost. Only when we've worked through this process – albeit with some stages lasting longer or being felt more deeply than others – and accepted the inevitable can we finally begin the climb back up out of our emotional trough.

If maintaining a healthy sense of identity and self in a mobile, cross-cultural life is *why* we need emotional resilience, and the expat transition phases are *where* we are and *when* in our cross-cultural journey, we might think of the Kübler-Ross change model stages as *what* we deal with as we go through those transition phases.

As with the expat transition phases, not all of us experience the change stages in exactly the same manner, order or for the same period of time. When faced with moving abroad – perhaps over and over again – some expats/ cross-culturals fixate on the denial or bargaining stages, while those around us may skim through them or skip them entirely. Others become mired in anger or irritation. Unfortunately, still others may find themselves trapped in the depression stage.

Virtually everyone feels some level of grief and sense of loss during the leaving, transition and entry phases of expat life. What is important for each of us is how long and to what extent these phases last. Becoming overwhelmed with these feelings may keep us stuck in the depression stage of the change model, precluding us from moving on to acceptance of where we are in our lives.

It is reaching the acceptance stage of our own personal change model experience which allows us to leave the expat transition phase and emerge into the expat entry phase, ready and willing to face the opportunities and challenges of making a new life in a new place. It is only in dealing with the often unsettling changes which occur upon entry, that we can ultimately reach the re-involvement phase where we begin to feel settled and more importantly, a sense of belonging.

CHAPTER 2: IDENTITY ISSUES IN EXPAT LIFE

With an initial understanding of the uniqueness of the expatriate/ cross-cultural life, definition of key terms, and an introduction to the phases of the transition cycle and the stages of the change model, we arrive at an important juncture – gaining insight into the wide range of difficult issues that tend to arise. In this chapter we will address identity-related challenges, in *CHAPTER 3: OTHER KEY ISSUES IN EXPAT LIFE*, we will look at additional potential problem areas.

ONE EXPAT'S STORY OF THE DOWNSIDE

"We have lived outside our birth country, in several locations, for 17 years. Our family initially relocated to the USA following a job offer from my husband's company. Being a 'glass half full', 'grabbing opportunities' kind of family, we jumped at the chance.

There were few resources for expats back then and no support from the company once the job contract was signed. Culture shock wasn't something we'd heard of, nor was it something we could have easily recognized. I look back and cringe at our naiveté and innocence. Alone in a foreign country, with no support group, no understanding of how anything worked, and not knowing the right questions to ask to get the answers we needed. It was a disaster waiting to happen.

As parents, we hold ourselves responsible for the consequences that initial expat move had on the health and well-being of our children, particularly our eldest son. Then aged 13, this loving, smart, enthusiastic, funny guy found himself unable to cope – depression, an eating disorder, giving up in school, few friends, and a descent into drugs and alcohol. He became a functioning alcoholic. Our dreams of a successful, happy life for him were reduced to praying he would survive – survive the times the paramedics came to revive him when he'd drunk himself to oblivion, the times he'd get behind the wheel of a car, any car, and smash it into something.

And those dark times when I'd wish, in the deepest despair, that he would succeed and find the peace he craved. A series of counselors and therapists, none of whom had experienced life out of their own state, let alone country, with no concept of 'expat life' made us feel more isolated. We knew his problems were caused by moving from a loving secure environment surrounded by family to a new life he was not emotionally equipped to deal with. We had no tools to help him.

We live with the emotional fall-out and guilt. What if we hadn't moved, what if we'd had better resources, what if we'd made this decision here or that decision there. At the end of the day, it is what it is and we have to accept it, we can only move forward. Our son continues to fight depression and every day is a battle not to have a drink.

The 'glass-full-to-the-brim' woman of 17 years ago now sees life very differently. I try to keep the glass half-full but sometimes life smashes the glass and sends it flying. There are times I get tired of 'keeping optimistic', 'being positive', 'looking on the bright side'. I don't share my stories with other people – who wants to be a Debbie Downer or Negative Nancy? In the expat world we want positive, upbeat, happy, lively people full of energy, who feel blessed to have had the expat experience. Where grief, loss, depression and anxiety are the dirty secrets very few acknowledge.

The flip side of the expat coin is a dark place and far more people struggle with depression and anxiety than anyone wants to admit. At the first sign of a downturn in mood I take some time for myself, unplug the phone, discontent the laptop and take long walks with the dog. Be kind to myself and nurture the simple things – baking, gardening, reading a book (often a much loved book from childhood) or just sitting feeling the sun on my face. Gentle, calming time away from people. I detach from the world, don't watch the news, don't read the papers, allowing myself to be still. In the stillness comes the healing. Taking these simple steps for maybe a day, a few days, however long it takes, can stop a depressive episode.

It's in the peace of these nurturing times I can look at the pieces of the shattered glass, and stick them back together. Once that's done the process of filling it up again can begin."

Elizabeth W., expat

Many of the issues we're discussing are not unique to living the expatriate, cross-cultural life – they can and do happen to those who spend their entire lives in established communities alongside family and friends with whom they grow up, live, and eventually die. However, there are also issues that can be attributed in part or in whole to the experience of living across cultures.

It is important there be no more dirty little secrets, or presenting a glossy version of expatriate life when the literature and life experience have told us there is also loss, longing and issues with identity. No more sugarcoating the lifestyle as carefree, glamorous, luxurious, and entirely without problems or potential emotional repercussions. No more painting the picture of what Elizabeth refers to as uniformly: *'positive, upbeat, happy, lively people full of energy, who feel blessed to have had the expat experience.'* It's time to shine the spotlight on the underside of what can be an exhilarating way of life – the part that is sometimes debilitating. We owe it to ourselves and others to be completely honest – there are ups and downs, highs and lows, shadows and light to life lived cross-culturally. Let's not be afraid to discuss the entire spectrum, openly and candidly.

IDENTITY AND WHY IT MATTERS

Nothing in cross-cultural life is more important than one's sense of identity. It goes to the very core of our being. In fact, many of the other key issues in expat/ cross-cultural life stem from identity issues.

HIERARCHY OF NEEDS (AND WANTS THAT BECOME NEEDS)

In general terms, identity is a collective presentation of the set of characteristics by which something or someone is recognizable or known. An important marker in the fields of sociology and psychology in the mid-20th century was Abraham Maslow's development of a human 'hierarchy of needs'. This pyramidal-shaped representation starts at the bottom with the most basic, physiological needs such as breathing, eating and sleeping, and moves up to more advanced levels of need including safety, love/ belonging, esteem and finally reaching self-actualization. The concept behind this model is that a human being – you, me or anyone else – must have their needs met at one level before being able to become concerned with meeting the needs of the next.

In layman's terms, when I've got food, shelter and clothing, I can then worry about whether I am safe. Safety refers not only to myself physically, but also emotionally, to my

> *'Our societal background is altered by transitioning to another country/ culture. Not only must our lower-level needs be met anew within that host environment, our sense of identity is affected too.'*

health, having employment, property, resources and basic morality (e.g., basic accepted definitions of right and wrong leading to legal systems such as 'rule of law'). When I'm safe, I can focus on caring about and feeling that I belong in my relationships with family and friends. When I 'belong' and feel love, I can consider higher-level needs such as being confident, respecting and being respected by others, feeling good about myself and seeking achievements. Only then can I turn to 'self-actualization' – essentially realizing the innate need to meet my fullest potential as a human being. Self-actualization can be reflected in creativity, problem-solving, behaving morally and lacking prejudice.

I share Maslow's needs hierarchy, because how we choose to fulfill these requirements speaks directly to our identity. If I think that morality – or religion, legality, education, business, philanthropy, cross-cultural connectedness, or whatever else – is most important, then I will use my time, energy, focus and natural talents toward achieving actualization of myself (my identity) toward those ends.

We have multiple needs at each level and so can aspire to reach the highest levels possible in whatever combination. But what is key is our individualism exists within the broader society, country and culture in which we find ourselves. Our societal background is altered by transitioning to another country/ culture. Not only must our lower-level needs be met anew within that host environment, our sense of identity is affected too.

An interesting note is that Dutch researcher Geert Hofstede, famed for his work in international and organizational cultures, maintains an ethnocentric vein runs through Maslow's work. For more than 40 years, Hofstede has categorized countries/ cultures on a number of important value scales, including whether they tend to be individualistic or collective. Hofstede believes Maslow's interpretation of human needs reflects an individualistic society perspective and not a collectivist one. In a collective society, actualization and improvement are focused significantly more on acceptance and the community view, rather than a self-oriented one. (More on Hofstede in *CHAPTER 6: CULTURAL INTELLIGENCE AND INTERCULTURAL COMPETENCE.*)

IDENTITY AND THE EXPAT

When you move abroad, it can seem that everything which distinguishes you as a unique person (e.g., your family, friends, connections, career, activities, community) suddenly vanishes. There's no tag around your neck, or tattoo on your forehead, outlining in detail the full being of your person. No one knows you were treasurer for your church/ mosque/ synagogue or ran seven marathons, that you raised thousands of dollars for charity or led a crusade for educational reform, that you were voted best history or pre-school teacher or were about to make partner at a prestigious law firm.

This may be particularly troubling if you are not the one whose employment brings you to your new country. Labeled an accompanying spouse, significant other or the ever-condescending trailing spouse, you arrive in a place where no one knows you or anything about you. No one realizes, nor do they particularly care, that prior to arrival you were an actively engaged individual in your own right. Suddenly you are relegated to 'wife/ partner of' status by the Human Resources division of your spouse's company or organization. Even the administrators and teachers at your children's school initially view you solely in terms of 'parent of' status.

Essentially you've become a blank slate.

It is not surprising people living in cross-cultural situations grapple with questions of identity. As mentioned previously, in their book on Third Culture Kids, interculturalist David Pollock and adult Third Culture Kid (ATCK) Ruth Van Reken focused on addressing what they considered these foundational questions of identity – *Who am I, Where do I belong, Where is home?*

As we learned earlier from Pollock and Van Reken, a Third Culture Kid is: *'a person who has spent a significant part of his or her developmental years outside their parents' culture(s).'* While TCKs may build relationships to all of the cultures in which they interact, they have full ownership in none. They aren't from their parents' culture(s) or the host culture(s) in which they find themselves living, but instead form a third intersection or interstitial Third Culture of: *'shared commonalities with those living the internationally mobile lifestyle.'*

'For TCKs, the moving back and forth from one culture to another happens before they have completed the critical developmental task of forming a sense of their own personal or cultural identity.'

Writing initially to the TCK, over time Pollock and Van Reken recognized that TCKs' backgrounds share many of the same aspects of the overarching group of cross-culturals, of which they are a subset. They find themselves: *trying to develop a sense of personal and cultural identity when the world around them mirrors back changing definitions of who they are.* Van Reken specifically added chapters in their revised edition describing this

> *'For TCKs, the moving back and forth from one culture to another happens before they have completed the critical developmental task of forming a sense of their own personal or cultural identity.'*

'cultural hybridization', thus opening up the discussion to include others in the cross-cultural camp.

In *The Global Nomad's Guide to University Transition*, Tina L. Quick builds upon the underpinnings of Pollock and Van Reken's work with TCKs and the cross-cultural experience. Quick recognizes the importance and impact of the underlying two-pronged reality which shapes the lives of TCKs (and indeed of many expats) – we live in a genuinely cross-cultural yet highly mobile world.

The beauty of Quick's book is its value not only to students intent on pursuing higher education opportunities, but to young expats/ cross-culturals heading into the work force, planning a gap year, or unsure of their next move. Indeed many young, and not so young, adults who grew up across cultures don't even know what an ATCK or ACCK is, let alone that they are one, and what it might mean in terms of addressing nagging identity questions they may have carried forward with them.

OUR CHILDREN MAY BECOME TCKs WITHOUT OUR REALIZING

"I must admit to entering into our first '2-4 year assignment' with great naivety, not realizing that within a remarkably short time we would morph into 'expats' with the associated cultural, emotional and psychological impact that goes along with this unnatural social construct. I think it was at least two years in that I first read anything about the expat experience, and Third Culture Kids made quite an impression. I realized I had unwittingly created three TCKs with little conscious thought about the impact it would have on their lives. I became more informed about and more conscious of the cycles and psychological effects of expat life, and have tried

to make decisions that help myself and my family members avoid some of the potential pitfalls associated with being an expat."

Sara C. American expat now living in the Netherlands after Australia and Scotland

Sara C. needn't worry that she and her husband were alone in failing to recognize how international transitions during their children's developmental years automatically inducted them into the little known club of 'TCKness'. We cannot know what we don't know, and for most of us it takes a move or two through the transition cycle, or a heavy bout of culture shock, to jolt us out of our complacency and send us scrambling for an introduction to the complexities of global life.

WHY IDENTITY MATTERS

Why does this matter? If we don't have a clear sense of identity – of who we are – as we continually move from place to place, we may struggle with the emotional fallout from the disruption and loss of relationships and connections. The high mobility aspect of expat life lends itself to unresolved feelings of loss and grief as we leave behind people, places, possessions and memories that matter. When we admit we miss a certain house, it usually isn't a materialistic lament for lost square footage, nice furnishings or the latest appliances – what we're really missing is how we felt, who we knew and the life we led while living there.

We mourn for these losses, and if we don't acknowledge and incorporate these feelings our identity development may be affected. We risk feeling alienated, helpless, lost. The cross-cultural aspect of the expat life adds additional layers of distance from our sense of our former self.

At our core we need to know who we are. Not the roles others ascribe to us, or the labels we give ourselves, but who we are in the very essence and fullness of our being. A sense of identity is crucial to one's mental and emotional health. Yet the cross-cultural, highly mobile world many of us live in, introduces challenges when we shift from one country/ culture to another, forcing us into transition. When someone goes through a traumatic event or period of turmoil (such as transitioning between/ among cultures), lack of emotional resilience can contribute to feelings of helplessness and depression.

Conversely, enhancing our emotional resilience can help us navigate our way through the transitions and changes present in our expat lives. This is precisely why the transition cycle and change model discussed earlier are directly relevant to the expat experience.

> 'Identity development is the search for congruence (i.e., agreement) in who we are, by integrating and resolving differences among who we see ourselves to be, who we thought we were, how others see us and who we'd like to become.'

IDENTITY DEVELOPMENT

The importance of identity is a common theme running through Robin Pascoe's expat books, from *A Broad Abroad: The Expat Wife's Guide to Living Abroad*, to *A Moveable Marriage: Relocate Your Relationship Without Breaking It*, to *Raising Global Nomads: Parenting Abroad in an On-Demand World*, to *Homeward Bound: A Spouse's Guide to Repatriation*. Each book addresses how living an expat/ cross-cultural life can affect not only how we are viewed but also how we view ourselves.

In *A Moveable Marriage*, Pascoe discusses how everything that distinguishes you as a person (e.g., career, friends, extended family, religion, community), seems to disappear when you move abroad, particularly if you are the accompanying spouse or partner. At times it can seem like a dream sequence in a cinematic thriller, one in which the characters awaken to find their identities have evaporated, no one knows (let alone understands) them, and with little understanding of how to set things right.

It is with regard to those having grown up in cross-cultural situations in their formative years, when an integrated sense of self is being forged, that this becomes more critical. Identity again plays a central role in Pascoe's *Raising Global Nomads*, where she includes an entire section by Barbara Schaetti on the importance of 'identity development'. Schaetti explains that for those living a globally nomadic life, identity development is the search for congruence (i.e., agreement) in who we are, by integrating and resolving differences among who we see ourselves to be, who we thought we were, how others see us and who we'd like to become.

Moving between and among cultures certainly qualifies as an event that tests our personal levels of emotional resilience. Most global nomads do successfully integrate their mobile childhoods into their adult identities, but some may become stuck along the way, suffering emotional pain and anguish. While Schaetti was specifically addressing TCKs/ global nomads at the time, the concept of identity development extends to all expats/ cross-culturals, regardless of age or background. We *all* seek to integrate who we thought we were with how we see ourselves, how others see us and who we hope to become.

If we don't address these issues, we risk emotional pain. We may struggle with the emotional fallout from disruption and loss of relationships and connections. This can lead to unresolved feelings of loss and grief as we leave people, places and memories that matter to us, or are similarly left behind by others. We mourn for our losses, and if we don't acknowledge and incorporate these feelings, we may feel alienated, helpless, lost. Tina Quick includes identity development as one of her 'Four Pearls' every TCK should be cognizant of and deal with as they move into adulthood, but the concept applies to all of us, regardless of where we spent our childhood.

In her essay, *Phoenix Rising: A Question of Cultural Identity*, Barbara Schaetti refers to the related concept of 'cultural marginality' – not quite fitting into any one culture in which we live but (hopefully) fitting comfortably on the edge or margins of each. When casually referred to by a relative as 'American', Schaetti writes of being shocked and unsettled as she saw herself very differently: ' *...an American-Swiss global nomad with a very European-influenced international background.'*

She explains why the precise wording matters so much to her: '*It has to do with fitting in and belonging, with my intent to be a part of society rather than apart from. It has to do with finding integrity and direction in my experience as a "cultural marginal".'*

So what is the lesson? Learning to recognize the personal truth of who we are, what we believe, regardless of – or perhaps more accurately, *because of* – whatever cultures in which we have lived.

'*It is valuable to be able to understand different truths as represented in different cultures, to withhold judgement and interpretation,'* Schaetti continues. '*At the same time, however, it is important for the adult global nomad to plant his or her feet in personal truth, one not dependent on circumstance.'*

Schaetti's words ring true. It is up to us as adults to consider the totality of our life experiences and seek congruence among the various parts of our identity. We must find agreement among who we have been, who we (and others) think we are, and who we wish to become. Similarly, we need to help our children as they develop their identities during the formative years.

SUPPORT, SELF-BELIEF AND A STRONG SENSE OF SELF

"Looking back over 12 years as an expat in several countries, I'd say that the key to surviving intact is to have a strong sense of who you are, unshakeable self-belief, and a good support network of people who nurture both these traits. Without these things I think it would be challenging for anyone to bounce back from the hard times.

Life as a regular expat (by which I mean those of us not on company relocation packages), is not always easy. As our work visas are tied to our employers there is little opportunity to switch jobs, regardless of the conditions you are faced with. Having spent a year working for someone I can only describe as a sociopath, I'd love to see this rule changed. I can honestly promise you that if you're looking to work abroad as a way to 'find yourself' this isn't the most promising place to consider!"

Val Hamer
British expat currently living in South Korea after Japan and Vietnam

Identity development and congruence aren't necessarily the easiest of processes. It is important that if we do find ourselves, or a family member, getting bogged down in a sense of overwhelming sadness, helplessness or depression that keeps us (or them) from taking action, we owe it to ourselves and our loved ones to consider seeking help, particularly from a psychologist, therapist or other mental health professional familiar with cross-cultural issues.

CULTURE SHOCK

Much has been written about culture shock, but essentially it is the physical and emotional discomfort, disorientation, or loss of bearings a person experiences when moving to/ from one culture to another. Culture shock is generally considered to have four phases, each of which can last anywhere from a few weeks to several months:

- **Honeymoon:** This is the initial period in which the novelty of differences between what we are experiencing in our new host culture and what we have known seem fresh, fascinating, deeply enthralling.

- **Negotiation:** This period reflects both definitions of this word, in that we are finding our way among cultural differences at the same time we are grappling with an internal bargaining as to how much we are willing to accept and/ or adjust.

- **Adjustment:** In this phase we have a sense of our place in our new culture and are feeling more accustomed to daily life.

- **Mastery:** By this phase we are engaging comfortably and operating fully within our host culture.

I consider it fortunate I was exposed to the concept of culture shock early in expat life, or I should say, early in my second round of expat life. When I studied abroad in Mexico many years ago, no one was talking about culture shock. Being young and adventurous, we simply jumped into the intercultural fray. It was exciting, colorful and new, but after a while most of the students in the program – myself included – began to encounter feelings of disorientation, unfamiliarity and overload. Some fell prey to ever growing homesickness. For me, it was wishing I could take a short break to reset my emotional bearings. At the time I may not have known culture shock existed or why it happens, but I sure knew how it felt.

The second time around I was a little more prepared, not because I recalled that disconcerting period in Mexico years earlier, but because I had finally learned what culture shock is and what it entails. I attended an orientation program designed specifically for parents of new students at my children's international school. ASH has a highly regarded, multi-faceted umbrella program called Safe Harbour, created in large part by then high school counselor Douglas Ota, a child and adolescent psychologist now in private practice. Safe Harbour focuses on the entry, involvement/ re-involvement and leaving phases of the transition process, with a series of ongoing programs providing education and support.

Once school began, parents were invited to weekly Monday Morning Networking meetings, which functioned both as 'how to' information sessions on a range of topics, and meet-and-greet opportunities to forge acquaintances with empathetic, experienced 'old hands' and other new arrivals in similar straits. These meetings were open to the community and guests welcomed, with parents sometimes bringing a friend or neighbor. They also proved popular with new expats whose children attended other local international schools, which offered little or nothing in the way of such assistance.

For some, these sessions were the temporary support they needed until they found their way. For others, they became a 'safe harbour' (pun fully intended) in which to seek calm, re-orient themselves, bolster their confidence, and share stories, laughs and the occasional tears. Ultimately many of these bonds blossomed into friendships.

SHOCKING FOR INDIVIDUALS

Given the generally self-oriented focus of most human beings, we tend to readily note the jarring nature of culture shock as we encounter differences in our host and previous cultures. We know to look out for the larger issues of difference such as religion, race and gender, form of government and degree of openness of society, language, history, geography. Often it's the little things that remind us we're no longer in our comfort zone.

SURPRISED BY DIFFERENCES IN SOCIALIZING

"What did I have difficulty with? Socialising in a new environment, missing my friends and places to hang out. Difficulties adapting to a new perception of friendship, camaraderie, solidarity and what having a good time entails. Coupled with this it was, and still is, difficult to fully grasp the impression of what is meant by, and the emotional significance of, what the Dutch call gezellig*

The new perception of friendship caused me to feel a sense of otherness, something I had not anticipated.

I went back home for a while, spoke to knowledgeable friends about my emotions. Afterwards I made my resolve – boy, if you want to settle down then it is time to find your feet in Holland. To do this you'll have to let go and adapt to the new situation. Make life a bit easy for yourself... It's time to be honest. Yes, you could call it being emotionally resilient, but with logical rationalism behind it.

One cultural shock was to keep track of what you are consuming while having a good time with friends – at the end of the evening you'll have to enumerate what you've consumed and foot the bill. How different! Back in the Caribbean we don't 'study' how much we are going to pay at the end of the evening, instead we focus on having a good time. We all have had a great time, in the end that is what counts. So Roy, want to enjoy yourself in Holland? You'll have to go with the flow!

One should not underestimate the impact of culture and to a limited degree ethnicity. In situations like this – cultural shocks – you forget academics, your knowledge and passion of social sciences, in my case anthropology and sociology. Emotions prevail!" (**Gezellig generally means cozy, sociable, convivial.*)

Roy Lie A. Tjam, Caribbean expat to the Netherlands

Some expats sail through the cultural orientation to another culture with little noticeable upset while others struggle. For some, the shock to their system doesn't hit them hard until they are on their third or fourth or seventh move. Just as no two people experience culture shock in precisely the same way, what shocks you in one culture may be entirely different in another.

Each of us experiences culture shock differently

"When I first moved to China, I was terrified. I had nightmares about Mao posters and beggars and Communists in the weeks leading up to our move. It took me more than a month to venture, alone, beyond a two-block radius from where we lived. I had intense social anxiety. I was terrified to be in any social situation without my husband. My husband once asked me to go to an event that would have required me to be at a table of people I didn't know, and I felt like I would vomit. I couldn't do it.

I didn't have the emotional reserves to manage the big changes in my life, to handle the culture shock, and to deal with being thrust into a whole new life. I didn't know it at the time, but culture shock was hitting me hard. So was adjusting to my new position as expat, as newlywed, as dependent."

Erica Knecht, Canadian expat (Japan, China, India, Switzerland, France) now living in Indonesia

At its worst, culture shock is literally that – an ongoing series of jolts to your system. Until we are able to process these shocks, we can find ourselves dealing with one negative issue or emotion overlaying another. It takes time, effort and yes, resiliency, to sort out the various pieces that cause upheaval and clamor for our attention.

CULTURE SHOCK CAN DEEPLY AFFECT YOUR SENSE OF IDENTITY

"Moving to Turkey was my first expat (lovepat) experience and I was completely naive and unprepared. If I had known how difficult it was going to be I would have set up a network ahead of time and had a plan for how to deal with the homesickness, culture shock, depression and identity crisis. But I was newly married and excited to start my new life with my Turkish husband. If I hadn't been so committed to my marriage I would have quit after the first year, but something inside me knew I was stronger than the circumstances I was in, and I tapped into my 'inner entrepreneur' to find solutions to the problems I was facing – loneliness, isolation, identity issues, language, depression and culture barriers."

Tara Agacayak, American expat living in Turkey

Strengthening or maintaining our levels of resiliency doesn't mean we'll avoid culture shock, but I do think it reassures us when we start to feel those uneasy twinges. It is important to know that virtually everyone encounters some form of this phenomenon and eventually makes their way through it – some sooner or with less turmoil or angst than others. Many may not realize what's happening, it's only with hindsight they can appreciate when and how they navigated through it.

SHOCKING FOR RELATIONSHIPS AND FAMILIES, TOO

As I indicated earlier, I've always been impressed with the prolific writing of seasoned expat/ repat author and speaker Robin Pascoe. It was the following two sentences in her book, *Raising Gobal Nomads: Parenting Abroad in an On-Demand World*, which grabbed and held my attention: *'Family culture shock is an often overlooked form of the (broader) phenomenon. It is a collective experience of loss: the loss of control over new surroundings and, later, over each member's behavior. As each individual family member struggles in their own way with the shock of regaining equilibrium, that person's behavior and moods can deeply affect others in the family.'*

'As each individual family member struggles in their own way with the shock of regaining equilibrium, that person's behavior and moods can deeply affect others in the family.'

Pascoe goes on to paint the all-too-common picture of how children may have a completely different perspective than their parents, or even their siblings. The children experience leaving one home and transitioning into a new one, having to become acquainted with a new school with different teachers and perhaps an altogether different curriculum. They start all over again with the challenge of making new acquaintances who, if all goes well, may or may not become friends. All the while they are trying desperately to fit in while hoping someone will actually look beyond the 'new kid' exterior and see – *really* see – the underlying strengths, talents and personality quirks that make each person a wholly distinct individual.

> 'The move can upset how the family relates to one another. As in any crisis, it takes time for a family to re-stabilize. Honest communication with one another, flexibility, and the ability to sit back and laugh about it. Children are not simply smaller versions of adults; they often lack the emotional frame of reference to put names to what they are seeing, feeling, experiencing.'

Often one parent heads off to work in a new situation while the other takes on the many tasks, big and small, required to help the family settle and function in their new environment, where the culture and often the language are entirely new. In the case of individuals, or when both adults are employed, the family may find itself struggling to get basic services connected, registrations handled and paperwork turned into the requisite authorities, new procedures learned and routines set up, leaving everyone tired, overwhelmed and in a state of uproar.

Everyone is doing their best (or not) to work their way through the various stages of culture shock (or not), often with the result of family members ending up in entirely different emotional places as they try to muddle through. Small wonder Pascoe turned to licensed marriage/ family therapist and ATCK Lois Bushong for this gentle reminder: *'The move can upset how the family relates to one another. As in any crisis, it takes time for a family to re-stabilize. And more than just time, honest communication with one another, flexibility, and the ability to sit back and laugh about it will be very helpful. Children, by definition, are not simply smaller versions of adults; as such they often lack the emotional frame of reference to put names to what they are seeing, feeling, experiencing.'*

I certainly found this to be the case as culture shock affected each member of our family in different ways and on different timelines. Husband arrived six months ahead of the rest of the family to start work with an international organization in which the primary workplace language was English. Long days were spent learning the nuances of how work was conducted and settling in; he had office colleagues to pose questions to regarding 'How do I…?' or 'Where do I find?' and could dash off a quick email to me or respond to mine.

Weekends were spent exploring our new city and its environs and, given the time difference, touching base with our family via Skype. Having arrived at the height of winter darkness and chill, he found himself buoyed by the expanding daylight and climbing temperatures. By the time we arrived he was enjoying the long days and in-city café culture of a perfect Dutch summer, ready to ride the bicycles we brought with us and show us the gorgeous beaches and surrounding countryside.

Son and I found ourselves going through what I would characterize as a relatively 'average' transition to cross-cultural life. He headed off to school and got to know classmates who eventually became good friends. Accepting it would take a little time to become comfortable and 'fit in', he joined the cross country team for camaraderie and enjoyed a greater degree of independence getting around by safe, inexpensive public transportation, and socializing in the more relaxed Dutch culture.

I, on the other hand, dove into learning Dutch, dutifully attended school-hosted orientation events and coffee hours, read up on this thing called 'culture shock', went easy on myself and essentially lowered my standards for the time being as to what constituted a productive day. There were a few days when I'd do the bare minimum and end up reading a book on the sofa, but generally I sensed if I kept plugging away I'd improve at speaking Dutch, become accustomed to life in a Dutch neighborhood, and find that some of those acquaintances would eventually become friends.

At that often awkward age of 13, Daughter was at a distinct disadvantage in moving during the tumultuous pre-adolescent years of middle school. While excited to get to know a new country and cultural ways, she found some of the other girls superficial in their interests and actions, and took far longer to search out others who would eventually become her close friends. Moreover, she deeply mourned the loss of the elite-level soccer-training path she had been on – a key component of her young identity.

Joining a Dutch club team satisfied her need to keep playing while giving her much-appreciated exposure to and interface with Dutch girls her age, but the differences in tactical style of play, and less serious dedication to intensive training, were continual reminders that her former life was over, and with it her dreams of playing at the highest level. Daughter's free fall into the deep trough of culture shock coincided with the advent of shorter, colder days. Overall, she suffered the most and was deeply unhappy for far longer than the rest of us.

That's why I feel an acutely personal sense of gratitude to Lois Bushong for filling a critical gap in expat/ cross-cultural therapy with her about-to-be-released book, *Belonging Everywhere and Nowhere: Insights into Counseling the Globally Mobile*. We'll explore more about the importance of assisting our children in identifying and naming their emotions later in this chapter, and ways to accomplish this in *CHAPTER 9: CONNECTING EXTERNALLY*.

HOME AND BELONGING

Poets, authors and musicians have been writing about the concept of home for millennia. No matter how humble or privileged our circumstances, we have an innate desire to create a place – a nest or haven – to be alone or with our families, safe from the outside world. It is where we can relax, recharge and regroup. Ideally our home is physically located where we feel a sense of belonging, of being part of a broader whole.

Our concept of home may change over time, based on our age, life stage and experiences. I was recently asked how I define home, and I shared this: *'It used to be people in a place. Things happened and memories were born. Along the way more people were added, more memories were created, and the place changed. And again, and again, on and on. So home became people, places and memories. With my son six time zones away attending university, out of the nest, I've come to believe that home is the feelings about those people, places, memories.'*

The question 'Where are you from?' may be simple to many people, but to expats/ cross-culturals it can be loaded with ambiguity and complexity. When you've lived in different numerous countries/ cultures for much of your life, determining where you come from can be downright complicated.

SOMETIMES THEY JUST DON'T GET IT

"When someone asks me where I come from, I answer '60% Holland, 35% New Zealand, and 5% Italy, Sweden, Dubai and Singapore.' Then they laugh and say 'Where do you REALLY come from?"

Rebecca Claudia Zijderveld, Dutch TCK/ repat currently living in the Netherlands after Italy, Sweden, Dubai and Singapore

While Rebecca has learned to apply levity and simplicity to make a complicated answer less so, it is poignant that so many times the rejoinder she receives reflects such disbelief. Imagine receiving a response like that, one which implies your 'story' deviates too far from what is expected, and is too complicated to be deemed truthful. Yet many of us deal with this over and over again.

Adult TCK Heidi Sand-Hart, author of one of my favorite books, *Home Keeps Moving: A Glimpse Into the Extraordinary Life of a Third Culture Kid*, and the child of missionary parents, grew up in England, Norway, Finland and India. She explains why it is so difficult to answer the standard question 'Where are you from?': '*It may sound ridiculous, but I often struggle with betraying myself if I tell people I am only from one country. The reason is that none of the countries of my upbringing fully represent who I am. I am definitely a blend of all the countries I am tied to, and I think I have taken certain parts of all the cultures and made them my own.*' For Sand-Hart and other TCK/ CCKs, limiting their answer to one place seems disloyal and would leave them feeling incomplete.

FINDING YOUR EMOTIONAL BASE WHEREVER YOU ARE

"My husband and I both had fairly transient childhoods and were raised by parents who were comfortably independent of their own extended families. Paul was an Army Brat and moved every few years. He really enjoyed living in Germany for his final three years of high school. I lived in four different states as a child, never in proximity to grandparents or extended family. So as children, both Paul and I lived in situations where emotional support was provided by our immediate families. Some of the expats I know who have struggled with living abroad grew up surrounded by extended family or in very stable communities with life-long friendships. For me, I have always felt that home is wherever my husband and kids and I are together. The strong support of my immediate family, along with the strong friendships that develop in expat communitie,s have provided the emotional base I've needed in each of my new communities."

Sara C. American expat now living in the Netherlands after Australia and Scotland

While the concept of home is in part literal in nature – the apartment or house in the place where you physically reside – for many it becomes more figurative with the passage of time. This is particularly true for expats/ cross-culturals living a mobile lifestyle.

CHOOSING YOUR OWN HOMES, HOWEVER MANY THEY MAY BE

"The flip side of belonging everywhere is that sometimes feel I belong nowhere, and this can be difficult at times. I have other Third Culture Kid friends who moved straight to their home country after high school and have stayed there, claiming their national culture and learning, better, how to fit it and belong. I made different life choices and decided not to do that, but I did spend a few years in New York City, learning what it was like to be American. Of course, New York City is the US's finest example of what it means to be American and at the same time from elsewhere, and American culture in general tolerates a great deal of multiculturalism, what with our nomenclatures of African-American, Indian-American, Italian-American, and so on.

I learned to be okay with not having a single 'home' location that I can claim in conversation and identify with. I answer the 'where are you from' question with the abbreviated truth, 'I'm American, but grew up in India, Kenya and Egypt,' and it communicates what I want without getting too personal. And I enjoy the absolute freedom of choosing my own homes – however many they may be."

Elie Calhoun, American ATCK who has lived most of her life in Africa, including Kenya, Egypt, Tanzania, Liberia and Senegal

While giving an evening presentation at ASH two years ago, Ruth Van Reken invited a panel of four high school students to share their stories of where they were 'from' and where they had lived in their mobile, global, expatriate lives. As she began discussing the importance of home, she turned to the students and asked whether they had a home base to which they one day expected to return. She was pleasantly surprised to learn the families of all four already had such a base in place, noting it was the first time in all her years of speaking around the world that this was the case.

The Korean student spoke of his family keeping their home back in Seoul and spending summers there. The Danish student's family were preparing to repatriate two years later and had purchased a house situated halfway between the two sets of grandparents, where they spent their summer and Christmas vacations. The son of a US foreign service officer would return to his family home in the American heartland which had been maintained for the entirety of their time abroad, and the Dutch student had repatriated to his family home after his expatriate years. Each student was able to comfortably and clearly state where 'home' was. Unfortunately, not every expat/ cross-cultural is able to do so.

THE BENEFIT OF HAVING A HOME BASE, IF NOT A SPECIFIC HOME

"We've also been fortunate to have strong ties to our extended families back in the US. We've made a point of spending a significant portion of our vacation time with our extended families in California, and I believe we have built stronger relationships with them than we would have if we'd remained in the US. This has provided an important 'home base' in the US for our children."

Sara C.
American expat now living in the Netherlands after Australia and Scotland

The concept of belonging is closely related to that of home, but it is more a sense of acceptance – that you fit in. Again, feeling as though we belong can be in relation to people and places, on an individual, group or societal basis. We all need to be able to say with some certainty 'this is my place in the world'.

YEARNING TO BELONG

"One of the biggest challenges I have faced in my expat life is the feeling of not belonging. Of course, as an expat you live somewhere that you do not have roots, but even returning to where you came from after a period away can be challenging.

It is well documented that when embarking upon life as an expat it takes time and effort to make new friends, to find work and to settle into a new place. Different cultures and traditions can seem overwhelming and getting to a stage where you feel confident carrying out daily tasks in a new country and language can, at times, feel impossible.

These problems often become seen as mere challenges however, because the excitement generated by the enormous life change protects our emotional well-being. A newly arrived expat faces a steep learning curve and the type of person who chooses to put themselves through that is usually someone who feels inspired and invigorated by such a change.

However, expat life is not the easy option that many perceive it to be. When you hit a rough patch, more often than not you hit it alone. Even if you are not entirely alone the people around are, more often than not, relatively new figures in your life. The strong support network from home is not there. Everyone everywhere has a bad day once in a while and even they can cause distress."

Liv Gaunt, an adult TCK now living in Turkey

We all want to feel we belong, but continual moving across cultures requires we start anew each time. If we can't initially find a sense of belonging in a place, is it possible, as with the concept of 'home,' to find it in a state of mind? I believe so.

BELONGING AS ACCEPTANCE OF WHERE YOU ARE RIGHT NOW

"Born in the Netherlands to long-term expat parents from the UK, I spent my first 18 years living on the outskirts of The Hague and going to Dutch schools. I moved to the UK to go to the University of Sheffield when I was 18. When I was 23 I spent a year in New Zealand, after which I returned to the Netherlands for two months to decide where to go next. I ended up in Bristol, UK, for six years.

Now, after living 'abroad' for 12 years, I am back in the Netherlands where I see myself staying for the time being. My parents still live in the Netherlands and since 2009, my brother, who had also spent a few years in the UK, lives here too.

I have moved around a bit and I have always wondered about where I am from and where my home is, but in the last couple of years I realise that home is much more than your physical location. It hasn't always been easy moving to a new place and building up a life for yourself from scratch, but it's not impossible either. Along the way I have learnt many things and I've found some tools and techniques that have helped me immensely, not only to settle into a new place, but also to cope with constant change."

Carrie Sanderson, Anglo-Dutch Adult TCK/ CCK living in the Netherlands

Accepting where we are as the new basis for how we envision home isn't always easy. We may be physically present yet feel emotionally detached, as if we're still elsewhere. It takes time, experience, and connections for a sense of belonging, of being home, to evolve.

NEITHER NATIVE TO OUR OLD HOME NOR LOCAL TO OUR NEW ONE

"It's true what they say. You don't really feel like you belong to either culture that you've grown up in. There is the slightest of divide between the culture you grew up in and the culture that you're from.

Some people say to me, 'Oh, you're so LA' – implying that I embody this idea of a laidback California girl with beachy waves in my hair. But this so-called personality of mine is only a result of current surroundings. I wasn't born in California and I didn't grow up on the beach.

Wherever the place was that I called home at the time, it never defined me or provided me with an identity. I was born in Hawaii, but leaving at less than a year old didn't give me props [i.e., proper respect] to be called a Hawaiian. I spent the next few years in Boston and Houston. Then we moved to Beijing.

My family and I had been going to China for a handful of summers so I knew what was different. I knew I didn't belong. I am Chinese, but I was cast as a foreigner, immediately known the minute I opened my mouth with slight 'American' accents to my fluent Mandarin. The international school I attended had other kids like me, their last home was somewhere else in the world too – most of us neither a native to our old home anymore nor a local to our new one.

Beijing did become home. It felt like home. It's where we grew up and hold our memories. But where do we belong? We're not Beijing locals. I've lived in Los Angeles for six years, yet I can't call it my home. It's a home. I don't suppose anywhere will truly feel like home if I'm always thinking about somewhere else. And the next time I move, people will assume I am 'so LA' because that's 'where I'm from'. But as any TCK knows, the last place you've lived doesn't make that your home, it doesn't just define who you are. Perhaps 'home' is just a feeling, not a place."

Annie Huang, Adult TCK now living in the US

Given the close relationships among our identity – how we were, how we now see ourselves, are seen by others or want to become – our sense of home and where we feel we belong, it is easy to see how our background and the life we lead contribute greatly to our perceptions of these three important themes. The more we move, especially when crossing cultures, the greater the effort required to integrate and make emotional sense of our experiences.

RESTLESSNESS AND ROOTLESSNESS

I'm reminded of the old adage about parents teaching our children to have 'roots and wings' so they know who they are and where they come from, but are also strong enough (and I would add resilient enough), to leave the nest and make their way in life. Years ago when my children were younger, we were visiting a friend's house for a family barbecue. As I was ducking into the powder room, a linen wall hanging in the nearby hallway caught my eye.

At the top was an embroidered oak tree, with thick branches of all sizes and strong roots growing deeply below the ground. Several birds in vibrant shades of blue and red sat perched in the upper branches. A particularly glorious yellow bird was caught in mid-flight, its open wings spanning the air as it glided away from the tree. What stopped me in my tracks was the embroidered saying beneath the tree:

'For you, my child, I wish two things: to give you roots and give you wings.'

To say these words resonated with me is an understatement. I experienced such a moment of clarity that I knew they captured the essence of not only childrearing, but of personal growth and exploration. I've since come to appreciate how much they also speak to the highly mobile, cross-cultural expatriate lifestyle. Various sources attribute the saying to Jonas Salk, Hodding Carter or an ancient Chinese proverb. I can't say for sure who wrote these words, I only know they touch people deeply.

Ever since, I've done my best to raise my children 'with roots and wings'. I believe we ground them by modeling in daily life the values we hold dear, instilling in them a sense of home and familial connection. This gives them the roots to feel secure in knowing who they are and from where they come. We also do well to prepare them to find their

> 'Yet home need not always be a place. It can be a territory, a relationship, a craft, a way of expression, an experience of belonging, a feeling of being whole and known, sometimes too close for comfort. It's those attachments that liberate us more than they constrain.'

own path in life – when we encourage them on that journey, they leave the family nest safe in the knowledge they are loved. Knowing we, as parents, offer them a safe harbor of emotional support, gives our children the priceless gifts of confidence and freedom to make their own way in the world.

Between the roots and wings, we foster a sense of resilience in our children. We help them learn to weather missteps, adversity, and difficult events which may occur, moving beyond such hardships with insight, new perspectives, strength and grace.

With good intentions, our best efforts, some trying moments and a particularly dark time along the way, our family have all come to appreciate our new life in a different country and culture, and the insights and opportunities it has afforded us. Like his parents, Son is now studying international affairs at university – both he and Daughter easily see themselves living abroad sometime in the years ahead.

In many ways having done so has brought us closer together. When you're adjusting to a new place, making new friends and learning new ways of doing things, even dealing with the toughest of times, you come to understand that 'home' is the people you care about and who care about you, rather than a physical structure or particular place. It is the safety of the nest, even if you've grown and are out on your own – you carry your 'nest' in your heart, and that is home.

'Restless' also can be double-edged in meaning – being so used to packing up and moving on that you become enamored of the fresh start. We risk developing a form of 'the grass is always greener' syndrome, itching to see and experience more, able to leave problems behind without resolution if we wait it out until we leave.

Many ATCKs/ ACCKs move around so much during childhood they find themselves, years later, experiencing feelings of homesickness or yearning for a homeland they may not be able to fully define. Even if they did have stable childhoods in established communities surrounded by family and friends, I believe the continuous moving of many expats/ cross-culturals in their adulthood also lends itself to this sense of yearning for an elusive place called 'home'.

YEARNING FOR THE HOMELAND

"I can certainly relate to this. The child of a Scottish father and Maltese mother, I had lived in five different countries, including Russia and Malaysia, before my ninth birthday. I rarely felt 'homesick' as I was used to seeing the world as a place you travelled through. You made friends and lived in different houses which you picked up from and said goodbye to as a matter of course. But I was left with a feeling, a restlessness, a yearning for a place to call home.

While on holiday in Portugal, I discovered a word which is the best I have found to describe this feeling: saudade.

The word is practically impossible to translate – look it up on the Internet, and you will get a wealth of detail around its history and meaning.

Associated with the Portuguese music genre fado, *it describes a vague yearning for something, which could be the homeland we long for and which lies truly nowhere, or elsewhere, or everywhere, or perhaps only somewhere deep within ourselves."*

Natasha Gunn
ATCK/ ACCK, now lives in the Netherlands after France and England

Gianpiero Petriglieri, an Italian-born professor of Organizational Behaviour with the international business school INSEAD, who lives in France with his British wife and their two multicultural children, is currently teaching in the United States. He spoke directly to the twin issues of restlessness and rootlessness in his blog post, *Moving Around Without Losing Your Roots*, last year for the Harvard Business Review online.

While he writes specifically about nomadic professionals and global business leaders, his sentiments and insights can be extrapolated more broadly to expats. Despite their transience and diversity, he finds they share far more in common than might be expected: '*I think of them as a peculiar tribe. A tribe for people unfit for tribalism. Their unwillingness or inability to settle – to embrace and be defined by one place only – draws them to each other. It makes them restless and curious. It helps them develop the sensitivity to perspectives and the ability to work across cultures... it also comes with a price. That price is struggling with the question of home and its troublesome acolytes, identity and belonging.*'

Few of us wish to be strangers, preferring instead to be known, accepted and embraced. Petriglieri acknowledges that extending roots in one or more places isn't always easy and requires a willingness to lay our hearts bare, including for eventual loss as we, or others, move on. Yet he makes a solid and surprisingly emotional case that while we may be nomadic professionals, we really don't want to become professional nomads. The distinction is important.

Petriglieri offers us this: '*Yet home need not always be a place. It can be a territory, a relationship, a craft, a way of expression. Home is an experience of belonging, a feeling of being whole and known, sometimes too close for comfort. It's those attachments that liberate us more than they constrain. As the expression suggests, home is where we are from – the place where we begin to be... This takes physical and emotional presence.*'

It takes time to settle into a new place, to make the connections and build the friendships, those attachments to which Petriglieri refers. We must remind ourselves to make the effort, but at the same time to be patient. These ties which bind us to a place do not happen overnight, they cannot be rushed. We must allow them to play out over time.

A CONTINUOUS FEELING OF DÉJÀ VU

"*Expat life is seen as adventurous by those who have not experienced it, with its constant changes and excitement. Perhaps when one first starts out as an 'expat' the feeling is one of adventure, but after 16 years of jumping from one country to another the adverse factor is 'boredom' – a continuous* déjà vu *feeling. This is both positive and negative. One of the most challenging factors is that people back home or even people locally do not understand any of the life you have lived...*

How does one deal with this déjà vu *feeling? Mainly by keeping a monthly goal in mind, an objective that supports either career or personal life, it can be a holiday, supporting development of people, getting rid of debt – yet it needs to be something that is part of your heart that will allow you to stay objective and positive.*"

Nicole Le Maire, Dutch serial expat (Germany, Italy, UK, Belgium, US, Kuwait, Saudi Arabia, Jordan)

Sometimes no matter how carefully we choose a place to call our own, no matter how deep the roots we establish, no matter how firmly we vocalize that we are 'home', we still cannot keep ourselves from wondering whether there is another place where we could be happier, another place that calls to us.

THE LIFE OF THE ETERNAL EXPAT

"There are vague memories. Half-constructed images with dream-like consistency that fade away into nothingness as I try to bring them into view, aided and almost preserved solely by the yellowish photographs that Mum keeps in a box somewhere. These memories are from a land that time forgot, England up till 1981, which was when we moved to my parents' homeland of Malta, in the Mediterranean.

The first real memories start to come to the fore here. I recall my father climbing into a large truck that somehow had all our furniture from England and he drove our car out of it. It looked unusual there – a familiar item parked on the street in front of my grandparents' house which is not where it usually belonged.

Days turned into months and before long I was in another foreign country – school – and had my fair share of trials and tribulations. One set of memories I had is of fitting in. Or perhaps of not fitting in. Despite my Maltese heritage, and despite my best efforts to integrate, I still felt different and to some extent I was different. I had this Ladybird book of London and for me, the places mentioned in the book were not foreign at all. I still had images of Buckingham Palace in my mind and could almost taste the Wimpy burger that my Dad and I ate before going to the cinema.

Life went on and I always spoke of myself as being British rather than Maltese. I almost added 'defiantly' to that last sentence and I'm not sure why that emotion popped into mind but I can recall being sidelined – bullied perhaps – as a result of being different so perhaps there was an element of pride in it.

Later on in life, I moved back to the UK after my studies. I settled into a quiet life in a country village in Suffolk, East Anglia. The difference from a dry and hot Mediterranean island could not have been greater and I enjoyed my life there. And yet...

And yet, I started to feel something else now. I would weave my way through the market stalls on a Saturday afternoon, crinkle up my nose and think to myself, 'You wouldn't find roast chicken in a market in Malta, you'd find an endless series of Maltese snacks'. Totally unfair comparison, I know, but I used to think to myself that the snacks were far superior than plain old chicken and if I had enough time and patience I would be able to put a stand together and make money selling Maltese treats to the locals while the roasted chickens remained unsold.

My jaunt back in the UK did not last long. I was back on the island inside of eighteen months for a marriage which did not quite work out as expected. In some ways, it felt like returning home. I know the place like the back of my hand. I've grown up in Malta after all and relate to local customs and quirks even if I don't quite speak Maltese as fluently as I should. And yet ...

And yet, I yearned to be back. I dreamt of living in London, someplace more vibrant than the quiet countryside of Suffolk. Perhaps moving to the countryside was a bad idea, I told myself. This time it will be different, I reassured myself. Ultimately, I did not end up moving back to the UK. Instead, I ended up in Belgium.

However, the thing about Belgium is that it is more English than Malta and more Maltese than England. It is jabberwocky country, with aspects from both sides of the looking glass. It is the comfort food of countries and consequently is rather appropriate for someone in my predicament.

And so here I am, an expat running away from being an expat by being an expat somewhere else. I enjoy my life here, I feel comfortable... and still ask I myself a key question whenever I travel to another city or country, 'Would I live here' In some cases I would and so I look forward to a life where I continue being the eternal expat."

Antoine, ACCK who writes under the name of The Unexpected Traveller, now living in the Czech Republic

Like a siren's song, sometimes the lure of change of place becomes too strong to resist. There is nothing wrong with that *per se*. Yet with each move we have more to integrate into our story of ourselves, and continually searching for the 'greener grass' can keep us from developing the emotional roots needed to feel grounded. Perpetual restlessness is not an easy burden to bear.

CAREER CHALLENGES FOR ACCOMPANYING PARTNERS

One of the most challenging issues to deal with overseas is that of employment, and more precisely, employment opportunities for accompanying partners, both male and female. I don't know how to say it any clearer than this – finding work in a different country/ culture as an accompanying partner is difficult. Not impossible, but difficult nonetheless.

How many expatriates/ cross-culturals are there in the world? It's hard to say. The World Bank estimates 215 million people are living outside their country of birth, while the United Nations estimates half are working and thus referred to as 'international migrants'. The deeper you drill down, the murkier the employment picture becomes. There is a large gap as the next best layer of information shifts from the international organization behemoths to large global mobility and relocation corporations such as Ernst & Young, Brookfield or Cartus, which poll companies operating internationally. It's quite a leap from international migrants to international assignments, and even then the total number of the latter – that is, actual people – is difficult to ascertain. We can safely say the number of people working overseas is somewhere in the vicinity of 100 million, and of these slightly more than half have accompanying partners, many of whom aren't working outside the home for pay.

Don't buy into the old stereotype of expat spouses living lives of pampered, chauffeured luxury, spending their days poolside or on the tennis courts, in shopping boutiques or throwing back glasses of wine at fancy luncheons. I'm sure there are some out there who may fit this profile, but they are few and far between. Most accompanying partners aren't. Anecdotal evidence, comments left on expat forums, websites and blogs, issues raised during presentations and discussions at the annual Families in Global Transitions conferences, and common wisdom gleaned from expat grapevines worldwide, tell us that most accompanying partners work before they head overseas, but once there, far fewer enter into the workforce.

The majority of these partners want to continue working, yet are often unaware of the seemingly endless obstacles and challenges that make it difficult to do so. These can include lack of work visas or employer support to gain them, the host culture not recognizing professional credentials or prior work experiences, language limitations, cultural barriers, child care which is prohibitively expensive, limited or non-existent, and/ or foregoing one's career while caring for family members, especially if the working partner travels extensively or works long hours.

That's where Scottish expat Evelyn Simpson and English expat Louise Wiles have fulfilled a pressing need. Working from different countries (Belgium and Portugal respectively), these two accompanying expat spouses and international business partners surveyed more than 300 accompanying partners in 59 countries around the world last year (2012) – exploring the decisions these partners make in relation to their own career choices when they relocate to accompany their partners in an international assignment.

As expats and professional entrepreneurs, Simpson and Wiles share a passion for coaching and working with accompanying partners as the latter take on the challenges of relocation and adaptation to their new lives abroad. Both Simpson and Wiles are seasoned accompanying partners with 40+ years of expat experience between them. They know what it's like to leave behind careers in other fields to support their spouses in overseas assignments. They've done the tough, yet necessary, business of relocating a family and helping members settle in during the expat transition cycle. They've each gone back to school for the obligatory coursework, training and accreditation, and successfully launched new careers for themselves.

In conducting this much-needed study and publishing the results, they combine all their talents, skills, training, experience and know-how to help create change that will benefit others who find themselves in the similar situation of accompanying partner. I for one am thrilled they conducted the *Career Choice and the Accompanying Partner Survey*, and have put together a highly effective report on their findings. If you're a current or aspiring expat, global nomad, international or transnational employee, accompanying partner, relocation/ mobility specialist, international Human Resources employee, expat coach or consultant, you may want to review the free Summary Report of the survey findings, and Simpson and Wiles' insights and assessments, at their site – www.ThrivingAbroad.com. By focusing on the wants, needs, challenges and opportunities of the relocating partner in general, and career development and employment options in particular, this survey goes a long way toward helping address the issues that can make or break an overseas assignment. They draw several important conclusions from the survey findings, shared here:

- *The majority of accompanying partners do want to work in some form whilst on assignment: This makes the challenge of recruitment and retention of employees who are a part of a dual career couple very real and relevant to organisations.*

- *There are some very real obstacles for accompanying partners to working whilst abroad in addition to the well documented and recognised challenge of work permits: Understanding these obstacles will help employers to target the resources they use to support accompanying partners in a more effective and cost efficient way.*

- *Assuming partners are happy in their supporting role is not always valid: Whether accompanying partners do not work due to circumstance or choice, it may have a negative impact on their level of assignment fulfillment.*

> 'Instead of seeing accompanying partners as an additional cost and a difficult issue, the study proposes partners be seen as an asset *in the relocation process'*

- *Accompanying partners require support: They would benefit from assistance identifying purpose and meaning in their assignment experience regardless of their ability or desire to work.*

I've read the entire report and find it accurate, thorough and comprehensive. Simpson and Wiles have conducted a thoughtful and in-depth analysis of the data provided in their survey results. In my opinion, perhaps the most important point they make is this: instead of seeing accompanying partners as an additional cost and a difficult issue, the study proposes partners be seen as an *asset* in the relocation process. You have no idea how refreshing that simple statement is, and how invaluable this report.

Hindsight is notoriously 20-20, so having read various reports about career challenges in expat life – particularly for the accompanying partner – I sought the insights of a long-term expatriate who has since repatriated. I was particularly interested in her perspective looking back on her years working abroad, and how that informed her employment upon return.

CAREER CHOICES: WHAT I'M GLAD I DID

" 'If only I'd known then what I know now' is something I rarely say, because I don't believe in crying over spilt milk and because the world changes so rapidly that often the solutions available today weren't available back then. But an upcoming webinar on portable careers for expat spouses got me thinking – what I would do the same if I were starting out today?

What I did then and would still do today:

- *I would be a stay-at-home mom until my son finished school. I am thankful that I had an opportunity to be both a working mum (before expatriation) and a SAHM (during expatriation) and to experience the joys and frustrations of both.*

- *I would study the local language. Even though I know now that hell will freeze over before I could work in another language, it is such an insight into the local culture and even just a few words and phrases make everyday life so much easier.*
- *I would do a lot of volunteer work. Looking back I can see I learned a hell of a lot doing things I didn't get paid for and with a bit of creativity they can be made to look quite impressive on a résumé. Nobody ever asks how much you got paid."*

Judy Rickatson, Canadian immigrant/ expat/ repat who lived in the UK, Azerbaijan, Egypt and UAE

Given the challenges our children face as they transition from one country/ culture to another, as well as the difficulties in finding the kind of work we seek, many accompanying partners find themselves electing to stay home with the children, at least initially if not longer. I did so for the first year, eager to make sure every member of my family had found their way and was settled in. Only then did I begin to enact the career change I'd come to realize I desired – even so, I started gradually, working part-time and at home. My career evolution continues and I'm pleased it has, but I don't regret the decision to step away from working outside the home when my children most needed it.

I also second Judy's recommendations to attempt to learn as much of the local language as possible and to seek out interesting and creative volunteer opportunities. More on these two topics in *PART III's CHAPTER 9: CONNECTING EXTERNALLY.*

CAREER CHOICES: WHAT I COULD HAVE DONE DIFFERENTLY

"Just as I considered what in my expat working career I would do the same if I were just starting out, I also asked myself what would I change?

What I would do differently today:

- *I would study more while I wasn't working. Distance learning when we first went overseas would have been difficult but not impossible, these days it's just a mouse click away and the choices are almost limitless.*

- *I would find a mentor or coach to brainstorm with from time-to-time. Like many expats I had no idea how long we would live overseas. Even those who have fixed term contracts often find they are extended or cancelled. I had never heard the term 'portable career' and I didn't realize that once my spouse had an international résumé, more international assignments would follow. Years slip away before you realize what's happening. If I were doing it again I would conduct an annual review of my situation and goals, ideally with someone who has expat experience, an unbiased opinion and enough guts to tell me what I need to hear (in other words, probably not a close friend).*

When I did finally return to the paid workforce overseas I would have looked harder for something related to my original profession. My personal experience, and what I've heard anecdotally from other expats, is that starting a new career when overseas often doesn't translate well when you return home. I found prospective employers here far more interested in what I did in Canada 15 years ago than what I did in Dubai one year ago. But maybe that's just me and Canada, and for those who never return to their country of origin it wouldn't apply anyway."

Judy Rickatson, Canadian immigrant/ expat/ repat who lived in the UK, Azerbaijan, Egypt and UAE

Consulting with an unbiased, outside expert, furthering your education and adding to your skillset are good suggestions. What I found of interest – even cautionary – is Judy's final recommendation of sticking with your initial career path. After all, it is the obstacles in the way of expat accompanying partners which keep them from doing precisely that. This is why the idea of transitioning to a new career is so appealing.

Jo Parfitt has been writing for years about the challenges of building and maintaining a career when heading abroad, either solo or as an accompanying partner. Her bestselling, *A Career in Your Suitcase*, was recently overhauled for its fourth edition, and in so doing, Parfitt turned to fellow expat and career consultant Colleen Reichrath-Smith to help co-author this update. They share:

'Today, few international corporations remain ignorant of the 'dual career' issue. It is on the agenda of almost every multinational corporation. Sadly though, many organisations find it a bit of a hot potato and offer the same kind of support they always have – with work

permits, language and training. But it is impossible to create a 'one-size-fits-all' solution to this dilemma. Few mobile spouses will be able to climb their chosen career ladder, stay in the same field, or even the same company. Few will find it easy to hop from permanent employment to permanent employment. For even if there were work available, other hurdles get in the way... it can be hard to find suitable work which fits round everything else... While there are many barriers likely to hinder your progress, there are skills to be learned and techniques that will support you to develop your own personally meaningful portable career.'

One of the key reasons why expats/ cross-culturals encounter such challenges when it comes to ensuring work is available for both parties in dual career couples, is because they themselves often don't give it much thought before moving abroad. They assume once they arrive it will sort itself out. *'Surely if I've been successful in my field at home (or in country X), my experience and education will help me find similar work when I live in Y'* they think. Little do they realize.

Brookfield GRS noted in their 2011 *Global Relocation Trends Study*, just how important the role of family dynamics is in the success of expatriate assignments. Partner resistance (47%) and problems with family adjustment (32%) top the list of impediments. Resistance on the part of accompanying partners can come from several sources, including the local country/ culture, dissatisfaction with quality of life, extensive hours and/ or travel associated with the expat partner's job and, of course, difficulty in finding meaningful work when desired.

CHAPTER 3: OTHER KEY ISSUES IN EXPAT LIFE

In *CHAPTER 2: IDENTITY ISSUES IN EXPAT LIFE*, we looked at identity and related issues in expatriate/ cross-cultural life. Now we will look at a number of additional challenges likely to present themselves. These may range from uncertainty, to changes in relationships, to guilt, to missing out.

UNCERTAINTY AND CONTINUAL CHANGE

Two of the most challenging aspects of expat life are becoming accustomed to a fairly high level of uncertainty and learning to deal well with ongoing change. Whether due to the vagaries of the international economy, a tenuous political or employment situation on the ground, the unraveling of a marriage/ relationship, or family considerations, time spent in another culture is fraught with uncertainty.

LEARNING TO ACCEPT FORWARD MOTION

"One of the issues I have struggled with over the years is the uncertainty that goes with expatriate living. I think it is made all the more difficult by being the accompanying partner. We have relocated five times in the last fifteen years because of my husband's jobs. At times we have known a move is possible/ probable but have not been certain about where it would take us and when. At these points there can be a dilemma between wondering 'do we leave things to fate and simply trust that the right thing will turn up' OR 'do we work hard to influence the outcome, and if so how?' *At these moments there is an inner battle between our desire to be and feel in control of our own destiny and the more intellectual reaction, which is that we can influence and do our best but never control everything.*

I have found over the years that at these points we have to be clear about what we want and do not want, then we work to decide how best we can influence the outcomes. This gives us a sense of 'control' and I have been surprised at how, when we have decided to work towards a specific outcome, we have eventually arrived there. This is not to say the journey is always easy, it rarely is, and I would never describe our experience as 'being in control' more simply being in forward motion."

Louise Wiles, British expat living in Portugal after Spain

Sometimes when we move overseas, we think we have a good sense of what to expect in our host culture. Other times we know where we're headed is vastly different from anything we've ever encountered. Either way, we're usually surprised a little. One pervasive belief on the part of families/ friends left behind – and occasionally by the expats themselves – is that the standard of living is almost always higher.

NOT ALWAYS THE LUXURIOUS EXPAT LIFESTYLE YOU MIGHT THINK

"In terms of difficulty, I would say adjusting to a different standard of living caused me some stress. Our rental accommodation needed an intensive clean, and compared to the luxury of our newly renovated home in the UK, it was shabby and disappointing. That, coupled with our inability to get a car thanks to exorbitant insurance meant that I felt demoted in the world somehow. While we found our financial feet, we had to do without many things that we'd been used to at home – telephone, cable, wheels...

I suppose you could say I felt my social status had been lowered and I had never considered that when thinking about moving abroad. You tend to concentrate on the positives, and expat life is stereotypically portrayed as luxurious. I've since discovered it's not unusual for expats to experience a drop in their standard of living, particularly if, like us, you still have the financial commitment of a house in your 'home' country. I must sound so snobby and I'm really not, but when you have to walk 25 minutes into town to do your grocery shop in snow and blizzard, you start to hate everyone else who takes their car for granted, especially when you were one of them back home. On the upside though, the whole experience taught me some valuable lessons about the pitfalls of material attachment and appreciating what you've got."

Aisha Ashraf, Irish expat living in Canada by way of the UK

One of the biggest challenges many expats/ cross-culturals face is dealing with our children growing up and preparing to head off into the world. It may sound trite, but it really can feel as though they grow up in the blink of an eye. One day you're holding their hand as they enter kindergarten, the next you're discussing boundaries and curfews as they navigate the tumult of teen years, and suddenly you're waving them off as they go to university or plunge into the work world.

PARENTING FROM OVERSEAS

"We are closer as a family unit than we would have been if we'd stayed 'at home' where other family members and friends would have diluted our time and attention from each other. People who haven't traveled and lived away from a support group might find our relationships with each other intense compared to theirs.

We were settled overseas, life was mapped out for us. The older two were at university but close enough to drive home when they wanted. Then fate intervened with a hurricane, which changed the course of our lives. Seven years later, with the youngest having now left home too, none of them lives in the same country as each other or us, yet all of us wish we did.

It has been a challenge for each of those seven years, parenting by phone and email, across time zones – one, seven and nine hours respectively. These days it's easier because of Skype and WhatsApp but the worry and anxiety for one or other child seems to be constant, even though they are grown. Finding their feet in college, the workplace, or dealing with serious health issues with no immediate support group, has been tough for them. As a parent it's said you are only ever as happy/ settled as your unhappiest/ unsettled child and to some degree that's true."

Jane Dean, Anglo/ American expat currently living in the Netherlands

'Two of the most challenging aspects of expat life are becoming accustomed to a fairly high level of uncertainty and learning to deal well with ongoing change. '

I remember well my own feelings about Son heading off to college two years ago. I thought I'd be a bit sad when he reached the milestone of graduating high school two months earlier, but sailed through that without so much as a tear shed. I was happy for him – happy he'd graduated, happy he'd been accepted at a good school, happy he was looking forward to going to university. It's what we do – we raise them to leave and make their way in the world. But sometimes our true feelings lie below the surface, as I found out when I sat down and wrote the following barely three weeks before he was to leave:

"Twenty three short days until Son reports to university and begins his college career. He's crossing an ocean to go to school in a different time zone, one that is six hours behind us. He's chosen to attend college back in the US. We know the school well, have visited before. He chose it because he said it 'felt right', and I could see that for myself. I know this is not the end of his being with us, living with us, sharing our daily lives. Plane reservations are already made to bring him home for the holidays at the end of the semester, interim holidays he'll spend visiting family in the US. We can jump on a plane and be there in less than a day if need be. In this wondrous age of modern technology, I know I'll be able to stay in touch with email, or catch him on Facebook. We can Skype face-to-face when I really need to see his smile, hear his voice, look into his eyes, read his emotions. It won't be exactly when and how I want to communicate with him, and I may have to wait longer to get my 'fix' of him. But still, the opportunities to stay connected are there.

I expect he will return at the end of the school year to spend next summer with us. We'll be able to share most meals together, pass each other on the stairs. We'll hear how his day went, ask him to walk the dog or take out the garbage or run some errand. We can discuss current events, watch a television show together. We'll have a sense of his comings and goings, who his new friends are, who he is becoming.

But I know that as he progresses on his journey, at some point it will cease to be him living with us and become him visiting us. And that is what is tearing me up inside."

'I had to accept the transience of relationships. The pattern was just a way of life. I had learnt not to miss people.'

I didn't know I would write those last two lines until I reached the end and they flowed out, along with my tears. But once they were written, a strange thing happened. I'd voiced my biggest fear and in doing so had released it into the cosmos. I let go of the building tension I'd been holding onto deep down inside, and was able to focus on enjoying the time we had together before he left for school.

> 'We are closer as a family unit than we would have been if we'd 'stayed at home'.'

One person I turned to for insights and experience on parenting from afar is Jane Dean. On her respected expat blog, www.wordgeyser.com, Jane has often written about parenting across time zones and continents. Her series of posts on parents preparing to send children off to university, or entry into the working world, and facing the resultant empty nest is particularly worthy of your time.

RELATIONSHIPS

You arrive in a new place – alone or with immediate family only – without the benefit of your friends. These are the people who matter – some you may have known for ages, others you've met and folded into the mix over the years, even the new one(s) you've discovered more recently and incorporated into your life. Now you've got to start over meeting and getting to know new people. At some point you have to determine whether any relationship is more than an acquaintanceship, has the makings of a full-fledged friendship, or is destined for the trash heap. Worse still, no one *knows* you – your quirky sense of humor or fear of heights, how you would drop anything and be there when a friend or family member is in need, that you're seldom on time but always arrive with an amusing story as to why you were late.

If you live a highly mobile life you may find yourself doing this again and again, starting over every few years. Often there is considerable pain and loss associated with coming and going. Anyone who has moved around a fair bit in life knows about the hurt of leaving, having to say goodbye to people, places, possessions, activities – even pets – which mean a lot to us.

One concern is that over time, you may start to ask yourself whether it's worth the effort – and yes, it does indeed take physical and emotional effort – to find and develop new friendships. Eventually some withdraw, retreating into the solace of immediate family and the ease of social media to remain in touch with loved ones around the world. In choosing to do so, however, we run the risk of 'gliding through life' rather than living it as fully as possible. We settle for superficial relationships, biding our time until we move on, repatriate or visit again. While understandable, this isn't healthy. It is light years from choosing to engage, adapt and thrive.

LEARNING NOT TO MISS PEOPLE

"I call myself an eternal expat – I was born in Dubai to English and Egyptian parents. I have no idea where I am from and have no concept of where home is.

From an early age I had to accept the transience of relationships when living in an expat hub. Many of my childhood friends' parents were on two-year contracts, so when we came back from summer holidays many of my friends would no longer be at school. The pattern was just a way of life. I moved myself a few times and eventually went to boarding school in the UK when I was 14. By this time I had learnt not to miss people. No one. Sometimes I'd think there was something wrong with me. I realised it was a necessary skill to adopt to cope with the distance and frequent separation and severance of relationships.

Don't get me wrong – I had a privileged childhood – I wouldn't wish to have been anything other than an expat. I'm now a citizen of the world – even if that does cause minor issues with people who can't relate. Most of my close friends have similar childhoods – we just 'get' each other. It does make you look at the world in a different way.

Years later I met John and we wanted to start a family. We were living in Dubai at the time. I was adamant I wanted my future children to grow up somewhere that wasn't transient, where they'd have rights in that country, and a place to call home. We moved to France three years ago and our daughter was born a year later. She is French, born in France and she speaks both French and English. I am still an expat and I'm not against the idea of living somewhere else one day – I think it's a great experience for anyone.

The hardest part of being an expat was when my daughter was born – the language barrier and being so far from family and friends was tough. It was equally hard when my sister recently had twins in Dubai. I felt so lost and resentful for being so far away from her. It was strange. You do miss out on a lot of events – Skype helps but it doesn't replace the day-to-day."

Ameena Falchetto
English/ Egyptian expat born in Dubai, now living in France

One notable aspect of expatriate life is our penchant for quickly forming intense, albeit (often) temporary, friendships. These have sometimes been regarded as convenient at best, superficial at worst. I tend to think this is a bit harsh. Yes, we may find ourselves spending time with people who aren't necessarily those we might hang out with were we 'back home' or in another place. But it doesn't have to mean these friendships don't serve a purpose – making emotional and social connections, however superficial they may appear, help both parties get through lean times. Sometimes all we need is an open mind to get to know someone we might not have considered a friend under different circumstances. If either party evolves out of the acquaintanceship, so be it. That's what adults do all the time – periodically realize they are growing away from some friends and toward others. So prune carefully, prune kindly, but prune accordingly.

MAGNIFIED, AMPLIFIED, MORE INTENSE

"A Yorkshire man, born in the early 60s, emotional resilience isn't something I have ever thought too much about: very much from the 'just get on with it' side of the fence. I am an only child, and from the age of 18 have lived away from home, frequently in a different country from my parents for long periods of time, and since 2005 we have been based full time in Almerimar, Spain.

If asked I would say I was emotionally resilient. I prefer my own company, can entertain myself for weeks on end, don't worry about the past, have very little need for the company of others, and the years have proven I can take most things in my stride and 'just get on with it'.

Little did I anticipate this background would equip me so well for life as an expat! When asked what it is like living an expat lifestyle I often liken it to living under a magnifying glass. In general things are amplified, made more intense. Relationships that take years to form in the normal world are formed (and broken) in a matter of weeks – one good session, a drunken heart to heart and bingo a new best friend, until next week when same bar, same discussion, same booze, different person reveals that the definition of 'in confidence' doesn't exist for the expat.

To live a successful expat lifestyle is to learn the art of compromise – people, events, types of food, cultural options are all different from those experienced and accessible at home. At some time you will be living amongst a hot bed of jealousy, resentment and bitterness, and with very few outlets for frustration it is easy to get in the firing line. If you stick it out for any length of time, inevitably you will be invited to significantly more funerals than weddings, given the aged demographic of many an expat community in Spain, very often for people you have only met infrequently in some bar or other, but you will be 'expected' to attend as one of the 'established expats'. Without a strong will your social diary will be controlled for you with a series of bland, boring and repetitive events trying to replicate the 'real thing' back home, and god help you when patriotic events such as the Royal Wedding, the Jubilee or a World Cup comes along when you will be expected to don face paint and a funny hat, as if you would ever do that at home!

Don't get me wrong, in small doses all the above can be fun (well, maybe not the funerals, although that said some of the best social events are at funerals when old friends and family from the UK have been known to turn up and bring a fresh conversation to the party), but the 'trick' to being a successful expat is to be your own person and do your own thing.

In all probability you aren't going to be a Yorkshire man and only child, so won't have the head start that I have, but you can develop an emotional resilience which will hold you in good stead."

Chris Marshall, British expat living in Spain

Mobility often makes for quickly formed, intense friendships. We don't want to waste time – literally – always fearing we or the other person will be leaving shortly. It's as if an unseen ticking clock demands we hurry along our friendships by sharing early and deeply.

It takes time to build a new life, and that includes a new circle of trusted friends. You've got to keep at it because in highly mobile expat life attrition runs high, you cannot afford to become complacent, assuming they will always be around. One day you're feeling fine, with a group of friends to call your own. The next thing you know, you look up and suddenly a few years have passed and either you or they are leaving.

GUILT

One of the most delicate issues we face is that of guilt, whether inflicted by family, friends or ourselves. We may feel guilt over being the one to leave, heading off into the world for whatever reason. We hear familiar refrains – why aren't we or our spouse looking for work 'back home'? Why can't we live near family and friends and satisfy our wanderlust with the occasional trip overseas? We feel guilt over not being there – wherever 'there' is – of not being part of things.

> 'Mobility often makes for quickly formed, intense friendships... an unseen ticking clock demands we hurry along our friendships by sharing early and deeply.'

We find ourselves missing important events and the frequent interactions that bind people together. We miss our nephew's wedding, or our cousin's graduation. We haven't met the newest additions to the family (babies, new spouses), and all they know of us is what they've been told. It's bad enough our families miss *us*, but how can we deprive them of the presence of our children, too? This is an especially sore subject between adult expats and their parents; by living so far away, we're made to feel – intentionally or not – that we're depriving our parents of their treasured relationship as grandparents to our child(ren). Both sides feel they've missed out on so much by our not being there, or at least not as often as we would if we still lived at 'home'.

The guilt felt at being so far away when loved ones need you is not something that is easily shared, yet is something many expats/ cross-culturals experience. That is certainly true in our case. We went from annual trips visiting my elderly in-laws and seeing my parents twice a year (often on their way to or from visiting my siblings and their families), to far fewer visits and making do with Skype sessions and email. If he traveled back to the US for work, Husband would tack on a side trip to check on his parents while I held down the home front. His parents were ten years older than mine, which has made for a bittersweet situation.

On the one hand it has meant we have gained experience in dealing with the demands and challenges of our parents' aging, illness/ injury, and ultimate passing. On the other, it has meant we have been doing so for more than a decade. During our time overseas we have lost both of his parents, most recently his mother at the beginning of this year. My parents are still alive and making the most of their golden years, but both are dealing with emotional and physical issues associated with advanced aging, and my father has been diagnosed with terminal cancer.

A particularly stressful time occurred several years ago when my mother-in-law had to be admitted to a dementia facility. She could no longer care for herself nor could my father-in-law care for her, she required around-the-clock supervision to ensure she didn't wander off. We were all fortunate, she included, that the form of dementia from which she suffered meant she was calm, content and surprisingly happy. Rather than forgetting everyone and everything, she still recognized her sons and their family members, and believed her mother, grandmother and others were still alive.

When you visited she would cheerfully explain you'd just missed her husband who had left for the office, and she was meeting her mother for lunch later in the day. Thankfully when lunchtime rolled around she would have forgotten her previous arrangements, and start looking forward eagerly to an (actual) musical concert in the facility's recreation room or (imaginary) dinner with husband and friends. The care she received was exemplary, we arranged for independent assessment and oversight, and visited her often. It helped assuage the guilt, but it certainly didn't eliminate it.

DON'T MAKE A DECISION YOU MIGHT REGRET

"The hardest thing for me as an expat has been when I felt conflicted about where I should be. Last year, my mother's battle with cancer reached its final stages, and I stayed on in California to be with her as she started hospice care. My husband and son returned home to the Netherlands to go back to school and work. My mother-in-law (who'd been an Army wife and lived far from her aging mother), gave me good advice. She told me that my guys could survive without me, but that I should be sure not to make a decision I'd regret later about caring for my mom. Ultimately, I kept extending my stay and was able to spend the last two months of my mom's life with her. It was difficult being away from my husband and son for that long, but I had the support of my sister, brother and daughter in the States. Also, my close friends back in the Netherlands looked after the guys. As an expat, I've had to learn to ask for and accept support from friends and family more than I did before I left the States."

Sara C.
American expat now living in the Netherlands after Australia and Scotland

The guilt stemming from not being there as family members age and/ or become ill is the bane of many an expat, especially for those of us in the 'sandwich generation' caught between caring for our children and our elderly parents. Even when children aren't involved, sometimes the needs of our parents can be overwhelming.

FEELING TORN AND NOTHING IS EVER QUITE ENOUGH

"The day before I moved to Turkey with my partner, Jack, I caught the end of a relocation programme on television. A young couple had moved to Sydney, Australia, and were faced with video footage of their parents, siblings and friends telling them how much they were missed. They stared at the screen, held hands and sobbed uncontrollably.

I felt sure I would never be in that position. Jack and I had worked through all the possible scenarios. We had justified why our move to Turkey was the right thing to do, and we knew our family and friends would understand. Of course they would, they loved us; they wanted the best for us.

Within a year of our move, my mum's health deteriorated and she was diagnosed with dementia. Dad struggled to cope with his ailing and confused wife. He was also caring for my younger brother who had multiple physical and learning difficulties. As my siblings stepped up to the plate to support Mum and Dad, my sense of guilt and uselessness grew exponentially.

I started to have nightmares about Mum and wrestled continuously with a growing sense of responsibility, and an overwhelming need to jet back to the UK and tell my parents I was there for them. But I wasn't there for them. I was 2,000 miles away immersed in a new life. I was stimulated, I had the perfect partner and I was happy. I was also an emotional wreck.

I decided on a series of mercy dashes back to the UK. As the months rushed by, my visits to London became more regular and more upsetting. I provided emergency TLC for Mum and Dad but wondered if I was actually doing more harm than good. It was all very well reassuring Mum she would be okay. Yes, I could massage her hands with lavender-scented hand cream, I could stroke her cheeks and tell her I loved her, I could make her feel good for a while, but I would always leave.

Two years on and I seemed to have found a solution, a way of coping with the huge emotional dilemma. It turned out to be a range of solutions, there was no panacea. Number one in my emotional resilience arsenal was my relationship with Jack – trusting my partner and venting my anger was crucial. Jack allowed me to rant and collapse in a heap of mush when I needed to, allowed me to cry and, for a time, to wallow in my misery.

After a melodramatic month or so, we turned to practical solutions. How sensible, affordable and effective was my current approach? Would we consider moving back to the UK and if so, how could we protect our life-work balance? What was the medium and long-term prognosis for Mum? What did I actually know about her condition and how would things impact on Dad over time? What was my role in all of this and how should I work with my siblings to provide Mum and Dad with the support they needed? Was it possible to provide the necessary care and consider our own needs at the same time?

What happened next was quite remarkable. Jack and I fought through the seemingly insoluble mess by acknowledging the emotional trauma and then getting practical. Armed with months' worth of research, financial calculations, scenario planning and discussions, I arrived at absolute clarity. I knew what to do.

We would return to the UK and try to balance the books without slinking back into full-time work. We would do the right thing because it was the only decision that would ultimately make us happy. Finally, and crucially, we set ourselves a challenge. At some time in the future, we would consider another move abroad. Nothing was forever; we could still have more adventures. We would move back for the right reasons, but we wouldn't get trapped.

Maybe some people have built-in survival mechanisms. Maybe some people can easily and quickly adapt to emotional roller-coasters. For the rest of us emotional resilience isn't something you 'have', it's something you develop; it's something you work at.

I have no idea what happened to that British couple in Sydney. I hope they realised it was fine to feel guilty, torn, desperate even. I also hope they worked together and found a way of protecting their dream. Emotion is a wonderful thing. It enriches us and it makes us human. Sometimes we should embrace it. Sometimes it can help decide where to go next."

Liam Brennan, UK expat, repatriated from Turkey

The more expats I talk with, the more I hear about feelings of guilt at not being near when loved ones are ill or dying. It has been part of our family experience, and while you do the best you can, it doesn't necessarily make it any easier. This is also the underlying theme of the story from 'Jo from USA/ England'. Sadly her grief was compounded by the callous treatment of unthinking – or simply uncaring – immigration officials upon her return to her host country.

GUILT OF DEALING WITH LOSS FROM AFAR

"Without question, the hardest part of living overseas has been the death of my parents. My father died a year after we moved abroad, my mother a decade later. I'm not sure I will ever lose the guilt I carry around, guilt at the knowledge I couldn't be near them in their final days.

Illogical? Of course. Even if I had been living in the same country as they were, I doubt I would have stayed at their bedsides for weeks on end, waiting for them to pass from this world into the next. My young family's commitments would have been just as demanding, the stop-start drive around London's M25 still the worst part of the journey.

But nevertheless, in my years away, these were the times when I asked myself if I had done the right thing in moving abroad. My experiences with immigration officials when I returned from the two funerals didn't help.

'Reason for visit to England?' barked one official, who then looked suitably discomforted as I muttered 'Mother's funeral' and tears welled in my eyes.

The experience after my father's funeral was even worse. Dragging behind me two toddlers who had been confined on a seven hour flight and were now ecstatic to be freed, I was confronted by a US immigration official who was having a bad day – although not as bad as mine, I'd be willing to bet. He didn't ask me why I had travelled to England. It would have been better if he had.

I handed him the immigration form; the wrong one, apparently. Already overwrought with the emotion from the last four days, I apologized profusely and, I daresay, incoherently. He told me, quite casually and with no empathy for a mother travelling on her own with two small children, that if I couldn't get my act together and control my overexcited offspring, he would send us to the back of the long immigration line.

A few kind or jocular words at that point would have made all the difference to my state of mind. Instead, for the next few months, I replayed this scene over and over in my head, and have never, before or since, wanted to be back in my own country so much."

Jo from USA/ England

Eventually we are able to resolve the guilt of having chosen to move away from those we love. But sometimes the guilt is over what happens to the loved ones who make the journey with us. The pain and suffering of hardships encountered and trials endured are too deep, too raw, for far too long to be dealt with quickly or easily. And sometimes the damage is so great it cannot be undone.

TIPPING POINT

If I had known
Hope and excitement would quietly evaporate
Under the pulsating heat of a foreign sun,
Would I have followed you?

If I had known
The currency our children would trade, drowning silently
Beneath relentless waves of disconnection
Would I have followed you?

If I had known
Twisted tendrils of loss and depression would devour them,
Torn from our scrabbling fingers as they sank
Would I have followed you?

If I had known
Our brittle remnants would be strewn across the globe,
Tightknit-love torn and shredded over continents
Would I have followed you?

If I had known,
Wrapped in the tangled sheets of our last night,
The unstitching of our family would begin here,
Would I have followed you?

If I had known
At journey's end we would stand face to face
Staring into the haunted eyes of who we once were,
Adrift and rudderless in a dark ocean of sadness
Would I have followed you?

Upbeat expat on a bad day

When our loved ones are hurting, guilt exposes itself as one of the strongest and most corrosive of human emotions. We're told when we feel guilt, we should make amends if they are warranted, but not every situation can be made right. We express what is in our hearts, lend our support, and hope for some sense of peace for all involved.

MISSING OUT

The flip side of the guilt coin is that of grieving for the life (or lives) we've left behind. Our parents don't stop being our parents, our brothers and/ or sisters remain our siblings. Our extended family is still that – relatives who know and love us, and for whom we care deeply.

What about dear friends, the kind we've laughed and cried with? Friends we've known for years, with whom we've celebrated good times and shouldered bad? We do our best when we leave such close friends behind, yet leave we do.

What few will share about life lived across cultures is that sometimes there is an undercurrent of feelings of rejection on the part of family and friends – we were the ones who chose to leave, therefore we couldn't care that much about them. Fellow expats/ cross-culturals leading a mobile lifestyle understand these comings and goings, but for those who don't, the sense of having been rejected can exist. In either case, for those we leave behind, life goes on. They continue to work and socialize as they did when we were there, but we aren't.

SMALL SADNESSES

"Family bereavements from afar are the worst-case scenario, but even what may seem a small sadness by comparison, such as not being able to attend a wedding or a birthday, can enhance the feeling of loneliness."

Liv Gaunt, an adult TCK now living in Turkey

When we do return for a visit, the holidays spent together, fun parties, celebrations and inside jokes – their shared history – give us a cumulative reminder of precisely what we've been missing. For every person who welcomes us back heartily, there is another who acts as if they only vaguely remember us. For them it seems to be a case of 'out of sight, out of mind'. No doubt about it, moving away means missing out, and it can sting.

NEED FOR EMOTIONAL SUPPORT

One theme running through virtually every expatriate/ cross-cultural experience is the desire for emotional support from those who matter to us. This is especially true in terms of those we leave behind when we decide to strike out on our international journey. As humans, we tend to be tribal creatures. We prefer being surrounded by fellow members of our 'tribe', family or affinity group. Yet when we cannot be with our group physically, we still crave those feelings of acceptance, belonging and connection. In short, we long for emotional support.

Perhaps the single strongest message we can receive, indeed the most powerful words known to mankind, are a simple, 'I love you'. As we grow up and mature into adulthood, this proclamation of love is joined by an equally powerful phrase, 'I am proud of you'. While many of us will not let the absence of these words stop us from pursuing our own particular path in life, most of us benefit greatly from hearing them.

'When our loved ones are hurting, guilt exposes itself as one of the strongest and most corrosive of human emotions.'

In some instances the stumbling block that keeps a family member or loved one from uttering these words is cultural in nature, for instance in cultures where such expressions are not common practice. In other instances, the barrier is generational ('your great grandparents were far too busy eking out a living to have time for such sentiments'), gender ('men don't say those sorts of things'), or simply personal ('I'm not one to express my feelings in words').

> *'Moving away means missing out, and it can sting.'*

Sometimes when we choose to leave the familiarity and comfort – some might add suffocation – of home, family and friends may feel rejected, as if we are publicly announcing they aren't enough, or they are lacking in some way. The emotional difficulties of not feeling wholly supported in our choice to move 'away' are not to be understated; they are painful and take their toll.

WHEN FAMILY MAKES US FEEL BADLY ABOUT LEAVING

"One of the most important (and challenging) aspects of expat life for me has been encountering, and learning how to deal with, negative family attitudes towards the decision to leave my home country. When my wife and I committed to leaving England in June 2003, we did so after three years living together. We both felt a need to satisfy a growing wanderlust and decided to emigrate to Canada under the skilled worker permanent resident visa program.

The decision to leave was never accepted by those close to us who saw the move as an act of betrayal and disloyalty. The fact my wife was not English confirmed long-held views this was a decision we would always make. Initially, disagreement in opinion manifested itself through increasingly negative conversations. Over time, the tone changed with the aim of pressing guilt upon us at having left the homeland and a sense 'we did wrong' and 'acted abnormally' compared to other 'normal families' who live near each other.

The impacts of these behaviours, and unease with our decision, have been profound. Early on, I struggled to cope with the situation. I had no way of figuring out how to address the guilt I felt at being separated from my UK family. After a while I began to lose faith in my decisions, basing future moves on how this would be seen by my English family. Over time my self-confidence was affected, unnecessary home-life issues and tension were created, and we considered moving back to the UK at various points. We felt alone, missing the support we needed from home, and constantly questioning whether we had made the right decision to leave.

I spoke with a friend based in New Zealand who was experiencing similar familial problems. I also spoke with other friends who had lived abroad and returned home because of related situations. In short, I turned to my support network of fellow expats. I learned through them that my actions were not at fault. The non-acceptance by my family of the initial decision to leave the UK, and the way my family had been brought up in a close network within a few kilometres of each other, had led them to act the way they did. Nothing I could say or do would change their perceptions or outlook on life.

I learned I had to accept certain levels of separation guilt on my part, but realised I hadn't acted badly or inappropriately in the course of living abroad. That I was not a bad person. That our decisions, made for the good of our own nuclear family, were right for us. That we would be better for it. That we were decent people. It took significant strength and resolve to overcome the feelings of guilt and self-criticism. I had to adapt my approach to my family, ensuring telephone conversations covered only certain topics, and frequent email contact was avoided for a while. I had finally started to understand that the attitude towards our decision to leave England was not the real issue. The issue concerned any decision we made to leave my hometown, regardless of how near or far we moved.

We got on with our life. We benefited from exploring our environment, socialising more, surrounding ourselves with positive people and most importantly, looking out for and protecting each other from the continual snipes and remarks. I wish I'd known all this earlier. If it hadn't been for the new knowledge the 'separation guilt' would have been constant and the burden of it too much to bear. Our life has often felt like having one foot placed in our current home and one foot placed in the country we'd left. It hasn't been conducive to a settled life lived abroad.

Am I mentally stronger now? More emotionally resilient from the experience? Perhaps. What I did learn was this – the decisions made by my wife and I must be based on our own immediate family unit. The only thing worse than living with a little 'natural' guilt is living with guilt and unhappiness at having not followed our life's path, because of the attitude and behaviour of others."

Russell V.J. Ward
British expat (Canada) now living in Australia

Choosing to make a life far away from loved ones is never easy. We were blessed with family members who understood our reasons for going abroad and didn't make us feel guilty about it. The choice may be entirely within our purview or out of our hands. Either way, we hope for emotional support to reinforce our decision. When that is

> 'The emotional difficulties of not feeling wholly supported in our choice to move 'away' are not to be understated; they are painful and take their toll.'

not forthcoming, it takes tenacity, steadfastness, and belief that we're doing the right thing to stay the course. Seeing us persevere and build a new life for ourselves, which still includes them, changes our loved ones' perspectives, ruffled feathers are smoothed and they come to realize life is too short to waste time poking and prodding us on our decision. Hopefully this is how it has been for you.

DEALING WITH SOCIAL, ECONOMIC AND CULTURAL INEQUITIES

One fallacy about expat life is that it always involves pleasant weather and good living conditions, otherwise why would we go? The reasons are numerous – business opportunities, diplomatic, military or missionary service, providing assistance to developing countries, working in the international aid arena or simply a sense of adventure. Yet whatever brings us to live in developing countries or hardship posts, the fact remains that day-to-day living can range from inconvenient, to difficult, to downright primitive.

WHEN MEDICAL CARE IS LACKING

"Emotional resilience was key for our life in Africa (three years), raising our first-born, welcoming to life our middle child, fearing the eminent epidemics of malaria. Due to a minor heart condition, I'd declined to receive the anti-malarial medicine during our official posting in Mozambique. It was a personal decision, and, despite the constant fear of eventually catching malaria during my work trips through the country, I have no regrets. We were fortunate enough to never have any major medical issues while posted in Africa. Raising kids is difficult enough on its own. Sick kids, when medical assistance is not always available, is even more challenging. We had a couple of medical evacuations to neighboring South Africa, and thankfully they were all very successful.

That's part of life. It comes with the package you sign off below the 'fine print' when deciding to live overseas with small children."

Raquel L. Miranda
US Foreign Service spouse in Bolivia after Mozambique and Brazil

Sometimes we find ourselves in circumstances which are entirely alien to us, and we aren't sure how to proceed. When options are limited, choices fewer, decisions tend to be easier. It is in the luxury of choice that we encounter economic, social and cultural inequities more fully. There may be societal expectations to maintain a certain standard of living, even as many in the local population live in poverty and appalling conditions. The dichotomy can be disconcerting and unsettling.

GETTING CAUGHT UP IN A WAY OF LIFE THAT ISN'T OURS

"It's difficult for me to pinpoint one specific part of expat life that has gone especially smoothly and easily. Expat life is hard, and the stresses of being away from home and adapting to a foreign culture tend to amplify character traits or tendencies that may cause your difficulty. Still, when I look back on the highs of expat life, these have been times when I have had a strong community of people around me, people who understand the challenges particular to expat life. Being part of a varied social network, getting to know people from all sorts of backgrounds and cultures has been a real high point for me.

One particular low point of expat life was our first foray into living abroad. My husband and I were young, just 24 and 26, we weren't yet married, and he got offered a job in Delhi. We had no idea what to expect, but went along, excited about the adventure, about career prospects in Asia.

We arrived, totally intimidated by our new lush surroundings in a luxury hotel, the fancy people, grownups who had money and drivers and housekeepers and expensive clothes. We couldn't square all this with the poverty so real and heartbreaking that we saw all around us. In that light, we didn't feel comfortable asking for a lot, and didn't know how to push for what we really needed. We ended up with a drafty, dusty, hot apartment without proper furniture and appliances (which, by the way, I feel totally ashamed to complain about considering we had food and a roof and riches untold compared to so many millions of others in India).

My husband and I had barely two pennies to rub together. He was starting a new job, I had none. Still, we felt we needed to keep up expat appearances and hire a helper, join a super expensive club, buy gadgets and gizmos, and eat in fancy restaurants, all with money we didn't have. We didn't have the emotional maturity, the good sense to understand we didn't need all that stuff to fit in, and if we did, then there was no sense hanging out with those sorts of people.

When the job turned into a disaster, and we left the country within 24 hours, we were left with mountains of debt, no plan. Thankfully that abrupt end put us on the path we are on now, and pushed us to get married rather sooner than later. In hindsight, I'm glad it all happened, but at the time, it was pretty crummy."

Erica Knecht
Canadian expat (Japan, China, India, Switzerland, France) now lives in Indonesia

One group of expatriates/ cross-culturals who experience firsthand the heartbreaking inequality of our world of haves and have-nots are international aid workers. They step into the fray of natural and manmade disasters, desiring to alleviate suffering from hunger, poverty, disease, loss of life, lack of resources, violence, treachery and conflict. Helping others in in the direst of circumstances assuredly requires specialized skills, the ability to work surrounded by human pain and misery, and enormous empathy, compassion and emotional resiliency.

HELPING OURSELVES IN ORDER TO HELP OTHERS

"Emotional resilience is something that can be cultivated, over time. It's something we all have, as humans – the ability to sustain a trauma, the ability to work through a tough situation. I think it's important aid workers do not confuse emotional resilience with beating ourselves up, though. If we're in a challenging environment and find ourselves feeling depleted and depressed, the best and most resilient thing we can do sometimes is to take a break.

Aid workers often have a toughness complex, which at times can become damagingly competitive. Sticking things out when you're not thriving isn't emotional resilience, it's self-destructive, especially if we compare ourselves to other professionals we think are tougher than us, or believe will judge us for our needs.

People in the aid industry are only now beginning to talk about the personal toll that development work can exact on a person, her family and her relationships. Because our job is one of service, by nature, we often ignore our own needs because those needs seem small or trivial compared to the needs of the populations we serve. What's so bad about crying in the morning, every morning, for example, if the people you compare yourself to are impoverished, single mothers, commercial sex workers with HIV?

No matter where we are or who we work with, it's crucial we remain compassionate and gentle with ourselves, and respond to what our bodies, minds and hearts ask for and need."

Elie Calhoun, American ATCK who has lived most of her life in Africa, including Kenya, Egypt, Tanzania, Liberia and Senegal.

Another group often experiencing the inequities of our world firsthand are missionaries and their families. As ATCK and child of missionary parents Heidi Sand-Hart mentioned in her book, *Home Keeps Moving: A Glimpse Into the Extraordinary Life of a Third Culture Kid: 'TCKs are often exposed to things at a tender age that many of their friends back home have never been faced with. Seeing drastic poverty, beggars and inhumane living conditions, has the potential to mature us a lot earlier on in life. Many of us live in parts of the world where tensions run high between ethnic groups, and it becomes everyday life to us, not just something seen on TV.'*

'Living and traveling abroad brings home to us the enormous gap between developing and developed nations on a deeply human level, in graphic detail and high definition colors, sounds and smells.'

We must rely on our personal sense of morality, what is right, and growing awareness of the need to help those less fortunate than ourselves. At the same time we must respect the existence of and navigate the intricacies of cultural, social and economic differences. Faced with such inequities, it isn't possible to turn a blind to the poverty and pervasive need in our surroundings, *nor should we.* Living and traveling abroad brings home to us the enormous gap between developing and developed nations on a deeply human level, in graphic detail and high definition colors, sounds and smells. It is up to us – individually and collectively – to educate ourselves on the issues, causes and possible solutions, and address need as best we can.

I would add a word of caution about falling into the trap of thinking cultures which handle challenges differently to how we're accustomed are somehow inferior, less intelligent or less caring. We would do well to engage our eyes and ears before our mouths, because an open mind holds far more understanding than a closed one. It is in the widest cultural chasms that sensitivity is most needed.

MENTAL AND EMOTIONAL HEALTH CHALLENGES

The US National Institute of Mental Health estimates approximately one quarter of the American population suffer from some form of mental illness each year. Similarly, the US Center for Disease Control estimates one in five of the population will suffer some form of mental illness at some point in their lives. Thankfully the percentage of Americans with mental illness which can be characterized as 'severe' is a fraction of that number, but it doesn't mean the others aren't stigmatized and struggling with pain and suffering.

There will be those who chalk up the numbers to the supposedly typical predilection of Americans for fixating on squishy 'emotions' and 'feelings' and a preoccupation with 'happiness' and psychotherapy. I suspect many other countries are right up there with the US in terms of mental illness, if they would only take the time and effort to calculate the numbers, and sufferers were encouraged, rather than discouraged, from seeking treatment.

How many expats/ cross-culturals deal with mental and emotional health challenges? Once again the numbers aren't clear, but anecdotally there is a sense they at least match the level of more stable populations, and more likely are higher. In the 2012 article, *Are Expats at Risk of Developing Mental Health Problems?* – highlighted on the Expat Info Desk website www.ExpatInfoDesk.com and itself based on Michele Rubin's article, *Expatriates at Higher Risk for Mental Health Issues and Substance Abuse Problems* at PRWeb – we can gain some insight.

> 'Expats are at increased risk compared to their home population for encountering stress, depression and anxiety.'

A study conducted by Chestnut Global Partners and The Truman Group, found American expats to be at higher risk than their US-based counterparts for internalizing mental health problems such as depression and anxiety, externalizing ones such as hyperactivity, attention deficit, conduct and impulse control, and substance abuse. The study's co-author, David Sharar Ph.D., noted the impact of stress on assignment failure rates, often stemming from 'cultural differences and demanding workloads'. Dr. Sharar went on to say that the findings: *'underscore the need to design programs and provide services that mitigate the challenges of living and working abroad.'*

This is in line with the previously mentioned 2011 *Global Relocation Trends Study* from Brookfield GRS, highlighting the role of family adjustment issues in making or breaking expatriate assignments. These studies underscore what expats have known for years. They are gaining attention and for good reason: expatriating and repatriating across cultures can be difficult. Working our way through the highs and lows of the transition process can leave many of us battling feelings of alienation, dislocation, anger, frustration, loneliness, lack of identity and rootlessness.

Certainly most expats come through on the other side just fine, or without lasting damage. But there is no doubt some do struggle. It isn't limited only to the expatriate employees themselves, as their family members can also be affected deeply by relocation pressures. Yet the resources to help support them before, during and after transition differ greatly depending on one's experience, running the gamut from decent to nil. I for one found greater transition support in the form of valuable information sessions, field trips, guest speaker programs and social opportunities from the international school Son and Daughter have attended than anything Husband's organization offered.

No wonder Dr. Sharar's co-author, Sean D. Truman Ph.D., licensed practicing psychologist and adult TCK, notes the: *'explicit need for programs and services that are comprehensive in scope and sensitive to the personal, interpersonal and professional dynamics that contribute to the overall well-being of expats and their family members.'*

Whatever the exact statistics, expats are at increased risk compared to their home population for encountering stress, depression and anxiety. By shedding light on mental illness in general, and in expatriate life in particular, we can go a long way in smashing stigmas associated with depression, anxiety and other mental health challenges. We can also encourage people to seek necessary support and treatment.

> 'You are perfectly normal if you experience loneliness. It is just a signal telling you to increase your social bonds in quality and quantity.'

We need to get the word out, at home and abroad. We need to be talking about these issues, writing about these issues, reading about these issues and sharing these issues. The growing body of expat literature reflects as much, as does informal evidence offered online in expat blogs and in the cafés, corridors and homes of expats/ cross-culturals sharing their own experiences and that of others they've known.

INTENSIFIED MY STRUGGLES AND REACTIONS

"When my husband and I decided to move overseas, it was a joint decision. He could teach and I could write. We had both lived overseas separately before we met and married, so we felt confident and excited about our move. For me, the game changer in my life as an expat came when I had children, as we lived in Thailand for several years before starting a family.

Looking back, I can now identify two major issues that occurred after my first son was born. First, living in the isolation of having a newborn without a lot of support, I realized what an isolated and solitary life I'd been living as an expat. Second, I also realized I didn't want to be a stay-at-home mom in the traditional sense, despite telling myself that would be my job when my son was born.

Almost four years later (and now a mom to two young sons) where am I at in my process of addressing the above issues? First and foremost, I worked with a mental health counsellor (who made house calls in those early days after my first child was born) who helped me become aware of and reframe my negative thoughts. I've worked with mental health counsellors in the past, even earlier in our time in Thailand, but for the first time in my adult life, I felt I was provided with real tools to make real changes in my life. Interestingly, the issues I addressed (negative thinking, low self-esteem) would have existed for me wherever I lived, though it's almost certain that life as an expat intensified my struggles and reactions.

In my work with the mental health counsellor, I also identified ways to start reaching out and building community. I've had to give myself permission to reach out and 'have no shame' when it comes to meeting others and building relationships. It's a work in progress, but I'm in a much better place these days.

This process has helped me realize that the new mom is a specific sub-set within the expat community that could benefit from more resources. Overall, having my children overseas has been an intense and life-changing experience, but one that has stretched me and, I think, made me a better, happier person."

Hope, expat currently living in Thailand

Culture shock can be hard enough to handle for most people; it is more difficult if you are prone to, or suffer from, mental or emotional challenges such as anxiety, depression and other diagnoses. Here are the insights of another expat for dealing with culture shock amid the added concern of triggering a relapse in positive mental health.

TIME AND TALKING ABOUT CULTURE SHOCK HELP

"I think my emotional resilience was strongly challenged by the double-whammy of the onset of culture-shock and my first Canadian winter. As a Borderline Personality Disorder sufferer, keeping a handle on my mood isn't easy and any challenge has the potential to plunge me into 'all or nothing', black-and-white thinking. I've come through a lot since leaving therapy seven years ago, even enduring a miscarriage without regressing, but culture-shock caused me to question, for the first time, whether I was succumbing to depression again.

I entered a prolonged period of listless, hopeless, sadness that just seemed cemented around me. I had known to expect some emotional difficulty but knowing doesn't make it go away. I confided my fears to my family doctor, who told me to make an appointment any time I needed to talk. Somehow, just getting it off my chest seemed to help and I never made an appointment. It lasted about three months. I was desperate for any small crumb of comfort, hoping every day when my husband came home from work he might have some 'good news' (quite what shape or form I expected that to take I was never clear on). Basically, I was looking for outside help in lifting my spirits. I couldn't seem to do it myself. When spring arrived, I began to feel more normal and by summer I knew I hadn't made a mistake – I was happy in Canada.

I don't know if my difficulties with culture-shock were because I'm less emotionally resilient than my husband and daughter or if it was just down to the added difficulty of

the BPD, but I did worry that I was overwhelmed by it when it was occurring."

Aisha Ashraf, Irish expat living in Canada by way of the UK

Moving abroad does not necessarily mean you will be at risk for encountering emotional difficulties or mental illness. By the same token, if you already suffer from, or have a genetic predisposition to such illnesses/ disorders, changing the scenery by heading overseas will not help you avoid them. In any case, the keys are awareness of the possibilities, careful self-monitoring (or by medical personnel as needed) and taking appropriate action – both preventive and responsive in nature – should such problems begin to arise.

EXPERIENCING NEGATIVE EMOTIONS

As discussed earlier, sadness, loneliness, alienation, anger, irritation, frustration, and depression are all negative emotions we may experience as we go through our transitions phases and the different stages of the change model.

In her book, *Turning International: How to Find Happiness and Feel at Home in a New Culture,* Ph.D. psychologist, researcher and expat Catherine Transler explains the chemistry of loneliness and how we humans are genetically wired to be tribal, connected individuals. Social neuroscience tells us that when we interact with others – in a romantic, familial or friendly manner – chemical reactions, including the release of the 'feel good' hormone oxytocin, occur. When we are deprived of social interaction and the relationships necessary to help us feel connected, anchored, involved in our surroundings, the lack of oxytocin contributes to our feeling sad, lonely, or blue.

Here Transler describes the damaging physical and emotional effects of continual loneliness: '...*you are perfectly normal if you experience loneliness. It is just a signal telling you to increase your social bonds in quality and quantity... The problem is that loneliness can become a chronic condition... The devastating effects of social isolation and chronic loneliness (the feeling of being left alone, even when in reality you have some good social connections) have been the focus of many epidemiological studies in recent decades... In people with similar numbers of social relationships, those who feel lonely often experience poorer health outcomes when compared to people who do not experience this feeling often.'*

When dealing with transition-rich change and/ or culture shock, we sometimes withdraw socially to give ourselves time to get our new bearings. However, if we aren't careful, it is easy to lapse into a cycle of what Transler refers to as, *'social isolation and chronic loneliness'*. So what do we do to avoid or break free of such a state? As we'll see in *PART II: PIECES OF THE EMOTIONAL RESILIENCE PUZZLE*, and *PART III: PUTTING IT ALL TOGETHER*, there is much we can do internally through mindfulness, meditation, visualization, and self-care. The external part of the equation is every bit as important, and includes taking actions which may feel counter-intuitive at a time when we might prefer hibernating. These encompass getting out into the community, making new connections, interacting with others, exploring our environment, becoming involved in new interests/ activities and being physically active.

Julia Simens is an educator, counselor, and speaker specializing in family therapy, early childhood education and international relocation. She's worked on five continents with relocating families, helping them to adjust to their global lifestyle. Author of the outstanding book, *Emotional Resilience and the Expat Child: Practical Tips and Storytelling Techniques That Will Strengthen the Global Family*, Simens has written what I consider a very important work which can help families with young (and not so young) children.

You'll notice I didn't say 'expat families'. That's because I believe this book is of use not only to parents when moving to a different country/ culture, but also in a variety of transitional situations. The underlying concepts of recognizing, acknowledging and sharing our emotions and establishing rituals to honor our memories and reflect our identities, are useful not only to young children but to teens and adults too.

A serial expat and member of the American Psychological Association, Simens has worked for years in international schools. She outlines the importance of healthy relationships for expat children to thrive, the need to accurately identify and deal with their emotions throughout their transitions, and the value of enriching our emotional stores through shared experiences, memory-making and recollections.

In her book Simens included psychologist Gordon Neufeld's six stages of attachment which form the basis for every relationship a child develops:

- Proximity
- Sameness
- Belonging/ loyalty
- Significance
- Love
- Being known

It isn't hard to see how deeply the vein of identity runs through each of these attachment stages, or that these needs follow us into adulthood and indeed throughout our lives.

I had the opportunity to interview Simens shortly after her book was published. I wondered whether there is a particular stage in which expats or cross-cultural children seem to have more trouble than their monocultural counterparts, and posed the question to her.

"Many expat children are quite adept at all stages and thrive in their cross-cultural awareness," she noted. "But I do see that it is hard for some to 'belong'. It is hard to be loyal to someplace if you feel you are just passing through. Since all children spend so much time in school or connected to school activities, it is important that parents foster this loyalty to the new school and new community."

An underlying theme is teaching children to acknowledge and accurately name their emotions. But what happens if they cannot?

"Through socialization, children learn how to express what they feel about the environment they are in and the people they are around. If they cannot do this, their social and emotional foundation is at risk. The chance of being misunderstood is greater. They might not have strong, healthy communicative relationships and therefore they may be isolated."

Whether child, adolescent, young adult or adult, each of us needs to recognize and appropriately display our emotions, even – some would argue especially – the negative ones. Otherwise we risk sublimating our feelings, bottling them up until they threaten to erupt, potentially with unfortunate consequences. We cannot have healthy relationships with ourselves or with others unless we are able to acknowledge and address negative emotions we may be experiencing.

Recently I contacted Rebecca Grappo, an experienced expat/ repat, parent of TCKs and international educational consultant specializing in university and overseas school placement, and other education solutions for the global expatriate community. Grappo has worked with hundreds of children and adolescents in the past two decades, and has seen when clients are thriving, and sadly, when they are not. I asked about her experiences working with TCKs and the importance of resiliency, a topic she has written on extensively.

"In looking at different interpretations of the definition, it's easy to see why 'resiliency' is such an important asset to cultivate in TCKs. When children and adolescents are resilient, they will be able to 'recoil or spring back into shape' after changing life circumstances. And in some cases, it's not hard at all to think of examples where kids have had to 'withstand or recover quickly from difficult conditions.'"

"Unfortunately, not all the young people I have worked with are 'poster children' for being a TCK. Rather, they offer insights into how difficult the lifestyle can be and how resiliency may be a concept that is illusive for them... those who seem to be struggling the most are lacking in one or more of these areas – they have a difficult time making connections, don't feel recognized for who they are, don't feel like they belong or fit in, and question their own identities."

In Grappo's Foreign Service Journal article, *Building Resiliency in Global Nomads*, she writes of our children dealing with issues of identity, self-esteem, belonging and the all-important finding and keeping of friends. To children, peer acceptance is of greater concern than how they are doing in school. Not adequately processing negative feelings can lead to other emotions including anger, denial, depression, withdrawal, rebellion and even self-destructive behaviors.

As adults we deal with these issues too, but with the benefit of having emerged from our developmental years with a core sense of identity intact. For the young, they are trying to sort out these important issues while still in the formative years of identity development.

Grappo shares warning signs of potential trouble parents must be on the lookout for – inability to focus in class, lack of interest in previous activities, regression in behavior, more frequent episodes of crying, anger, sadness, depression.

Additionally, in her more recent article, *Promoting Your Child's Emotional Health*, Grappo warns that what Pollock and Van Reken refer to as 'the chronic cycle of separation', in which children experience repeated loss and grief due to the mobile nature of expat/ cross-cultural life, can lead to some developing issues associated with moving on from problems, rather than learning to deal with them directly.

Later in the article, something Grappo wrote chilled me to the bone: '*Two mistakes I see parents make over and over are being too hopeful that things will turn around on their own, and waiting too long to take action.*' This can apply to adults and children alike. Sadly, I could see our family in that statement. Despite the best of intentions, we didn't fully appreciate the warning signs of a loved one's struggle with depression and anxiety. It wasn't until the bad days outnumbered the good that we realized the extent of the situation, and then they were struggling.

DEPRESSION AND ANXIETY

As a writer and expat blogger who chronicles issues of interest to those living across cultures, I receive emails from readers or someone who has stumbled upon my blog while doing research. Some are from aspiring expats with questions about moving abroad. Others are expats-to-be, headed over to _Nederland_ or elsewhere, excited and worried at the same time, with slightly different questions and concerns.

I truly believe that awareness of the challenges of expat life (transitions, culture shock, continual change, loss and unresolved grief from seemingly always having to say goodbye or hello), is important. I believe sharing the good, the bad and even the ugly about living cross-culturally can help people understand some of the difficulties and prepare accordingly. It serves as a reminder of things to keep an eye on. You know the old adage 'forewarned is forearmed'. I feel it's the right thing to do. There are many wonderful positives about living a global life, but to gloss over the downside seems irresponsible. In his famous saying, '*An ounce of prevention is worth a pound of cure*', Benjamin Franklin captures this perfectly.

INFORMING MYSELF WAS VITAL

"What helped me? Managing my expectations. Reading all the Robin Pascoe books so that I knew it was okay to have a low period and that it would pass. To inform myself about the culture shock cycle and to know I was neither alone nor mad. Informing myself was vital. The more I knew the easier it was to accept what I was going through. I realised I could not avoid the bad bits, but that bad bits were normal. I attended lectures and conferences and read the books on the topic. That made ALL the difference."

Jo Parfitt
English expat (Oman, Norway, Dubai, Brunei) now living in the Netherlands

Then there are the emails I've received from expats in emotional pain. They may be mourning the loss of family, friends and places they used to live, or finding it difficult to summon energy or enthusiasm to move on. They might be on their first or second posting, or settling in to their fifth country in eight years.

They may have said goodbye to one too many close friends. Or they've woken up one day and realized they don't have it in them any more to start over, learning their way around a new country and new culture with a new language. They can't bear having to meet new people and try to make new friends yet again. Some are overwhelmed, and others are plain tired. Some are going through a bad patch they understand will pass. Others are in a far worse place. These emails are sometimes difficult to read, but I am humbled to receive them. And I am appreciative they have reached out to share their deepest feelings, whether it be with me or someone else.

I'd like to make clear this isn't a litmus test of strength or weakness, as if some people are tougher, smarter, savvier or worthier. We're not being graded by 'pass' and 'fail' here, and there is no 'right' way to handle difficulties. Everyone's situation is unique, complete with different backgrounds, challenges, stressors and other factors. No two people may encounter exactly the same experience, yet we can sometimes see the patterns there, if only in retrospect.

Their experiences reflect what I've observed and what has been shared with me by my own friends and fellow expats. Sometimes you get the blues and need time and tenderness to work your way through the transitions of your life. This is true of anyone, and isn't limited to the expat lifestyle. But sometimes you may be nearing the bottom of the emotional well and need assistance. Sometimes you don't even realize which situation you're in.

FILLING OUR EMOTIONAL RESERVOIRS

"In preparation for life as an expat, I would highly recommend taking a good hard look at your behavioral tendencies in your day-to-day life. Do you rise to challenge? Do unexpected changes leave you unsettled or tearful? Do events or people who don't conform to your ideas make you angry? Does adversity make you turn inward and put up walls? Look at how you react under pressure. I can almost guarantee that these unsavory tendencies, which, let's face it, we all have, will be louder and more pronounced as you settle into your new life abroad.

Also, if you have any suspicion you may have depressive or anxious tendencies, get a plan in place before you go. Because that, too, will become louder and more difficult to manage when you're away from home.

I think that I can offer a unique perspective here. I've had the privilege of seeing expat life from the point of view of a very emotionally un-resilient person. I've also had the chance to live abroad with greater emotional resources, fuller emotional reservoirs. I recently sought treatment for anxiety/ depression, and part of my treatment has included medication. I can now see that many of the things I used to get upset about were trivial. This is particularly true of my experiences in China.

China is enterprising, entrepreneurial, and gritty. Everyone is looking to get ahead, regardless of who they leave in their wake. This is something I very much admire about the country, but while I was living there, I used to seethe at the old ladies who would elbow me out of their way as they literally RAN into the subway train to get a prime seat. I fumed as mobs of people rushed towards the single cashier without regard for the fact that I. WAS. HERE. FIRST! I would shake with anger when a taxi driver cut me off, thinking, 'Why does he not follow traffic laws!' As if I were dictating to the Chinese the proper way to behave in their own country.

As I said, expat life is stressful. The frequent moves, the lack of social support, the unexpected challenges that crop up, language barriers, cultural barriers, and all sorts of frustrations make simple things so much more difficult. Being basically mute, deaf and illiterate is hard. It makes something simple, like buying milk, a huge challenge. I think all of these stressors can work together to build pressure. Each stress, like a brick, is piled up upon the body. If you don't have a solid foundation, cracks form, and walls may crumble.

I wish I had known that it's not them, it's me. That my frustration with the people in my host country was mine. That I did not, at the time, have the tools to deal with all of the changes in my life and so small things, like pushing on the subway, or losing 50 cents to the taxi driver seemed like personal attacks. I wish I would have known it didn't need to be so hard, that it wasn't 'us vs them', that I could have taken steps to build my resilience reservoirs. I wish I would have had a massive attitude adjustment way earlier in my expat career.

Now with the perspective of more balanced levels of serotonin and less generalized anxiety, I'm much more equipped to handle the foibles of my host country, I still don't understand them, or even like them, but they no longer cause me to crumple into a flood of tears."

Erica Knecht, Canadian expat
(Japan, China, India, Switzerland, France) now lives in Indonesia

I am not a medical doctor, psychologist or therapist, but when people write to me and share their difficult feelings, I can tell when they are in pain. I also have a healthy appreciation for when you must encourage, gently cajole or even insist they speak to a professional and seek more specific and tailored assistance.

It is for them and others in similar straits I share these links – www.webmd.com/depression/depression-health-check/,WebMD's Depression Health Check and – www.mayoclinic.com/health/depression/MH00103_D, the Mayo Clinic Depression Self-Assessment. These sites and others have plenty of information to help you or someone you care about get a sense of what is happening, whether to see a health professional, the questions to ask and the sort of details which are important to share with them. Another good resource is www.InternationalTherapistDirectory.com, which lists psychiatrists, psychologists and counselors familiar with expatriate/ cross-cultural experiences in general, and the challenges of identity development for TCKs/ CCKs in particular.

There should be no stigma attached to someone recognizing things have gone off track and seeking help. I think it is courageous and wise, and a sign of strength. We ought to encourage and support them in doing so. Why do I feel so strongly about this? Because it became our personal story when a loved one began suffering from depression and anxiety.

In that vein, one of the most revealing books on depression to hit the expat/ cross-cultural genre is Laura J. Stephens *An Inconvenient Posting: An Expat Wife's Memoir of Identity.* Stephens has written an emotionally candid depiction of the downward spiral into depression. A licensed therapist and second-time expat at the time, she chronicles her bout with depression on relocating

> 'The emotional upheaval which accompanies transitioning from one culture to another can bring unease, feeling adrift, unresolved grief, even anxiety and depression.'

from England to Houston, Texas, and her slow, steady climb back. Even therapists are not immune to the vagaries of expat life, which can batter and besiege our confidence, sense of well-being and most importantly the core of who we are/ how we see ourselves – our identity.

Within expat circles it is quietly common knowledge that continuous moving means leaving the friends and support structures we've worked hard to build (and/ or being the one left behind as others repatriate or move on). The emotional upheaval which accompanies transitioning from one culture to another can bring unease, feeling adrift, unresolved grief, even anxiety and depression. For far too many, it is the insidious little secret not talked about as openly, honestly and at length as it should be.

Stephens has bravely owned up to having dealt with a full-blown depression, capturing in detail the slippery slide from loneliness, feeling disconnected from the basic actions of everyday life and being lost into a deep, dark, ongoing funk. Equally courageous are her descriptions of how it impacted her marriage and relationships with her children and friends.

She makes her way back to emotional and mental well-being, sharing how therapy, journaling and various self-care measures associated with emotional resilience made the difference for her. Her situation may have been all too common – hesitantly agreeing to a move for the sake of her spouse's career, interruption of her own deeply cherished career aspirations, wrangling with transitional issues in a new environment, trying to keep a stiff upper lip while being overtaken by an insidious depressive episode. It is the overlay of contributing factors, stemming from sudden immersion in a new and often unexpectedly bewildering cross-cultural situation, that makes this intimate memoir ring true for many expatriates.

When I read Stephens' book, I felt her descent into depression was reminiscent of the frightening, pre-tornado scenes of *The Wizard of Oz*, shot in black and white, entirely devoid of color. Similarly her painstakingly slow recuperation, and re-entry back into a healthier, more positive mental state, evokes Dorothy's awakening into a strange, new, colorful world.

Another aspect I valued highly is that Stephens wasn't afraid to own up to irritation, frustration and exasperation with any and all aspects of her Houston life during her dark days. This makes her later appreciation of, and delight in, many of those same cultural nuances and differences ring all the more true. Who among us hasn't had similar feelings when we were going through culture shock, feeling out of sorts in a new country, usually going on to embrace and enjoy what may once have bothered us?

It is to Stephen's immense credit that *An Inconvenient Posting* is a no-holds-barred account of both her physical and emotional decline and her victorious re-emergence into a newer, stronger, wiser, more grateful version of her old self. It serves as a beacon of light in the darkness of depression and despair others may be feeling. I cannot help but think such a book might assist struggling expats like the contributor of the next story.

IN DENIAL ABOUT DEPRESSION

"Our son, despite being born one month premature, was healthy and blooming and six weeks after giving birth we moved to Egypt. After settling into our new home in Cairo I began to feel sick. I spent more and more time in bed. I relied on our Sudanese nanny to take care of my son. I went to see a doctor. I saw five. They all came to the same conclusion; there was nothing wrong with me.

What amazes my husband now is how long it took him to realise anything was 'wrong'. I never told him I spent most of the day in bed, getting up an hour or so before he got home from the office. He noticed I had no interest in social activities and went to bed early most nights, but he put that down to motherhood. He was, and is, a fabulous dad, and spent most of his free time with our son reading and playing with him.

I knew I had not really bonded with my son and yet I lacked the energy to do anything about it. I loved him, no doubt at all. I just had no energy. I was always exhausted. I was in denial. We were a happy, healthy family who were living the good life. I was just tired.

After a year we returned to Holland for home-leave – September 11, 2001. My first reaction was not to return to Egypt, I was genuinely afraid. For months afterwards I had nightmares. I was terrified our son would be kidnapped, that we would have to evacuate, that my husband would have to stay behind. Our world was on terrorist alert and our lives were on hold. I had a suitcase permanently packed and slept with a huge diving knife next to my bed – just in case.

Some months later tragedy struck again – my father passed away three months after being diagnosed with pancreatic cancer. Twice in those three months my son and I flew to Hungary to be with my father. I wanted him to hold my son. Sadly, the final phone call came too late. Papa passed away without any of his children by his side. Two days later I was back in Egypt.

Still feeling sick, I saw more doctors. Each one would prescribe medicine against nausea or stomach ache, sometimes it would give relief but it never completely went away.

The following year was the turning point. On holiday in the south of France I fell ill and my husband took me to see a doctor who prescribed the usual nausea and stomach tablets. I finally found the courage to confess to my husband that while he was at work I stayed in bed, and this was probably more than an upset stomach. I had grown up in the tropics and must have picked up something there. On our return to Egypt I would see a tropical disease specialist. This naïve self-diagnosis ended up being a lifesaver.

The doctor let me talk. He asked me about my life rather than my symptoms. I spoke about the challenges of our move to Egypt with a young baby, losing my support system, the effects of 9/11 and my father. The doctor assured me I had neither amoebas nor any other tropical horrors. He advised me to seek a therapist.

Two years after my son was born I went into therapy and was able to process all the changes in my life and give them closure. I learnt the human mind has the capacity to process only so much in a particular period of time, and my brain was on overload. Rather than admitting I could not cope, subconsciously it seemed more acceptable to have a stomach ache or to feel sick.

My depression – yes, I was depressed – was likely triggered by an overload of major changes happening in the period before, and up to two years after, the birth of my son.

My stomach aches ceased, my energy returned and I was able to enjoy the simple things in life again. I became a mother to my son and as my senses returned I realised how much I loved my husband. The previous two years must have been really hard and confusing for him. His caring nature is his strength, but he later admitted it hadn't been easy. At times he had misunderstood my lethargy as disinterest, and yet he never once let me down.

Five years ago I noticed I was 'falling' again when we moved to a new posting in South America. I recognized the symptoms – lethargy, sleeping during the day, emotional numbness. I immediately sought help. A few sessions with a good therapist were enough.

The important thing is to acknowledge when you need help and get it. I had a friend make the appointment for me as she'd been through it herself.

Expat life is wonderful, but the constant changes it brings are not always easy to process and I have not met an expat spouse (including men), who have come out of it completely unscathed."

Reina Rácz, Dutch-Hungarian adult TCK (England, Austria, Germany, Gabon, Oman, Pakistan, Hungary, US, Egypt, Chile) now repatriated to the Netherlands

Unscathed? Perhaps not. Wiser? Stronger? I'd like to think so.

We've examined expatriate/ cross-cultural life more closely, including the challenges of transitions, change, culture shock, identity-related and other specific issues inherent in a highly mobile, international lifestyle. The need for building, maintaining and replenishing our personal stocks of emotional resiliency is great. Now we will look in depth at emotional resilience and some of the tools available to bolster it.

PART II:

PIECES OF THE EMOTIONAL
RESILIENCE PUZZLE

'One's destination is never a place, but a new way of seeing things.'
Henry Miller

HOWLING WINDS

Watching Daughter dart her way through the throngs of pre-weekend shoppers, I struggled to keep up with the pace of youth.

"Wait up," I said. "If you don't slow down, I'm going to lose you in this crowd."

The North Carolina shopping mall was enormous and bright, July sun flooding in through skylights and two-story windows. It was only three weeks after the conversation with Husband in the kitchen of our home in the Netherlands, but for all that had occurred in the meantime, it might as well have been half a lifetime ago.

Weaving my way through the shopping hordes, my mind drifted back to Husband's and my discussion of a job possibility in Geneva. I had risen early the following day to call an international school there, to discuss the possibility of securing Daughter a place for the fall semester. With the truncated timeline and necessary paperwork the school required, I spent the day on my computer completing the online application and forwarding scanned copies of Daughter's birth certificate and passport. I swapped emails with her current school, outlining the pressing need to send official transcripts and required recommendations to the school in Geneva. The requisite teachers were aware of the urgency to complete the latter over the weekend, before they headed off for their summer break.

Congratulations, read the email from the admissions director at the school in Geneva. *You've broken our previous record of 48 hours to get everything submitted. And you did it over a weekend!* The last of the electronic recommendations had been submitted that morning by Daughter's departing math teacher. He had taken time out of a hectic weekend of packing and farewell parties to dash off the necessary assessment.

Twenty feet ahead, Daughter tossed a quick look back over her right shoulder, her lightly furrowed brow expressing mild irritation that I was holding her back. She and I had been back in the US almost two weeks of what was turning out to be a month-long whirlwind of activity. We'd begun with a visit to my parents at their home in Florida before heading north to Virginia. Daughter's university search was in its infancy, and we'd visited several campuses in the preceding week, before arriving in Durham the previous day. She had wasted no time in letting me know the extent of the back-to-school shopping she envisioned.

Not to the school in Geneva, where we'd worked so hard to secure her a place, but her current one in the Netherlands. In the intervening weeks following our kitchen discussion, Husband had flown to Geneva for an initial interview, followed up by a phone interview. It was down to another candidate and him, nothing to do but wait. We'd learned long ago that living in limbo is a common occurrence for expats.

In a Skype conversation with him the previous night, Husband had mentioned he'd been informed they were going with the other candidate.

"Seems two males had been promoted within the same part of the organization recently, so my chances were essentially nil. Of course my source wasn't aware of this earlier, and would never admit to this publicly."

I marveled at his matter-of-fact acceptance of the vagaries of dealing with an international organization. I was more than a bit peeved my family, staff members from two schools, and I, had been forced to jump through hoops on the off chance the stars aligned and the job offer came through. Not to mention the drain of mental energy in thinking we might be gearing up for another unexpected international move. It would have been nice had they not strongly encouraged him to apply in the beginning, saving us all the aggravation. At least we now had our answer and could move on with life.

Brrrng, brrrng.

My cell phone rang and I reached into my pocket to retrieve it, checking the number, heart racing. My father was in the middle of a seven-hour surgery to remove a cancerous tumor, and I was expecting a status update from my brother. I motioned to Daughter I needed to stop and take the call. She nodded and turned to do some window-shopping. I deftly sidestepped the gaggle of laughing teenaged girls, laden with shopping bags and Starbucks *machiattos* headed my way, and moved toward a quiet spot on the balcony overlooking the shopping hordes on the lower level.

"Hey, didn't think you'd be calling this early," I said, aware of the tight knot of anxiety beginning to form in my chest. "Any word yet? How's Mom doing?"

Instead of his usual witty retort, I heard a deep sigh followed by silence as he struggled to collect himself.

"He's already done," he answered, his voice catching. "The surgeon opened him up... said there's nothing she could do... closed him back up."

I grabbed the balcony railing as my knees started to buckle. Glancing over at me from the doorway of a nearby store, Daughter registered the stunned look on my face and stood still. Steadying myself, I took a few breaths. Trying to focus, I caught sight of a makeup consultant at a kiosk below, carefully applying eyeliner on an older customer. The two chatted amiably, amid the passing shoppers, oblivious to my world being turned upside down.

"How... but I thought... do they think?" I managed to get out a few words in the confusion. "Now, what...?" my voice trailed off, as I fought a rising wave of nausea. Beads of sweat broke out on my forehead, the clamminess spreading across my body. I felt light-headed, and it took all the concentration I could muster to avoid fainting.

What had begun as an emergency appendectomy at Easter had managed, over the course of the ensuing months, to spiral into discussions of a tumor, likely cancerous, very near the pancreas. Concern was so great no one was worrying about the simultaneous discovery of recurrent prostate cancer.

During pre-op testing for the scheduled tumor surgery, they'd found a pulmonary embolism. The precious weeks it had taken to dissolve the embolism, get him stabilized, and remove him from blood thinners in preparation for the delayed surgery, had taken their toll physically and mentally.

Jumbled thoughts crowded my mind – delaying flights, changing plans, extending our four-week visit stateside, interspersed with images of my parents, concern about how my mother would cope, what my father faced in the months ahead...

"Okay, tell them I love them," I whispered hoarsely. "I'll call Mom later."

I fought back tears as I ended the call and shakily turned toward Daughter. She knew instinctively the shopping expedition was done, and silently made her way to my side.

It had been an incredibly difficult year, beginning with my father-in-law passing away the previous autumn. Husband's mother remained in a nursing home for patients suffering from dementia, unaware of her husband's death, and we'd been dealing with aging issues with my parents before my father's current situation came to light. We made our way down the escalator, stumbled out into the blinding sunshine, and headed across the hot asphalt of the parking lot toward the rental car.

Two days later I received an email from Husband: *I'll take care of cancelling the vacation plans and changing the dog's kennel reservations on this end. Son and I are flying back to meet you at your parents on the 3rd as we discussed. Tell them we send our love. Hang in there.*

I was hanging alright, but whether it was 'in there' or by a thread remained to be seen. I had plans the next day to visit my dear friend Hannah and wasn't sure how I'd pull it together to see her. Hannah was fighting her own losing battle with brain cancer.

cultural resilience +
job loss /fear of job
loss.

CHAPTER 4: EMOTIONAL RESILIENCE

In this *PART* we will look at various pieces of the emotional resilience puzzle, including concepts and developments in the primary areas of emotional resilience, emotional and social intelligence, cultural intelligence and intercultural competence, brain-body connections and positive psychology. We begin with resilience itself: how it is defined, why it matters – especially in expat/ cross-cultural life – and one expat/ counselor's perspective.

DEFINING EMOTIONAL RESILIENCE

Resilience is generally defined as the ability to recover from and/ or adjust to negative events or significant change. Emotional resilience focuses not only on the psychological ability to adapt to the challenges, misfortunes and set-backs life throws our way, but also to maintaining or returning to a positive view of oneself during and after such turmoil. I've come to believe that developing and enhancing our emotional resilience is important for everyone, but becomes essential to those living overseas.

For an expat, emotional resilience may be tested in the form of dealing with a sudden job transfer due to the weakened state of the global economy, in handling the transition into a new culture and language vastly different than one's own, or in facing a medical crisis while overseas. Understanding that the universe is not singling us out, that these events happen, and that we are not at fault or in any way deserving of bad news or difficulties – all are part of emotional resilience.

We accept we'll do the best we can under trying circumstances, and we don't berate ourselves over how quickly or well we manage each step in the process. Exhibiting emotional resilience doesn't mean we won't get upset or overwhelmed at times. Instead, we acknowledge these feelings and work our way through them. The need for awareness of our own and our family members' emotions is the underlying theme of Julia Simens'

'Exhibiting emotional resilience doesn't mean we won't get upset or overwhelmed at times. Instead, we acknowledge these feelings and work our way through them.'

book, *Emotional Resilience and the Expat Child*. Simens outlines the importance of healthy relationships for expat children to develop and thrive, and the benefits of accurately identifying and dealing with their emotions throughout the transition process.

To put it all in context, as expats, we are the *Who* in this equation, and *What* is the turmoil and upheaval we face resulting from the cross-cultural, mobile life in which we find ourselves. Healthy identity development and congruence are the important reasons *Why* we need emotional resilience. Emotional, social and cultural intelligence skills, positive psychology and other tools are *How* we enhance our emotional resilience – they help us handle our experiences as we go through the Kübler-Ross change model that helps identify *Which* stage we're in, and *When* and *Where* we happen to be in our transition phases.

I've spent more than two years reading and researching emotional resilience, expatriate life/ cross-cultural life, transitions, culture shock, emotional/ social/ cultural intelligence, mindfulness and related topics in this book. My objective was to put it all into a cohesive framework to make the strongest case regarding the need for emotional resilience and ways to promote it in expat life. I was able to do this – developing the *'Who, What, When, Where, Why, How* and *Which'* guiding statement and the concept of FACTORS™ – within the first few months. I knew what I wanted to write about, had my framework and a detailed outline.

Throughout this project I have read more than 70 books and countless articles, the most relevant of which I share in the References/ Resources section at the end of this book. I followed countless information trails branching off from the main avenues of thought, to better understand how all the pieces fit together, trying to ensure coverage of the most important points. I deliberately chose to *not* read any of the books on emotional resilience (other than Julia Simens' on expat children) until the first draft was completed. In this way I've allowed my ideas to percolate without being unduly influenced by others.

So how do others view resilience? When it comes to the subject, corporations and business/ management schools have been interested for quite some time. Companies and employees must plan for, react, and respond to economic, technological, market, resource and industry-driven change. They also recognize the human element – helping employees deal with the associated stress. One of the best articles addressing work-life resilience I've found is the Harvard Business Review's, *How Resilience Works*. Senior editor Diane Coutu outlined three practices of resilient people:

- Acknowledge reality
- Search for meaning
- Continually improvise

Rather than drifting into denial, take a sobering view of what you're up against. This bolsters your ability to endure, a necessity if you are to prevail. Recognize bad things happen to everyone. Reject the 'victim' label, stop rationalizing and begin to find deeper meaning, life lessons – even an upside – in difficult experiences. Coutu credits French anthropologist Claude Levi-Strauss with using the word *bricolage* to refer to the third aspect of resilience – inventiveness or constructing creative solutions with few resources at hand.

In her book, *It's Not the End of the World: Developing Resilience in Times of Change*, Joan Borysenko builds on Coutu's three components for emotional resilience, emphasizing the need to be flexible, adaptive and creative in dealing with change. We can choose to view change as a challenge – although sometimes a difficult one – instead of automatically perceiving it as negative or unwelcome. Borysenko also includes considerable information on utilizing brain-body research to help us develop new neural pathways to shift from negative thinking to positive. This knowledge is also addressed in books by Daniel Amen (mind-body connections), Martin Seligman (positive psychology), and Barbara Frederickson (broaden-to-build positive emotions), among others, and will be discussed in greater detail in subsequent chapters.

Al Siebert makes a strong mind-body connection among knowledge, motivation and action to enhance resilience. In his book, *The Resiliency Advantage: Master Change, Thrive Under Pressure, and Bounce Back From Setbacks*, he outlines commonalities among highly resilient people: dedication to health and well-being, sharpened problem-solving skills, strong internal sense of self, a curious, hopeful approach, and a talent for making good come out of bad. He goes on to offer a set of eight principles affecting resilience:

- Change ensures we cannot remain the same – it's up to us to determine whether we become bitter or better
- Our mind and existing habits can create barriers or bridges to a more positive future state

- Blaming others causes us to retain a non-responsive 'victim' mindset
- Life's unfairness helps build resilience as we seek ways to overcome challenges
- Self-motivated, self-managed learning from adversity strengthens our resilience
- Self-observation, experimentation and receptivity to feedback contribute to self-knowledge and a personalized approach to resilience
- Making conscious choices about how we interact in the world contributes to independence and control over our actions
- The more resilient we become, the easier, faster and more effectively we handle change and setbacks

These principles are affected by our attitudes, beliefs and values, but we have the ability to make adjustments in how we view events, and a choice in how we respond to adversity.

Karen Reivich and Andrew Shatté take a more mind-centered approach, sorting resilience-enhancing skills into the two categories of self-knowledge and self-change, and applying these skills to marriage, parenting, work and life. In their book, *The Resilience Factor: Seven Keys to Finding Your Inner Strength and Overcoming Life's Hurdles*, they identify seven skills integral to resilience:

- Understanding how our individual hot button issues and beliefs can impact our behavior and actions in the Adversity-Beliefs-Consequences model
- Avoiding or changing negative assumptions ('thinking traps')
- Detecting subconscious, underlying beliefs ('icebergs')
- Challenging our beliefs
- Putting things into perspective
- Learning to quiet our emotions through self-calming and focus (mindfulness)
- Being resilient in real-time by challenging beliefs and using perspective simultaneously

There are some wonderful books on emotional resilience out there, although none specifically relating to expat life other than this and Simens' book. I'm pleased that while we don't all cover exactly the same information, there is sufficient overlap to make me feel I've captured the most essential material. There is also considerable unique content in this book geared specifically to people living across cultures, thus ensuring I've met my objective.

I think it is important to note there is no moral high ground with regard to emotional resilience. Those who naturally possess more emotional resilience than others are not necessarily smarter, better, tougher or savvier. If you are fortunate enough to have a naturally positive outlook on life, are able to roll with the punches and bounce back quickly from the minor ups and downs we experience throughout life, then good for you. Consider yourself blessed, but certainly don't take it for granted. Life throws us curve balls at the oddest times. A downturn you might shrug off and move on from quickly at one point in your life, may be a crushing blow if it's the latest in a series of difficult setbacks. If a resilient nature doesn't come easily to you, don't throw up your hands and assume you have no recourse to increase your resiliency. Rest assured there is much you can do to change your approach and how you handle tough times.

WHY EMOTIONAL RESILIENCE MATTERS

As a writer, I spend a considerable amount of time communicating the significance of emotional resilience in everyday life. I'm often called upon to share how those of us living cross-cultural lives (including, but not limited to, expats), can benefit greatly by developing and enhancing our personal reserves. As an expat, I know firsthand how valuable this can be.

For the most part, gone are the languid, slow-paced days of the expatriate life of the past. Life today in this globally interconnected, cross-cultural world is fast moving and frenetic. More and more, people choose to head overseas for employment, experience, education, better standard of living, adventure and wanderlust. Sometimes the choice is made for them, as in the case of economic recession, corporate restructuring, downsizing and organizational reassignment.

To better understand how emotional resilience can help expats, I think it's helpful to discuss the possible risks we face if we lack in this crucial area. Some people are motivated more by outlining the benefits of taking a particular course of action, while others respond better to warnings about the potential dangers of not doing that same thing:

- **Identity Incongruence:** Our sense of identity is critical to our mental and emotional health. When the way we see ourselves is in alignment with how others see us, we're said to have congruence in our identity development. The high-mobility aspect of expat life means we may feel as though we're always leaving or arriving in a continual loop of transition from one country/ culture to the next. During these transitions we encounter the confusion of leaving one environment and plunging into a different one with the increased likelihood of our identity being out of sync. The cross-cultural feature of expat life also impacts our sense of self, continually challenging us to find our way, fit in and adapt to new people and surroundings. Without a clear sense of integrated identity, of who we are as we continually move from place to place, we may find ourselves suffering from identity incongruence. Without sufficient emotional resilience, we find it hard to navigate our way through the transition phases inherent in the

> 'Sense of identity is critical to our mental and emotional health. When the way we see ourselves is in alignment with how others see us, we're said to have congruence in our identity development.'

expat experience (involvement in the old culture, leaving, transition, entry and re-involvement in the new culture), with our identity congruence intact.

- **Unresolved Loss and Grief:** Virtually everyone feels some level of grief and sense of loss during the leaving, transition and entry phases. What is important for each of us is how deeply we feel these emotions and to what extent these phases last. As we move through these transitional phases, we tend to go through the Kübler-Ross emotional change model of denial, anger/ frustration, bargaining, depression and acceptance. In dealing with transitional challenges, we struggle with emotional fallout from the continual disruption and ending of relationships and connections, as we find ourselves on the move. The comings and goings of expat life lend themselves to unresolved feelings of loss and grief as we leave behind people, places and memories that matter. If we don't acknowledge and incorporate these feelings as we mourn our losses, our identity development and congruence may be affected, and we may not be able to move on to the acceptance stage of the change model. We risk becoming stuck in this painful limbo of unresolved grief.

- **Lack of a Sense of Belonging:** In order to be emotionally resilient, we draw upon our emotional intelligence – self-awareness of what we're feeling and why, and being able to manage our emotions appropriately. Part of how we feel about ourselves is a function of our social intelligence (i.e., how we relate to and deal with others, and in turn how they relate to, and interact, with us). When we are lacking in emotional and/ or social intelligence, or these skills are hindered by the shift in cultural environments, we can find ourselves out of sorts, in a confusing, situational free fall. While most of us do integrate ourselves into the new culture, thereby reaching the re-involvement phase, it can sometimes come at great emotional expense. If we don't reach the acceptance stage of our own personal change model experience, we become trapped in the expat entry phase and cannot reach the re-involvement phase, where we begin to feel settled and experience a sense of belonging. We risk feeling alienated, helpless, lost, if we don't feel we belong.

- **Difficulty in Making/ Maintaining Connections:** When exposed to both the constant change and cross-cultural aspects of expat life, we risk not effectively engaging others as we transit from place to place. If we haven't allowed those we knew and connected with previously to know we cared about them,

> 'The comings and goings of expat life lend themselves to unresolved feelings of loss and grief as we leave behind people, places and memories that matter.'

or didn't allow them to express how they felt about us, we risk feeling as though they never cared. We find it harder to connect with those we interact with in our new environment, and start to withdraw. We protect ourselves, disengaging while keeping others at an emotional distance. We risk becoming ships that pass in the night, not allowing others to get close enough to know the real us.

- **Sadness, Anger and Depression:** For an expat, emotional resilience may be tested in many forms – facing a sudden job/ family transfer due to political upheaval, economic downturn or natural disaster, in handling the transition into a new language and culture which may differ vastly from one's own, or in dealing with a medical crisis involving themselves or their loved ones while overseas. If we are already carrying feelings of unresolved grief and loss, we may find ourselves emotionally overwhelmed and stuck in the depression stage of the change model. Lacking sufficient reserves of emotional resilience when faced with these additional challenging events, we risk not acknowledging our feelings and being unable to work our way through them. We may unnecessarily view ourselves as weak, and berate ourselves for not dealing well under such trying circumstances. Overwhelmed and sinking further into depression, we find it difficult to find meaning and a sense of accomplishment in daily life.

- **Negative and/ or Destructive Behaviors:** When we are in pain, we tend to try to ignore or suppress those painful and negative emotions in whatever manner works. This ignores our human need for resolution and closure, and sets us up for repeating similar negative behaviors in the days, months and even years ahead. When we are unhappy, grieving and/ or depressed, we risk employing negative tactics (withdrawal, avoidance, denial), unhealthy crutches (alcohol, prescription or non-prescription drugs, food), or acting out with other inappropriate

> 'When we are in pain, we tend to try to ignore or suppress those painful and negative emotions. This ignores our human need for resolution and closure, and sets us up for repeating similar negative behaviors.'

behaviors (sexual promiscuity, screaming, physical or emotional abuse). We seem to lose the critical ability to identify subtle differences among the emotions we may be feeling and to properly label them (and if need be, help family members to do so), to deal with those emotions, to choose our actions wisely, and to interact with others in a healthy manner.

A series of individual events can accumulate over time, sapping our resilience reserves and snowballing. Everyone has their own 'tipping point', the moment when it all gets too much to handle. Many of us are fortunate to never quite reach that point, but for some, being walloped with one crisis or stressful event after another can end up pushing us over into depression. The contributor of the next story shares the series of events which proved too much.

CUMULATIVE CHALLENGES TAKE THEIR TOLL

"Having post natal depression, then post-traumatic stress disorder following a major car crash (both within the space of four months), and moving internationally for the second time – and my fourth home in less than two years – wasn't the best time I spent as an expat.

I became depressed following relocation from a country we enjoyed and felt we still had so much more to experience, back to a country where we'd lived previously but had been ready to leave after two years. I found this relocation the toughest as it highlighted everything I thought I'd escaped from, and it would be harder to make a new life somewhere I didn't want to be. This was compounded by damaging my ankle and limiting my normal active lifestyle.

Especially hard was coming to terms with having a disabled child with learning issues, whilst living in a foreign country and having difficulty finding support for his needs because of a second language issue and the school's inability or unwillingness to acknowledge there was a problem."

Nicola McCall, British expat/ repat

As we see in these stories and those that follow, some of the difficulties expats/ cross-culturals experience are unique to this way of life (culture shock, cultural transition, facing a new language). However, many are the same challenges we might face in a stable, non-mobile lifestyle. People everywhere may encounter accidents, illnesses, learning disabilities, and the deaths of loved ones. It is being removed from our usual support systems that can exacerbate the situation, causing us to draw further upon our resilience reserves.

ONE EXPAT AND COUNSELOR'S LOOK AT RESILIENCY

PREPARING OURSELVES FOR THE WORST

"During the past fourteen years, I have relocated internationally five times with my husband and three (now) teenage children. We have lived in England, Bahrain, France, Holland and Qatar – twice. The excitement, adventure and life changing learning I have experienced have gone hand in hand with traumatic events happening to close family and friends, or to my community. My family has faced several traumatic bereavements, cancer, emergency repatriation due to the outbreak of war, and extreme bullying, on top of the continual good-byes to those we love.

Like many expat parents, one key motivation for moving abroad was the desire to build a better quality of life for my children. I hoped to gain a wealth of time, experiences and choices, to enjoy my children and be there for them in the short time they are entrusted to my care. I have heard parents describe expat life as, 'Great! But it's not real life, is it?' I wonder what they mean.

There is a wealth of material to help you and your children adapt during transitions, but this lifestyle will not protect you from adversity. Truly tragic things happen to good people everywhere, all the time.

I am an optimistic person, but my experience of adversity has taught me the value of the other side of the coin – what we can learn from viewing the glass as half-empty. Not in a morbid way, but a truth that can help build resiliency during quieter times, in preparation for the storms ahead. Dr. Phil McGraw, in his book, Real Life: Preparing for the Seven Worst Days of Your Life, *says we should proactively prepare for devastating crises.*

During my most recent relocation, my family faced another 'worst day' identified by Dr. Phil – the day addiction takes hold of you or a family member. Our past pain and suffering have become the stepping-stones which are turning what should be a tsunami into a wave. We are getting our feet wet but are experiencing indescribable peace as we muster our hard learned resiliency and move forward into a better life for us all, again.

The reality is the glass is both half-full and half-empty. We need both perspectives to be spiritually and psychologically resilient. Honestly facing the half-empty glass has made me aware of the courage, tenacity and love that have grown in us despite the pain.

When my children were recently showered with school prizes for their outstanding achievements in leadership, diligence, and progress, my family can honestly state we know that, '... suffering produces perseverance; perseverance, character; and character, hope. And hope does not disappoint us...'*

Neither will your expat adventure in giving you and your children extraordinary opportunities to develop vital resiliency skills."
(**Romans 5: 3-5*, New International Version of the Bible*)*

Sarah Koblow, counsellor, social worker, longtime expat, currently in Qatar

Finally, I would like to conclude with this: expat life offers wonderful opportunities to explore and experience the enchanting excitement of a culturally diverse world, yet it is not without its challenges. If we do find ourselves, a family member or friend, getting bogged down in a sense of overwhelming sadness, helplessness or depression, which keeps us (or them) from taking action, we owe it to ourselves and to them to consider seeking help, particularly from a psychologist or therapist familiar with issues in expat/ cross-cultural life.

> *'Some of the difficulties expats/ cross-culturals experience are unique to this way of life (culture shock, cultural transition, facing a new language). Being removed from our usual support systems can exacerbate the situation.'*

CHAPTER 5: EMOTIONAL AND SOCIAL INTELLIGENCE

Emotional intelligence and its counterpart, social intelligence, are two of the most effective tools we have available to develop, enhance and restore our emotional resilience reserves. In this chapter we will learn what these types of intelligence are, when we might need them in expatriate/ cross-cultural life, and how to improve our skills in employing them.

WHAT ARE EMOTIONAL AND SOCIAL INTELLIGENCE?

Few of us live a life that glides along smoothly with nary a concern. Most of us regularly deal with the minor troubles and hassles which pop up along the way. Others face difficult and potentially life-altering events including death of a loved one, life-threatening illness or debilitating disease, divorce, disability, job loss, and yes, relocating from one country/ culture to another.

Regardless of whatever situation you find yourself in, we all benefit from enhancing our levels of emotional resilience. This is every bit as true for children as it is for adults. In fact, the earlier we learn to stoke the fires of emotional resilience, the better prepared we may be to handle difficult situations and work our way back to a sense of normalcy. One way to increase our emotional resilience reserves is to focus on improving our emotional intelligence.

Emotional intelligence has its roots in the species survival and adaptation work of Charles Darwin, but the term 'emotional intelligence' is generally attributed to Peter Salovey and John D. Mayer in 1990. They, along with David R. Caruso, went on to develop the well-known Mayer-Salovey-Caruso Emotional Intelligence Test (MSCEIT™) for measuring a person's ability to perceive, understand, use and manage their emotions.

'Emotional intelligence and its counterpart, social intelligence, are two of the most effective tools we have available to develop, enhance and restore our emotional resilience reserves.'

It was Daniel Goleman, building on Salovey and Mayer's work and earlier research, who made the field well-known with his 1996 bestseller, *Emotional Intelligence: Why It Can Matter More Than IQ*. A psychologist and former science journalist for Psychology Today magazine and the New York Times, Goleman initially defined emotional intelligence as a series of competencies and skills including self-control (regulation), persistence, self-motivation, compassion (empathy), social (management), and zeal (achievement). His is considered a mixed model in that it combines an underlying level of basic innate talent with learned capabilities.

Goleman has made it his life's work to continue the research, writing numerous books on emotional intelligence and related topics. In 2006 he introduced another breakthrough book, *Social Intelligence: The New Science of Human Relationships*, in which he split his earlier definition apart with emotional intelligence being inwardly focused (dealing with ourselves), and renaming the outwardly focused aspects social intelligence (dealing with others):

- **Emotional intelligence is now generally defined as self-awareness and self-management:** Identifying, understanding, using and managing our emotions in positive, constructive ways.

- **Social intelligence is considered 'other-centered' social awareness and social management:** Leveraging perception and understanding of how others are feeling/ acting to engage in social interactions/ relationships in ways that are healthy for all involved.

Today Goleman remains active in expanding the field of what is now often referred to as 'social and emotional learning' (SEL), to help educators teach children the requisite skills of emotional and social intelligence.

In order to be emotionally resilient, we draw upon our emotional intelligence. How we feel about ourselves is a function of how we relate to others (and how they relate to us), employing our social intelligence can also aid in enhancing our emotional resilience. Similarly, how we relate to others can impact how we feel about ourselves.

Julia Simens makes this important connection between what we, or family members, are feeling (self and social awareness), and the need for developing emotional resilience in her book, *Emotional Resilience and the Expat Child*. While she focuses primarily on pre-adolescent expat children, and the parents and other adults who interact with them, Simens' message easily translates to teens and adults. The importance of

> 'Emotional intelligence is now generally defined as self-awareness and self-management and Social intelligence is considered 'other-centered' social awareness and social management.'

identifying the subtle differences between emotions and properly labeling them – and helping those we care about to do the same – is essential in order to deal with those emotions, choose our actions, and interact with others in a healthy manner.

ENHANCING EMOTIONAL INTELLIGENCE

Let's look first at the emotional intelligence half of the emotional/ social intelligence coin. Increased awareness of our feelings and emotions, and being able to better manage them, contribute greatly to how emotionally resilient we are, or can be. How we feel about ourselves can impact how we relate to and interact with others. The reverse is also true – the way in which we relate to others and how they relate to us affect how we feel about ourselves.

When are emotional intelligence skills helpful? In a word, *always*. If we've recently moved to a new country or culture and are feeling disoriented and out of sorts as we go through the expat transition cycle. When our children don't feel understood, act out in frustration or anger, lament the inability to find friends they 'click' with, or feel bullied. Whenever we face change of any sort in our life, being in touch with our emotions and feeling good about ourselves are important cornerstones to our behavior.

The key to emotional intelligence lies in reading our own feelings and emotions to help ourselves act in a healthy and socially acceptable manner as we interface with others. The following are ways in which we can enhance our emotional intelligence skills:

> 'The key to emotional intelligence lies in reading our own feelings and emotions to help ourselves act in a healthy and socially acceptable manner as we interface with others.'

- **Recognize our own emotional state and its impact on our thoughts, perceptions, potential actions:**
  - Periodically assess what we are thinking and why, especially if we find ourselves feeling negatively (e.g., stressed, angry, frustrated, irritated, jealous, depressed).

- **Learn to break the feeling/ thought/ action cycle:**
  - Feelings can affect thoughts and in turn actions, but we can recognize and rationalize at each step to interrupt, redirect or intervene.

- **Don't be too hard on ourselves:**
  - It is one thing to set challenging goals and objectives and to expect our best effort, but entirely another to be overly demanding or to criticize and berate ourselves for not measuring up.
  - We'll find we are more generous in our assessment of others if we are generous with ourselves.

- **We all tend to behave best when others believe in us, so start by practicing self-kindness:**
  - Doing so reduces negative feelings that contribute to stress, which can exacerbate feelings of anger, anxiety, sadness and depression.
  - Feeling better about ourselves helps foster feelings of kindness towards others.
  - Feeling positively toward someone not only makes it easier to behave more positively toward them, it also allows us to feel better about ourselves.

- **Employ positive behaviors and take care of ourselves:**
  - Make sure to get adequate rest, eat healthy food, exercise moderately and engage in some form of regular reflection or contemplation.

- **If we want to encourage our own positive feelings, thoughts and actions, actively practice the ability to empathize (i.e., the capacity to recognize feelings in others):**
  - When we feel empathy, it becomes easier to view others as similar to ourselves and harder to dismiss others as different or apart.
  - Consider how they may be feeling and why.
  - Notice their words and deeds, and ask ourselves why they might be acting in that way.
  - Put ourselves in their place and consider how we would feel in that situation.

- As empathy grows, so does our capacity for feeling compassion (i.e., going beyond feeling sympathy for others' misfortunes by desiring to help alleviate their pain):
  - When we feel compassion it becomes easier to act in a helpful manner and harder to act negatively.
  - The release of those chemical endorphins which make us feel good can be triggered both by engaging in physical activity such as brisk walking and exercise, AND by helping others.

- Feeling good about ourselves can result in improved emotional well-being and make us more receptive to feelings of satisfaction and joyfulness:
  - Positive self-feelings are also considered conducive to healing and improved immune function.

- Feeling positively in general (optimism) leads to becoming more hopeful, forward-looking and future-oriented:
  - When we have things to look forward to, we tend to feel happier and more settled.

- Gain perspective by looking at the bigger picture:
  - Remember that many challenges and difficulties are temporary.
  - Cultivate patience while we consider actions to improve our situation.

Emotional intelligence has tremendous value in helping us – cross-culturalists and monoculturalists alike – feel better about ourselves, our current situation, and our future. It also helps us interact more positively with others. There is now a growing trend toward introducing the concept to children, as evidenced by the next story.

DEDICATED TO TEACHING EMOTIONAL INTELLIGENCE

"Emotional Intelligence Education – http://www.emotional-intelligence-education. com is a website that helps parents and teachers to learn more about emotional intelligence and how learning these skills can help develop happier, healthier children and adults. I created this site because of my passion for the topic and the lack of resources available specifically looking at children and emotions.

I feel that emotional intelligence (EI) is such an important topic in today's ever-changing world. The great thing about EI is it can be learned, and research shows that teaching children these skills results in better academic performance and a happier outlook. Teaching children to manage stress is one of the skills we explore in depth on the site. This is important as we learn more and more about the harmful effects of being overly stressed on the body. We also explore different activities using drama, art, music and more to help build skills in conflict management, reducing bullying and building motivation."

Helen Maffini, serial expat and founder of the Emotional Intelligence Education website, now living in her eleventh country

Emotional intelligence helps us identify, acknowledge and manage the varied emotions we are feeling, so we are able to act in a more positive, less stressful manner. Now let's shift that perspective from ourselves to others by examining social intelligence.

STRENGTHENING SOCIAL INTELLIGENCE

If emotional intelligence is oriented toward oneself (i.e., self-awareness and self-management in which we identify, understand, use and manage our emotions in positive, constructive ways), then social intelligence is the 'other-centered' half of the emotional/social intelligence coin (i.e., social awareness and social management of relationships by engaging with other people in ways that are healthy for all involved).

Increased awareness of the feelings and emotions of others, and being able to better interface with them, also contribute to how emotionally resilient we are or can be. The manner in which we relate to others, and how they relate to us, affect how we feel about ourselves – just as how we feel about ourselves can impact on how we relate to, and interact, with others.

When do we benefit by employing sound social intelligence skills? As with emotional intelligence skills, the answer is *always*. When we are new to a place or culture and interact with others as we get to know our neighborhood, school, place of employment, or community. When our children seek help in dealing with difficult emotions, or with friends, teachers, dating, bullies. Moments

> 'The key to social intelligence lies in reading the feelings, emotions and actions of others to help ourselves act, or react, in a socially acceptable manner as we interface with them.'

of change, challenge and difficulty tend to put us in social situations where our words, actions and behavior can greatly benefit us, or contribute to misunderstanding, uneasiness, awkwardness or pain.

The key to social intelligence lies in reading the feelings, emotions and actions of others to help ourselves act, or react, in a socially acceptable manner as we interface with them. The following are ways in which we can enhance our social intelligence skills:

- **Present ourselves in a positive manner to receive positivity back:**
  - Be receptive to others by being welcoming – make eye contact, smile and be approachable.
  - Being thoughtful of the feelings of others leads us to be more thoughtful in our own actions.

- **During conversation give the other person(s) our undivided attention to help convey that what they say matters:**
  - Maintain eye contact.
  - Listen intently, without interruption.
  - Lean forward slightly to indicate we don't want to miss anything they say.
  - Occasionally nod our head in agreement to show we are taking in what they are saying.
  - Make receptive comments in a supportive manner.
  - Be gentle when asking questions, not demanding, insistent or interrogative.

- **Work on regulating our emotions to act appropriately:**
  - Think before speaking to avoid unnecessarily instigating negative interactions.
  - Break the negative feeling/ thought/ action cycle to avoid whining, gossiping, lashing out in irritation or anger.
  - Take deep breaths, count to twenty, refrain from speaking, or remove ourselves from a situation if we feel unable to interact in a positive manner.

- **Be open to learning about the world in general and others in particular:**
  - By embracing new knowledge and information, we expand our horizons.

- **'Read' people's emotions and behavior by employing empathy (i.e., the capacity to recognize feelings in others):**
  - Make an effort to understand not only the words spoken, but also the tone and use of body language.

- ○ Consider the situations others may face, and the feelings and emotions behind them.
- ○ Ask ourselves why they might be acting as they are and what could be motivating them.
- ○ Put ourselves in their place and consider how we would feel in that situation.

- **As empathy grows so does our capacity for feeling compassion (i.e., sympathy for others' misfortunes and wanting to help):**
  - ○ Empathy makes it easier to relate to and understand others, and is necessary for feeling compassion.
  - ○ Compassion helps us refrain from acting negatively, encourages our wanting to help others, and can result in our acting in a more considerate, supportive manner.

- **If we want to understand and interact better with the outer world, practice gratitude:**
  - ○ Regularly reflect on what we have to be grateful for.
  - ○ Make a list to remind ourselves of the abundance in our life, or journal about them.
  - ○ Actively express appreciation to ourselves and others.

- **Working with others on a common project, cause or organization allows us to get to know others better and to feel greater ease in social situations:**
  - ○ Seek out such opportunities at school, in the workplace, neighborhood or the wider community.

- **Volunteering helps shift our focus onto the plight of others while helping reinforce feelings of appreciation and gratitude for our own situation:**
  - ○ Offer your time and skills to assist in making a difference in the lives of others.

Empathy plays a significant role in both emotional and social intelligence. By recognizing and relating to the feelings of others, we make a connection. We understand we aren't alone in our feelings, that others aren't as different as they may seem. We have far more in common than we might have thought. Heidi Sand-Hart captures this sense of empathy in this passage: '*Through my childhood experiences, a real empathy has stayed with me for refugees, the odd ones out, and I suppose it is because I have spent much of my life as just that – the new girl in class, the blond-haired in a multitude of black, the brown-eyed in a sea of blue. Accepted to a degree, but never fully in.*'

Without empathy (understanding how another feels), we cannot have compassion (feeling moved to help alleviate their suffering). It is also important to practice empathy and compassion on ourselves as well as others. When it comes to difficult public experiences, such as the one shared below, we can all benefit from taking a few deep breaths and reminding ourselves that a positive presentation helps encourage a positive reception. Even when others respond in what we perceive to be a less-than-amiable fashion, it is important we interrupt any negative feelings and thoughts we experience, to avoid acting in a way we may later regret.

COMPASSION, TOLERANCE AND PATIENCE

"My daughter's first day at school comes to mind. I stood there surrounded by other families. My daughter and I stood alone, slightly apart from the rest. We were living in a conservative village at the time and I spoke English to the small white-haired child holding my hand. Mothers turned around and seemed to stare or glare. I heard the mutterings of 'foreigner... should speak Dutch to her child...'

I ignored the feeling of loneliness though it engulfed me like a tsunami wave. My daughter's first day and I felt extremely alone. Her Dutch father was on a business trip. His family did not believe in 'fussing', and I longed for my dead mother to be alive. I longed for somebody to stand with us. My daughter, luckily enough, was oblivious to my emotions. She quickly joined the other children as we all followed the animated group into their classrooms. Groups of Dutch mothers and fathers closed ranks on their children. My daughter smiled at me and sat down contentedly. The teacher could not pronounce her name and I corrected her. It didn't help that I chose a very Irish name for our daughter. My cheeks reddened as I felt everybody was taking note of the foreigner and her daughter. I spoke in my best Dutch and small sniggers exploded in the classroom, eventually reaching proportions of – what I thought to be – hysterical laughter. Was I imagining this? Was I really here in this conservative village? Will my daughter survive? Will I survive? Am I being too sensitive?

It was time to leave the children and I blew my daughter a kiss as my mother had with me on my first day at school. There were no tears. My daughter was ready to be in school. Other children started crying. I was lucky. I was grateful I did not have to deal with the emotion of tears as well. I was grateful to walk out of the classroom at a very steady pace and very grateful my bicycle was parked conveniently near the school gates. I rushed, almost in blind panic, to the parked bike. I heard parents' footsteps behind me. I didn't want to talk to anybody. It was clear I was an outsider. I just wanted to get home to my little sanctuary.

I closed the door of the white villa, the background of windmills, like a chocolate box setting. I sat down and heard a strange noise coming from somewhere. I realized it was me. It was a deep, sad resonance coming from deep inside. As the fat tears dripped on the new dining table, I looked at the clock on the wall, ticking. I could collect her in three hours. I waited.

In hindsight, I think I was not in a good place with myself, regardless of the circumstances. I suppose I took everything very personally. I don't think the Dutch parents were laughing at me, but it felt that way. I just wanted to 'fit in' and be like the rest. The reality is I am not Dutch and never will be. I have spent 25 years in the Netherlands and have re-defined what resilience is. It is 'being yourself'. It is taking the positives out of the situations that occur daily. It is the perception of how you deal with your own emotions. Now, I have a better idea of who I am and am quite happy living in The Hague. However, living in a country village was extremely difficult at the time. There were very few foreigners and instead of blending in, I was the focus. Luckily, my daughter never had a problem with it. She blended in wonderfully and made lots of friends. I think emotional resilience is taking yourself as you are, wherever you live and accepting it. It enriches who you are as a person and does make you stronger. I do not take anything personally now. I realize we are a mirror of each other and usually, if there is a problem, it is about the other person's story. I have learned compassion and tolerance. I have learned patience and being non-judgmental. These are wonderful gifts I would not have readily embraced if I had not lived in another country."

Niamh Ni Bhroin, Irish expat (Greece) now living in the Netherlands

In the end, we can only control our own thoughts, feelings, and actions, not those of others. When faced with the perception of negative behavior, such as the sniggering at mispronounced language in the story above, our feelings may be initially hurt. It helps to remember our perceptions aren't always accurate. Even if they were, such behavior says far more about those insensitive enough to act that way, than on our attempts to speak a new language. Don't give others a power they don't deserve by allowing their actions to make us feel badly about ourselves. Better to shrug it off and move on.

As we have learned, emotional and social intelligence offer us constructive ways to improve our current and future environment. By presenting a positive, approachable demeanor and taking the time to listen, observe, and read the social and physical cues of others, we are better able to appreciate new and different cultural situations –

> 'When we make an effort to assess what we – and others – are feeling and why, we are more inclined to be patient, caring and respectful of them.'

and interface in ways that reflect connection, empathy, compassion and understanding. When we make an effort to assess what we – and others – are feeling and why, we are more inclined to be patient, caring and respectful of them as well as ourselves. In turn, this leads to a more hopeful, positive, forward-leaning approach to identifying solutions to our immediate problems, and gaining perspective of the temporary nature of many of our difficulties.

CHAPTER 6: CULTURAL INTELLIGENCE AND INTERCULTURAL COMPETENCE

Cultural anthropologists have long studied cultures and human societies, and the variations among them. In the past century research has grown to encompass other disciplines such as psychology, sociology, communications, linguistics, geography, history, international business, education and training, for an interdisciplinary approach to cultural competency. Cross-cultural competency remains difficult to define let alone measure, but at a minimum it includes awareness, assessment, and cognitive, behavioral and affective (emotional) components.

RESPECT FOR YOURSELF AND OTHERS

The field of intercultural competency, especially learning to adapt and work successfully overseas, has grown primarily out of work spanning the last 60 years. Researchers have gleaned much from the experiences of missionaries, Peace Corps and other international volunteers, as well as more traditional government, military and corporate expats. Intellectual curiosity and concern for failure rates on overseas assignments – due in part to intercultural challenges faced by employees and their family members – have fueled significant research into this broad genre.

In recent years, work by researchers such as Geert Hofstede (intercultural understanding, cross-cultural competency in international business), Milton J. Bennett (intercultural sensitivity), Janet Bennett (intercultural communication), Michael Paige (intercultural competence), Darla Deardorf (interdisciplinary definition of intercultural competence), Anne Copeland (cultural transitions), Carly Dodd (intercultural assessment) and many others, has helped inform the study of cross-cultural readiness, effectiveness and competence.

In 1980, Dutch Geert Hofstede introduced 'dimensions of culture', and in the process affirmed the important role of culture at all three societal levels: individual, organizational and country/ national. Hofstede defines culture as: *'the collective programming of the mind that distinguishes the members of one group or category of people from others.'*

In his book on intercultural understanding, *Culture's Consequences: Comparing Values, Behaviors, Institutions and Organizations Across Nations,* he writes of the 'mental programs' of culture, and values we each possess on the individual, interpersonal and collective levels of our self. Our personal mental program is rooted in childhood, derived from both nature and nurture, and is a salute to relational identity. In relational identity, each of us seeks to integrate the various aspects of who we are in terms of the relationships we have with others, and the roles we inhabit in those relationships. These relational roles can be both interpersonal (e.g., parent, partner, sibling, child, cousin, friend, neighbor), and group-oriented in nature (e.g., female, Canadian, business owner, Muslim, Caucasian, conservative, athlete, middle-aged). Our mental programs are reinforced through our relationships and roles with others – individuals, family, groups, organizations and institutions – and contain components of national culture. They are expressed in the dominant values espoused by members of our country/ society.

Using as his research study pool the hundreds of thousands of international business employees of IBM, from more than 40 countries around the world, Hofstede was able to plot where individuals – and by extension, organizations – fall on a continuum from weak to strong for each of five crucial pairs of cultural dimension. This approach, often referred to as the Hofstede Cultural Orientation Model, measures proximity to power, uncertainty avoidance, individualism/collectivism, masculinity, and time horizon orientation. Hofstede's later work extended his model to the level of national culture by including countries/ societies, and added a sixth dimension (gratification) based on Michael Minkov's work with *World Values Survey* data. The six dimensions of national culture are:

- **Distance from power:** This measures the level of acceptance of authority, social inequality and the distribution of influence. In countries with significant political, economic and social inequality, the distance from power is much further than for countries having greater equality.

- **Uncertainty avoidance:** This measures how comfortable or anxious a culture is in dealing with ambiguity, rigidity, laws and regimentation, creativity and abstraction.

- **Individualism and collectivism:** Whether a society tends to be more self- or group-oriented in affinity and sense of responsibility.

- **Masculinity:** Whether a culture leans more toward values traditionally considered masculine (e.g., dominant, assertive, decisive), or feminine (e.g., caring, inclusive, relationship-oriented), in emotional roles and behavior.

- **Societal orientation:** This is the orientation a society takes – short-term or long-term – regarding planning, spending, resource consumption and delayed gratification for the common good.

- **Gratification:** Whether a culture leans toward indulgence or restraint of the gratification of basic and natural drives for seeking enjoyment in life.

As with individuals and organizations, Hofstede's findings of where countries/ societies fit according to these cultural dimensions are not absolute, but rather reflect tendencies and trends at each level.

Why are Hofstede's cultural dimensions, and the cultural orientation model, relevant to enhancing emotional resilience in expat life? If we have a sense of how the country/ society in which we live compares to the one(s) in which we were raised or previously lived, we gain valuable insight into similarities and differences in our respective cultural values, attitudes, behavior and beliefs. This knowledge allows us to better understand potential areas of agreement, solidarity, friction or conflict.

Suppose I grew up in a culture where time is considered linear and precious, punctuality and precision are revered, and people are expected to mean exactly what they say. I may find it disconcerting to find myself living in a culture where the approach to time is more relaxed and elastic, saving face is preferred over sharing bad news, and the response 'maybe tomorrow' can mean anything from two days to two weeks to never. Similarly, a person from this culture might find people in my home culture abrupt, impatient, demanding and self-centered.

In her book, *Turning International*: *How to Find Happiness and Feel at Home in a New Culture*, Catherine Transler also believes awareness of where we fall on Hofstede's dimensions of culture compared to other cultures – including the one in which we currently live – can offer insight and information useful in interacting across cultures. '*Understanding these cultural differences better is a huge step towards adapting your own*

'If we have a sense of how the country/ society in which we live compares to the one(s) in which we were raised or previously lived, we gain valuable insight into similarities and differences in our respective cultural values, attitudes, behavior and beliefs.'

behavior. This is not about changing yourself or your values to become like the people of the host country, it is simply about having more options... Cross-cultural knowledge is useful in new situations and, in the long term, it boosts your openness and mental flexibility.'

As we'll see in *CHAPTER 7: BRAIN-BODY CONNECTIONS AND POSITIVE PSYCHOLOGY*, and later in *CHAPTER 12: VISUALIZATION* and *CHAPTER 13: OPTIMISM*, we need not be ruled by our thoughts and feelings. Rather than expect those around me to miraculously change the behaviors I may find confusing, irritating or offensive – or continue to beat my head against a wall in frustration when they don't – I can identify and choose to interrupt negative thoughts before they become bad feelings, and vice versa. I can also cultivate more positive thinking and emotions. I can adjust my behavior accordingly. I can't control how life works in another culture, but I can take steps to control my reactions, responses and conduct.

One of the key points made repeatedly by intercultural competency academics and researchers, is that handing a list of cultural do's and don'ts to relocating expatriate employees is not sufficient to ensure appropriate, effective communication and behavior in cross-cultural situations. Knowledge and superficial skills only take us so far. We may do some of the right things or temporarily avoid doing wrong things, which may disrupt or damage intercultural effectiveness. Yet without a foundational understanding of cultural differences and underlying attitudes, values, and behaviors – *our own as well as those of others* – our effectiveness is illusory at best and detrimental at worst. Recognizing and addressing differences in attitudes, beliefs and ways of interaction is critical to maintaining and enhancing cultural competence, and identifying them requires assessment.

'Understanding these cultural differences better is a huge step towards adapting your own behavior. Cross-cultural knowledge is useful in new situations and, in the long term, it boosts your openness and mental flexibility.'

In looking at assessment tools used by psychologists and businesses (e.g., Myer-Briggs Type Indicator, Minnesota Multiphasic Personality Inventory, NEO personality domains), to identify characteristics likely to ensure workplace success, researchers have recognized the need for assessment tools that can predict performance and adaptive skills in intercultural situations. For example, two decades of concentrated research and testing by Carly Dodd, Ph.D., of Abilene Christian University, have yielded the Intercultural Readiness Assessment (2007), and the Go Culture Assessment (2011). These assessment tools, along with others, identify and measure capabilities, which can be useful in tailoring training to increase effectiveness in cross-cultural environments.

Why the need for assessing and understanding cross-cultural values, attitudes, behaviors and beliefs? Consider the example of giving a large and varied group of people the task of planning and throwing a birthday party for a good friend. On the surface their common affection for the friend, and interest in celebrating the occasion, would seem to be sufficient cause for them to excel in this joint endeavor. That is, until the person who enjoys museums and quiet dinners with the friend hears the suggestions of the one who goes dancing and clubbing with him/ her every weekend. They, in turn, are flummoxed by the ideas of the one who spends Sunday evenings with the friend, at home on the couch with a take-out and old movies. One person regularly attends gala events and high society fundraisers with him/ her. Someone else has other ideas from their hiking and camping experiences.

Some may insist on certain things because 'that's how we celebrate birthdays here'. Others respond that local traditions aren't necessary, relevant or appropriate in this situation. A few have no clue what these mysterious traditions may be. The extroverts may dominate the conversation, while the more introverted group members struggle to share their vision of the perfect party. Each person has a different view of the friend's personality, interests, tastes and preferences. They also bring their own experiences, opinions, biases and party-giving customs to the project. Individually they may each excel at organizing birthday parties, but collectively confusion reigns. Lingering resentment, bruised egos and feelings of exasperation, puzzlement and marginalization may remain long after the party takes place.

This brings us to the concept of Cultural Intelligence. Cultural Intelligence, also known as Cultural Quotient (CQ), is a measure of a person's capacity to function effectively in a multi-cultural environment. It comes from a multi-disciplinary perspective, incorporating anthropology, sociology, psychology, linguistics, education and business, including corporate,

'Without a foundational understanding of cultural differences and underlying attitudes, values, and behaviors – our own as well as those of others – our effectiveness is illusory at best and detrimental at worst. '

'Cultural intelligence marries the cognitive (knowledge and understanding), with the motivational (what drives us, our interests, desired outcomes), and the behavioral (mindful awareness, employing our senses to adapt our actions).'

organizational, and mission experience and literature. Building on the extensive work of P. Christopher Early, Soon Ang, Linn Van Dyne, and David A. Livermore – all scholars contributing to this relatively new field – CQ offers a construct with cognitive, behavioral and motivational aspects, which build on the more traditional elements of cultural knowledge, skills and abilities.

Cultural intelligence calls for us to recognize and understand the values, attitudes, beliefs and behaviors of ourselves and others, and then apply that knowledge to achieve specific results, such as developing cross-cultural relationships and operating in culturally diverse situations. Employed well, CQ enhances cross-cultural connections and encourages awareness, understanding, respect and tolerance. It is developed through a mix of cognitive, physical and motivational means – learning about our own and other cultures (cultural diversity), using our senses and body awareness to adapt, and achieving emotional goals such as acceptance, inclusion and belonging. Livermore and others suggest CQ picks up where EQ leaves off, in that it focuses on interacting with people, environments and circumstances unfamiliar in context.

Cross-cultural competence tends to focus on understanding differences in cultural values and how they affect the way we relate to those cultures. Such effectiveness across cultures includes a respectful approach to learning and interacting, and can include appropriate practices and taboos. However, cultural intelligence seeks to give cross-cultural competence a framework for understanding the interrelation of cultural knowledge, values, and information, with our aspirations and motivations to develop appropriate cross-cultural behavior. In other words, cultural intelligence marries the cognitive (knowledge and understanding), with the motivational (what drives us, our interests, desired outcomes), and the behavioral (mindful awareness, employing our senses to adapt our actions). Efforts have been made to measure CQ on a scale just as we can our IQ and EQ.

In Livermore's book, *Cultural Intelligence: Improving Your CQ to Engage Our Multicultural World*, he identified the four leading factors of CQ as knowledge, interpretive, perseverance and behavioral. Less than a year later he released his subsequent book, *Leading With Cultural Intelligence: The New Secret to Success*, and had relabeled the last three factors as strategy, drive and action. Livermore posits that through self-awareness and self-assessment, we can measure our CQ capabilities in the following four, interrelated areas:

- **Drive:** Interest in gaining and enjoying the benefits of cross-cultural interaction – including acceptance and a sense of belonging – and to confidently be effective.

- **Knowledge:** Understanding of political, economic and social values, beliefs and norms, and verbal and non-verbal means of expression.

- **Strategy:** Mindful awareness of, preparing for, evaluating and making sense of intercultural experiences.

- **Action:** Ability to adapt verbal expression and non-verbal behavior in various situations across diverse cultures.

Livermore considers: '*the beauty of the cultural intelligence model is that it links thinking and cross-cultural understanding to action*' with the strategy/ interpretive factor as the link between knowledge and action.

David C. Thomas and Kerr Inkson also envision mindfulness as an integral part of cultural intelligence. In their book, *Cultural Intelligence: Living and Working Globally*, they assert that learning to deal effectively in different cultures and/ or with people from other cultural backgrounds calls for perception, contextual interpretation and perspective, in addition to knowledge and skills. Ideally this becomes an iterative, experiential process in which we continually review and assess our interactions, and adjust accordingly.

As with emotional resilience and emotional/ social intelligence, we all have some base level of cultural intelligence. We are able to improve these capabilities by acquiring verbal, written and auditory knowledge, mindful observation, training, direct experience, practice, role-playing, careful miming, evaluation, and eliciting feedback.

However, when it comes to cross-cultural competency it seems a fairly large gap remains between *knowing* and *doing*. In their *Academy of International Business* article, published in the Journal of International Business Studies, James P. Johnson, Tomasz Lenartowicz and Salvador Apud maintain there is inadequate conceptualization of the definition of cross-cultural competency. Instead, emphasis is placed on the knowledge, skills and attributes – which they agree are building blocks of such intercultural competence, but not the competency itself. Until CQ is more fully defined, measurement will remain limited. They

> '*The beauty of the cultural intelligence model is that it links thinking and cross-cultural understanding to action.*'

> 'The CQ model must address measurement of performance (i.e., doing), in addition to the knowledge, skills and attributes contributing to that performance (i.e., the knowledge or learning).'

acknowledge the contribution cultural intelligence brings to the cross-cultural model, but it remains more focused on *learning* rather than *doing*. To be fully successful the CQ model must address measurement of performance (i.e., doing), in addition to the knowledge, skills and attributes contributing to that performance (i.e., the knowledge or learning). With the world becoming more interconnected by the day, thankfully research continues.

The good news is that, as with emotional resilience and emotional/ social intelligence, we can enhance our personal levels of cultural intelligence and intercultural competency. We are able to do this not only for the specific culture in which we find ourselves, but also to develop a greater general capability for interacting across a wide range of cultures. This bodes well for those of us living and working across cultures.

HUMILITY, APPRECIATION, FINDING COMMON GROUND

"What I learned by being a foreigner in Turkey is humility and that if I took everything personally I'd run myself into the ground. What I developed was a deeper appreciation and respect for both (all) cultures, even if I didn't agree with or understand them. I could accept that just as my own culture influences me, the same is true for all those around me. It's best to find common ground to connect on and be tolerant of the things I don't necessarily agree with. And adopt the things that are best in all cultures that suit me."

Tara Agacayak, American expat living in Turkey

While most people would agree respecting cultural differences is a valuable asset when living abroad, sometimes it is easier said than done. The first step is recognizing the tremendous influence culture has over each of us. Moving *across* cultures reinforces this awareness, and hopefully we respond not only with curiosity, but also with an openness to understanding without judgment. The next contributor knows the importance of being receptive to others,

> 'Because I empathize, understand and can work within all my resident cultures, I am able to act as a bridge for those on one side or the other.'

having lived in several countries where lack of respect among cultures and sub-cultures led to violence and war.

SENSITIVITY, RECEPTIVITY AND LEARNING

"Always be sensitive and receptive towards other cultures – mutual respect is all important and we can learn so much from each other."

Nicky Sully, South African expat (Rwanda, Tanzania, Cambodia) now living in the Netherlands

Ambiguity can refer to uncertainty or doubt in interpretation, but it can also mean the ability to express more than one explanation or understanding. The desire of the next story's contributor to move beyond the cultural chameleon role of 'fitting in', to bridging differences, reflects cultural intelligence in action.

LEARNING TO VALUE AMBIGUITY

"I've been an expat all of my life, a perpetual being-on-the-outside of my resident culture that has shaped who I am and how I interact in relationships and community. When I was growing up, this always in-between wasn't something I noticed, since my friends and the families in my community were in the same space of being-from-somewhere-else. I noticed, for myself and for my friends, that as we got older we claimed our resident culture more and more, and our links to our national culture became something that was more negotiable. For me, that meant claiming and feeling more cultural affinity with Egypt than with the US. Of course, it can easily go the other way, with an American in Cairo feeling more affinity for the US than for Egypt, but either cultural expression was a matter of choice and, because of that, ambiguous.

It is that ambiguity I value so much now, as an adult. Because I fit into all the cultures I have lived in, and at the same time, belong 'authentically' to none, I am able to be a chameleon and adapt very quickly to fit in wherever I am. But it's more than just being able to pass. Because I empathize, understand and can work within all my resident cultures, I am able to act as a bridge for those on one side or the other. Cross-cultural interactions often become polarized, so this bridging is an extremely useful service for me to perform in my relationships and within a community. In the last decade, it has been particularly valuable to be able to express values and world views from Egypt to Americans, and vice versa."

Elie Calhoun, American ATCK who has lived most of her life in Africa, including Kenya, Egypt, Tanzania, Liberia and Senegal

At the core of all positive cross-cultural interactions lies a curiosity, an awareness of one's self in relation to others, and an inquisitive nature as to how we and 'they' are both similar and different. Open mindedness helps facilitate this awareness, which we put into context with cultural knowledge, language and information gained. Combined, these translate into intercultural skills, and help promote understanding, acceptance, and the willingness and interest in promoting continued interactions and relationship building, and the cycle continues.

WE ARE MORE ALIKE THAN DIFFERENT

American writer Matt Krause was traveling overseas for business when he met 'the one'. Taking a chance on love, he followed the object of his affection to her native Turkey. Love paid off, in marriage to the woman and what can only be described as a deep and discerning love affair with her country. He has chronicled their years together living in Turkey, in the beautifully written and moving memoir of short stories, *A Tight Wide-Open Place*.

WHEN THINGS GET TOUGH, OPT TO OBSERVE RATHER THAN FEEL

"The best moments of my life have come while living abroad. Unfortunately, the lowest moments of my life have come while living abroad, too. I used to think the intensity of those low moments meant I was not cut out for expat life, but at some point I got tired of beating myself up for my 'unfitness'. I realized without the bad times I couldn't have the good ones, so I had no choice but to learn how to get through the tough spots.

One technique I've used over the years to get through those tough spots has been to feel less and observe more.

Wherever we are in the world, the people around us are going through very significant milestones in their lives, and those milestones are usually the same ones we know from back home – births, deaths, graduations, weddings, promotions, illnesses. When it comes to how people respond to those events, the trimmings may be different from one culture to the next, but the meat is pretty much the same. People celebrate births. They mourn deaths. They dance at weddings.

So when I am feeling dislocated and lonely, I focus on the people around me and notice how the way they respond to the events in their lives is similar to the way people back home respond to theirs. This pulls me closer to the people around me and counteracts my feelings of dislocation and loneliness. But there's more...

I try to articulate those similarities to the people back home.

Living abroad is unusual. When we are surrounded by expats, living abroad might not seem so special, but most people live their entire lives and never get to experience what we experience as expats. They dream about living in a foreign land, sure, but it remains that, a dream. We owe it to them to show them a world they might not get to experience otherwise. It is our duty to report back on what we see.

Why do I prefer talking about the similarities, rather than articulating the differences? Human nature being what it is, people tend to notice differences first anyway. They notice differences even when those differences are less significant than the similarities. They notice differences in religions even when other people are basically worshipping the same god. They notice differences in cuisine even though what really matters is people like to eat together. Our knowledge of the foreign culture puts us in a unique position to refocus the folks back home on the similarities and remind them foreigners aren't really as foreign as we sometimes think.

Understanding a foreign culture requires very careful observation though, and it is very hard to observe and feel at the same time. When observing we focus on the world around us. When feeling, we focus on ourselves. So the more energy we spend observing, the less we have available for feeling. And the less we have available for feeling, the easier it is to get through those bad days."

Matt Krause, American expat who walked 1,305 miles across Turkey

Choosing observation over feeling seems counterintuitive. Wouldn't we want to embrace our feelings and deal with them? Yes, but sometimes our feelings are all over the place and we're not sure why. As we will see in the section on mindfulness in *PART III, CHAPTER 12: VISUALIZATION*, being open, and eventually adapting, requires we orient ourselves toward the immediate experiences unfolding before us. It is in observation that we can begin to understand the similarities, to accept the differences and ultimately to connect with our fellow man.

THE SIMILARITIES OUTWEIGH THE DIFFERENCES

"In July 1997 following a coup in Cambodia, fighting broke out and Cambodian refugees fled into Thailand. It was a short-lived conflict thanks to international interventions, which allowed the return of refugees. Enter myself, a staff of the UN Refugee Agency, UNHCR, dispatched to help with that return.

I worked alongside one lively, energetic Khmer man named Ravi, who had lived through the Pol Pot era, worked with the UN in the years after the war and was a key source for all things Cambodian. One day we were talking about our families – families are important to Cambodians, but some traditions had broken down in the face of years of war and the Khmer Rouge policies.

Ravi explained how, during the Pol Pot years, he was forced to work in one farm area while his parents worked in another. One day he got word of his mother's illness and requested permission to leave his workstation and go to her. By the time the permission was granted and he had managed to travel, his mother had died. He gave a matter-of-fact account while I looked at him in shock.

I told him about my mother who I had lost nearly three years before to cancer. It was a feeble attempt to show some understanding of his experience. I had been working in Sri Lanka with UNHCR and she died before I could reach home. I was still grappling with her death, the guilt of not being there, and being so far from home and family and missing her more, rather than less, as time progressed.

Ravi's reaction took me by surprise. He grabbed my hand and told me how sorry he was, how terrible my loss. I looked at him in astonishment. 'My mother died in a hospital,' I said, 'surrounded by family, killed by a disease. Your mother died alone in a field!' He shook his head with sorrow, convinced there was no difference in our grief.

His ability to show such sympathy deeply impressed me. As sad and tragic as my loss was, it in no way compared to his story; his family and life destroyed by his own government.

I was astounded at his ability to empathize when the circumstances of our losses could not have been more different. But it also comforted me. Ravi and I, from entirely different worlds and circumstance, suffered the same devastating losses of our mothers, made worse by our absences. If he can live with his experience, I can surely live with mine.

I didn't stop grieving for my mother, but Ravi helped put it in perspective. We are more alike than we may realize. Ravi showed incredible compassion for a fellow child who had lost their parent."

Tracey Buckenmeyer
American international humanitarian aid worker for two decades

The story below is from a young adult TCK accustomed to moving across cultures. Despite looking as if she belongs in her 'home' culture, that is where she feels most foreign. This is an example of what Pollock and Van Reken referred to as being a 'hidden immigrant'. More and more, in our increasingly internationalized, cross-cultural world, we are coming to see what is on the outside does not automatically reflect – or determine – what is on the inside.

COLOR OF MY HEART

"At the check-in counter of the Penang International Airport, I watch four years of my life, packed in suitcases, roll away on the conveyor belts into the mass hysteria of baggage hidden behind the wall. I graduated from high school three days ago, and now I am leaving Malaysia. Having lived overseas for 15 years in five different countries, I've lost count of how many times I moved. As a TCK, it's hard to find anything that's 'constant' in life.

Throughout it all, airports have been constant for me. I spend a lot of time on the moving walkways observing the things going on around me. Even though I can feel the tension of transition in the air, I'm relaxed. I think about where I've been, and where

I'm going. This time, I'm on my way to the US. I instantly feel a pang in my gut. I've usually disliked the month I spend there every summer. I hate the culture shock. I hate the feeling of foreignness. Wait. Do I feel like I fit in more in an Asian country? I look at myself in the reflection of the glass window in front of me. Yup, tall, white, curvy and long red hair. I totally blend in Asia! I wish my reflection showed what color my heart looked like."

Cat Foster, American ATCK (Southeast Asia) now living in the US (excerpted piece, originally published on DenizenMag.com, used with permission)

With cultural intelligence and cross-cultural competence we understand and respect cultural differences, adapting effectively to our environment without necessarily taking on the values, attitudes and behaviors as our own. Being able to accurately articulate the beliefs of others, to value the ambiguity in alternative views, and to put ourselves in another's position are all critical skills in intercultural life.

> *'Being able to accurately articulate the beliefs of others, to value the ambiguity in alternative views, and to put ourselves in another's position are all critical skills in intercultural life.'*

CHAPTER 7: BRAIN-BODY CONNECTIONS AND POSITIVE PSYCHOLOGY

Our nervous system is a network of neuron cells transmitting signals from the brain to coordinate the voluntary and involuntary functions of our body. Extensive health, psychological and neuroscientific research efforts into the nervous and other systems, and related areas, continue to reveal developments in how the brain and body interact. The findings have implications for helping us live healthier, more satisfying lives.

UNDERSTANDING BRAIN-BODY CONNECTIONS

In his books, *Change Your Brain, Change Your Life: The Breakthrough Program for Anxiety, Depression, Obsessiveness, Anger and Impulsiveness,* and *Change Your Brain, Change Your Body: Use Your Brain to Get and Keep the Body You Have Always Wanted*, psychiatrist and medical doctor Daniel G. Amen outlines a number of recent developments in brain-body connections, with significant implications. If we want our body and mind to be healthy, we must begin with our brain. His work in single photon emission-computed tomography, which scans the brain and measures how it functions, has led to better understanding of diagnosis, treatment and prevention of disease as well as how to improve brain function to improve overall quality of life.

If activity is low in our prefrontal cortex – responsible for planning, forethought, decision-making, impulse control, follow-through and empathy – stimulating that part of the brain can increase our attention span and control over our actions, while reducing our impulsivity and tendency toward procrastination. If prefrontal cortex activity is too high, calming this area

> 'Research efforts continue to reveal developments in how the brain and body interact. The findings have implications for helping us live healthier, more satisfying lives.'

'If we want our body and mind to be healthy, we must begin with our brain.'

and boosting the level of serotonin – the neurotransmitter chemical naturally released when we accomplish something or earn the respect of others – can help people who are nervous, anxious or under chronic stress. An overactive deep limbic system – the brain part responsible for setting our emotional tone – can contribute to feelings of negativity, guilt, sadness, depression, helplessness and low self-esteem, and have been associated with mood disorders. Lessening activity in this situation can help encourage a more positive, hopeful state of mind.

Worry, anxiety, low energy and physical stress symptoms may indicate high activity in our basal ganglia, the part of our brain involved with integrating feelings, thoughts and movement, motivation and setting our level of anxiety. Low activity in the basal ganglia can lessen motivation and increase feelings of pleasure associated with overeating or drug use. The anterior cingulate gyrus helps us shift our attention, be adaptable, and initiate change when needed – too much activity here can leave us worried, argumentative and fixated on negative thoughts and actions. It has also been linked to obsessive-compulsive disorders.

Our temporal lobes deal with short-term memory, language, and mood stability, so concern there can include problems with memory, moodiness and temper. The parietal lobes are involved with sensory processing and our sense of direction. Damage to the parietal lobes can cause a tendency to get lost, and is one indicator of Alzheimer's disease. It has also been associated with eating and body distortion disorders. Our occipital lobes are involved with vision and visual processing. The cerebellum deals with physical and thought coordination and processing – and with the pre-frontal cortex – judgment and impulse control. Doing coordination exercises can improve these two areas of the brain.

Amen maintains that the more 'brain reserve' we have – the cushion of healthy brain function to deal with injuries or stressful events – the better able we are to cope with unexpected difficulties and serious life challenges: '*When you have ample brain reserve, it builds resilience and makes it easier for you to deal with life's unexpected twists and turns.*' Brain reserve can be diminished through negative behaviors such as drinking or taking drugs, poor nutrition, and any injury to our brain, no matter how minor it may seem at the time. Conversely, positive behaviors including healthy eating, exercise, meditating, maintaining healthy relationships and avoiding stress, smoking, drugs and alcohol, can increase brain reserve.

Interference with other brain-body connections can contribute to poor health. Chronic inflammation, in response to infection or injury in our body, constricts the blood flow to our heart and brain – it is now thought to contribute to diseases such as obesity, heart disease, Alzheimer's and diabetes. Lack of exercise also decreases blood flow to the brain and body parts, negatively affecting overall health. Caffeine similarly constricts the body-brain blood flow, while dehydrating our brain, body and skin, and interfering with sleep.

Chronic stress causes our brain to instruct our body to secrete cortisol – the stress hormone – which can increase the appetite, muscle tension, blood pressure, chronic pain, and puts us at risk for other serious health conditions. Negative thoughts can lower healthy brain activity, cause our heart to beat faster, raise blood pressure and impact other body systems in harmful ways.

Al Siebert, author of *The Resiliency Advantage: Master Change, Thrive Under Pressure, and Bounce Back From Setbacks*, also writes about mind-body connections impacting resilience. He outlines three strengths which serve as 'gatekeepers' for access to a higher level of resilience. Siebert maintains that as every feeling, thought and action has a physiological component in addition to a psychological one, each of these strengths is associated with one of the major nervous systems in our bodies. According to Siebert, the strengths and corresponding originating nervous systems are:

- Self-confidence – from the somatic nervous system associated with controlling body movements and physical action
- Self-esteem – from the autonomic nervous system which governs involuntary body actions such as our heartbeat, breathing and digestion
- Self-concept – (i.e., identity), from the central nervous system (brain, spinal cord and corresponding nerve cells), responsible for thinking, speaking and physical activity

If these 'inner selves' are weak or underdeveloped, we can be rocked by sudden or sustained change. By developing and sustaining them, we are better able to cope with challenges and difficult situations. Just as importantly, Siebert argues, we need to care for, and strengthen, the corresponding responsible nervous systems.

In her book, *Meet Your Happy Chemicals: Dopamine, Endorphin, Oxytocin, Serotonin*, Loretta Graziano Breuning, Ph.D., explains

> 'The body's secretion of these four 'feel good' chemicals can affect moods, concentration, sleep, weight and other activities.'

the impact on the mind of the body's secretion of these four 'feel good' chemicals. Dopamine and serotonin are neurotransmitters which send messages between nerve cells (neurons), throughout the brain and body. They deliver instructions (e.g., telling the heart to beat and the lungs to breathe), and can also affect moods, concentration, sleep, weight and other activities. Endorphins and oxytocin are hormones released by our endocrine glands to help stimulate action in other parts of the body.

During exercise our body releases endorphin hormones, which give us a sense of euphoria. This positive feeling is referred to in running circles as 'runner's high,' and has been shown to lessen our ability to register pain and discomfort. When we socialize with others, cuddle with our babies, and fall in love, the hormone oxytocin is released eliciting warm feelings of bonding and social alliance. When we solve a puzzle or figure out something we find difficult, the neurotransmitter dopamine causes us to feel that 'Eureka!' or 'aha!' moment. Similarly, a release of the neurotransmitter serotonin causes us to feel proud and experience a sense of accomplishment when we complete a challenging project or otherwise earn the respect of others. If we want to feel good, we can partake in the kinds of activities which trigger the release of these chemicals.

Putting together all this information on how the brain and body interact, we can come up with a list of actions to help keep us healthy and safe. In general:

- Eat a healthy, nutritious diet of fruits, vegetables, nuts, lean protein and healthy fats such as olive oil. Avoid overeating and stay properly hydrated.

- Take daily vitamins, minerals and Omega-3 fish oil (the latter helps with chronic inflammation).

- Exercise regularly, stay fit, maintain a healthy weight and practice safe, emotionally healthy sex.

- Get sufficient, restful sleep.

- Meditation activates your brain and can help contribute to making better decision-making.

- Practice stress-reduction techniques and learn to relax.

- Practicing gratitude helps us become more positive, improves our coordination and how our brain works, and makes us feel better.

- Protect our brain by wearing protective gear as necessary and avoiding head injuries.

- Avoid alcohol, smoking, drug abuse, eating disorders and other risky behaviors.

By understanding these important brain-body connections, we can make decisions that may help us live healthier, better lives.

OPTIMISM

Martin Seligman, of the University of Pennsylvania, is seen by many as the founder of modern day positive psychology, a branch of psychology focusing on the empirical study of positive emotions, strengths-based character and healthy institutions. Positive psychology has seen significant growth in the past 20 years, with central theories in the field continuing to evolve, and theoretical concepts driving new research. Prior to that, as Seligman had seen in his work trying to understand and identify interventions to lessen depression, the field of psychology tended to work from a disease model, concerned primarily with alleviating suffering. While a noble intent, this treatment-heavy approach of reducing negativity, and attendant damage after the fact, ignores the potent, prevention-focused half of the equation – positivity by cultivating human flourishing.

In his book, *Learned Optimism: How to Change Your Mind and Your Life*, Seligman made a case for positive psychology with the argument that optimism – which he defined as reacting to setbacks from a presumption of personal power – can be both measured and enhanced.

In a follow-on book, *Authentic Happiness: Using the New Positive Psychology to Realize Your Potential for Lasting Fulfillment*, he demonstrated how understanding the tenets of optimism could help achieve a greater sense of fulfillment. In this authentic happiness theory, Seligman believed the goal of positive psychology to be one of increasing the level of happiness in our own life and the lives of others.

'To experience healthy, vigorous growth, we need interest and involvement in expanding our horizons through continual learning. We also need to feel our lives are valuable and what we do with them worthwhile.'

what about joy?

> 'Positive emotions tend to increase our awareness, encourage exploration, and widen our consideration of new and different ideas, thoughts and actions. This broadened behavioral repertoire can lead to new skills and resources, including knowledge and social relationships.'

However, in his most recent book, *Flourish: A Visionary New Understanding of Happiness and Well-Being*, Seligman puts forward a more refined construct of well-being based on the concepts of positive emotions, engagement, positive relationships, finding meaning, and accomplishment. The goal of well-being theory, then, centers on increasing the amount of 'flourishing' (thriving) in our lives and on the planet. We must possess all five of these features in order to be seen to flourish. It isn't enough to have a romantic relationship and friends, or to feel good about ourselves and others. In order to experience healthy, vigorous growth, we need interest and involvement in expanding our horizons through continual learning. We also need to feel our lives are valuable and what we do with them worthwhile. Positive psychology remains a high-growth field with initiatives expanding into other disciplines such as health, education, psychotherapy and neuroscience.

In a related development in the study of emotions in positive psychology, social psychologist and University of North Carolina researcher Barbara Frederickson is credited with formulating the 'broaden-and-build' theory of positive emotions. Negative emotions have a tendency to limit our behavioral options, focusing on a survival-oriented fight, flight or freeze mentality. On the other hand, the ten positive emotions Frederickson regularly works with – joy, love, hope, gratitude, interest, inspiration, pride, amusement, serenity and awe – tend to increase our awareness, encourage exploration, and widen our consideration of new and different ideas, thoughts and actions. This broadened behavioral repertoire can lead to new skills and resources, including knowledge and social relationships.

Frederickson views positivity as a means rather than an end in itself. In her book, *Positivity: Groundbreaking Resource Reveals How to Embrace the Hidden Strength of Positive Emotions, Overcome Negativity, and Thrive*, she asserts positivity is a choice, and can be turned 'on' with conscious thought. Not only will practicing positivity broaden our minds and help us create the kind of life to which we aspire, it also helps us enhance our emotional resilience to bounce back from adversity and life's challenges.

Psychologist Marcial Losada developed a mathematical model of Frederickson's 'broaden-and-build' positive emotions theory. Working together, they identified and tested a 3-to-

1 positivity/ negativity ratio for the tipping point between flourishing and languishing. If we can increase the numerator (positivity), and decrease the denominator (negativity), we can improve our personal ratio. False or insincere positivity is more than empty words – it acts as negativity in disguise. Subsequent research of individuals, married couples and business teams has borne out this 3-to-1 ratio.

> '*Regardless of our circumstances, we can choose to find ways to eliminate gratuitous forms of negativity and increase heartfelt positivity.*'

What this means for us is regardless of our circumstances, we can choose to find ways to eliminate gratuitous forms of negativity and increase heartfelt positivity. According to Frederickson, we can do so by:

- Focusing our habitual thought patterns on finding more positive meaning in daily life
- Savoring the good
- Counting our blessings (i.e., practicing gratitude)
- Recognizing kindness
- Following our interests and passions
- Using our strengths
- Visualizing our future
- Connecting with others
- Opening our mind (i.e., employing mindfulness and mindful meditation)
- Appreciating nature
- Open-heartedness toward ever-widening circle of community (i.e., practicing 'loving-kindness' meditation)

Selecting and carrying out one or two simple activities in a few of these categories can make a difference. The cumulative effect of implementing several actions in all of them can be significant and inspiring.

THE CONCEPT OF FLOW

If Martin Seligman is the founder of modern positive psychology, Mihaly Csikszentmihalyi, a Hungarian émigré to the US, is often considered the father based on his earlier work in creativity and optimal experience. Author of, *Flow: The Psychology of Optimal Experience*, and other books on creativity and happiness, Csikszentmihalyi

'Flow is a state of mind, or experience we feel, when we are totally involved in what we are doing. We are engaged in an activity and enjoy it so much, we become lost in the moment.'

describes the latter as 'flow experience'. He sees flow as a state of mind, or experience we feel, when we are totally involved in what we are doing. We are engaged in an activity and enjoy it so much, we become lost in the moment. Many in the throes of flow do lose track of time.

Csikszentmihalyi describes the characteristics of our being in the flow as extremely focused, with a clear goal which is neither overly difficult nor too easy, a finely-tuned balance of challenge against our matching type and level of expertise. We receive immediate feedback from what we're doing, sensing whether something is working or right and when it is not, yet our concentration is so intense, we seem to step out of our immediate reality. We can easily find examples of flow in artists lost in the reverie of putting paint to canvas, musicians caught up in the rapture of creating music, an athlete operating fully at his/ her skill level – each completely 'in the zone'. Csikszentmihalyi maintains we can also learn to put ourselves in the flow for more mundane tasks, thereby making them more enjoyable.

Csikszentmihalyi also refers to the 'anatomy of consciousness', in which the aforementioned intense concentration engages our mind's capacity to process mentally what we are observing. What goes into our consciousness has significant impact on our quality of life, and we are able to choose much of the content we allow in. We need only recall the phrase 'garbage in, garbage out' to realize the importance of ensuring what we focus on is worthy of our time and attention. We want to choose wisely, practice mindfulness (*CHAPTER 12: VISUALIZATION*), and not fritter away our time with mindless – or worse, mind-numbing – activities. After all, it can affect our well-being.

How might this concept of flow benefit us in terms of strengthening or restoring our emotional resilience reserves? Find something we enjoy and are reasonably good at, then improve our skills to be able to do it at more challenging levels. This offers us the possibility of becoming caught up in a pleasant, optimal experience. It makes us feel good, it makes us feel accomplished, and it makes us feel happy. This positivity then carries over into other parts of our life.

PART III:

PUTTING IT ALL TOGETHER

'All the art of living lies in a fine mingling of letting go and holding on.'
Henry Ellis

LIGHTNING UNLEASHED

When Daughter headed to Thailand on a school break service trip, to work with Burmese refugee families, I took the opportunity to make a quick visit back to the US to see my parents. It was good to spend time with them, and allowed me to revert back to the primary role of a daughter, if only for a few days. It gave us a chance to talk, and just be together. We tried to maintain their usual schedule as best we could, but as was only to be expected, occasionally the interruption of their routine rattled them. There was also the tendency of something as emotionally charged as cancer to take center stage. How could it not?

Everyone handles such crises differently; there is no one way these things unfold. Some choose to ignore it, believing to do so will keep it at bay. Others stoically insist on maintaining a positive attitude, hopeful of a cure or significantly slowed advancement. Still others want to talk about it, taking strength from being able to discuss it. Advancing age makes it all the harder. Sometimes denial creeps in as we attempt to wrap our minds around the reality of illness, growing older, dying. Often it is a combination of these and other emotions, tumbling out like water gushing down a mountain stream. It has been draining, and there have been times we've each felt overwhelmed. This is particularly true for my mother as the primary caregiver, contending with her own health issues while trying to buoy my father's spirits and deal with each new development.

Leaving them was particularly difficult.

True to form, my father was outside, standing sentinel over my suitcase in the driveway, awaiting the taxi to the airport. My mother and I paused in the foyer for a more private farewell.

"It's been so good having you here, honey, we're going to miss you so much," my mother whispered, leaning in as I drew her close for a long hug.

"I know, it's been good being here. I wish it could be longer…" I replied, feeling the lump rise in my throat. I willed myself to remain calm, not wishing to add to the heightened emotions of the moment. Then came the question I knew was coming, yet it stung nevertheless.

"When will we see you again?" she asked, her eyes sweeping hopefully over my face for signs of an answer. "We can't wait for you to come back, we miss you so much. Maybe we could come visit you before Dad starts his chemotherapy. We had such fun the last time."

"I'm not sure, Mom," I said, my voice husky with emotion. I struggled to find the words, knowing they'd ring hollow and disappoint. We both knew they wouldn't be making another trip to the Netherlands. Not now, not ever.

"We'll figure something out," I continued, gently. "It's just we've got to balance everything with Husband's work and Daughter's school, and then there's Janet..." The mention of my mother-in-law, ten years older than her and confined to a dementia facility, reminded my mother we were dealing with other sensitive issues, too.

"I know, I know," she replied, fighting back tears as she hugged me tighter. "You've got a lot on your plate. We'll Skype on Sunday. I just hate to see you go."

You can't help but feel awash in guilt for going – at times it feels like escaping – while they are left to carry on in a nightmare not of their making. Add to that a heavy dose of feeling nothing you do is ever quite good enough – you don't stay long enough, you won't be returning fast enough, you fail to bite your tongue that one time, you rush from here to there. It's all juggling, doing your best, trying to help and making do. You're the meat in the multigenerational sandwich and no matter what you do, it is *never* enough.

I arrived back in The Hague, grateful for the time with my parents yet glad to be back with my own family. Within a week things had spiraled downward, and then the latest blow came. "It's moderate depression combined with anxiety." I tried to concentrate on the words coming from the other end of the telephone line. "... needs time to heal... medication combined with therapy sessions... ongoing treatment will take a while... "

A member of my own family, who had seemingly been coping with low level depression and mild anxiety in previous months, hit the proverbial wall.

My mind reeled as I scrambled to take it all in. This was big, a game-changer. Until now, much of the worst of things had been happening to others, outside the cordon of my immediate family. This was real, and it was on my own doorstep. I felt completely out of my depth, unsure of what to do, how to help, how to proceed, yet with an almost feral need to somehow, in some way, make things better.

Anxiety and depression, I've come to learn, are two very different medical beasts, which often join forces to cause considerable emotional mayhem. I don't know that we ever learn precisely what brings on deep depression or worsens anxiety. Sometimes genetics are a contributing factor, or they can be triggered by emotionally difficult events such as death, divorce, illness or accident. It can be exacerbated by such things as living 'in limbo' as we transition from one place to another, being torn away from friends who themselves have scattered across the globe.

Perhaps we encounter overwhelming stress due to an insurmountable workload, trying to get by in a demanding environment or overly competitive world. Then there are the ways in which we each are wired. This is particularly true of over-striving, relentlessly driven perfectionists who cannot seem to cut themselves a break. Not wanting to disappoint others, they demand excellence yet barely register achievements and successes, instead fixating only on the next minor bump along the way. And then there are sensitive souls for whom it all becomes too much.

It can be a combination of factors. Sometimes it's all of the above, or something else entirely. The building stress in early depression and anxiety can also contribute to altering our ability to hear what is meant through a cacophony of words and images warped by the prism of pain. Chicken or egg – which comes first – it isn't easy to sort out causes from effects, or contributing factors amid considerations. Sometimes you're simply left with a mess to work through.

While causes may prove more difficult to pin down, we do know a fair amount about treating depression and anxiety. The most important thing is to recognize it isn't only the problem of the affected person. It is the responsibility of the entire family and loved ones to understand they are part of an emotional tapestry which has frayed, and work together to mend the distressed fabric. While the individuals suffering from such illnesses must do the heavy lifting in terms of participating in counseling and learning coping skills, there is much family and close friends can do to assist – and in some cases, adjust. Therapy sessions can be priceless in terms of unearthing valuable information and educating family members on best courses of action, and what to avoid.

CHAPTER 8: ENHANCING EMOTIONAL RESILIENCE

It is time now to take what we have learned and put it to good use. We can apply the knowledge, research, and experience shared in the first half of this book to build, enhance and replenish our reserves of emotional resilience for increased well-being. This is where we shift from *knowing* what it takes to be resilient to *doing*.

WHO, WHAT, WHEN, WHERE, WHY, WHICH AND HOW

In *PART I* we looked at expatriate/ cross-cultural life, up close and personal. We shared many of the pluses and minuses, the benefits and detractions, the beauty and, in the case of the key issues, the difficult underbelly. Chief among the key issues is figuring how to incorporate our expat life experiences into a healthy identity, one in which who we see ourselves to be is in alignment with how others see us, how we used to view ourselves, and perhaps most important, who we truly wish to become.

We covered the phases of the transition process (involvement, leaving, transition, entry and re-involvement), and how we can become temporarily trapped in one or more of these phases as we move on to the next place, are left by others who mean much to us, or return to what once held the essence of 'home' for us. We discussed how the Kübler-Ross change model stages (denial, anger, bargaining, depression, and acceptance), reflect what we are actually experiencing, at least to some degree, while we move through the transition phases.

In *PART II* we focused on a deeper understanding of emotional resilience before turning to a number of concepts and fields of study, including important brain-body connections, which inform our discussion and present us with opportunities to develop, strengthen, and restore our resiliency.

> 'It is time to take what we have learned and put it to good use for increased well-being. This is where we shift from knowing what it takes to be resilient to doing.'

In *PART III*, we now take a look at a range of concrete, specific, actionable ways in which we can enhance our emotional resiliency.

> *'We can practice resilience consciously and conscientiously.'*

All of this comes together to complete the '*Who, What, When, Where, Why, Which* and *How*' statement, originally mentioned in the Introduction, which reflects the overarching framework of this book:

- **Who:** We, as expats/ cross-culturals
- **What:** Impacted by our intercultural, mobile way of life
- **When:** An approximation based on the order of the transition process phases
- **Where:** The particular phase in the transition process
- **Why:** We need emotional resilience – for healthy identity development and congruence
- **Which:** Stage of the Kübler-Ross change model we're in as we navigate the transition process
- **How:** Tools and techniques to increase, enhance and restore emotional resilience

PUTTING EMOTIONAL RESILIENCE INTO ACTION

Before we get started on ways we can augment our emotional resilience, let's review four fundamental points we've learned so far:

- Everyone everywhere needs emotional resilience
- Possessing emotional resilience doesn't protect us from hardship, misfortune, turmoil or strife, but can help us deal with them
- We can maintain, enhance, and renew our levels of resilience
- We can practice resilience consciously and conscientiously

We need to acknowledge and embrace all four of these precepts if we are to act in an emotionally resilient manner. The next story shows how one longtime international aid work incorporates these points into her stressful daily life.

HEALTHY BOUNDARIES, BEING OF SERVICE AND REACHING OUT

"Emotional resilience has, without a shadow of a doubt, been the single most important factor in my life for determining serenity and happiness.

I define emotional resilience as the ability to hold space for myself through challenging events and environments, and to take the time and use the resources I need to process and work through their physical, emotional and mental impacts.
Emotional resilience also lets me use my own experiences of these challenges for the good of my friends, family and community, as I'm able to empathize, share and support when others experience these challenges in their own way. My own experiences become ways I can be of service to the community, a community that will in turn be a resource to me when I need it.

Key to my own resilience is the ability to step away to create and respect healthy boundaries for myself. I need to be able to call upon a wealth of resources that I've gathered to have on hand for just such challenges – phone numbers of friends, yoga teachers, trusted guides and mentors, masseuses, food delivery, and a few weekend getaway spots. It's a very comprehensive support network.

For me, it's important also not to feel guilty when I start to react to challenges that call upon my emotional resilience. Instead of thinking that I'm weak or wrong to feel a certain way, I try to recognize I need extra support to move through something and grow. I look at the challenge as a valuable lesson to learn, work and move through, as an opportunity to expand and evolve my own life experience. And then I reach out – reaching out, for me, has been key."

Elie Calhoun, American ATCK who has lived most of her life in Africa, including Kenya, Egypt, Tanzania, Liberia and Senegal

In looking at the various actions we can take to enhance emotional resilience, I have grouped them into the following five broad categories:

> *'Key to my own resilience is the ability to step away to create and respect healthy boundaries for myself.'*

- **Connecting Externally:** Purposefully reaching out and interacting with others, exploring our environment, expanding our interests and becoming a part of our community.

- **Connecting Internally:** Understanding and monitoring ourselves and our closest relationships, especially during times of transition and difficulty.

> 'These five concepts – connecting externally, connecting internally, communication, visualization and optimism – form a strong foundation on which to base efforts to enhance our emotional resilience.'

- **Communication:** Letting others know who we truly are (and they us) verbally, in writing and through shared experiences.

- **Visualization:** Envisioning improvement in our current situation through stress management techniques, self-care, creative expression and reviewing our past to determine the best course of action.

- **Optimism:** Taking a more hopeful, positive, future-oriented approach, finding meaning, setting goals, taking action and expressing gratitude.

Taken together, these five concepts – connecting externally, connecting internally, communication, visualization and optimism – form a strong foundation on which to base efforts to enhance our emotional resilience. We'll explore each of these in greater detail in the following chapters.

CHAPTER 9: CONNECTING EXTERNALLY

Connection is the perhaps the deepest human need we can experience. It goes to the very heart of belonging and related concepts of home, friendship, love, family, and sense of community. In our relationships with ourselves, our family, friends and the outside world, we all need to feel wanted, valued and loved. We reach out to others to establish and nurture connections of all types, perhaps risking rejection but buoyed by the belief the opposite is more likely.

We find ways to share ourselves with others and to encourage their sharing themselves with us, in order to know each other more deeply and profoundly. We acknowledge differences and learn to accept them, secure in the knowledge our similarities are far greater. We treasure rituals as reflections of what matters to us, and to honor our memories and ourselves. We focus on empathy, compassion, how others are feeling, and how they make us feel:

- Reach out to others – build new friendships on an individual or small group basis
- Seek out newcomer, expat or international clubs and groups that share information and facilitate meeting others
- Explore your new home and beyond – look for the positives, don't focus on negatives
- Make an effort to meet and interact with neighbors, colleagues and others you meet
- Check with local international schools, community organizations and religious houses of worship for programs and activities open to the public
- Expand your interests – study the local language, acquire a new skill, take a class
- Volunteer in your community – service to others provides surprisingly strong, positive benefits to all

> 'Connection goes to the very heart of belonging and related concepts of home, friendship, love, family, and sense of community. In our relationships with ourselves, our family, friends and the outside world, we all need to feel wanted, valued and loved.'

- Celebrate your own rituals and develop new ones to reflect who and where you are
- Create new memories through experiences, not things
- Remember we don't build friendships overnight, widen your circle, be present and be patient
- Circumstances may alter the quality and quantity of our relationships so grow and feed them as you would stoke a fire

The next story demonstrates the importance of putting into action many of the suggestions, listed above, to build our human connections.

NETWORKING, FACE-TO-FACE

"I wish I had known how important it was to manage expectations. I wish I had realised how much my own mood would affect my kids, even if I did not say anything – they knew! I wish everyone could find the strength to recognise what matters to them and what they value, so they can ensure those things do travel with them to a new place. I wish I had realised that face-to-face contact is much more powerful than cyber contact. You get energy from being physically close to people and staying behind a computer, keeping in touch with people on Facebook is not enough, for me at least. Networking groups have been the most help without a doubt. Also, starting a writers' circle so I met like-minded folk who shared my passion was key to my starting to be happy in a new place."

Jo Parfitt
English expat (Oman, Norway, Dubai, Brunei) now living in the Netherlands

In the course of discussions with contributors to this book, I asked Dorota Klop-Sowinska, owner of DoSo! Coaching & Counseling, what she has seen as the biggest challenge faced by many of her expat clients. Her reply was immediate and direct, "Self-confidence."

STRUGGLE FOR SELF-CONFIDENCE, ESPECIALLY IN THE BEGINNING

"Looking at my coaching clients I notice almost all of them struggle in the beginning. I see that in many cases the recurring problem is loss of self-confidence. This translates

itself into problems in relationships, problems with getting a new job or with making new contacts. I guess many of them do not realize they are in the same boat as other expats. They often feel ashamed to admit their 'weakness'. The drop in their self-confidence often comes when they are temporarily without a job, do not understand the language and the new culture, and from the fact their whole support system (family and friends) is miles away.

I notice those clients who take full ownership of their decisions and feel in control of their lives, are those who – generally – find it easier to overcome the difficult times. They want to act and change things. Once they start acting the perspective changes, they meet others, start to feel more self-confident and they start the positive spiral of actions."

Dorota Klop-Sowinska
Polish expat (Brazil and Mexico) now lives in the Netherlands

When we are new to a culture, place or situation, the realization we have few or no friends there can be daunting. Isolating ourselves won't bring new acquaintances to our doorstep, we've got to take a deep breath, tell ourselves our future friends are out there, and go find them. We do this by putting ourselves into situations where we are forced to interact with others, and we show that we are interested in, and receptive to, meeting and getting to know them. For many of us, there is an element of truth to the saying, 'fake it 'til you make it'.

FIND YOUR TRIBE OR BUILD YOUR OWN

Friends, acquaintances, pals, potential dates and BFFs ('best friends forever') don't grow on trees. You've got to go looking for them. The perennial lament of expatriates everywhere is that you look up one day and realize half of your circle of friends, acquaintances and what I affectionately call POPIs – persons of potential interest – are gone. They've headed off to new locales as a result of better opportunities, reassignments, empty nests or repatriation.

'I notice those who take full ownership of their decisions and feel in control of their lives, are those who – generally – find it easier to overcome the difficult times.'

'One enduring lesson of life is about finding your tribe in whatever location you may be. If you can't find your tribe, then it's up to you to build one.'

One enduring lesson of life is about finding your tribe in whatever location you may be. If you can't find your tribe, then it's up to you to build one. It sounds so simple, yet over and over I've heard from expats, global nomads and cross-culturals about the difficulties in seeking out new friends. You might begin by making contact with fellow internationals, both of your own nationality and others.

INCLUDE OTHER EXPATS IN YOUR TRIBE

"Making expat friends in the host country makes everything seem more manageable as you can draw from their experience and pull out your hair together. Find an expat community to connect with (e.g., FAWCO, available worldwide). Before the move, ask a contact some of your moving questions and then take her for coffee when you meet. Friends and support are the keys for a successful move and settling in happily."

Laura, American expat living in the UK

By all means, explore the possibilities of friendship with other internationals, but don't limit yourself to that group only or you'll find yourself caught up in an 'expat bubble'. You may share much in common with fellow expats/ cross-culturals (think 'Third Culture'), but sometimes too much time spent with people who see themselves, or are seen as, 'other' serves to reinforce a sense of displacement or alienation. In making connections with locals, you begin to forge deeper ties to a place, community, culture. Some may not be as interested in, or willing to develop, such relationships with foreigners who are likely to be leaving somewhere down the line, but others appreciate the richness such intercultural interaction can bring.

'To my mind, friendships are built on three vital components – shared experiences, shared self, and shared receptivity.'

To my mind, friendships are built on three vital components – shared experiences, shared self, and shared receptivity. The first two tend to play out over time, and the length of that timespan isn't fixed but is fluid and flexible. The third is hit or miss.

You get to know a person by engaging them in some endeavor. It can be as simple as meeting for coffee after the morning school run, lunch at a favorite café or for drinks after work, or as elaborate as getting tickets to a sporting event or concert, attending an opening at an art gallery, throwing a birthday or holiday party, or planning a day trip to some local spot of interest. Dinner parties weren't invented for people to show off cooking or conversational skills or simply to eat great food. They exist to bring a group together to break bread and break down barriers.

It isn't so much *what* you do as that you do it, and do it together. You can bond as much over things you enjoy as you do over things you barely tolerate. Who among us hasn't found a kindred spirit to chat with at some boring office gathering where both of you are there as 'partner of' and don't know another soul? I guarantee your pleasant surprise at tolerating the corporate bash has less to do with the *hors d'oeuvres* or the tedious speech and more with the two of you giggling over the stifled yawns and watch-checking of the other attendees.

It's the same principle in motion when you host a party to watch a special televised event. Those who enjoy the featured sports championship or the season finale of the latest hit show will crowd around the television, while those who don't will carry on in another room. We build our social connections in our own way, and everyone goes home happy.

BUILDING A COMMUNITY OF FRIENDS

"One of the benefits of traveling or living abroad is the freedom it grants you. There is no opportunity for personal development that could ever compare to leaving behind every influence that shaped you, everyone that knows you, and every box you've been put in. When you move abroad, it is the ultimate chance to start over, to experiment, to be that amazing exciting person you never felt you could be at home. The roles created for you by family, friends and colleagues are erased, and your ability to reinvent yourself is bound only by your desires and imagination.

The problem is that sometimes we need these boundaries, these boxes, to keep ourselves grounded. When everything you know is oceans away, it's easy to get lost, and once you get lost, you're surrounded by strangers who may not be able to guide you back. At times I struggle with choices I've made, and I question myself frequently. Building a strong community of trustworthy friends has been paramount, but is not an easy or fast undertaking. Finding new friends that somehow know you who truly are and can help keep you on the right track is essential. Don't try to be too independent when living abroad, or limit yourself by rejecting friendships with other expats. Seek out friends of all cultures, share with them, listen when they share, and build quality relationships."

The Over-thinking Expat, living in the United Arab Emirates

The second component of friendship – sharing of self – also takes time. You don't stroll up to a newly introduced soul, spill your darkest secrets and expect them to embrace you as their new best friend. Instead, you do what I think of as 'the onion dance'. You start with perfunctory chit chat about the weather or some equally innocuous topic, then – over time, of course, remembering the importance of a series of shared experiences – you graduate up to current events, favored activities, preferences, dislikes, pet peeves. Peeling the onion back layer by layer, bit by bit, you figure out which issues are ripe for discussion and which you'd best avoid for any relationship to continue.

The interesting thing is that with the advent of the Internet and social media, you needn't meet in person to go through the onion dance online. I remember a flesh and blood friend telling me ten years ago that she'd become friendly with a couple of people she 'talked' with nightly in a chat room for fellow sufferers of a particular medical condition. I remember thinking how odd that sounded. Surely you couldn't forge a connection with someone you've never met? Over time I've learned you can.

You can stay in touch with someone you knew vaguely from younger days or your last posting, or were introduced to through family or friends, and over time get to know each other a little better on Facebook or Twitter. Similarly, you can find a blog or website or social media venue you like and follow along. You get to know some of the fellow visitors or forum participants, find you have more in common with some than others, and 'converse' more frequently. Nowadays it's not unusual to canvas the online scene of websites, blogs, forums and meeting groups in your next location as part of your research, often leading to the names of a few friendly faces on the ground when you arrive.

I've come to know many people online, some better than others, a few extremely well. I've even had the pleasure of eventually meeting a few in the flesh. Last autumn I attended a book launch party and saw a familiar face. We both smiled and made our way across the room to talk. Several minutes into the conversation we both realized that despite living in the same city we'd never been introduced, we just knew each other from several expat sites and forums online.

> 'Being in groups of people I can relate to has been essential in understanding myself and my local culture better.'

It was the same at the 2013 conference of the Families in Global Transition (FIGT) organization I recently attended; I was able to physically meet several people I've engaged with online or via email. I'm not saying you should limit yourself to online 'virtual' friends, only that you never know when virtual friends may well become 'real'.

I'm a firm believer in finding potential new friends anywhere. I met one of my closest Dutch friends one spring day on the corner of a busy intersection, waiting for the light to change. I was out walking my dog, Oli, and Katja was coming back from a lunchtime jog. The owner of two dogs herself, she petted Oli and we began chatting. She was taking up jogging to prepare for the upcoming Royal 5km run and I was looking to get back into jogging. Our conversation continued, she invited me to meet her for what became thoroughly enjoyable talk-and-train sessions, and a friendship was born.

SEEK OTHERS YOU CAN RELATE TO ALONG THE WAY

"I am inspired and encouraged by hearing others' stories about how they overcame adversity. Being in groups of people I can relate to has been essential in understanding myself and my local culture better, and understanding how I fit in (or don't). So having a strong network of people to share accomplishments and go to for support has been extremely important."

Tara Agacayak, American expat living in Turkey

We'd like to think that once we find a few friends, a lover, or spouse/ significant other it all falls easily into place. Sometimes it does, sometimes it doesn't. We need to remain aware of how the people in our lives make us feel (and vice versa). If it isn't positive and uplifting, then we've got some work to do.

COURAGE TO CHANGE YOUR TRIBE

"From my experience emotional resilience is very personal. Others can affect it, but ultimately we control it and it's up to us to tailor it to our specific needs, nurture it and own it. We can nurture it through developing a supportive tribe around us.

I moved to the UK from the US when I was 21. Moving away from everyone I had ever known made me realise how much I had underestimated the importance of having a supportive tribe around me. My British boyfriend – later husband – and his family were my main network and they were not equipped to deal with a young expat. When I suffered culture shock and homesickness, I was labelled 'difficult' and people distanced themselves or began to complain about me. No allowances were made for my not understanding the system they had lived in all their lives.

My friends were his friends, and eventually my self-confidence faded, my emotional resilience weakened and I stopped bouncing back – instead I was knocked back again and again. I gained weight. I lost my ambitions. I became a two-dimensional person.

And yet, some emotional resilience must have remained, a survival instinct or a memory of what I had been, and after nearly ten years I started going to a gym and after three months of hard work I looked amazing, but my husband begrudged the time I spent at the gym. I started talking about going back to university. Other people encouraged me, but my husband said, 'What will you do with our daughter?' instead of 'Great idea! How can I help make this happen?'

I complained about him and my life to my dad and once, when visiting my family in the States, my dad turned to me and said, 'So what are you going to do about it?' I was instantly silenced. I needed a tribe member to knock me out of that cycle of complaining-without-action.

My dad's comment was the key to my emotional resilience and I grabbed it. When my husband got a job a couple of hours away I told him I wouldn't be moving with him. We divorced and I began to search for a new tribe – friends who would be healthy for me. Now, 12 years later, I am who I was supposed to be – happy, healthy and successful, re-married and with a wonderful group of family and friends around me. And still an expat. I am convinced I have more emotional resilience than before because I had to work at it and rebuild it and learn through experience.

You need a heck of a lot of emotional resilience to survive if you end up in the wrong tribe, but if your emotional resilience fades, you can rebuild it and get back on your feet. I had no idea how important a good network would be in life. As an only child I grew up feeling I could get through on my own, but when you need direction, ideas, support or just a place to have fun and relax, a great group of family and friends are essential.

We are clan or tribe creatures by nature. Our evolution has not caught up with our lifestyles where people move far away from family and friends for jobs or adventure. My experience has shown me we need each other, but that we need to choose the right tribe or it's better to be alone."

Michelle Garrett, American expat living in England

There is nothing nicer than building a life of strong, rewarding emotional connections, and being fully involved. When we move, the transition process begins again as we leave the familiar, enter a new space and seek involvement. Of course we can – and should – stay in touch with those we leave (or who leave us), but in terms of relationships 'on the ground' we must start all over again. Doing this in another culture presents its own challenges.

FINDING AND MAKING FRIENDS IN A DIFFERENT CULTURE

"Moving abroad can be exhilarating, but it can also be one of the loneliest times of your life. Initially everything is new and exciting but there comes a point where you long for something familiar that you accept unconditionally because you understand it. When you build friendships with local people in your new country you open yourself up to a greater understanding of your new home and that, to me, is the key to creating an enjoyable life somewhere new because when you stop questioning the differences and instead comprehend and enjoy them you can move forward. Local friends helped me to understand and ultimately love living in Turkey.

Turkish is a language unlike any other I have experienced. I studied French, German and Spanish at school but still could not guess anything in Turkish. The longer I lived in Turkey the more of the language I picked up with help from my Turkish friends. They were endlessly kind and would gently correct me, and sometimes poke fun at me, while I butchered their language. I will always be grateful to them for their patience and good humour. But beyond language, even spending time with people and feeling comfortable enough to question their habits helps you to understand a way of life different to your own, and that greater understanding helps you settle in. With time I noticed that Turks do not wear outdoor footwear inside their homes, they often hang large glass eyes near building entrances for good luck, hoot their car-horns at just about everything and Turkish men often speak to each other in a way that looks like they are having an intense argument but suddenly burst out laughing.

In short, when you befriend locals you develop a greater understanding of your new country through your daily activities and your interactions with them. It is one of the best ways to learn about life in your new country and hopefully settle in easily."

Liv Gaunt, an adult TCK now living in Turkey

Long-term, deep friendships are important because those are the people who know us best, including many or all of the versions of ourselves we've been along the way to who we are now. Still, we need to keep in mind that most of us require more than one group of friends to invigorate us to grow and flourish. We end up developing different pockets of friends, acquaintances and colleagues to address the different parts of our identity.

I find the final component of friendship – shared receptivity – in many ways to be the most important. It means being open to meeting and interacting with people in any situations, from all walks of life, regardless of whether you think you'll become friends or not. You do it for the social intercourse, for the connection, no matter how fleeting. Why? Because it broadens your horizons, it bolsters your confidence in your ability to make the most of any social situation, it passes the time, and you feel good thanks to the oxytocin your body releases when you interact with others.

The irony is you never know when your interest in meeting and conversing with another person is shared until it is. But if you're holed up at home, watching lousy television shows for yet another evening, and lamenting the fact that you're lonely and without many friends (or acquaintance and POPIs), at some point you'll have to acknowledge you're part of the problem and thus need to be part of the solution. The same holds

Even circle group

true for making assumptions about people and writing them off before you've given them a chance.

Telling lonely people to get out and take advantage of whatever opportunities exist for interaction with others may sound trite, but it happens to be true. What's promising is that our definition for 'getting out' is broader than it used to be.

FINDING YOUR TRIBE

"I find myself looking forward to the time when my children go to school, because you immediately have more (and more frequent) opportunities to connect within the community. I've also been attempting to find work that is meaningful to me, and to come to terms with the fact that working is good for me. It can be tough and isolating at times, as most of the moms in my community stay at home. As much as I enjoy the company of other moms, I still haven't found my 'tribe,' at least in the sense of moms/ women who want to and are working. As a writer and a trailing spouse, I consider myself blessed that I can pursue one of my passions without having to worry about legalities or visas."

Heather Van Deest, American expat living in Thailand

It takes time to locate your circles of connection, and not all acquaintances need become friends. At the same time, those we socialize with may change over time as we become involved in more and different activities. We may find ourselves 'editing out' people here or there, and they us, as we add new faces to the mix.

FINDING YOUR OWN CORNER OF THE PLAYGROUND

"Travel may well broaden the mind but upping sticks and relocating to a foreign field can blow it completely. The best-laid plans may not prepare you for having the cultural rug pulled from under your feet, something that can throw the most balanced person off kilter. Becoming a novice expat is like the first day of school. All those childhood fears come flooding back. Will I fit in? Will people like me? Am I wearing the right kind of clothes? Am I as good as them?

As the naïve new kids on the block, we made the classic mistake of chucking ourselves into the well-rooted and largely insular expat community that clung to the iridescent coast of Aegean Turkey. We didn't dip our toes into the water to test the temperature. Oh no. We leapt in with eyes slammed shut, noses held and hopes raised. It was a salutary lesson in what not to do. The expat soap opera was a life-sapping experience and negativity stalked the smoky bars and over-crowded beaches. We spent the first six months trying to get to know people and the next six months trying to get rid of many of them. In retrospect, I don't know why I expected a disparate group of people thrown together purely by chance to be our cup of tea.

Four years down the line our burnt fingers had healed and we enjoyed the sparkling company of a small cohort of like-minded people. As with many things in life, less is more. Ironically, just as we'd reserved our own corner of the playground with a hand-picked gang, we returned back to Blighty to be grown-ups again."

Jack Scott, British expat/ repat after living in Turkey

Tina Quick has spent years writing and speaking about TCK relationships, another of her 'Four Pearls' each young global nomad should understand about themselves and carry forward with them in life. One aspect noted by Quick (and Pollock and Van Reken) is that of TCKs – and adult expats/ cross-culturals too – taking care not to come across in conversations about their lives as bragging, showing off or even worse, lying. This 'arrogance' may be real or simply perceived, as when they mention exotic locales visited or traveled to, fascinating people they met or amazing adventures they encountered. Someone who hasn't experienced these types of situations may respond initially with suspicion or disbelief, which in turn embarrasses or offends the expat/ cross-cultural, sending any chance of establishing a friendship down in flames.

I STOPPED TELLING MY STORY

"I was born in Burma and grew up on five continents. When I was 18 I went to college in the USA, my passport country. It was a very difficult adjustment for me. I was usually very careful when I moved to a new place – I would hold back and observe... I knew how to adapt and adjust. But this was different.

My roommate had never been out of her home state except to come to college. She spent her time telling stories about how wild she was in high school. I thought as she was telling her stories, I could tell mine. I made a mistake – I told. I learned to drink beer at the Hofbraühaus in Munich. I skied at St Moritz. I'd been to the Parthenon and Knossos. She told everybody I was a liar. I was ostracized and ignored. I thought there was something wrong with me.

Halfway through my freshman year an old friend from high school showed up for a visit, and as soon as I saw him I knew everything was going to be all right. He knew exactly what I was talking about. Eventually I made other friends and things turned out okay. However, I stopped telling my story. To this day, I never volunteer anything about myself unless I know the other person's story first. Then I usually adapt mine to theirs in a way they can relate to it."

Kathleen Gamble, American ATCK (Burma, Mexico, Colombia, Nigeria, Switzerland, Netherlands, Russia) now living in the US

In making social connections, we wish to know and be known. However, we do well to remember this is a process which unfolds over time. Due to the cultural backgrounds of those involved, the comfort levels of each party may differ as to how long that process takes, what and how much is shared, and when.

Quick offers this advice: *'It may take time to build relationships with (home-country) peers. Try not to judge them... Just as home-country peers need to understand you in order to accept you, you need to make an effort to understand them. Be genuinely interested in other people's lives. Listen to other people's stories – everyone has one to tell... Go easy on yourself and others, extending a bit of grace to all concerned as you reach out to build relationships.'*

Quick's words remind me of the late Stephen Covey's *Seven Habits of Highly Effective People: Powerful lessons in Personal Change*, one of the habits is: *'seek first to understand... then to be understood.'* Keeping this in mind will hold us all in good stead throughout life.

> *'Listen to other people's stories – everyone has one to tell... Go easy on yourself and others, extending a bit of grace to all concerned as you reach out to build relationships.'*

MAKE A HOME

Where we decide to live and what type of housing we choose are very personal decisions. Regardless of the size, style or location of our accommodations, we need to make a nest, a haven, a refuge, out of whatever physical structure in which we happen to reside. This is what transforms a house into a home, a place where we can refresh and recharge. It's important to make this space our own by decorating it as we see fit. This helps us feel we're putting down roots rather than living in a transitory stage.

DESIGN YOUR OWN SPACE

"When I arrive in a new country, it is like a holiday. My family always spends the first month or so acting like tourists, discovering the country and making it a fun place to be. Finding a house and moving in has always been made fun, not a chore. When we look for a house, we stay in a nice hotel, and check out the area, like a discoverer finding new land. When we find a house, it is our tradition for the kids to play table tennis against the walls of the empty rooms, and discuss and imagine possibilities for our 'dream' house arrangement of furniture. I get to 'design' my own room, enthusiastic to take my stuff out of the boxes, rediscovering all my lovely possessions and popping bubble wrap. When we finish with the boxes, we have a tradition to keep a few big boxes to build forts and paint on. Moving into a house is a potentially negative chore, but we make it a whole lot of fun."

Rebecca Claudia Zijderveld, Dutch TCK/ repat currently living in the Netherlands after Italy, Sweden, Dubai and Singapore

I particularly love how Rebecca's family has created rituals (e.g., playing Ping-Pong in the empty rooms, each member sharing what furniture they would put where, building forts) and incorporated them into their househunting forays. Before we arrived in The Hague, Daughter interrogated Husband on the dimensions and layout of her room, then spent hours considering various options for placement of furniture. These rituals help each person settle in after entry into a new place.

MAKE YOUR HOME APPEALING

"Take the time to find an appealing home and surround yourself with photographs and meaningful memorabilia – coming home must always feel good."

Nicky Sully, South African expat (Rwanda, Tanzania, Cambodia) now living in the Netherlands

Don't underestimate the importance of doing little things to help make your home your sanctuary. I remember reading a friend's blog in which she shared that she hadn't bothered to put up artwork or mirrors, because they were waiting to hear news of her husband's next assignment. What was expected to be a quick decision ended up taking far longer than anticipated. Weeks can stretch into months, and living in limbo in your physical surroundings, in addition to your emotional state, can add to the unsettled, disruptive feelings. Don't allow yourself to wallow in feelings of being stuck between coming and going, here and there, or here and somewhere to-be-named.

TAKING THE TIME AND EFFORT

"One of the most important things in building a life away from home is creating a new home space. Set aside a budget for making your new home comfortable. It doesn't have to be super fancy or expensive, but you'll want your house or apartment to be a refuge of sorts. Make it feel as homey, as light, and as calm as possible.

Oh, and also figure out where to get imported foods ASAP. It's great and exciting to discover new tastes and aromas (believe me this is, hands down, my favorite part about traveling), but finding a way to eat a familiar meal when you are stressed and overwhelmed will be a great comfort. If it means paying double or triple the price for a box of mac and cheese, well, do it, once in a while. Fluorescent yellow cheese on industrial noodles can sometimes make you feel so much better."

Erica Knecht, Canadian expat (Japan, China, India, Switzerland, France) now lives in Indonesia

Moving house from one country to another is no small undertaking. To this day I still refer to the six-month period in which Husband came over to the Netherlands to start his new job, while I stayed back in the US to prepare for the move, as 'That About Which We Do Not Speak'. I had to remind myself, often, that we'd agreed to this as a family and would soon be back together. In the end it all worked out, but I still have a visceral reaction when I recall that time.

CHOOSING TO STAY TOGETHER AS A FAMILY IS MORE IMPORTANT

"Perspective has been the most powerful tool for dealing with the challenges of expat life. As a 'trailing spouse' (urgh, that label!) it is easy to fall into the trap of feeling sorry for yourself. You've sacrificed your social network/ career/ home/ life to follow your partner while they enhance theirs. They seem to get all the help and the perks while you're just one of the 'back-room boys', doing all the behind the scenes work – making a home, setting up schools, doctors, dentists – basically, establishing a new life. I had already made a mental note to myself before we left England, that if I ever felt resentful, I needed to remember that I had made this choice. The kids and I could have stayed behind and kept our life in England running as usual, we'd done this while K worked in Libya. But I knew from experience, sticking together as a family was more important. Wherever we were, as long as we were together, we'd get through it. Being apart was harder. Whenever things were crappy, I'd think 'I'm here because I chose to be'. It made me feel a bit more in control of my life when my usual reference points were in turmoil. It also spurred me to feel more determined to make it work."

Aisha Ashraf, Irish expat living in Canada by way of the UK

With the advent of email, Internet and social media venues, researching places to live, sizing up neighborhoods and finding accommodations from afar has never been easier. A reconnaissance trip is recommended, but not everyone is in the position to make one. We'll never know for sure whether it's the right place or not until we're there and ensconced in our new home, but it sure beats the way things used to be done. Regardless, we learn to make the best of the situation and get on with life.

TECHNOLOGY MAKES HOUSEHUNTING EASIER

"Having been our first overseas move, it went extremely well. I think having a wealth of information on the Internet, as well as the technology available to 'talk' (Skype, etc.) with others who have had this experience was a key to this. For example, access to property listings on the Internet, made the move much easier as we could see available properties and associated costs."

Rose P., an American expat living in the Netherlands

Experienced expats who relocate regularly learn lessons, tips and shortcuts to make it easier with each move. With time and practice, they know to travel lightly, see the bigger picture, focus on what's important, and minimize stress by not getting bogged down by the minutiae.

DITCH THE PERFECTIONISM

"I think I now know not become too frazzled and stressed about the actual move, it will work out. I am a bit of a perfectionist so it is hard to stop, but I have realized there is no point in worrying that I may not ship something I need. I can find pretty much everything I need or a close substitute in every place we have been, or I can have someone send it to me if I really need it and can't find it. The important things are the kids and my husband and our health and well-being."

Helen Maffini, serial expat living in her eleventh country

Having lived in a variety of cultures, many expats know the emotional journey taken as we slowly make our new accommodations into 'home'. Once we've relocated, we begin the physical and mental processes of moving in.

> 'Having lived in a variety of cultures, many expats know the emotional journey taken as we slowly make our new accommodations into 'home'.

FILLING IN THE SILENCE

"An expat life is one of contrasts and being able to balance on a tightrope between those contrasts. First there is the transit-house silence when so recently life had been full of noise, packers, leaving parties, jet engines. This goes hand in hand with loneliness when once there were family, friends, work colleagues. An empty calendar shows free weekends where once every date was full.

Then suddenly your belongings arrive, your new house is filled with boxes where once footsteps echoed as you walked. Why do I need all these things, you wonder in amazement when you have survived on air freight for six weeks. And where am I going to put them?

A wish for a lack of materialism disappears as you shop for souvenirs in the local markets, it is after all a 'must' to have a wooden hornbill from Sarawak. Coffee mornings, clubs, St. Andrews balls and holidays, soon your diary is looking as full as ever. You look at the newcomers and recognise their needs, the desire to be settled. Suddenly you realise that this is your home and there is no longer silence."

Sareen McLay, Scottish expat (Oman, Malaysia) now living in the Netherlands and preparing to repatriate

When I asked Susan Zijderveld how she has handled settling in after seven moves across Asia, Australasia, Europe and the Middle East, her response below was immediate, emphatic and teeming with excellent suggestions.

ONE SERIAL EXPAT'S TOP TEN LESSONS IN MOVING

- *"**Get a house you love:** If it takes you six months to find it, no problem. Life can be worse than living in a hotel :) Real estate agents might hate you for it; buy them dinner and apologize for being a fusspot, but make sure you get a house that makes your heart sing. You do not get points for finding a house on your initial looksee (those four days is for an introduction to the housing market and locations, choosing furnished temporary accommodation and seeing schools). After you move, the focus should be securing your husband and kids' happiness in their respective* *work/ school. Looking at houses needs to be a leisurely, fun and interesting activity if you are going to do it every three years.*

- **Compensate:** *If it is a lousy climate buy woolly underwear, turn up the central heating (in Sweden I kept it on all summer) and light candles. In Dubai we had a midnight swim tradition (more like a bath). In Holland I have the most beautiful (and expensive) raincoat on the planet – possibly universe – and I wear it even when it is not raining. Since we always rent and we are very house oriented people I pretend that we own the house and invest a lot of time and money into the house (though we sign three-year leases).*

- **Feather your bed:** *Every country presents different opportunities – you can change everything – or nothing. In Holland I have found the most extraordinary neighbourhood – who knew! Holland is known for great modern things so I have bought ultramodern lighting and I'm now on the search for old Dutch paintings. Eat local – I am 95% stomach so this one works for me. I suppose for other people this might translate as getting a hobby (something you love, or something that is available only in that country). We always get a house very characteristically local knowing we only have to tolerate the negatives for a few years – but, oh the memories!*

- **Routines and traditions:** *Moving stress is hugely reduced by maintaining some routines and traditions no matter what. We always take the birthday hat in hand luggage, along with Ping-Pong bats and balls for the kids to play Ping-Pong on the walls of the empty house. All our houses have the same colour scheme and I take every stick of furniture with me right down to the dishcloths. Friday we eat out local (in Dubai shwarma, Singapore Peranakan, NL Indonesian, NZ fish and chips). It always feels like home, even when it is a hotel.*

- **Focus on people, not things:** *Your kids and your husband's job are what matter. Curtains are on the lowest of the lowest list. Small things are just that. Friends are the jewels, but it is really worthwhile to put the energy into mining for friends early on for you, and for your children and husband. Do not forget the people at home or relatives, but do not go home in the first year – it is not home anymore and will just mess with your head.*

- *It takes a year to get your rhythm:* I always seem to sleep more in that first year and no matter how careful, gain a stone. Thank goodness I do not move every year! I tend to allow myself to have a glass of wine every night as a reward. But it is important to move heaven and earth to create the kind of life you want in that first year as you will get cumulative returns, and just have faith that when you have rebuilt this new world things will get better. At the one-year point the clouds start to part and sunlight shines in. If you have not done so, then that is generally the implode time.

- *Catastrophise and manipulate:* It is very important for me to catastrophise well in advance. Everything works out sooooo much better than I thought when I do this. When I arrive with the kids and hubbie for the looksee my role is chief manipulator. I am the centre of the family and whatever emotional baggage I have needs to have been predigested, because my job is to create a virtual world that my family can call home. This is my job. Nowhere can be horrible when you have this mindset. My family looks to me for attitude. I do not gloss over problems though, we see them as challenges to deal with.

- *Apply for schools before you have your looksee:* Most good schools have waiting lists of more than one year. Apply before you are even sure you are going as most will refund the fees if they do not get you a place (and it is a small amount in comparison with the hell that is the unhappy children with Ds in their reports).

- *God sent you to be creative:* If it is not there in your new country, create it. The world does not owe you a living. Locals have their own life and you have to prove yourself (over and over and over again). Be the solution not the problem. It's not them – it's you.

- *Take the light and pass it on:* I have been incredibly humbled by the overwhelming generosity of people when I have been stupid, inexperienced or just plain new. They show me through demonstrating 'right behavior', inclusive, open, hospitable, patient. They show me, I show you, you show the next person – that's the expat woman's mafia code."

Susan Zijderveld
serial expat now living in the Netherlands

Susan's recommendation to apply to schools early in the relocation process is a crucial one. We found this out the hard way when we considered schools while moving to the Netherlands. Son didn't have the right qualifications to undertake the International Baccalaureate diploma, and the only international school in The Hague offering an American diploma program (and where Daughter had been accepted), didn't have a spot for him.

> 'It is important to move heaven and earth to create the kind of life you want in that first year as you will get cumulative returns, and just have faith that when you have rebuilt this new world things will get better.'

Only after several conversations with the Admissions Office and tense weeks of waiting, the school administration finally voted to raise the cap on students in his grade. Ours had a happy ending, but many other expat/ cross-culturals aren't always as fortunate. When we seriously considered a subsequent move to another country, you can bet the very first actions I took were to research schools, talk with admissions staff and submit the requisite applications.

There aren't many books available on selecting schools during overseas moves, but a particularly helpful one is Kathleen McAnear Smith's, *Parents on the Move!: Preparing Your Family for a Successful and Creative Relocation*. McAnear Smith has developed a clever seven-level approach to international moves, ranging from one in which a family wishes to operate within their own cultural bounds as much as possible (a level one relocation), to a one or two passport family preferring their children become part of the international community (a level three or four relocation depending on future plans), to total immersion in the new culture (levels six A, B and seven relocations).

By getting us and our family members to carefully consider our own background experience, as well as what we wish to get out of a move abroad, McAnear Smith is able to help steer us to the appropriate kinds of schools (differing by style, type, environment and expectations in academic programs), and the social and community support we might seek out. Only then can we delve deeper with McAnear Smith's detailed questions and checklists to find the best fit.

I think it is also wise to have an extension of home for those moments when you need a break, a place to hang out or simply a second home (but without the mortgage). This idea of a 'home away from home' reminds me of the American television comedy *Cheers*, popular in the 1980s and early 90s.

> 'A recurring theme in the stories from expats all over the world is that of making an effort, of getting to know your surroundings and forging connections.'

The theme song, written by Gary Portnoy and Judy Hart Angelo, speaks of a place – in this instance, a neighborhood bar – '*where everyone knows you're name and they're always glad you came.*' It needn't be a bar – for you it may be a favorite café, bookstore, fitness center, library, or nearby park.

HOME AND AN ESCAPE FROM HOME

"Sometimes there is nothing more comforting than hearing the front door click behind me as the stresses of the day disappear in the quiet of my apartment. However, since I live alone most of the time, in moments of anxiety and loneliness my home can feel empty, and the peaceful quiet is replaced by my thoughts and worries echoing off the walls. All expats need a place to go when home is not the refuge it should be. For me, it's a local coffee shop where I can always count on a warm welcome, as little or as much company as I desire, and free Wi-Fi. My biggest secret to survival here was finding my second sanctuary. One should always have at least two shelters when living abroad – home, and escape from home."

**Kimberly Burcher-Curling,
American expat in the United Arab Emirates**

I once interviewed an artist in the lobby of a neighborhood boutique hotel here in The Hague. I was greeted not only by the subject of my interview, but also the hotel manager/ barista who welcomed me warmly and took my *koffie* order. The two were on a first-name basis, interacted with ease and clearly knew each other fairly well. It seems the artist, a recent widower, had made the miniscule lobby his own home away from home.

MAKE AN EFFORT

Once you've made your home your personal oasis, don't make the mistake of holing up there by yourself. You didn't relocate 500 or 5,000 miles or more to stay within your own four walls. If that were your intention when you moved to a new country/ culture, you needn't have bothered leaving!

EXPLORE AND DISCOVER

Rather than become housebound, now is the time to explore and get to know your surroundings. For me, this meant grabbing a map and the dog's leash and starting to walk in ever-widening concentric circles from our house. Each day I'd venture further, becoming comfortable with our street, then the adjacent ones, the local shopping street and tram/ bus stops, before expanding my treks outward to new neighborhoods, nearby parks and so on.

A recurring theme in the stories from expats all over the world is that of making an effort, of getting to know your surroundings and forging connections.

FINDING COMMON CONVERSATIONAL GROUND

"Get good social skills. Develop a one liner to describe yourself when they ask 'so what do you do?' and 'where do you come from?' and 'where do you live?' and 'how long have you lived here?' The questions under these questions are really, 'give me a subject that you like so we can have a nice chat'. So for instance you say, 'I live in Swiss Club Road but I miss being close to the hawker markets' which tells a person you love food and the local culture. These answers should also be ones that the children develop.

My rule of thumb is to be pragmatic. When I am talking to Dutch people I will always tell them I am a New Zealander as they all love it there and love me for being exotic, but if I had told them British it might not have gone so well. People who I have already sized up as possible friends will probably be trusted with the whole and long truth to give them an opportunity to run away while there is still time!"

Susan Zijderveld, serial expat now living in the Netherlands

When you make the effort, you remain open and curious. You work with what you have, seeking opportunities to try new activities, meet new people and become familiar with your new locale.

CREATIVE CHAMELEON

"My husband was a Russian American who grew up speaking Russian at home and had relatives in Moscow and St. Petersburg. He decided to open his own business in Moscow. This was the 1990s and everybody was doing it. I moved to Moscow not

knowing much about it and not knowing the language at all. I landed there with no support system. I was on my own. My husband was working most of the time or out with his Russian buddies.

I was horribly unhappy at first but what I ended up doing, and what saved me, were two things. I cooked and I wrote. I made everything from scratch (no convenience items available) plus substitution became my norm. I could rarely find what I was looking for so I improvised. I pored over cookbooks. My husband was always dragging people home for dinner – mostly Russians who were happy to eat anything I fed them. I think I fed half of Moscow. I was fearless. Everybody was a potential guinea pig. I made berry pies, hazelnut tortes, tortillas, English muffins, pita bread, cakes, Stroganoff, chicken Kiev, eggplant parmesan, pizza, you name it, I made it. And then by a weird twist of fate I became the editor of the American Women's Organization newsletter.

In the end it all came together and I edited, designed and produced the AWO Moscow cookbook. By that time I was an old hand and everybody knew me. I was satisfied and I was content. I had carved out my new persona.
Growing up as a chameleon taught me to have inner strength and to be creative. We never had all the things we needed or wanted, but we found ways to get around that. If Christmas trees were not available, we made one out of paper or cards or cloth. We always made each other birthday cards. We rarely had TV so we read, or played cards, or listened to music. When we lived in Lagos and I only spent summer vacation there, I didn't have any friends or any place to hang out and meet people, but there were always new things to see and experience and learn from all around me. I never felt lonely or bored.

You become such a tight family unit that it doesn't really matter. I think that is why I had such a hard time in the beginning in Moscow and in college. I didn't have the support system people need in those situations. Whether it is an old friend or a family member who has been through it all with you, or a new friend who 'gets' you, as long as there is somebody there telling you, 'No, you haven't lost your mind', it really helps. But if there is no support system, then find something you really love to do and enjoy the ride. An open and curious mind always helps."

Kathleen Gamble, American ATCK (Burma, Mexico, Colombia, Nigeria, Switzerland, Netherlands, Russia) now living in the US

Making an effort extends to all areas of life, including the workplace. This is true whether things are going well or not, but it is even more important when it is the latter. Differences of opinion in style and substance, stressful working arrangements and disagreements can – and do – occur anywhere. However, working in a cross-cultural environment may add additional layers of possible confusion and misunderstanding.

MAKING THE MOST OF A TOUGH SITUATION

"My husband was in a role he loved and was pulled back to a role he didn't enjoy, in a country he didn't want to be in, and offered no reason why. He felt it was his fault, something he'd done. But he decided to make the best effort he could in the role he'd had to take, and not let his managers see he was stressed, his family life was in bits and that he wasn't capable of delivering, no matter what. I saw him succeed in it and emotionally become stronger and get more out of the role than he'd anticipated."

Nicola McCall, British expat/ repat

Even serial expats occasionally need to be reminded not to lose sight of what's right before them. As they reminisce about the many places they've been, the people they've encountered and the experiences they've had, they don't want to miss out on the opportunities, adventures, and friendships that await them where they currently are.

INVEST IN YOURSELF

"I should say that I am not fond of the terms 'expat' and 'expat life'. I do not believe in labeling people. There are people who decide to go live abroad only for professional reasons. They are offered a lucrative contract abroad and accept the offer. They sometimes

take their family along in that venture. Their stay has a clear beginning and an end. They usually look forward to returning home. Maybe these people are expatriates. But I will not say more about them because I do not belong to that category and I believe one should not talk about the things he does not know.

I am an international teacher who as always wanted to live abroad. I left Canada for the first time when I was 17 years old. I went to Paris for a summer on a short-term student/ work visa. I found a flat, and a job as a waiter in a restaurant. I made new friends and travelled all over France. When I returned home, I had a good idea of what it was like to be French. It was very different from being a Canadian (or a Quebeçois). After that experience, going to places for a short-term vacation was not satisfying for me anymore. I did not see the point of going somewhere if I did not have the time to get to know the people who live there and share their lifestyle.

I went to teacher's college knowing that I would work and live abroad. That was my goal. My first job as a full-time teacher was in Neuchatel, Switzerland. Even though Switzerland is very much part of the Western world, it is also very foreign. Swiss people have their own ways and I have loved discovering them. However, as one often does, I also spent a lot of time criticizing and blaming them. I was young! Instead of embracing the culture, I often fought it. I was looking for nightlife and a laid-back French bistro culture in a country where people seldom get drunk in public. Instead of hiking the gorgeous Alps and Jura mountains, I used the money I earned to fly out of the country every time I had a chance. Later on, I regretted not taking advantage of what was right there under my eyes.

Since then I try to be more aware of my behaviors and mind set when I live abroad. In Prague, unlike many expats, I resisted the temptation of criticizing the Czechs because I knew that one day I would regret that.... and now I live in Tunisia, I do. I miss the Czechs. For the same reason, since I moved to Tunisia, I try to say and think nothing but positive things about this wonderful country. I am making an effort to branch out, to meet locals, to invest myself in this country where I chose to live.... because I know that one day, I will miss Tunisia."

Phillippe, Canadian expat (England, France, Malaysia, Switzerland, Czech Republic) now living in Tunisia

Philippe's message is a good one. Remaining open-minded about the culture in which you live – and the people, customs and traditions you encounter – is essential. If you look for positives, you'll find them, in the same way if you focus on negatives, you'll soon be drowning in them. Don't make the mistake of criticizing every little detail of a place, you waste the chance to experience what is special and unique about this place in this time.

GIVE BACK

One of the most rewarding things you can do is to give back – to the community in which you live, on a regional or national level, even globally. It is not surprising expats/ cross-culturals often become involved in helping address needs in their host cultures. They give freely of their 'time, talent, and treasure' (i.e., hard work, skills and monetary and/ or other donations), volunteering for worthy causes.

Often high schools make graduation contingent upon mandatory volunteer efforts benefitting the local community. Schools have long pulled in parents to tutor students, help out in classrooms, accompany classes on field trips, lead fundraising or other projects, and temporarily house visiting speakers/ students participating in academic, artistic or athletic events. As it is with so many, I juggle working with holding down the home front, but I do try to identify one or two projects each year to offer my assistance to at Daughter's school, and we have housed visiting students many times.

Those intending to stay more than a couple of years may decide to become more heavily involved in school-related roles dealing with policy and program oversight, participate in Parent Teacher Associations or run for School Board posts. Others choose to make use of their experience, skill sets and interests by getting involved in local charities or developmental projects to support the greater good. One such example is American Tara Agacayak, who lives in Turkey and is involved in women's business and empowerment issues. She serves on the Advisory Board of what is envisioned to be the first national Women's Awareness Conference in that country.

It is also common for many international expatriate groups to partner with and support local voluntary organizations. In most countries and larger cities, there are expat clubs and associations, even nationally affiliated groups, many of which are heavily involved in volunteering and charitable activities.

Opportunities abound to become personally involved in helping others overseas. Many schools and religious organizations sponsor service trips. At Daughter's school, several staff members have a long-standing relationship with an international charity helping Burmese refugee families in Thailand. Each year they take a small group of high

> 'When it comes to charitable work, even the busiest among us can find the intersection of what we enjoy doing and what needs to be done.'

school students, along with donated clothing, educational materials and equipment, to spend a week volunteering at childcare centers and the elementary school. They see firsthand how the refugees make their living in shrimp farms and rubber plantations, and spend time in their homes. They realize the sacrifices made by refugee families in order for their children to continue their education past middle school. They develop friendships with their Burmese teen counterparts, which last long after their visits. Additionally, each student is required to raise several hundred euros to help meet the school's commitment to fund the child and infant feeding program year round. Other students go to Tanzania to help construct houses and community buildings.

Dr. Othniel J. Seiden, veteran volunteer on numerous medical missions throughout the world, was asked how to get involved in charitable efforts so often he wrote a book on the subject. The result was *The Joy of Volunteering: Working and Surviving in Developing Countries*, and shares his experiences, observations, and insights. He stresses the need to observe and listen, keep an open mind, and become comfortable with the need to adapt as necessary. In discussing what he has learned, even under the most primitive conditions, Seiden mentions: *'how to make do, how to improvise, how to prioritize, how to survive, how to utilize, how to transpose, how to simplify, how to facilitate, how to substitute, how to, how to... I have learned a lot more than I've ever taught.'*

On a local level, I know of several people who volunteer regularly to help provide meals to the homeless, including one parent who has arranged with her children's school to take a different small group of middle school students each month to work one half-day in a local soup kitchen. One friend offers her time and services at a home for the elderly, another volunteers weekly at a shelter for homeless dogs and cats. Several others combine their love of running or cycling and enter races to regularly raise money for various charities.

For many of us, helping others has become incorporated into everyday life. When turning in plastic bottles while shopping at my *Albert Heijn* grocery store, I contribute the small deposit I get back to the monthly-featured charity. I can take a bag of gently worn clothing to a drop-off bin at our glass and paper recycling station. Books and furniture no longer needed are donated to school or neighborhood fund-raising activities. The doorbell rings at least once a month with registered volunteers collecting small change or larger contributions for international aid efforts dealing with poverty, medical missions, hunger, literacy, and disaster relief. Individual actions such as these may seem small, but when repeated over and over all around the world, the cumulative effect can produce dramatic results.

The reasons we give our time, money, effort – or all three – are legion. Some of us do it to fill a specific, urgent need in an underprivileged community. For others it satisfies a strong desire to help others, or allows us to show gratitude for the benefits and blessings of our own lives. We do it to assuage guilt, remind ourselves of the incredible disparity among haves and have-nots, and to regain perspective or reflect personal priorities. When it comes to charitable work, even the busiest among us can find the intersection of what we enjoy doing and what needs to be done.

LEARN THE LANGUAGE (EVEN IF ONLY A LITTLE)

There are not many topics among those living across cultures as divisive as that of whether or not to learn the local language. It's a personal decision based on individual circumstances, but in general, I do think it helps to make an effort. The next story reflects several reasons why.

A GRASP OF THE LANGUAGE

"I remember the first few months as full of excitement – everything was fresh and new. The life, the people, the energy were unlike anything back home. Two in the morning no longer signaled the end of the evening and best of all I didn't have to drive. Conversations no longer started with, 'What do you do?' but rather, 'Where are you from?' My days no longer consisted of the same old routine, but instead offered a new adventure as I explored some new nook of Barcelona that I discovered accidentally. It had been a long time since I felt so energized.

But, just as nothing in life lasts forever, the same goes for the rush of living in a new city, and around my sixth month the sheen wore off. Feelings of loneliness crept in. Living alone in a foreign land with a strange tongue made basic communication seem like mission impossible sometimes. Even if I used the right word, my pronunciation would have people grimacing as I butchered their language, and there were many times I ended up buying something I didn't need or want just to get out of a store before facing further embarrassment. After facing situations like this, I thought about the life I had left, my family, my friends and my ability to communicate freely and confidently. But as my old boss once told me, 'What you miss no longer exists'. He was right. Life was fluid and not static, and all it took was a call home to reconfirm this. Of course, knowing this didn't make it any easier. So what did?

For me, it was getting out and reminding myself of why I had chosen to move to Barcelona. I'd wander the streets and get lost in its beauty, ending the day with a beer outside and some people-watching. I also found some solace in the two medieval churches – the Santa Maria del Mar and the Gothic Cathedral back when it was free. Far from a religious man, I was nevertheless happy when the holy water didn't burn, and sitting in such magnificent buildings brought a certain serenity and peace to my confused mind.

I also broke my promise to avoid all things expat or English, and completely immerse myself in Spanish culture. Enough nights going out and not catching a single word made the need to sit and have a chat a priority. It was at the English pubs where I befriended not only expats, who had decided to make Barcelona home, but Spaniards and Catalans, who were interested in improving their English and helping me with my Spanish. And, by the end of my first year, the foundation of building a life in a foreign country had been accomplished – some favorite spots to collect your thoughts, a network of friends to help and support you through the ups and downs, and a basic grasp of the language to lessen the moments of embarrassment."

Jeremy Holland, Anglo-American ATCK (Philippines, Saudi Arabia, England) living in the Netherlands after Spain

From the moment I arrived in the Netherlands, I have done my best to learn as much of the Dutch language as possible. Six weeks after arrival I began a month-long intensive course and a shorter follow-up course a few months later. That gave me a good base, and I've been building on it ever since. It is slow going at times, but I keep plugging away.

I listen to Dutch radio while driving in my car. Whenever I hear a new word or want to know how to say a phrase I use often in English, I look it up online at Google Translate – www.translate.google.com, or Babel Fish – www.babelfish.com, or in an old-fashioned

Dutch-English dictionary. I'll pick up one of the local Dutch newspapers and plod through a few paragraphs, sometimes an article, trying to glean as much information as I can. Believe me, pictures do help. Sometimes I'll follow the Dutch subtitles if I'm watching a television show in English. This is especially good for learning idioms and unusual expressions.

I've sought out Dutch friends who encourage me and are willing to speak with me at my lesser level. I live in a Dutch neighborhood, so I make an effort to speak with a few of my neighbors in their own language. Well, perhaps that is overstating it a bit. I should say I make an effort to exchange social pleasantries and as much conversational back and forth as I can muster, before sputtering to a stop. If I learn a new word every day, I am thrilled. I am ecstatic if I can remember that same word two weeks later.

Thank heavens my Dutch friends and neighbors are a patient lot. Over time, I've gotten better. Not great, just better. I've definitely lowered my expectations over the years. When I first learned we would be moving here, I vowed to myself I would become fluent in Dutch. Once I arrived and had some time and experience under my belt, I realized I'd do well to become proficient. Nowadays I'll settle for moving from reasonably intermediate to solidly intermediate, with a side order of being able to converse longer than two minutes with people talking much faster than I can. I'm not there yet, but I aspire to be.

I am able to get around and function in most situations. I can usually figure out which track my train is on, that it's running late, but I may not necessarily understand the reason for the delay. I can understand traffic on the A12 is backed up three kilometers because of an accident, and have a decent handle on what's going on with the weather. I get that the plumber will be coming Tuesday after 3 pm. I can make most appointments, seek simple directions, place an order in a restaurant, and inquire whether the store carries a particular item.

I can describe. Perhaps my descriptions include words at the pre-teen level, but you can get my drift. Sometimes I can act out whatever I don't know how to say. I can pantomime with the best of them. I ask questions, lots of them, often repeating the same ones. Most days I muddle through. Some days I fail spectacularly.

'By the end of my first year, the foundation of building a life in a foreign country had been accomplished – some favorite spots to collect your thoughts, a network of friends to help and support you through the ups and downs, and a basic grasp of the language to lessen the moments of embarrassment.'

I may not speak or understand Dutch extensively, even when I'm pulling as many visual cues from a situation as possible. But what little I can understand and speak, I try to do with a decent Dutch accent. That's always a useful lesson to remember – if you can't manage substance, at least go for style.

So why do I keep putting myself out there, subjecting myself to the long pauses, quizzical looks, odd stares and occasional outright laughter? Just as the contributor of the previous story, I hope to build a fuller, deeper life here. I want to feel a part of this place. And when I read the next story, I knew precisely what this contributor meant.

VULNERABLE, MOVING AND UNSETTLING

"Language learning puts you in a very vulnerable place. It isn't easy, it takes considerable effort. It can take years, and your accent may still not be completely right. But for me, it's deeply moving and unsettling not to be able to communicate well."

Norm Viss, American repat after three decades away (Nigeria, Netherlands)

Everybody has their reasons as to why they may or may not attempt to learn the local language, or to what extent they are willing or able to go in that endeavor. Some are deeply personal, some are situational, but all are unique to the individual. This isn't about judgment ('thou shalt learn the local language'), but about making an effort. It helps us feel part of a community, and makes everyday life a little bit easier. It demonstrates awareness of our surroundings and signals honor of cultural differences. For most of us, having someone try to speak our language is a sign of cultural respect.

If you're still not convinced of the benefits of learning a foreign language, it appears it can benefit you from a neuroscientific perspective.

LEARNING LANGUAGES AS BRAIN FOOD

As longtime Science magazine staff writer Yudhijit Bhattacharjee wrote in *The Benefits of Bilingualism: Are Bilinguals Smarter?* (New York Times Sunday Review), speaking a second language or more: *'can have a profound effect on your brain, improving cognitive skills not related to language, and even shielding against dementia in old age.'*

While researchers, academics and policy makers have tended to view bi- and multilingualism as interfering with cognitive learning, and even intellectual development, due to continual switching back and forth within the brain, it seems: '*this interference isn't so much a handicap as a blessing in disguise. It forces the brain to resolve internal conflict, giving the mind a workout that strengthens its cognitive muscles.*'

According to Bhattacharjee, collective evidence from several studies: '*suggests that the bilingual experience improves the brain's so-called executive function – a command system that directs the attention processes that we use for planning, solving problems, and performing various other mentally demanding tasks.*' Those who can speak two or more languages may be more adept at certain mental puzzles, and the benefits may help delay the onset of dementia and other symptoms of Alzheimer's.

Similarly, an article by The Guardian's science correspondent Alok Jha, *Being Bilingual May Delay Alzheimer's and Boost Brain Power*, pointed to the growing benefits of speaking multiple languages beyond postponing dementia. He cited recent studies at York University in Canada and Penn State University in the United States, which demonstrate that bilinguals were able to better edit out irrelevant details, focus on important information, prioritize and multi-task.

So why not at least *try* to learn the local language, if only to build and continually add to a repertoire of words and phrases that help you along?

MAKE A LIFE

Finding our tribe of friends, creating a comfortable home, and making an effort to become part of the society in which we live, go far towards building what we *really* seek – a full, rich, balanced life. We know our identity comes out of congruency between how we see ourselves and how we are seen – past, present and future – and that the groups, activities and issues we involve ourselves with contribute further. Being part of the community around us is integral to making a life. Otherwise we're simply gliding along, doing what we please in a self-oriented daze, without truly feeling anchored.

DON'T JUST FIND YOUR PLACE IN LIFE, MAKE IT

"A piece of advice given to me by an American friend in her 70s, and whom I see as my mentor, was that you don't just find your place (in life), you make it. She also said you don't walk your path, you are the path. Knowing this has helped me in my darkest moments and given me faith – life is what we make of it and we can create magical moments no matter where we are."

Carrie Sanderson, Anglo-Dutch Adult TCK/ CCK living in the Netherlands

Just as the previous story underlines the importance of creating the life we wish to lead, the next offers a suggestion as to how to do that. It begins with adjusting our mindset, because as we've already learned, thoughts can become actions.

LIVE AS THOUGH YOU'LL BE THERE FOREVER

"As a fairly new expat, I received a great piece of advice from an Australian woman who'd returned home after more than a decade away. She said, 'wherever you are, always act as though you will be there forever, and live your life accordingly'. She'd had a bad first assignment in England where the duration of her assignment was uncertain and extended in small increments. She'd always been waiting to move on. When her husband received his next assignment to the US it was to be for 18 months. She refused to go until she had secured her green card enabling her to work in the US. When she got there, she started a business and enjoyed that entrepreneurial challenge for more than ten years, selling the business when her husband's career took them back to Australia."

Sara C., American expat now living in the Netherlands after Australia and Scotland

Can you honestly imagine telling someone else, 'wait, don't grow, put your life on hold, don't explore, don't meet people or make new friendships'? Of course you wouldn't. Yet sometimes we find ourselves doing precisely that when we find ourselves in a situation that isn't to our liking. Not all expats have the opportunity

'New expats can teach themselves to love every fresh encounter and laugh off the frustrations.'

to decide where they will be living – their employer decides when and where they will move, and for how long.

This next story is a good reminder that while we may think we know where we'll be and for how long, circumstances can change. By making the effort to live as if we'll be there forever (or at least for many years), we tend to drop some of the superficiality that can come with thinking we're only in a place temporarily. We can begin living on a deeper, more involved level.

WHEN SHORT-TERM BECOMES LONG-TERM

"When I became an expatriate, I was riding an emotional high. A man I met during a semester in London had turned out to be the love of my life, someone I'd follow anywhere. I was also in love with London, but when his work sent him to Hong Kong, I decided to follow him there instead. It was romantic and exotic to run off to Asia for him. We would explore the Far East, get some great CV-building experience, and then return to London where we first fell in love.

Two years into my Asian expatriation, the European job prospects showed no signs of improvement. It became clearer every day that we were in Hong Kong for the long haul. The extended separation from my home and culture became more taxing when I realized this wasn't just a short-term adventure. My career goals would also have to take a different form than I had expected.

When I was just moving to Asia for a year or two, everything was novel and exciting. New expats can teach themselves to love every fresh encounter and laugh off the frustrations. But now I need to develop the resilience to continue to love this city when it isn't new anymore, and when I know I won't live near my family again. The long-term expat needs a particular type of emotional resilience to deal with the future, not just the present. We are lucky because our entire lives can be an adventure, but adventures are exhausting. We need to embrace the new culture, but also establish space to take a break from it and nurture ourselves so we can handle the lows as wells as the highs. When the initial fire of the romance burns out, we need to settle into a marriage of respect and contentment with our new home."

Shannon Young
American expat currently living in Hong Kong, after England.

It may not be easy to look in the mirror and convince ourselves to go out and make the best of it, yet that is exactly what we need to do. Withdrawing into the physical shell of our home and the emotional shell of our mind, and foregoing chances to learn more about our surroundings, are neither practical nor healthy.

MOVE OUTSIDE YOUR COMFORT ZONE

"Find ways to integrate with people – move out of your comfort zone and reach out to people in the community through volunteer work or leisure activities. With our fourth move (to the Netherlands) I made a stout effort to keep in contact with old friends and I have sought new acquaintances through volunteer work and enrolling in art and language courses. I have been fortunate in finding work as a part-time language teacher in The Hague, a job I love and which gives me a sense of community as well as a sense of flexibility.

Living as an expat provides the opportunity of meeting people from many different countries and I have found this hugely enriching on a personal level. It's a privilege to spend time in far flung places learning from different cultures, and I look forward to looking back on my years as an expat which has been full of colourful memories and quirky experiences."

Nicky Sully, South African expat (Rwanda, Tanzania, Cambodia) now living in the Netherlands

I can attest firsthand that Nicky follows her own advice. Our husbands both work for the same international organization, and in conversation they discovered we live in the same neighborhood, *Statenkwartier*. Over a 'get-to-know-you' lunch, Nicky mentioned that when she arrived in The Hague, she had become active in an English language expat radio station. Responsible for hosting short, weekly stories about arts and cultural topics to the large international community here, she believed my contribution of a chapter of a soon-to-be-released book about global women entrepreneurs would interest her audience. A week later we were in the studio taping a short interview.

But it hasn't ended there. Enjoying each other's company, Nicky and I continue to meet periodically for *koffie* and a chance to catch up. It's always fun to get together with her as she is a charming, upbeat woman whose personality reflects her positive outlook.

I distinctly remember sitting in the garden section of a favorite café last year when she shared excitedly that her volunteer work teaching English had developed into a paid position. The flush of excitement on her face and the tumble of the words spilling out as she spoke reflected the pride and immense enjoyment she takes from her work. Moving out of her comfort zone? Reaching out to people in the community? I'd say so. She is a woman who sees opportunities and possibilities, not obstacles and problems.

> 'When the initial fire of the romance burns out, we need to settle into a marriage of respect and contentment with our new home.'

I know many expats don't necessarily consider the importance of building a support system for help in difficult times. Such a network doesn't appear overnight, it takes time, attention and effort to create. When the going gets rocky, they'll wish they had.

DRAWING COMFORT AND STRENGTH FROM FRIENDS AND COMMUNITY

"I had been living in Japan for several years when my mother's health declined rapidly. Sadly she died as I was halfway through the journey home to say goodbye. This was an incredibly difficult time for me, complicated by the cultural mores regarding privacy and 'face' in my adopted country. As heartbreaking as that time was, I drew comfort and strength from a wonderful group of friends. Ironically enough, the separation between public and private life actually gave me much needed time to grieve on my own terms. Perhaps it helped that I felt part of the Japanese community, aligned to their cultural values without losing my sense of Britishness completely."

Val Hamer
British expat currently living in South Korea after Japan and Vietnam

In the next story, one repat shares how some expatriates feel 'different' from the rest of the expatriate world when they have a harder time than others adjusting to their host culture. Similarly, some expats have difficulties repatriating to their home countries once they have sampled the outbound life. Actually, they're not so different after all.

EXPLORING HOW YOU RELATE TO YOUR ENVIRONMENT

"It is important to remember we are all playing the game of 'Who Am I?' We are all unique in the way we approach our individual life, but we are the same in that we all depend on one person – The Self. It is The Self who holds the tools to help us survive life in the most fulfilling way. We are each responsible for our own lives and what happens in them, regardless of age, cultural background, wealth, condition or talent. Not taking responsibility for your own life means you inevitably make yourself dependent on others, on what they say, on what they want you to do, on how they make you feel. And that applies whether you live in another culture or in the society you've been part of all your life.

You may say, 'But how can I be responsible for things outside of me? This is not my country, not my culture, this isn't me. How can I adopt the customs of a whole group when I don't feel comfortable with them and am used to doing things differently?' The answer is you don't. It's not a matter of 'if you can't beat them, join them'. It's a matter of how you, as a person, relate to your environment.

A prerequisite to be part of the culture you live in is to bond with it and not reject it when you see something you don't like or feel doesn't fit with your values. You don't have to agree with it. Yet by rejecting it the only one you isolate is you; and you can't blame others for that.

I lived in Singapore, which I found hard, because as an expat spouse I wasn't allowed to work. It was the first time I hadn't worked. I was in my thirties and that's tough for a workaholic. It made me feel uncomfortable and gave me plenty of time to look around me and observe. I disliked the 'loss of face' aspect of the local culture. In my very Dutch approach to life I often felt 'things were being kept from me'. The Dutch are known for our bluntness in expressing ourselves, while the Singaporeans often practise patience behind a smile without letting you in on what they really think.

I isolated myself from the Singaporean society by criticizing it. Rather than enjoying myself sampling the wide variety of cultures Singapore has to offer in such a small area, I spent much of my time lying at the pool reading a book or entertaining visitors. I wasn't present in Singapore; I was rejecting it. I lived there but 'I' had gone into hiding because 'I' didn't want this.

Twenty years later and perhaps somewhat wiser, I realise whatever it was I saw in Singapore had nothing to do with me. I wasted time being angry, (which is often the result of being scared), while I could have explored and developed myself within that culture. I could have taken Indian cooking courses, done voluntary work, explored what I could give back to the environment I was living in. I didn't have to like Lee Kuan Yew, the President, to like the Singaporean neighbour across the street. However, since I

didn't like Lee Kuan Yew, I didn't bond with the neighbour across the street and stuck to my pool, other expats and visitors.

To bond with where you live, and explore how you relate to where you live is the prime target in personal development. It helps the process of adjusting to change and filtering those things that can be of help in sustaining your own life in a positive way, which in turn creates contentment and happiness."

Ingrid Schippers
Dutch repat, Yoga-based personal development instructor and author

How we choose to make a life for ourselves differs for each of us. For some, the thought of leaving behind all that is known and cherished is unimaginable. But as many expats/cross-culturals have found, there is something thrilling in taking the plunge into a place and culture different from the one we're used to. It may be daunting, but it is stimulating too.

ONE SMALL STEP, ONE GIANT LEAP

"Like all great stories we need to start with the 'Once Upon A Time' stuff. I was born in Brisbane, (Australia) almost two weeks after Neil Armstrong took his one small step for man. While I spent my childhood in Queensland, I consider myself a Melbourne girl. It is an amazing city of food, sport, culture and outdoor living. I went to secondary school and built my career there, climbing the corporate ladder and enjoying the fruits of my hard work along the way – travelling, shopping, theatre, dining out and stepping onto the much sought-after property ladder. Two of the closest people to me on the planet – Mum and my little sister – still live there. And those that tell me they are considering a move to Australia's southern shores are greeted with my glowing litany about one of the World's Most Liveable Cities.

I spent most of my adult life there feeling confident, comfortable, empowered... and that I didn't quite fit. No one who knew me would have told you that. They would probably have told you about the golden girl, one of life's go-getters who seemed to take life on with a conviction that it was short and there to be made the most of, and that's true.

But I felt isolated by Australia's distance from the rest of the world – both in geography and philosophy. Smothered by that easy-going, homogeneous approach to life that meant a 'she'll be all right' was the answer to any difference of opinion. Frustrated by a political climate and economy that rode on the coat-tails of others. All under-pinned by a deep-seated feeling that there must be 'more'.

Maybe that's why, when I decided to move to London in 2003 after a wildly uncharacteristic fling, the only one not surprised was me. Maybe it took a stranger who didn't know all of the other stuff about me to hear what was unsaid, what I had kept buried for fear of hurting the people who cared about me most. That it didn't feel like 'home'.

Two and a half months later I arrived at Heathrow Airport, two suitcases beside me, half a dozen boxes to follow and my worldly possessions in a shipping container about to set sail. I knew one person (the fling who, despite his prior assurances, was not terribly helpful) and had a couple of email addresses on the back page of my diary. Nothing prepared me for the fear and loneliness of being unknown. But at the same time, the feeling of anonymity was intoxicating. And it felt 'right' to be here.

It's almost eight and a half years since that moment at Heathrow. A lot of the trappings and lifestyle choices have gone. My career took a bit of a beating and it's been confronting to be asked to prove myself over and over again. And I'm well and truly off the property ladder. But I've become a competent and confident cook. I relish a good deal, whether it's finding literary booty in a charity bookshop, enjoying a previously unknown movie or play, discovering the delights of a new neighbourhood, or marvelling at new places and faces in the snatched moment of a work trip. I have retreated to lick many a wound but know that my broken heart will mend again. I am brutal with friendships, letting go of those that don't respect my need for privacy and space and holding fiercely on to those that do. I appreciate the quiet moments, the peace I've found. I am surprised by how much strength I keep finding within to take those innumerable small steps every day. And best of all? I'm home."

Kym Hamer, Australian expat living in England

Every bit as important as knowing ourselves in order to find our way in intercultural life are the ability – and willingness – to learn from others. Finding the right people who inform and inspire us helps us build our personal sense of community.

GOING ALONG, AS COMMUNITY

"What has helped me the most in terms of developing emotional resilience has been the example of others. I've always looked for people who have knowledge and experience, have lived in a place much longer, who have a broader perspective. Although I may not always agree with all their opinions or attitudes, or even some of their actions, I learn from their experience and insight. People who don't have that, who don't become real learners, who have an inability to learn from others, sometimes have an arrogance about them. They tend to find cross-cultural life difficult, and often just don't make it. Hands down the thing that is the most helpful is to be in contact with people who have gone before me or are going along with me, so we can really do it as community."

Norm Viss, American repat after three decades away (Nigeria, Netherlands)

In emphasizing the importance of building community in a well-rounded life, we are actually talking about *communities*, plural – extensions of the interests and groups with which we associate ourselves. Out of the broader society in which we live, we seek to become part of several communities or create our own, each reflecting an important aspect of our identity.

FIND AND FEED OUR VARIOUS COMMUNITIES

"Emotional resilience and living within community are two of my biggest resources. The first, I feed within myself. The second, I find and feed with my participation and service. Growing up as a teenager and young woman in Cairo honed my emotional resilience and made me recognize the necessity of community. As the Egyptian press has been writing about a lot lately, sexual harassment on the streets of Cairo is a major issue affecting all women, not just foreigners. Even veiled women experience sexual harassment on the streets, and Egyptian women are increasingly speaking out to shift this gender-based violence that so deeply affects our quality of life.

As a teenager, I began to learn to access community resources when I felt overwhelmed, going to a friend's house, a quiet café or restaurant, or just spending time on my own to let the feelings process and pass. When I was at university, I increasingly called on a community of other women to help me in this process and we became a resource for one another, holding space for each other as we managed our reactions and feelings around this difficult situation. Learning to respond to stress as part of a community was invaluable.

Since then, I've recognized and valued the communities that we create and strengthen around us. They are of value to everyone, but especially to expats. Our nomadic lifestyle means that long-term communities may not be physically available to us, so it's up to us to find other ways –Skype, email, visits – to call on them, and to find and feed the communities that exist where we are, here and now."

Elie Calhoun, American ATCK who has lived most of her life in Africa, including Kenya, Egypt, Tanzania, Liberia and Senegal.

I'd like to end with this upbeat story about establishing your support network, thriving on change and redefining 'home'.

WHEN YOUR SENSE OF 'HOME' SHIFTS

"Strangely enough, my biggest challenge as an expat came when faced with the prospect of returning to my native country. In 2009, after I'd been away from England since 1998, my job at the company I had been working for was moved to England. I'd worked at the company for over 16 years, and it was the job that drew me initially to move to a foreign country. The natural thing to do both financially and career-wise was to return 'home', yet the situation led me to analyse what the experience of being an expat really meant to me.

I realised that the positive aspects of daily difference of language and culture were something my character thrived on – and I'd hardened myself to the difficult aspects, such as dealing with healthcare and arranging telephone, electricity and other utilities. I'd also established a strong, compact network of friends who took the role of family and support when things were both good or tough. I bought a house in Amsterdam, which gave a strong sense of permanence, and had improved my Dutch to a reasonable level.

In contrast, I'd heard about others who had returned finding it difficult to fit back in. Getting an Internet connection installed is just a hassle wherever you are, and not related to country. I myself had been a bit shocked on meeting up with a big group in the UK that year, finding a disconnection with English humour and a lack of awareness of what most English people chatted about.

Conclusion? My sense of 'home' had completely shifted to Amsterdam. That realisation itself came with both a sense of loss and of excitement. The journey I began in 1998 was intended to be a little adventure for a couple of years, yet had resulted in me losing my connection with England. I'd found a new home – it just wasn't the one I'd grown up in.

Deciding to cast yourself adrift 'for good' is not a light decision. Naturally I knew that it was a decision I could reverse at any time. Even so, such a gold-plated opportunity to return to England, with removal costs paid and a ready-made well-paid job to drop into, would probably be unlikely. The strength to take that challenge on and to embrace finally the reality of 'no going back' certainly came partly from 11 years of dealing with unusual circumstances and finding good people to help me through them.

I chose to stay in Amsterdam and keep facing those daily surprises, and have not looked back since, as the choice in itself proved to be a freeing moment in my life. I travelled the world, then returned to write a book about my favourite city, called Amsterdam... The Essence. I also met my girlfriend at a writers' group, and we have had a baby together – not something I expected at the age of 45! Being brave and resolutely sticking to the expat path, even when shunted firmly in the direction of a native return, has proven the best thing I could possibly have done."

David Beckett, British expat living in the Netherlands

I think this story reflects the entwined themes of the importance of community and of building a life quite nicely.

'Our nomadic lifestyle means that long-term communities may not be physically available to us, so it's up to us to find other ways to call on them, and to find and feed the communities that exist where we are, here and now.'

CAREER CONSIDERATIONS

In *CHAPTER 2: IDENTITY ISSUES IN EXPAT LIFE*, we discussed some of the obstacles accompanying partners – male and female – face trying to work abroad in their chosen field. Now we'll look at how several expats have handled such obstacles based on the situations they faced.

> *'One of the key aspects of remaining emotionally resilient is the ability to maintain a connection to your professional purpose.'*

REVIEW, RETHINK AND (POSSIBLY) REDIRECT

"Before you relocate take time to really think about what your career means to you. If you have a profession you know you want to continue whilst abroad, investigate the reality of doing so in your new location. If the idea of a career break seems at first an attractive proposition – great! But take time to consider whether not working for the duration of the assignment is also attractive.

From working with accompanying partners, and being one myself, I have seen how quickly the attraction of 'no work' can fade. Suddenly the reality of the new location, the absence of friends, family and social networks/ community that give meaning to your life back home is no longer there. There can be a sense of isolation, a loss of identity and a desire to find something that gives a sense of meaning and purposeful involvement to the new life. For some it comes down to this issue of contribution – making a valuable contribution through the roles in which they participate – of which work may be only one. And of course for many accompanying partners there is a financial need to work – and this makes the challenge of doing so whilst living abroad even more frustrating.

For those who do not feel a financial pressure to work, for some, the support role for the partner and family is sufficient. For others it is not. Neither response is right or wrong – and yet accompanying partners do seem to carry around this weight or guilt around in terms of can I, should I, expect to be able to have a career abroad. My response is 'why not?' You may need to be creative, inventive and a little patient in what form that career takes and how it develops, but the answer should not be to give up. In the research results from our Career Choice and the Accompanying Partner Survey, (see CHAPTER 2: IDENTITY ISSUES IN EXPAT LIFE, CAREER CHALLENGES FOR THE ACCOMPANYING PARTNER) those who could look back on their assignment experiences positively in relation to work, often talked about the opportunity provided by the assignment period to review, rethink and redirect their careers – regarding this as a very positive outcome."

Louise Wiles, British expat living in Portugal after Spain

Throughout this chapter I have reiterated the theme of building your external connections, getting to know people, making a concerted effort to become involved and focusing on finding or creating communities of which you become a part. This next story exemplifies the benefits of doing so with your career, and the risks of not.

NEED FOR POSITIVE SOCIAL CONNECTIONS

"My career went well in Dubai because I was brave and 'went for it'. I was not afraid to ask not only for work, but also for help. As a result my career took off big time here as I tried many different things. Things were baaad in Norway because I did not want to go, I had the wrong attitude from the start. Made no effort, got a bit down, did not ask for help and wallowed in what is sometimes called 'woundology'. We can feel united when sharing our wounds and moaning with others. I joined Stitch and Bitch for the first time. I learned I needed to surround myself with positive people and to take action and then things improved.

I did not want to be happy, I guess, so I made little effort to connect. I realised that without social connections I lose any chance of resilience and one day in the school playground, my one friend said to me, 'Jo, you know that you don't look anyone in the eye, don't you? That is why you are not connecting with people.' It was a hard lesson, but I realise now that I find resilience in my support team and when I do not try to connect I lose my strength."

Jo Parfitt
English expat (Oman, Norway, Dubai, Brunei) now living in the Netherlands

It is challenging to be the accompanying partner of a diplomat or businessperson whose work requires continual moves, and nowhere is this more evident than in trying to establish and maintain a career of your own. It seems just as you become familiar with the local/ national labor market, find a job, figure out how things are done in your new place of employment, begin accomplishing your intended objectives and hit your stride, it's time to move and start all over again.

DIPLOMACY AND DEDICATION

"Our first family post was Mozambique where I worked as an eligible family member with an American NGO on the response to the HIV/ AIDS epidemics. All in all, it was an extremely positive experience, with unconditional support from all my American counterparts, supervisors and managers. And yet there were also some challenges – working with the Ministry of Health and its branches, was tricky and demanded around-the-clock diplomacy, particularly when it came to suggesting better ways for the Ministry to conduct certain operations. During my final year in Mozambique, the Ministry appeared to be of the belief that expats were 'stealing' highly qualified jobs from Mozambicans. I watched several colleagues and partners lose both their jobs and their work visas, effectively forcing them to return home. Special work authorizations had to be requested from the Ministry of Labor, in a continuous process of renewals.

When my husband completed his tour and had to return to Washington for his next assignment, we agreed I would stay behind to finish my commitment to the contractor. I had started a national staff-training program, and needed to see it through. Was it difficult to be separated for almost an entire year, with two little children? Absolutely. But it was also well worth the sacrifices we all made. The experience gave me a sense of confidence, responsibility and self-respect.

Recently, back into the work force but this time in Brazil, wasn't easy. Our family arrived in the country in 2010, with two toddlers and a baby on the way. Just a few months after our youngest child was born, I began working full-time as a math and science teacher at the American School of Recife. In coordination with the school principal, I launched an experimental program to expose elementary school children to science. During our posting, I contributed to a project called Future Scientists, hosted by the Northeastern Center of Technology (CETENE).

The program encourages female students in public high schools to pursue a career in science. This program has been supported by Brazil's national government, as well as by the US consulate. The original idea came from the joint interest of the Brazilian government to establish innovative ways to stimulate the participation of young adult women in Science and Technology. My duty was to share experiences as a woman of science, working, researching and teaching in Brazil, and to discuss the challenges and alternatives to overcoming the difficulties.

'Is it possible to keep a career, without losing track of your personal life as a wife and mother, reminding yourself about your personal needs as somebody with a heart and mind, despite the constant moves?', I'm often asked by other expats and local fellows. My answer – 'Absolutely you can!' With the right guidance and support from family, friends and co-workers, a large dose of self-esteem, self-respect and the will to make a difference."

Raquel L. Miranda
US Foreign Service spouse in Bolivia after Mozambique and Brazil

When moving abroad, so many different aspects contributing to your identity are in flux all at the same time – home, friends and social life, job, favorite activities, language, sense of community. Often we begin to fill in the blanks and find our career takes the toughest hit of all, especially when credentials or experience aren't valued in the same way. It helps to have a strong sense of self, of your talents, skills and abilities, and what you can bring to a new situation so you're not starting over completely.

STAYING CONNECTED TO YOUR PROFESSIONAL PURPOSE

"One of the key aspects of remaining emotionally resilient is the ability to maintain a connection to your professional purpose. This can take the form of working, starting your own business, or volunteering. Living in a new environment can create uncertainty in many areas. One way to maintain a sense of self is to utilize your professional skills, which creates continuity with your previous life. With the technology available today it is easier and cheaper than ever to set up an online presence that will allow you to continue to make a contribution and find meaning in your work."

Stephanie Ward
American expat living in the Netherlands

Typical workplace problems exist everywhere, but working abroad often means there is an overlay of cultural issues, which can add to miscommunication and contribute to an already stressful situation. Rather than withdraw or suffer in silence, it helps to build a rapport with others, seek assistance as needed and try to take a broader perspective of what is going on.

WORKING THROUGH WORK DIFFICULTIES

"I recently had some difficulty with my supervisor. If I were in the States, I would have given my notice and quit. However, having my family relying on me for this job and not many backup opportunities available, I have had to stay at the job and try to work out the difficulty. This has definitely taken an emotional toll and required much emotional resilience, which at times was high and other times low. Also coming into play is the fact that my spouse is not working. This places more pressure on me to work things out at the office.

What has helped the most is having my family here with me (husband and two children). We're in this together and it has definitely brought us much closer. Also cultivating strong relationships at work has helped with settling in. And feeling okay with reaching out to folks and asking lots of questions has been key for me in acclimating to a new place."

Rose P., American expat living in the Netherlands

Earlier in this chapter we addressed the importance of giving back to your local community. I would also like to note in this section on career considerations that volunteering is not only important for emotional and social connections, but especially for professional well-being.

In her recent memoir *Expat Life: Slice by Slice*, I love that Apple Gidley titled one chapter *Volunteering is Work*. It is. Too often we forget this simple truth, bowing to societal pressures and the insecurities of others telling us that unpaid work is somehow inferior, trivial or lacking in value, when in reality it is often anything but. I'm reminded of an American expat, Carrie W., whom I got to know in the year she lived in Amsterdam. In a situation similar to that of many expats/ cross-culturals worldwide, Carrie's credentials in social work weren't recognized in her host country. Rather than let that stop her, she spent her time volunteering for an international non-governmental organization and a global foundation focused on helping refugees and women in conflict.

Just as a job opportunity in one of the organizations opened up, Carrie and her husband were heading back to the US for his job reassignment there. While job-hunting in New York City right before their return, she was pleasantly surprised to find it was her volunteer

> 'While job-hunting it was her volunteer experience which led to the job of her dreams. "Never underestimate the power and reach of your network."'

experience in the Netherlands which led to the job of her dreams. As Carrie says, "Never underestimate the power and reach of your network."

CHAPTER 10: CONNECTING INTERNALLY

We've considered many ways to build connections with the world around us. Now we'll look at developing our personal connections more deeply. We'll also discuss how to create and celebrate rituals honoring our experiences and memories, handle the trials and tribulations of transitions, and if repatriation is in the cards, prepare for returning home.

MAINTAIN YOUR UNION

There is no doubt maintaining a good relationship with your significant other takes considerable care and effort. It's easier to stay connected when things are going along well, and there is sufficient time and attention for each other. As we become busier and daily life becomes more complicated and hectic – often coinciding with major transitional changes such as the arrival of children, new job(s), a(nother) move abroad – many couples report that time for each other seems to fall by the wayside.

FINDING YOUR ROLE MODEL IN YOUR PARTNER

"For me, what helps in cross-cultural life is to find role models – people I can look up to, who challenge me, who show the same characteristics that are important to me. I think it's essential. The best scenario is if you can find that in your partner, which I certainly have been able to do."

Norm Viss, American repat after three decades away (Nigeria, Netherlands)

Highly mobile, global life holds plenty of opportunities that can contribute towards partners drifting apart, often without either realizing. Job pressures can include extensive travel (falling on both the traveler and the one left on the home front), worries over job loss or constant organization restructuring, dealing with cultural challenges in an international workplace or the emotional and/ or financial challenge of a partner not finding suitable employment. Your youngest child is suddenly diagnosed with a learning disability. Your middle-schooler doesn't want to move *again*. Your teen withdraws or acts out as they grapple with who they are and what they want to do in life. Whether it's you or your friends moving, no one likes having to say goodbye. Accidents, illnesses, issues with elderly parents – all contribute to your pile of concerns. On top of it all, a cross-cultural overlay permeates every aspect of daily life, adding another dimension of potential stress. The result can be two people working so hard to get through the day, they lose sight of what brought them together in the first place.

The first of 'Expert Expat' Robin Pascoe's books I read was, *Raising Global Nomads: Parenting Abroad in an On-Demand World*. Her worldly experience, complete candor, illustrative stories, and knack for getting to the crux of what matters in complicated issues drew me in. By the time I was a third of the way through, I knew I would also be buying her book on safeguarding and strengthening relationships while abroad.

I devoured *that* book, *Moveable Marriage: Relocate Your Relationship Without Breaking It*, in chunks as I did daily diligence on the exercise bike. I felt I had a pretty solid marriage with Husband, but the stresses of the previous year weren't to be ignored. I'd weathered six months of solo-parenting while Husband went ahead of the family to start his job. I got the house ready to put on the market, sold the cars and orchestrated an intercontinental move. I made sure Son and Daughter were situated in a new home, new school and new way of life. I survived culture shock while keeping a keen eye on the rest of the family, and reassured my parents and family members we were all doing fine. While I didn't particularly miss the job I'd left, I did find myself missing my career and lamenting the loss of my professional identity. After all that, I figured it wouldn't hurt to see what eye-opening insights Pascoe had in store for me on the marital front.

The beauty of Pascoe's writing is she doesn't shy away from discussing the tough stuff that can throw a relationship off-kilter, especially when living across cultures and time zones – balance of power issues, intimacy, irritation, resentment, isolation, loneliness, dependence, parenting challenges. I was hoping for the same frankness of her parenting book and wasn't disappointed.

Writing about the hustle and bustle to unpack, put the furniture and belongings in their proper places and settle into life in a new place, she mentioned how she and her husband would sit back to survey their progress and immediately fall into an argument over something trivial: *'While we discovered the appropriate cupboards and closets in which to put our belongings, we conveniently overlooked finding the right spot for our feelings. Everything was in its place except our marriage.'*

> 'No matter what you go through in expat/ cross-cultural life, at some point you realize you and your significant other are either in this together – or you're not.'

It doesn't get more forthright than that, and once again Pascoe delivered up savvy advice and real-life examples in her easygoing, straightforward manner. Small wonder I've kept her books near at hand these past few years.

No matter what you go through in expat/ cross-cultural life, at some point you realize you and your significant other are either in this together – or you're not.

A UNITED FRONT

"The stewardess closed the airplane door. Fighting a sudden feeling of claustrophobia I looked at my husband. He smiled and shrugged his shoulders as if to say, Here we go, it'll be okay.

My two eldest daughters were strapped into the huge seats that made them seem younger than their four and two years. My youngest daughter, only three months old, slept soundly in the cot provided by the airline, hanging on the wall in front of me. 'This is going to be some adventure, especially with these three little ones,' I thought to myself. At that moment all I could think of was how to get through the flight. The girls were awake but tired after their early start. Over the next twelve hours my husband and I took turns with the girls – playing, reading, feeding, trips to the toilet, walking up and down the plane. Our daughters were already experienced travellers but that didn't stop them being fed up on planes.

I looked around and saw other passengers reading, sleeping or watching films. I hadn't even bothered to bring a book – I knew there would be no point. And with all the baby bottles, nappies, spare clothes, etc. there was no space in my carry-on rucksack for anything else. Now and again my husband and I talked to each other – one or the other of us asking for a toy, snack or something for one of the girls. In that plane with hundreds of other people we were a small, self-contained unit, working quietly together to keep our daughters happy.

Finally the plane touched down and I stood up to stretch and retrieve my rucksack from the overhead locker. An elderly man who had been sitting a few rows behind us passed me and said, 'Your husband and you make a great team'.

I looked at him and smiled. I felt exhausted and we still had to get off the plane, through the airport, hire a car and get to our apartment, but his comment lifted my spirits. Yes, we are a good team I thought, looking over to where my husband was helping one of the girls to put on her coat.

It was good to know we were in all this together."

Sareen McLay, Scottish expat (Oman, Malaysia) now living in the Netherlands and preparing to repatriate

So many contributors shared stories of adversity, from illness to house fire to job loss to desperate loneliness. Not every relationship survived the turmoil and tribulations, but for some, the adversity they faced together strengthened their union.

GAINING A RESILIENT RELATIONSHIP

"What I gained from my expat experience is a resilient relationship with my partner. We've been through so much together in our lives in the past ten years, more than we'd ever have weathered if we had remained a couple in London back in 2002.

I think both of us should be very proud of having maintained our relationship and love through some personal and family difficulties and despite – at times – loud verbal reasoning and positioning (normal speak – arguing!). We've managed to retain a sense of humour and to revisit regularly what it was that made us find the other an attractive individual and the person we wanted to be with, as well appreciate what we give to each other now. That's helped a great deal. So I'd like to celebrate the resilient nature of love and relationships too."

Nicola McCall, British expat/ repat

A relationship can fall apart anywhere, leaving pain, destruction and emotional upheaval. When it happens in a different country or culture, far away from family, it can be all the more devastating, with tremendous repercussions rippling behind in its wake. We've all heard the horror stories, sometimes hitting closer to home than we'd prefer.

> 'Some expat families bond more with each other. Perhaps that is because you draw on each other more. I think we are closer from our experience.'

The husband who thought wedding vows didn't count when he traveled for business. The spouse who dallied with a teacher at the children's school. The husband who went ahead to the next assignment, then told his wife (and daughter) not to bother coming, they had grown apart and he'd found a new relationship. People caught unaware, sometimes without access to funds, work prospects, legal authority to make decisions or a visa. Each tale is a cautionary one – be prepared, be proactive, take the emotional pulse of your relationship often, try to stay closely connected if possible.

If the primary relationship within a family suffers, the relationships between parents and children will likely suffer too. We must strengthen and protect our union as much as humanly possible, for the sake of all involved. However, despite everyone's best efforts, sometimes separation and divorce are inevitable. If this is the case, both parties need to put aside differences and hard feelings, and focus on remaining a viable, centering presence in their children's lives.

It's easy to only focus on the difficulties that can befall expatriate/ cross-cultural families (e.g., culture shock, loneliness, loss of people and places along the way, unresolved grief). It's also important to keep in mind many relationships – and indeed entire families – are closer for having lived a mobile, international way of life.

CLOSER AS A RESULT

"Count your blessings as to how fortunate you are to be mentally stimulated in a new environment and learning something new every day. Someone told me expat families bond more with each other. Perhaps that is because you draw on each other more as you move around. I think we are closer from our experience of living abroad."

Laura, American expat living in the UK

As the overall number of expats/ cross-culturals increases, so do the number of those falling in love with someone of another culture or nationality. Often referred to as 'lovepats', Canadian expat Wendy Williams prefers the term 'GloLos' in her entertaining and educational book on multicultural relationships, *The Globalisation of Love*. Williams covers much territory (pun intended), addressing how differences in nationality, culture, values, religion, language and 'GloLo Colours' – her preferred label for issues of race, ethnicity and diversity – may play out in the relationships of intercultural couples and their families. In her book, *Black and (A)broad: Traveling Beyond the Limitations of Identity*, American Carolyn Vines offers insights into how issues of race, family, loss and identity eventually led to a cross-cultural marriage and new life in the Netherlands. Hers is a candid, deeply personal account of asking – and answering – those lingering questions of home, belonging, identity and love. Whether you're involved in an intercultural union or not, or know someone who is, Williams' and Vines' books are definitely worth reading.

MAINTAIN CONNECTIONS THAT MATTER

We're miles, oceans and time zones away. We do have technology to help stay connected and for that I'm grateful. But it does take effort to use, and to stay abreast of new developments and options available. It can also be confusing trying to remember who prefers to remain in contact via which method(s).

The younger generations have preferences when it comes to maintaining their connectivity with others (e.g., texting and online social media are in, email and calling on phones are out). I can text Daughter if she's out with friends, and only actually call her if necessary. With Son back in the US I send him Facebook messages, always remembering to *never* post on his FB wall out of respect for his privacy. Yet I want eye contact, the ability to observe his facial expressions and body language as well as hear his voice. So we augment FB messages with biweekly Skype sessions. It does all of us good to see each other face to face.

Often members of older generations have little or no level of comfort downloading or installing software and using tools such as Skype, Facebook, Twitter, Google+, even email. And why would they? They grew up with archaic 'snail mail' and telephones as their main avenues of interface.
The advent of the Internet, and subsequent technological advances in online social media connectivity, have come *after* they left the workplace during what for many – although certainly not all – represents their peak years for taking in significant

amounts of new information and acquiring additional skills. They simply haven't had the access to, or experience with, the barrage of social media developments of recent years. We've experienced this firsthand with my elderly parents and in-laws. It becomes more challenging as they age and become more forgetful, let alone face dementia and Alzheimer's.

> 'There is no point pining for a past time or previous location as things will have changed since the memories you made there were formed.'

SEEING YOUR HOME COUNTRY THROUGH ROSE-TINTED GLASSES

"It is all too easy for an expat to view their home country through rose-tinted spectacles, especially if life in the new country is more challenging than expected. Visits home are wonderful because you see the people you miss, everyone makes time to see you as you are only there for a limited time and you enjoy all the things that you love about your country.

Often however, when you return to your home country and the friends and family that remained there after you moved, you can sometimes feel your departure was of little significance to them. Of course the life that has changed most is your own, and nobody wants to hear their loved ones say that life is not the same since you left, but being faced with your friends and family continuing their lives without you, can leave you without a sense of belonging even at home.

This has a different effect on different people. It feels more poignant to those who have a deep-felt fondness for their home country or who are from close families. It is certainly hardest to come to terms with the first time you visit home after living overseas.

They say it is the people who make the place, and I believe that is the reason the continued feeling of belonging can be hard to sustain. It took me a long time to understand and accept that a place is rarely the same revisited after a period of time has passed. My light bulb moment was when I realised that is because the people have changed. The world's population is more global than ever before and it is common for people to move internationally. I have taught myself to make the most of the people and things around me each and every day. There is no point pining for a past time or previous location as things will have changed since the memories you made there were formed.

Personally, I embrace my mostly nomadic lifestyle. I have come to terms with the fact that things are always a little different when I return 'home' for a visit. I have been fortunate enough to call several different countries home, to enjoy many varied experiences and make friends with lots of wonderful people from a whole host of places. As a result I feel perhaps not quite 'at home' but certainly very comfortable in several places.

I still have days when I really miss people who are far away though. The Internet has made expat life a million times easier. I regularly use email to stay in touch with people and Voice Over Internet Protocol (VOIP) and webcams to talk live to friends and family who are miles away. I love sharing photos via Facebook and the included feeling you get from seeing your friends' wedding photos and pictures of their children. It heightens the feeling of involvement if, because you have chosen to live life as an expat, you cannot be somewhere in person."

Liv Gaunt, an adult TCK now living in Turkey

I think the key phrase in the last story is 'it heightens the feeling of involvement'. When we are away from family and friends *feeling involved* is what we are seeking. We may not be able to be with them physically, at least not as often as we'd like, but there are things we can do to bridge the distance. We have to be prepared to meet our loved ones on whatever communication terms they feel most comfortable – if it means calling your parents on the phone, Skyping with your siblings, chatting on FB with your friends and writing Aunt Georgina an old-fashioned letter, so be it. Small price to pay in time, money and effort to remain connected.

'We can see our children visibly relax after the long journey when they reach one of their grandparents' homes. The feeling of security, familiarity and routine alongside a strong relationship has been worth every minute of every flight we have travelled.'

MAINTAINING FAMILIAL CONNECTIONS

"Our family life was never going to be one where grandparents lived along the road from us and we could pop in and see them whenever we wanted. Work had brought us to live in the East coast of Scotland, quite a drive from our parents' homes in the West. Visits happened only every few months and a gradual awareness grew in me

that the relationship between my children and their grandparents could never be close at this rate.

Surprisingly enough it took a move to Oman in the Middle East for us to create a pattern for a solid relationship between our parents and their grandchildren. Although the visits were still only a couple of times a year, the amount of time spent on each visit lengthened. Our family came out to visit us and stayed for at least two weeks at a time. This meant the grandparents became familiar with the daily routines of our children and the grandparents themselves were familiar to our children.

It was with pride our children introduced their grandparents to new experiences and countries and were delighted at the gifts brought to them from 'home'. Who knew an imported packet of Smarties could build a relationship?

In return my husband and I took advantage of the longer holidays from work now available and every summer travelled to our home base, the UK. There we stayed for at least a week at a time with each set of parents. Aware that we were both lucky to be able to do this, as our family get on pretty well with each other, the other option would have been to rent a house for this period.

After returning to the UK every year for the past twelve years we can see our children visibly relax after the long journey when they reach one of their grandparents' homes. The feeling of security, familiarity and routine alongside a strong relationship with their grandparents has been worth every minute of every flight we have travelled with them."

Sareen McLay, Scottish expat (Oman, Malaysia) now living in the Netherlands and preparing to repatriate

Maintaining relationships with people we care about but are no longer with is important, but keep in mind it ought not be at the expense of our meeting and making new friends. I'm reminded of the line from a song I learned as a Girl Scout years ago: *'Make new friends, but keep the old; one is silver and the other gold.'* Treasure both.

> *'Maintaining and adding to rituals picked up along our journeys reflect the places we've been and the people we've loved.'*

NOT NEEDING TO HANG ON QUITE AS TIGHTLY

"When I first arrived here, I wanted to hang on to all of my friendships I had left behind in the States. This resulted in some exorbitant phone bills. Thank God for the Internet. I spent hours posting my pictures and a sort of blog on Google+ to share my experience with those I'd left behind. That really helped me to not be so lonely. In time I became immersed in everyday life here, and I don't need to hang on to those back home quite as tightly. I still keep in touch, but it's definitely at a more reasonable pace now."

Patti Tito, American expat living in the Netherlands

What matters is not so much the quantity of interactions with those we care about as the quality of our involvement. We don't want to become overly involved in the goings on of family/ friends in other places, especially at the expense of developing new connections where we find ourselves now, but we don't have to relegate them to the occasional contact. Finding the balance can be tricky, but if we use as a guide how we feel about them – and how they make us feel – it tends to work itself out.

VALUE RITUALS

Rituals are ceremonial rites, practices or observances we use to honor our history, cultural traditions, social customs, religious beliefs and values. They are important because of their meaning to us, and can also include food, clothing, symbols, objects, songs or sounds. Rituals are especially important to create a climate of support, security and belonging as expats travel around the world. Maintaining and adding to rituals picked up along our journeys reflect the places we've been and the people we've loved. Similarly, shared time and experiences help create a sense of togetherness with family and friends.

One thing I adore about Julia Simens's book, *Emotional Resilience and the Expat Child* – aside from its emphasis on emotional resilience – is her respect for rituals. I interviewed her for my expat blog and learned more about her views.

"I feel rituals are valuable because they are a way to develop a sense of shared joys and positive memories, but perhaps the most important thing a family ritual can provide is the space and time for emotional healing if the family relationships need that time. Good memories help eclipse the upsetting ones. Rituals provide a sense of security and can be soothing."

How does Simens suggest you might go about creating family rituals?

"A family ritual is anything your family does together deliberately. The routine of whatever you do is what counts. Just make sure you do it consistently. Rituals can and do evolve over time. Start with acknowledging how special something felt, and the verbalization that you'd like to do more of this same activity in the future."

> 'Rituals are valuable because they are a way to develop a sense of shared joys and positive memories, but perhaps the most important thing is the space and time for emotional healing if the family relationships need that. Good memories help eclipse the upsetting ones. Rituals provide a sense of security and can be soothing.'

Rituals abound in life, and it doesn't so much matter *what* you choose to do as that you *do* it. One friend has a tradition of having her family photographed standing in the same exact position – often wearing shirts of the same color – no matter where they are in the world. They share these photos with family/ friends and then place them in a digital picture frame in their home to enjoy memories of the places they've lived and visited. Another family volunteers at a different local charity each year on the father's birthday. One serial expat runs 10 km in every country she lives and has made a quilt out of the race T-shirts. Many expats throw celebrations to mark the national day of their birth/ home country.

We have made a conscious effort in our family to celebrate rituals, melding the old with the new. Cooking up a big Thanksgiving dinner with a (smaller) turkey and the trimmings is a given, even though it means hunting down certain ingredients or making do with substitutions. Wherever we have lived, our Christmas decorations have made us feel at home; wherever we travel, we pick up a new ornament to add to the collection, and we've woven in some traditions of the Dutch *Sinterklaas*. I also pick up decorative thimbles on our travels – they connect me to the memory of my grandmother; her simple one I inherited has pride of place in the collection.

Here in The Hague we always take visiting family and friends, or mark end-of-school year milestones, at 'our' Greek restaurant. There's something special about setting out from our house together, chatting on the tram ride with anticipation building, poring over the menu and recommending favorite dishes, enjoying a leisurely meal and the company of those we love.

HANDLING TRANSITIONS

Despite the wide range of positive attributes a global lifestyle may entail, there is no doubt the comings and goings of expat transitions can be difficult. Continual loss is painful; the cumulative effect can be disorienting, even heart-rending. Regardless of whether you are heading for a new destination or remaining behind while others around you leave, there's a reason why David Pollock and Ruth Van Reken wrote of the need to 'leave well to enter well', encouraging us in *Third Culture Kids* to make the time and effort to 'build a **RAFT**':

- **Reconciliation:** Reconciliation is making sure we part from people, places and situations on the best possible terms. This means dealing with any tension in our relationships, resolving disagreements, and doing our best not to 'lean away' from others as we prepare to leave or be left. This is integral to ensuring we don't merely ignore difficulties or block bad feelings; doing so ignores the need for resolution and closure, and sets us up for repeating similar negative behaviors in the days and years ahead.

- **Affirmation:** Affirmation is acknowledging that each person in a relationship matters. In action, it means letting others know what they mean to us, and allowing others to share what we mean to them. If we don't, we can feel as though people never really cared about us. We risk keeping our relationships casual, not letting others get close and know the real us.

- **Farewells:** Farewells call for saying goodbye to the aforementioned significant people, places, pets and possessions for whom we care deeply. Have coffee or go to lunch with your closest friends, write them a card or letter telling how and why you treasure their friendship. Children can bake cookies or burn a CD for friends, sign their yearbooks and 'friendship journals,' make a photo montage, get together for a last movie or pizza party.

As a family, visit your favorite restaurant, the park or places you used to go. Take pictures, and buy souvenirs which mean something to you and will remind you of the pleasant times and deep ties you have enjoyed. Be sure each family member takes their own treasured items along. These items themselves aren't what is important, it's what they *represent* that matters.

Don't underestimate the pain and grief that comes with no longer being able to see, speak and spend time with friends and family members. The loss of these immediate connections can be overwhelming. Sometimes the grief hits you full on, as if you've run into a wall, other times it is like the tide, waves and waves of sadness and loneliness washing over you. Wherever possible, it is important to put in place arrangements for staying in touch *before* you (or they) leave.

> 'Part of emotional resilience to me is to simply have faith in our ability to cope. We live through tough emotional times, times we need to feel, but ultimately we work through them and come out the other side.'

Embrace technology to help maintain connections through email, Skype, Facebook, Twitter, Google+, WhatsApp for text messaging, and of course telephone calls. Knowing you can catch up with your best friend on Facebook, check your email for a message from your former neighbor, or you will Skype with the grandparents every Sunday evening are the little lifelines which help us stay connected and ease our transitions, regardless of whether we're the ones doing the leaving or not.

- **Think Destination:** As you build the other three parts of your RAFT, you can begin looking ahead to where you're going. In addition to books and articles, the Internet affords us a plethora of expat, cross-cultural and travel web directories, websites, forums and blogs full of the kind of information and feedback to help you explore and get to know your next location in detail. Deal with the practical matters (e.g., housing, employment, schools), but don't neglect emotional considerations.

For those staying behind, your destination may not be changing, but this step still remains important and worthy of your attention. It entails the difficult process of envisioning life without those who are leaving, what holes in our lives they will leave. Don't wait until you are heading out the door for your weekly tea time (or tee time) with a good friend to realize this ritual is no longer available to you. Prepare ahead to help ease the pain by thinking how your life will be changed, even in the smallest of ways. Acknowledge the loss, appreciate what it has meant to you, and start planning a new project, hobby, class or excursion.

APPRECIATION AS AFFIRMATION

"The body's and mind's abilities to heal themselves are incredible and part of emotional resilience to me is to simply have faith in our ability to cope. We will live through tough

emotional times, times that we need to feel, but ultimately we work through them and come out the other side – appreciative of the friendships and times we all had, and looking forward to new friendships and planning our visits in years to come, and meanwhile learning to relate through Facebook and emails rather than over dinner face-to-face."

Louise Wiles, British expat living in Portugal after Spain

Several months ago I caught Tina Quick's webinar *TCKs, Cross-Cultural Kids and the University Transition*, sponsored by the organization USA Girl Scouts Overseas. In my notes I captured Quick's comments regarding unresolved grief (another of her 'Four Pearls'): *'Good grief is naming our loss, to mourn it, grow from it and move on.'*

YOU ARE NEVER ALONE

"Any feeling you're going through right now, someone else has experienced before. You are never alone. That's the most important thing to remember, and the most dangerous thing you can do is to assume you are alone, and retreat into yourself.

Hundreds of thousands of people go through cultural transitions every single day, and have gone through what you are experiencing. Make the effort to go out and find them, whether it is at your school, new community, or even online. They will be your support network, and you will be exponentially happier because of them.

Just because you've left a place does not mean you've left the people behind. I've moved so many times in my life and the one thing that has helped me keep it together is an incredible support network of friends, all over the world. Online tools have made it easy to find and keep in touch with people – there are no excuses for not reaching out.

The people in my support network come from all different stages of my life and remind me of who I am and where I come from. These relationships are like a comfy couch you can settle into it at any time. But, they also serve as a reminder there are great friends to be made anywhere you go. You just need to go out and find them."

Steph Yiu, Canadian ATCK (Hong Kong, Taiwan, Singapore) now living in the US after Scotland

The key to making an emotionally healthy transition in a resilient manner is not to hide your sadness or stress, but to acknowledge and face these feelings and what they represent. An

> *'Good grief is naming our loss, to mourn it, grow from it and move on.'*

important part of your life – regardless of whether you enjoyed it or not – is coming to an end. You can take the friendships and the memories forward, but to ease into your next phase, you have to admit to the pain of saying goodbye.

HELPING CHILDREN WITH TRANSITIONS

The beauty of a growing body of expat literature is that it eventually becomes big enough to branch off into niches. One such niche is children's books. For younger children, Helen Maffini, creator of www.emotional-intelligence-education.com, wrote *Sammy's Next Move*. Emmanuelle Payot Karpathakis published *Pixie's New Home* last year (2012), and followed up this year with *Pixie's Holidays*, about a child whose family returns 'back home' for holidays/ vacations to find much has changed in their absence. Simone Costa Eriksson and Ana Serra's *The Mission of Detective Mike: Moving Abroad*, is another good story to which children can relate.

For teens, Pollock and Van Reken's *Third Culture Kids*, and Julia Simens' *Emotional Resilience and the Expat Child*, are excellent books to help prepare both young and adolescent children for transitions, whether they are the ones leaving or not. Similarly, *Robin Pascoe's Raising Global Nomads*, Tina Quick's *The Global Nomad's Guide to University Transition*, and Dr. Lisa Pittman and Diana Smit's book *Expat Teens Talk: Peers, Parents, and Professionals Offer Support, Advice and Solutions in Response to Expat Life Challenges as Shared by Expat Teens*, are great resources for teens.

While written for TCKs/ global nomads preparing for university, Quick's book is particularly helpful for any teen or young adult facing a major transition such as moving to a new place, repatriating, changing schools, taking a gap year or diving into the working world. Quick reminds readers they're not alone, everyone encounters bumpy times, even those who have lived in their home culture their entire lives: *'Even though you have decided to become a part of this new place, you will still experience many emotional highs and lows. It takes time to settle in and feel normal again, but you will get there... Treat it as though you expect it to be different.'*

> *'You can take the friendships and the memories forward, but to ease into your next phase, you have to admit to the pain of saying goodbye.'*

HELP CHILDREN EXPRESS FEELINGS AND EMOTIONS

"I believe it is very important to say proper goodbyes and to ensure your kids have that opportunity. I have written a children's book, Sammy's Next Move, because I wanted a story my kids could relate to about moving abroad, and the feelings and emotions a child is likely to experience. I couldn't find one and the story grew in my mind. I hope it helps other children to be able to express their feelings and to know they are not alone and their feelings are normal.

I definitely think talking and giving children the chance to express their opinions is essential as well. Even if their opinion is they don't want to move, talking, and looking at the pros and cons can help a child to be more accepting of a move they are resisting."

Helen Maffini, serial expat now living in her eleventh country

All but the very youngest children can be encouraged to put their feelings into words, and reading a book together, or conversing around the dinner table, can help start the conversation. Don't expect everything they share to be positive and upbeat. They need an accepting environment in which to voice their fears and concerns. In coaxing them to express themselves, you lay the groundwork for helping them work through these difficult issues.

If at all possible, try to arrange for house pets to make the transition with you. Expat memoirs abound with sad tales of having to leave behind a beloved pet. In a new place where you don't yet know a soul, it's comforting to have the family dog, cat or guinea pig around.

PETS CAN HELP COMPLETE US

"Bringing our pet with us was important to us. It was expensive and a bit of a hassle, but definitely worth it. We felt more complete and more settled once he arrived."

Laura, American expat living in the UK

Have your children identify an item or items to take along which are meaningful to them. To you it may be a silly paper hat from a birthday party, a concert poster, inexpensive bracelet or polished stone from the beach, but to your child it embodies memories of the treasured friendship he or she shared with the a special friend. We'll discuss more about helping our children share their feelings in *CHAPTER 11: COMMUNICATION*.

IF REPATRIATING, PREPARE FOR LANDING

For those of us who intend to return at some point to our birth/ passport country – or a favorite place we found along the way – there is a tendency to think in terms of 'going home'. While obviously there are elements of the country and culture which will be familiar, it is important to remember that after years of living in other cultures, the one we thought we knew will seem far different – alien, even – than expected. Time has moved on, people and places have changed. *We've* changed.

In hindsight, repatriation is viewed by many as the most difficult transition of all. I can't tell you the number of repats who talk of it taking a good two years or more before they felt settled, let alone 'at home'. Once again we have Robin Pascoe to thank for writing a truthful account of the ups and downs of 'going home' in, *Homeward Bound: A Spouse's Guide to Repatriation*. She captures the other side of the culture shock coin in 're-entry shock'. She writes of the immobilizing nature of dealing with too much change, and the adjustment to differing cultural values when expats/ cross-culturals return to communities primarily comprised of less traveled, seemingly more insulated folk. As Pascoe wisely points out, a 'good' repatriation – if one can be had – is comprised of three parts: closure with both your last overseas residence and your cross-cultural lifestyle; chaos and limbo while transitioning; and ultimately a period of reconnecting with your former country/ culture.

We do well to start thinking about repatriation long before it arrives. For many of us, we have at least some idea when that might be. Often this coincides with milestones in our children's lives – returning for high school or university education, or when they leave the nest – or our own employment opportunities or retirement plans. Repatriation can be hastened along when our children start to marry and have children, or family members become ill, incapacitated or advanced in age. This

> 'Talking and giving children the chance to express their opinions is essential. Even if their opinion is they don't want to move, talking, and looking at the pros and cons can help a child to be more accepting of a move they are resisting.'

is particularly true for those of us at the point in life when we're sandwiched between the needs of our children and our elderly parents. For some, we reach a point where we've had enough of periodically moving and starting over, and realize it's time to settle down.

Whether repatriation sneaks up on us or is planned for assiduously, there is much we can do to ease our transition and make it less difficult, less painful, less overwhelming. In order to make our way through Robin Pascoe's aforementioned three parts of repatriation, we would do well to focus on enhancing and maintaining resilience in preparing emotionally to leave well, transition, and build the new life we desire and deserve. In order to take leave well of our last home, we already know to employ Pollock and Van Reken's **RAFT** (**R**econciliation, **A**ffirmation, **F**arewells and **T**hink Destination), outlined in the preceding section, to help guide us.

Preparing to repatriate is likely to be more a more emotionally challenging transition than any previous move. We've got to acknowledge our cross-cultural lifestyle is coming to a close, while simultaneously adjusting mentally to the notion we're entering a new stage in our lives. This is quite a shift in thinking, and we ought not underestimate its impact. We are building a new, more permanent life in which the thought of eventually moving on is no longer present in the back of our minds.

EMOTIONALLY PREPARING FOR EVENTUAL RETURN

"When I first went to Australia with my young family, I wanted to spend as much time as possible establishing roots there and exploring new and exciting places on the other side of the globe. I reluctantly scheduled a couple of weeks a year to visit family back in the US. I was happy to embrace our new life abroad and did not feel strong pulls to return. Midway through my expat experience, I began to worry about my lack of desire to ever return to the US. My new external perspective made me quite critical of American culture and politics. In recent years, aging parents, college searches, kids returning to the US to attend university, and the purchase of a vacation home in California have resulted in us spending much more time in the US. At first I was annoyed that my heartstrings were being pulled and I was feeling forced to spend more time than I'd like back in the US – there is still so much of the world I want to see! Now, though, I've come to look on this new phase as a good thing. I'm being emotionally prepared for an eventual return to the US, and building more ties there."

Sara C.
American expat now living in the Netherlands after Australia and Scotland

Preparing ourselves emotionally for repatriation also means facing the realization our identity is undergoing a major overhaul. For years we've been of thinking of ourselves as expats, cross-culturals or global nomads, reinforced by logistics, passports, residency cards, visas and requisite explanations whenever we travel. We're become used to those little events which remind us we're not entirely embedded in our host cultures, but

> 'A 'good' repatriation is comprised of closure with both your last overseas residence and your cross-cultural lifestyle; chaos and limbo while transitioning; and ultimately a period of reconnecting with your former country/ culture.'

have learned to shrug them off with the comforting thought 'it's to be expected in expat life'. Now we're headed to a country/ culture which seems familiar but slightly out of focus, as if we're looking through a telescope with the wrong lens.

We may well have family and friends there, but each relationship will undergo an adjustment as it begins to sink in we're back for good. As we negotiate the new ground rules for our relationships, we may find them permanently altered, not always for the good. In the case of previous friendships, we may pick up where we left off with some, or we may find the bonds have weakened or dissolved. We may find ourselves in different stages of life, with varying interests and less in common. It happens. The sooner we admit and accept that, the sooner we can get on with constructing our new life.

Identity congruence is an important factor during repatriation, especially as both how we see ourselves and how others see us are undergoing significant change. How will we spend our days? What will become our life's work? What is our broader purpose? With whom will we connect, spend time, become friends? What are our interests and activities? Some questions are more philosophical and existential than others, yet they all need to be answered. It won't happen overnight, either. It takes time to mull over the options and possibilities, envision ourselves in our new environment, make choices on the path we want to take. One thing is clear: the identity agreement we create must somehow incorporate our having lived across cultures. Hopefully we use the fourth part of our identity – who we would like to become – as a template for fashioning our new existence.

Another integral aspect of repatriation is where we will be living. In *CHAPTER 2: IDENTITY ISSUES IN EXPAT LIFE*, I shared the story of Ruth Van Reken asking serial expat high school students whether their families had a physical 'home' back in their birth/ passport country, where they could spend summers, holidays or time between moves. She raised this issue during a presentation for international parents to highlight the importance, if at all possible, of maintaining a place of stability within such a mobile lifestyle. Having a home to spend time at, and return to, helps reinforce connections to family, friends, country and culture. Not everyone has the opportunity to have such a place, but for those who do, it will make the emotional (and physical) part of repatriation that much easier.

> 'It behooves us to view repatriation as the move to a new country and culture that it is.'

It needn't be a home you own yourself. Several expats told of using their parents' home or a family property as their 'permanent' base. The families of two of Daughter's friends, and another of Son's, return regularly to properties purchased in the home countries of one or both of the parents. I have friends who have done the same. As one put it, "Through twelve years and moves to four other countries, we have returned to this farm whenever possible. My sons have come to see this place as their home. Now that we all live in different countries, returning to the farm where I was born and grew up, and where they spent childhood holidays and summers, is the closest we will ever get to living together again. It *is* our home."

Another expat friend began the process of identifying a place to serve as the family's base when her children went off to university back in their home country. She and her husband are still living abroad and will continue to do so for several years until retirement. They talked it over and decided to focus on purchasing a particular style of house in a specific neighborhood of the city they loved most. Eventually they found exactly what they were looking for, and as they spend more time there – individually and as a family – it has become the 'home' they had hoped, and to which they will retire.

When and if repatriation does happen, it behooves us to do our best to view our repatriation as the move to a new country and culture that it is.

CHAPTER 11: COMMUNICATION

I am using the concept of communication to cover a wide range of personal interactions in which we learn to feel safe sharing our feelings, thoughts, concerns and needs. It is conducting an inventory of our emotions in order to properly identify them, and calming ourselves to decrease personal distress when our emotions threaten to overwhelm us. It includes observing ourselves, and others, for signs that we or someone we care about is disoriented, confused, having difficulty. It is being 'heard'. This can be done verbally, in writing, wordlessly sharing an experience together or through other forms of interaction. We let people 'know' who we are, and they us:

- **Accurately identify and acknowledge your emotions:** Honestly admitting we're lonely or frustrated helps us reach out.

- **Understand we are not alone:** It is common to feel alienated, adrift or sad at times during transitions from people/ places we care about to new situations.

- **Employ self-calming techniques:** They help us quiet negative self-beliefs, regain our composure, clear our heads and feel better.

- **Pick up on signals in ourselves or someone else:** If they indicate unhappiness, loneliness or a struggle with transitions and change, we are better able to respond appropriately.

- **Be heard and understood:** Make it a point to share our thoughts and feelings verbally, in writing or by experiencing activities or events with others.

- **Embrace technology:** Research and learn more about what we may be going through, as well as for country, cultural and region-specific information.

- **Stay in touch with family/ friends:** Email, Skype, Facebook, Twitter, text messaging and phone calls encourage connections, but ought not be at the expense of building new ones.

- **Above all, we practice empathy and compassion, on ourselves and with others.**

EMBRACING OUR EMOTIONS AND IDENTITY

Embracing our emotions is often easier said than done, especially when they are negative. As humans we seem to do well at expressing happiness or love or gratitude or contentment. We are in our element when we feel cared for, respected, listened to, cherished. But when it comes to the less appealing emotions – jealousy, envy, anger, fear, unworthiness, embarrassment – we feel isolated, lonely and small.

In his foreword to Julia Simens' book, *Emotional Resilience and the Expat Child*, NIP child and adolescent psychologist Doug Ota wrote: '... *"understanding ourselves" is a skill that verges on art, and one that only a minority of the human population ever truly masters. Not understanding ourselves lies at the root of not being able to understand the other, and not being able to understand the other resides at the root of all human conflict.*'

An American expat-turned-immigrant living in the Netherlands, and a counselor for many years at the American School of The Hague, Ota knows about understanding emotions and dealing with shifting identity. Having experienced the sudden death of his beloved brother as a young adult, and watched colleagues, students and friends come and go over the years, he knows firsthand how 'transitions tear our stories'. It's what drove him to play an instrumental role in creating Safe Harbour, ASH's outstanding transitions program.

He has spent much of his working life observing, thinking, experiencing and dealing with both the negative emotions of transitions (sadness, loss, grief) and the positive (love, friendship, connection, belonging). As a psychologist and family therapist now in private practice, he still deals with these issues. It is a good part of the reason he is currently writing a handbook for building supportive transition programs at international schools around the world.

Last year I had the opportunity to hear Ota give a presentation to expat parents at the Passionate Parenting program in The Hague – http://www.passionateparenting.nl/. In the course of the evening he shared many lessons of transitions and loss, ending with the following summation:

> 'Above all, we practice empathy and compassion, on ourselves and with others.'

"Transitions create loss. Unseen losses hurt more. Many feel they must choose either one disconnected loyalty or another. Validation lets grieving heal disconnection. When both (all) loyalties are embraced, worlds link, leading to growth... As night precedes day, grief precedes growth."

And *that* is why we need to honor our emotions, share our stories, admit our grief, give and receive validation, embrace loyalties and ensure growth.

> 'Transitions create loss. Unseen losses hurt more. Many feel they must choose either one disconnected loyalty or another. Validation lets grieving heal disconnection. When both (all) loyalties are embraced, worlds link, leading to growth... As night precedes day, grief precedes growth.'

FACE WHAT YOU FEAR, ACCEPT AND MOVE ON

"I found being isolated from a bigger supportive network meant I had to deal with things often more internally than would have been the case if I had stayed in my home country. For a long time I'd felt no one believed me or saw me or had any interest in me, that my self-esteem had been severely warped. I made myself get on with things, and face the things I felt I couldn't and not complain about it. Things were always going to get better and I think I had an inner sense of the resilience my mother had shown, in her life and childhood particularly, and the feeling of 'it is what it is' – accept and move on."

Nicola McCall, British expat/repat

Often some of the answers to dealing with difficult situations lie within us. When we look deep within, identify how we're feeling and analyze why, we find the strengths and skills we possess which can be used to craft solutions. Doing so uses emotional intelligence to bolster our resilience.

FACING CULTURAL TRANSITION WITH SELF-KNOWLEDGE

"On the Keirsey Temperament Sorter* I'm an INFJ which means I'm extremely sensitive, emotional and self-deprecating. Because I'm an introvert, all these negative voices are trapped in my head. But I also have a strong set of analytical skills that kept questioning those voices and kept me looking for logical and practical solutions to my

problems. It was my search for sanity that helped me out of the difficulty."
(*A personality assessment test similar to the Myers-Briggs Type Indicator®)

Tara Agacayak, American expat living in Turkey

Most of us hit a rough patch along the way. It takes a little time, self-care and effort, but we eventually regain our equilibrium. For some, the cumulative effect of shock upon shock, disruption upon disruption, loss upon loss ends in a downward spiral, eventually hitting bottom.

LOSING YOURSELF AND HITTING BOTTOM

"On my first serious expat stint, Southeast Asia in the 90s, I achieved a state of photographic oblivion. When I set out from Los Angeles I was already solidly unemployed, unproductive, and unmotivated. I had a capricious romance to see me through.

In Asia, life losses piled up – heirlooms ransacked at the container yard, the cruel theft of a puppy, the unfathomable demise of my best friend. I did not write about any of these things. Too much shock, no support. Turns out capricious romance isn't the best fallback in a crisis. Language and cultural barriers prevented me from bonding with the Chinese, Malays, Tamils and Thais around me. My reactions were miscalibrated. I laughed when introduced to a person with the name of a celebrated American boxer – a common moniker in Malaysia — and took offense at the quickly-retracted handshake of a traditional Malay greeting. I expected dinner party banter at gatherings that instead seemed to focus on the scarfing of food in silence.

Soon enough I was as unrecognizable as my new world. My own body was erasing me. A spongy, knee-less Southern Italian genetic inheritance asserted itself with the help of a greasy local diet, while my hair frizzed mercilessly in the tropical air. Friends who knew me during cosmopolitan past lives in New York, California, and Italy wouldn't identify me as the 30-pounds heavier creature with the ill-fitting clothes and unschooled haircut photographed in jungles and palaces. Uprooted from my milieu, in a harsh climate and surrounded by perpetual strangers, I was desperate to locate comfort whatever the cost.

My Asia photographs are stowed, an expat adventure distressing to recall, impossible to frame. Yet, scraping bottom (especially on the far side of the world) has a benefit. It's easy to see which way is up."

Anastasia Ashman
American expat (Italy, Malaysia, Turkey) now repatriated to the US

Anyone familiar with Anastasia Ashman knows that, as the Phoenix rising from the ashes, it wasn't long before she found her way. Moving to Istanbul with her Turkish husband, she went on to co-edit (with Jennifer Eaton Gökmen) the popular non-fiction anthology *Tales from the Expat Harem: Foreign Women in Modern Turkey*, and later to found www.expat+Harem.com, a group blog and online community of global citizens, identity adventurers and intentional travelers. Today she is a cultural producer, essayist, editor, and co-founder (with Tara Agacayak) of the transformational business/life

> *'I've finally found my perpetual peers and a theoretical home for both my literary career and my life abroad. I have a way to nurture and sustain my most valuable expatriate possession – my sense of self – no matter where I am.'*

solutions start-up www.GlobalNiche.net. Not bad for someone who, in her own words, was 'scraping bottom' years earlier. Ashman goes on to share what these activities and accomplishments have done for her.

MOST VALUABLE EXPATRIATE POSSESSION

"In a wide world of strangers I've finally found my perpetual peers and a theoretical home for both my literary career and my life abroad. Now I have a way to nurture and sustain my most valuable expatriate possession – my sense of self – no matter where I am, or what heights or depths I face."

Anastasia Ashman
American expat (Italy, Malaysia, Turkey) now repatriated to the US

Debra R. Bryson and Charise M. Hoge addressed the topic of dealing with circumstances which challenge our sense of identity in their workbook, *A Portable Identity: A Woman's*

Guide to Maintaining a Sense of Self While Moving Overseas. They discussed reconstructing our identity during difficult transitions by executing the following steps – make a commitment, assess personal resources and pick up necessary tools – over and over again, so your sense of self becomes what you envision it to be. In particular, I found this passage especially useful: *'In essence, by creating*

> *'As we undergo transitions and live in countries/ cultures other than our own, healthy sharing is crucial to our established relationships and in making new connections.'*

a shell that "fits" you bring resolution to the state of transition your identity has been in. The results of your efforts are twofold. First, you put back into place the four facets of your identity (internal view, external factors, roles and relationships) altered by the move... Second, your identity becomes portable. You'll have an identity rooted to your sense of self which can thrive outside your home country and culture.'

HEALTHY SHARING

Communication is a large part of how we connect with others. Initially we chat about superficial subjects and exchange information, and if we are interested in expanding the connection, over time we begin to include some of a more personal nature. As we become closer, we tend to reveal more about ourselves. This is how we build relationships, whether friendly or romantic. As we undergo transitions and live in countries/ cultures other than our own, healthy sharing is crucial to our established relationships and in making new connections.

The term 'healthy sharing' means not disclosing too much, too soon, or to the wrong person. We avoid revealing overly personal information until a bond has been established and tested, there is a good reason to do so, and both parties trust the other to be truthful *and* not divulge sensitive information. Telling someone you just met intimate details of your life isn't healthy – it's inappropriate and awkward.

COMMUNICATE, SUSPEND JUDGMENT AND GIVE IT TIME

"The best advice I could give someone else considering expat life would be to keep the channels of communication open in your immediate family. Talk about everything. That means the bad as well as the good – any resentments, regrets or fears. It's important to stop yourself from feeling isolated and misunderstood. In a new country with no social

network or support system, you have to be there for each other – there IS no one else.

You also need to suspend judgement for a while. It's natural to feel that things in your new location don't quite match up to how they were back home, but once you get past that limiting viewpoint, it's interesting to see how others deal with a problem, the solutions that occur to other people. It's a different world out there. Don't close the door on it before you've even begun.

Lastly, give it time. It's surprising how differently you can feel about something with the passing of time, so go easy on yourself and don't make any rash decisions.

I think our positive attitude and preparation helped the children. I also believe that the fact the difficulties brought us closer together was thanks to our emotional resilience. We supported each other, vocalised our feelings and provided opportunities for each other to do the same. Apart from the two youngest members of the family, we all experienced some degree of culture shock, some more intense than others – each in our own way, I suppose. But our emotional resilience enabled us to work through it and come out the other end. We never regretted our move and never blamed each other for our difficulties."

Aisha Ashraf, Irish expat living in Canada by way of the UK

There are times we need to vent about frustrations when moving internationally – painful goodbyes, loneliness upon arrival, embarrassment at being linguistically and culturally misunderstood. A quick chat with family members and close friends, or sending an email message or letter, is often enough to offer perspective and regain our bearings.

VOICE YOUR FEELINGS, DON'T BOTTLE THEM UP

"Communication is key. For me it was important to find someone to talk to about my feelings, to voice them and not bottle them up so that they fester. I also write about my feelings regularly as it's a way to get them out of my system. Even when I have been in a different country, staying in touch with my family has been crucial in ensuring I have a support network. Thankfully these days it's much easier to do this through smart-phones, emails and Skype. When I first moved to university in 1999, technology wasn't

so far advanced, so letters and postcards from my family and friends back 'home' were well received."

Carrie Sanderson, Anglo-Dutch Adult TCK/ CCK living in the Netherlands

Healthy sharing goes both ways, with both parties feeling their needs are being met. It also means not taking advantage of the other person by 'dumping' on them. None of us like feeling taken advantage of, or put in a position where we don't know what to do with unsettling information.

HEALTHY SHARING IS BOTH MUTUAL AND UPLIFTING

"So many couples come to Portugal in search of a better life. Some on a wing and a financial prayer, hoping to find work in the sun, retirees following their dream and others who have just remarried and want to start afresh.

Whatever the reason, in the early days I used to befriend everyone and listen to their problems. My husband said I was a soft touch, and perhaps he was right, but in a way (I'm still thinking this one through) I could not turn my back on someone who was unhappy.

However, that said, did I hear from any of these women once they returned home? They sapped my inner strength, I hugged them, cried with them, listened to all their marital problems and tales of depression or alcoholism – no, of course not. We were just ships in the night and they were on the first boat home when the going got tough.

Husband is relieved I've learned to distance myself from people, but there is still a caring streak in me that wants to reach out... but I know the consequences...

To be honest, I don't have enough fingers and toes to count all the casualties of expat life here in Portugal. It sounds tough and even uncaring, but I'm not. I feel emotionally drained."

Carole, British expat in Portugal

Accepting what we cannot control and learning to live with the uncertainty in such a transitory lifestyle are two comments heard repeatedly in conversations with expats. Should it become overwhelming, turning to a professional for help can make the difference.

> '*When we can be honest about how we are feeling and fine tune it to the correct emotion for that situation, we are growing and building emotional resilience.*'

COMPASSIONATE, SKILLED LISTENER TO HELP

"I think letting go of what once was and accepting things sooner, and learning to live the long term 'not knowing' would have made things easier. I'm a planner and an organiser and like to know where I'm heading and why – aims, goals, outcomes, energy expelled in proportion to gains, etc. Living the role of an expat spouse long-term made this difficult but I learnt to readjust my horizons and get what I could from the way I was having to live.

I also had coaching and counseling during my expatriate life to help with making sense of things when I felt I couldn't manage to do this on my own. Having a compassionate, skilled listener who was unconnected to my story helped to sort what I could and should let go of and how to progress on the things I wanted or needed to deal with."

Nicola McCall, British expat/ repat

Healthy sharing is not limited to confiding your worries, fears or disappointments with a close friend or two, although most of us find this extremely beneficial. It can also mean knowing when the challenges seem too overwhelming to resolve on your own. That is the time to reach out to your doctor or seek the counsel of a therapist. Remember, doing so does *not* imply weakness, it's a sign of strength to get the assistance you need and deserve.

HELPING CHILDREN SHARE

As parents, some of the most valuable gifts we can share – and important responsibilities we must fulfill – are to help our children learn to handle uncomfortable change, weather tough times and acknowledge and address the accompanying negative feelings and emotions which may result.

DEALING WITH DIFFICULT EMOTIONS

Two years ago I had the opportunity to interview Julia Simens shortly after the publication of her book, *Emotional Resilience and the Expat Child*. She shared with me that in addition to successfully identifying and naming their emotions, "Children need self-calming skills which allow them to reflect on the reasons for their emotions and to modify their reactions in the future."

When asked what advice she would offer a family preparing to move overseas for the first time, Simens replied, "Ernest Hemingway said he could write a story in six words. My story to expats moving overseas for the first time would be 'nomadic lifestyle requires lots of love.'"

"It is never too late to work on building emotional resilience... Regardless of your child's age, I believe the building up of the emotional vocabulary is the right way to start building this skill. When we can be honest about how we are feeling and fine tune it to the correct emotion for that situation, we are growing and building emotional resilience."

While Simens writes primarily about young children in her book, she was clear the message can be extrapolated to teens and young adults. "The interactions between parents and their children are full of disruptions, miscommunication, and misunderstandings. This is the reality of all of our lives. What makes a relationship feel secure is the ability to 'repair.'"

"Your child can feel safe in the understanding that when mistakes or disagreements happen, you will pay attention to the cues they are sending, try to understand what they need, and come back again. There is always another chance to connect," Simens added. "This ability to bounce back after a problem or concern is what resilience is all about."

"I tell parents that they must target the strengths of their child," she continued. "If parents target things that highlight the strengths of their child,

> *'Having a compassionate, skilled listener who was unconnected to my story helped to sort what I could and should let go of and how to progress on the things I wanted or needed to deal with.'*

they will see more self-determination and strength from that child. Empowerment results from being treated with respect and having your strengths acknowledged and enhanced. This is the best way to enhance emotional resilience."

> *'I always tell parents to stop saying 'I know how you feel'. What kids need to know is, 'I hear what you are saying, how can I help?'*

Some expat/ cross-cultural children will find themselves overwhelmed and unable to develop the emotional resilience they require. What would Simens recommend to parents in this situation?

"Comments or actions should not be treated lightly or brushed off with words like 'you only have a few more classes' or 'you're very popular and have friends'. What the child needs is to be heard and know that the parents care about those feelings," she explained. "I always tell parents to stop saying 'I know how you feel'. What kids need to know is, 'I hear what you are saying, how can I help?'"

Simens also recommended asking yourself what messages you may inadvertently be sending out to others. "Children learn by watching their role models in life. When expats move around so much, the parents become the main role models so the messages we send our child are paramount... Is it okay to ask for help? Is it okay to be overwhelmed? Are you an honest person about your feelings or do you mask it so the family seems okay?"

"In the end, trust your gut... if it feels like you need to intervene, tell them it is your job as a parent to seek help when a family needs it. International therapists or experts who work with expats and transitions are becoming more and more common as we have more and more global nomads in the world."

STRUCTURE, EMOTIONAL SUPPORT, CONNECTIONS AND INTERESTS

Children need structure, order, routines, familiarity – particularly at home and especially when experiencing transitions such as moving, changing schools, loss of close friends, parental separation or divorce, major illness or accident involving loved one(s) or themselves, death in the family, relocating to a new country/ culture or other significant change. When I reread the sentence I just typed, I realize how many of the people who have confided they or a loved one have suffered from depression, were experiencing many of these pivotal events, one upon the other.

Children also need love and emotional support, to know they have a safe haven to come home to where they are cherished and nurtured, comforted and encouraged. As Pollock and Van Reken and Julia Simens remind us, to ensure our children feel heard and understood in their most difficult times, we need to be careful that we offer 'comfort *before* encouragement'. Providing encouragement without *truly* hearing what is upsetting our children (or our partners, other family members, friends), can send the unintended message that their feelings don't matter or are somehow wrong.

> '*Every child – and adult for that matter – needs to have some skill, talent, activity or interest of their own. This is important not only for the joy or satisfaction it brings to the individual, but to offer a bridge to others who share a similar interest.*'

They need connections that buoy them, from parents and siblings to friends and collegial classmates, or teammates or bandmates or castmates, from supportive teachers and instructors to favorite coaches or encouraging bosses.

Every child – and adult for that matter – needs to have some skill, talent, activity or interest of their own. This is important not only for the joy or satisfaction it brings to the individual, but to offer a bridge to others who share a similar interest. For some it may be fluency in languages, competency in advanced math, theatrical talent or skill on the playing field or in the swimming pool. For others it could be wizardry at chess, songwriting, singing or playing a musical instrument, or an affinity for yoga or martial arts.

Children can bond over preferred music, poring over lyrics for meaning and sharing favorite songs. They can also find kindred spirits who enjoy reading and writing as much as they do, swapping books and seeking out poetry contests or working on the staff of a school newspaper or yearbook. They may share a favorite sports team, or enjoy building model cars or sailing. The child who loves going to the movies might end up a film critic or make his or her own features.

Similarly, video game buffs may seek each other out for camaraderie, to hone their skills and share gaming strategies; computer geeks can hang out together learning software code and discussing the latest technological innovations. Artistic types will flock together, haunting museums and sharing their latest creations. Collectors compile whatever they're passionate about – stamps, coins, sporting cards, what have you. Others enjoy tutoring or mentoring younger children, working with animals, volunteering with charities or organizations helping those in need.

Finding things that make us feel good while doing them, which build our confidence and allow us to bond with others, is crucial to healthy identity development. For Daughter, it meant seeking out a Dutch *voetbal* team with whom to continue her high-level training. If you want to help your child handle transitions and whatever else life throws at them, encourage them to find what makes them happy and support them as they grow that skill, ability or interest.

Supporting Our TCK/ CCK Teens

Parents of global teens will welcome Dr. Lisa Pittman and Diana Smit's book, *Expat Teens Talk*, a balanced, honest look at how some TCKs really feel.

Practicing Psychologist Pittman and Educational Therapist, expat mother of TCKs and co-author Smit, have significant experience and insight into TCK teens, what they're thinking and what they've got to say. It turns out, it's quite a bit.

Pittman and Smit talked with a large group of TCKs directly, and share their stories in the teens' own words. At times that language can seem clichéd or overly cheery, then suddenly it veers into the reflective and heartrending. As the mother of two expat teens, I recognized many of the word choices and the feelings behind them. Sometimes they are tough to read:

'Being an expat teen means you have more than one home'

'You know you're an expat teen when the answer to 'where is home?' is 'I don't know''

'At times I genuinely thought I was depressed/ suicidal because I felt so lost in a world so different from the one I knew'

'I don't have anyone to talk to and I feel alone... one second I'm so angry and the next I'm crying'

'I find it very difficult to constantly say goodbye. Teachers, friends, people you know are always leaving... people and relationships seem to be temporary in expat life'

This book accurately reflects the wide range of emotions experienced by these TCK teens, and Pittman and Smit are to be lauded for not shying away from the tough discussions about the more negative feelings expressed. They also include insights and suggestions from parents and professionals who work with, and care about, TCKs. It is a simple truth that there are pros and cons to growing up globally, and this book does well in laying it all out for examination. It is a wonderful resource to read and share with an expat teen, serving as a good starting point from which to begin the conversation.

Another serial expat/ repat who has worked closely with teens is international education consultant Rebecca Grappo, who shares her observations from TCKs and their families, "I've worked with scores of children and adolescents in my 20 plus year career in international education and have seen so many who have not only transitioned well to an international location, but seem to have thrived in this globally nomadic lifestyle. They are the poster children of how we like to think about TCKs – flexible and eager to seek more culturally dynamic and interesting experiences. They are the ones who are symbols of resiliency."

"The TCKs I have worked with that are doing beautifully seem to be those who have **connected** to their new environments and people in their schools and communities, are **recognized** by others for their unique talents, gifts, and personalities, feel a sense of **belonging** to their families, schools, and communities, and have a strong sense of **identity**."

"Each person is their own complex case study into the human psyche and how humans adapt to change and new environments. Some seem to do it easily and are amazingly resilient. Yet others struggle with the challenges of shifting sands. How do you know how your child will fare? Is this something we can predict? In some cases, yes, we can predict it, and in those cases, one tries to encourage resiliency and head off trouble. But sometimes a parent doesn't see the train wreck in the making. This is every parent's nightmare."

So what are we as parents to do?

"My suggestion is to do your best to help your child feel like they belong, are connected, recognized for who they are, and happy with their self-identity. Strengthen your own family and relationship with your child. Read all you can about the normal development of children and adolescents."

Grappo also recommends empathizing with your child and acknowledging the loss and grief they may be feeling. She echoes Pollock, Van Reken and

'The TCKs I have worked with that are doing beautifully seem to be those who have connected to their new environments and people in their schools and communities, are recognized by others for their unique talents, gifts, and personalities, feel a sense of belonging to their families, schools, and communities, and have a strong sense of identity.'

Simens in saying parents would do well to offer 'comfort before encouragement' as it helps them talk and give voice to their feelings and emotions. Finally, if the situation doesn't improve or it worsens, seek help immediately.

"If your heart tells you things are not what they should be, don't wait too long or remain too hopeful that serious problems will resolve by themselves with time. Talk to your child's teacher, school counselor, a mental health professional, or an educational consultant about your observations and concerns. But don't let something as important as resiliency be left to chance."

One expat friend shared with me a little about her own tale of dealing privately with anxiety attacks and depression a few years ago. Something she shared stays with me, "None of my friends, even now, know the depth of my depression or despair at the time... But now when I look at them and they are feeling down, I look deeper and listen more."

Sometimes it takes us longer than we'd like to connect the dots in difficult situations. As many of us are prone to do, we may spend too long trying to reassure and bolster ourselves or others, rather than contacting a doctor or therapist. In hindsight, we simply may not realize – and perhaps there is an element of subconsciously not wanting to acknowledge – what is going on. I hope if you find yourself or someone you love in a similar situation, please err on the side of intervening earlier to seek help.

ACCENTUATING THE POSITIVE

"I think at times my teenage daughter has felt overwhelmed. She misses the friends she has accumulated in each country and the things that are unique to that place, but she always overcomes the feelings of despair to realise how lucky she is to have met those people and had those experiences in the first place."

Helen Maffini, serial expat now living in her eleventh country

When we're mourning the loss of our home and access to friends and family members, it's easy to lose sight of the wonderful people and experiences we've encountered along the way. That's why this lovely quote by famed American children's book author Theodor Seuss Geisel (also known as Dr. Seuss) is so apt:

'Don't cry because it's over, smile because it happened.'

I believe we would do well to teach our children this vital lesson and, just as importantly, to model it ourselves.

CHAPTER 12: VISUALIZATION

Visualization is more than painting a rosy picture in our mind and hoping it comes true. It consists of concrete actions we can take to make that vision a reality. Whether we 'see' our way forward to get through a tough day, find a more productive state of mind, or develop a better life situation, visualization can take many forms. These include imagining improvement, searching for clues in past behavior to determine best courses of action, writing, keeping a journal, and talking our way through challenges.

If we expect good results, we open ourselves to being more receptive to ways that help make them happen. I also include in this category efforts contributing to the better life we envision – physical and emotional self-care, stress management or relaxation techniques, prayer, meditation, mindfulness and learning to resolve conflict in a positive manner:

- **Review past behavior/ experience from relevant situations:** This reinforces confidence, and helps us determine best courses of action, then plan steps to move ahead.

- **Imagine improvement and expect good results:** This helps make us receptive to bringing about change.

- **Self-care is crucial:** Stay active (endorphins help mood), get sufficient rest, eat/drink sensibly and avoid risky behaviors.

- **Utilize stress management or relaxation techniques, meditation, mindfulness, prayer.**

- **Learn to resolve conflict in positive ways:** These can range from counting to ten (or fifty) before talking things through, rephrasing by using 'I feel' rather than 'You make me feel' statements, making a concerted effort to consider the other person's perspective, or agreeing to a cooling off period.

- **Write, talk or act your way through challenges:** Be creative with a journal, writing, poetry, painting, drawing, music, singing, or dance.

> *'Imagine improvement and expect good results. This helps make us receptive to bringing about change.'*

- **Don't ignore or suppress bad feelings:** Address them directly to allow for resolution and closure rather than repeating negative behaviors.

BOUNCEABILITY AND SELF-COMPASSION

"*I think of resilience the way I think of any trait – it's a product of both nature and nurture. The resilience matter in our DNA is like raw clay that can be shaped in many different ways over the course of our lives. I'm not sure whether I was born with resilience or not, but fortunately, my own children seem to be much more resilient than me. I attribute this in part to their TCK experience, which I consider to be on-the-job resilience training. Multiple moves, adjusting to new cultures, making new friends at new schools, learning a foreign language – these were things they struggled with initially, but after every setback, they picked themselves up and kept going. I'm in awe of people with that kind of bounceability.*

In contrast, when something goes wrong, my tendency is to withdraw so I can lick my wounds and try to regroup – the operative word being 'try'. I might get back out there again, but if I do, I hold something back.

One incident in particular stands out. We'd been in France maybe a month, and I was still very unsure of my language skills. One daughter was invited to a birthday party in a village outside of town. Having no car, I called for a cab. Phone calls are always difficult for language learners because of the absence of physical cues, so I was really nervous. The conversation went well... until the dispatcher asked me for a number. I recited my phone number, but that wasn't what he wanted. I gave him our house number and the number of the friend's house – nope, not those either. His tone, which had been polite in the beginning, took on a harder edge. My blood pressure rose every time he demanded this mystery number, but I just couldn't understand what he was talking about. He abruptly hung up on me. I can't describe the frustration, anger, shame, and utter worthlessness I felt at that moment. I sobbed for hours.

I'd like to tell you I bounced back from this unpleasant experience, but that would be lying. I never called for a taxi in France again. Instead, I worked hard on my French until I became comfortable talking on the phone. And I became very familiar with the public transit system. So maybe you could say I bounced sideways?

Psychological traits never operate in isolation. I'm pretty neurotic, and I'm not sure this quality can comfortably co-exist with resilience. One is about learning from mistakes and moving on; the other is about brooding over mistakes and internalizing them to the point that the brooder becomes the mistake. On an emotional level, 'walk it off' is a foreign concept for me, and yet that's exactly what resilience is all about."

Maria Foley, Canadian repat after Australia, Singapore, France (twice)

I couldn't resist following up with Maria to ask, "What *was* the number the taxi dispatcher wanted?" Her reply? "I never found out. It tortured me for months, but in the end, I had to let it go." Her insight about 'bouncing sideways' is a particularly helpful one as the way in which we are resilient is unique to each of us. The entire point of enhancing emotional resilience is to figure out what works best for *us*, to build or restore *our* reserves. As such, it is always a work in progress.

STRESS MANAGEMENT AND RELAXATION TECHNIQUES

An important aspect of building emotional resilience in expat life is learning tactics and techniques to relax, calm ourselves and handle stress. One of the most powerful of these is mindfulness.

MINDFULNESS

Mindfulness is essentially continuous, intentional observance without judgment. It is being aware of, paying attention to, and being completely in the present. This awareness and focus on what we are experiencing *right now* is often referred to as 'being in the moment'. More importantly, when being mindful we do not evaluate or decipher what or why a situation occurs. We simply observe while suspending judgment.

Mindfulness welcomes curiosity, openness, and acceptance by regulating our attention to the immediate experience before us. Rather than attempt to empty our minds, or focus our minds on problem solving,

> '*Mindfulness is essentially continuous, intentional observance without judgment and being completely in the present.*'

mindfulness seeks only conscious awareness of our thoughts, feelings, and surroundings in a deliberate, purposeful manner.

Mindfulness can be either secular or non-secular in nature. It is a tenet in several cultural and religious belief systems and traditions, including Buddhism, where it is the seventh element in the Noble Eightfold Path. Whether approached from a secular or religious perspective, mindfulness encourages us to set aside niggling worries and petty concerns of what *could* or *might* happen, to focus on what is happening *now*. It can be effective in interrupting negative thoughts, stemming unnecessary or unhelpful projections, and quieting the inner critic which revels in telling us what we do wrong.

Yet as much as mindfulness helps with eliminating negativity, it is also about gaining clarity, savoring expectation and positive feelings, and being aware of looking forward to things in the future. Who among us hasn't hurtled through a busy day, week or month anticipating some special event? That is precisely what I did for much of the six months' preparation to move overseas. Most of my energy and effort went toward resolving details needed to get us to the Netherlands. Being so future-oriented may have been necessary at the time, but I didn't enjoy it.

Putting our heads down and 'getting through' the packed calendar may be terrific for focused *action*, but not for focused *attention*. We miss out on so much if we do this constantly. This doesn't mean we cannot live in anticipation of pleasurable moments. Practicing mindfulness simply reminds us to be conscious of looking forward to such experiences, as well as the more mundane goings on of daily life. In seeking to live our lives as mindfully as possible, we choose to experience life as it is, taking the good with the bad, moment by moment.

Since 1979, medical professor and mindfulness pioneer Dr. Jon Kabat-Zinn, of the University of Massachusetts Medical Center's Stress Reduction Clinic, has been teaching others to help take control of their health and well-being through Mindfulness-Based Stress Reduction (MBSR) training. Dr. Kabat-Zinn is founding director of both the Stress Reduction Clinic and the UMass Center for Mindfulness in Medicine, Health Care and Society, and instructs others in the practice he calls 'mindful meditation'.

mindfulness app.

> 'Mindfulness offers us awareness, self-knowledge, perspective and choices for our actions and reactions.'

In his book, *Mindfulness for Beginners: Reclaiming the Present Moment and Your Life*, Kabat-Zinn asserts the immense power of mindful awareness as: '*our only capacity robust enough to balance thinking.*' Most of us have learned to think our way out of difficult or painful situations, but sometimes it is our thoughts that keep us mired in difficulty. Focusing on what is going on around and inside us can give us context, perspective and balance regarding our thoughts.

Mindfulness offers us awareness, self-knowledge, perspective and choices for our actions and reactions. Rather than ignoring negative thoughts or rushing to deny them, we can benefit from taking the time to acknowledge them, and becoming aware of the actions and experiences that might trigger them. By recognizing our default responses to certain events or situations, we can choose to either encourage or discourage such orientations. In this manner, observation can inform our ability to reinforce or to change.

Detaching ourselves from immediate reactions allows for a more considered approach to response, problem-solving and overall well-being. Mindfulness has been found to be effective in dealing with typical stresses and the more run-of-the-mill negative thoughts we all tend to have, as well as interrupting and defusing depressive and/ or anxious thoughts. Practicing mindfulness has also been associated with reducing the levels of the stress hormone cortisol, released by the body, and with decreasing emotional distress, anxiety, depression, insomnia, asthma and some symptoms of autoimmune illnesses.

In the context of cross-cultural living, the benefits of mindfulness make it a powerful tool during every phase of expatriate life. We can use it when we're packing up and taking leave of people and places that matter to us. We can employ it while transitioning into new countries and cultures, and while learning our way around and establishing new routines. Mindfulness encourages emotional and physical connections, which can help make a place 'home'. Whether moving on or moving back (repatriating), mindfulness has an important role to play in our daily lives.

Bringing our complete attention to the present and what we're experiencing is initially harder than you might think – we must quell the almost automatic desires to analyze, understand and solve. Yet with repetition, we can learn to master this and achieve the very worthwhile benefits.

MEDITATION AND OTHER RELAXATION TECHNIQUES

Relaxation techniques are self-employed practices to voluntarily calm the mind and body. In addition to mindfulness and meditation, these can include breathing exercises, progressive muscle relaxation, relaxation imagery, body scans for stress, visualization, yoga and tai chi.

According to Merriam-Webster's dictionary, meditation is: *'the engagement in contemplation, reflection or mental exercise (such as repetition of a mantra, or concentration on one's breathing or a visual image) to reach a heightened level of spiritual awareness.'* It costs nothing to meditate, and you don't need special clothing or equipment. At first it can seem difficult to stay focused on the meditation itself without letting your mind stray, but with a little practice you can see significant improvement quickly. It can be done almost anywhere, anytime – provided you hone your powers of attention to ignore your surroundings.

The benefits of meditation are impressive. According to Amanda L. Chan in her recent article, *Mindfulness Meditation Benefits: Twenty Reasons Why It's Good for Your Mental and Physical Health*, in The Huffington Post online, these include improved memory, relaxation, better sleep and awareness of ourselves and our bodies, and the lessening of fatigue, severity and duration of colds, loneliness and the risk and severity of depression. Meditation can help decrease levels of the stress hormone cortisol, increase brain signaling connections and the protective tissue myelin, and regulate attention and emotion. It has also been linked with increased compassion and helping others. In short, it can make us feel good and is good for us.

A compassion-oriented practice is often referred to as 'loving kindness' meditation. We train our thoughts and emotions toward tender, empathetic feelings of others. As we enhance our feelings of caring and empathy, we take on a more compassionate perspective as well.

Practicing mindful meditation and MBSR can also help to change the way our brains work. In her book, *The Mindfulness Breakthrough: The Revolutionary Approach to Dealing with Stress, Anxiety and Depression* (which includes a foreword written by Dr. Jon Kabat-Zinn), Sarah Silverton discusses how neuroscientific research has shown how we use our brain can change its structure and neuroplasticity (i.e., its level of activity), including emotion regulation.

During an eight-week MBSR program conducted in 2003 at the UMass Stress Reduction Clinic, Dr. Richard Davidson, Dr. Kabat-Zinn and colleagues showed that meditation as part of such a program caused shifts in activation from the right side to the left, in parts of the brain tied to emotion regulation: *'suggesting an increase in ability to deal with situations in a more positive and balanced way.'* Subsequent studies have demonstrated meditation can slow the natural aging of various parts of the brain.

'The benefits of meditation include improved memory, relaxation, better sleep and awareness of ourselves and our bodies, and the lessening of fatigue, severity and duration of colds, loneliness and the risk and severity of depression.'

RELAXATION TECHNIQUES HELP COPE WITH STRESS

"I have learnt to use relaxation techniques to cope with stress in healthy ways. They have played a major role in developing my emotional resilience. I use simple breathing techniques, meditation, relaxation CDs, and yoga. Whenever I feel stressed, or overwhelmed, I make time in my day to sit somewhere quietly, focusing on my breathing or I lie down and listen to a relaxation CD. Afterwards I always feel refreshed and ready to handle things. Running also helps me to deal with stress."

Carrie Sanderson, Anglo-Dutch Adult TCK/ CCK living in the Netherlands

There are many books, articles and websites to help you learn to mediate or employ other body relaxation techniques. www.FreeMindfulness.org offers a collection of free downloads and images for mindfulness-based meditation. Similarly, the Kansas State University website offers biofeedback audio files of breathing, imagery and phrasing for body relaxation techniques, and www.HelpGuide.org has a number of relaxation techniques for stress relief based on how you react to stress.

MINDFULNESS AND MINDFUL MEDITATION TO TREAT DEPRESSION

Mindfulness and mindful meditation from Kabat-Zinn's Mindfulness-Based Stress Reduction have also been adapted and combined with practices from Cognitive Behavioral Therapy (CBT) to form Mindfulness-Based Cognitive Therapy (MBCT). CBT married cognitive therapy (overcoming difficulties by recognizing and changing dysfunctional thought and emotional responses) and behavioral therapy (recognizing and modifying inappropriate or unhealthy actions), to focus on the full scope of emotions, thought processes, thought content, and behaviors. By adding mindfulness and mindful meditation to CBT, MBCT has been found to be effective in helping people with a history of recurring depressive events prevent relapses and maintain mental health.

For those interested in learning more about using mindfulness to deal with depression, expat Aisha Ashraf has written a number of informative articles on her blog, www. expatlog.com. In the series, Ashraf shares her personal experiences taking part in a Canadian MBCT-based program entitled, Mindfulness in Depression Relapse Prevention. She talks candidly about her prior depression and mental health issues and the need to practice many of the techniques she has learned to help prevent and/ or lessen the severity of recurrence.

YOGA

Yoga is another very popular relaxation technique. As with meditation and mindfulness, it can be practiced from either a secular or spiritual basis. Merriam-Webster's dictionary defines Yoga (with a capital Y) as a '*Hindu theistic philosophy teaching the suppression of all activity of body, mind and will*' so that one's true self can be liberated from them. However, yoga (with a small y) is '*a system of physical postures, breathing techniques and meditation derived from Yoga but often practiced independently... to promote bodily or mental control and well-being.*'

YOGA ENCOURAGES MINDFULNESS

"*For me yoga helps to bring about inner peace and stillness of my mind. The subtle movements and postures work my body in ways that no other physical activity does, forcing me to be mindful and concentrate on what I am doing, otherwise I would lose my balance. My body feels strong and I feel empowered whenever I do yoga, particularly doing The Warrior pose.*"

Carrie Sanderson
Anglo-Dutch Adult TCK/ CCK living in the Netherlands

The previous story demonstrates how yoga – breathing, movements, meditation – can reinforce mindfulness and build physical strength. The next speaks to the philosophical aim in Yoga of connecting to and freeing one's true self.

CONNECTING TO THE SELF THROUGH YOGA

"Many of us (myself included) find it very hard to do a daily regime of exercise. We don't have the time, the opportunity, the room, or we wouldn't know which specific exercises we could do. Many excuses apply. The secret of Yoga lies in one prerequisite only – the ability to move (as opposed to staying put). It doesn't matter what you do, as long as you do it. As long as you are moved by, or moving with, what happens in your life. Just as you would dance to the rhythm of music, dance to the rhythm of life.

Going back to what matters, becoming aware of what you say, eat and initiate; giving your Self breathing space; feeling connected to the Self, that's what Yoga is about. And the simple way to get there is to get up. Move, stretch out, and start exploring."

Ingrid Schippers
Dutch repat, Yoga-based personal development instructor and author

'Yoga incorporates mindfulness, meditation and exercise, so for many the practice is a cornerstone of their efforts to enhance emotional resilience.'

Several expats/ cross-culturals I've spoken with swear by yoga to help with some of life's stresses. It incorporates mindfulness, meditation and exercise, so for many the practice of yoga is a cornerstone of their efforts to enhance emotional resilience. Another yoga instructor, also an expat, elaborates below.

YOGA AND EMOTIONAL RESILIENCE

"A regular yoga practice, consisting of all the parts originally included in this ancient tradition – that is the pranayama (the breathing exercises), the asana's (the postures, the more physical part), the meditation and the integration of the philosophy of yoga into not only your daily practice but also your day to day life – is definitely one of the greatest tools in developing any type of resilience.

The meditation is often portrayed in popular media as this intensely peaceful and blissful state where you are enjoying an empty mind – well, that is not really what is going on! In meditation you allow yourself to do nothing and just watch what comes up, welcoming whatever is being thrown at you. While sitting there, with time, you learn to move from observing to discerning – and with a sharpened ability to discern as well as discriminate, you find your own direction. Next to that you are building up the ability to make choices and decisions from a solid base no matter where in the world you physically are, as you are your own home.

With the integration of the philosophy of yoga, on and off your mat, you gain the ability to see things within the larger perspective, 'wide eyes' as they are called in some ancient texts. Through this ability you won't feel so locked up in your own boundaries and locked out of other peoples or situation boundaries – which for me, at least, was always the first thing that happened after the honeymoon period in the new destination was over and 'real life' set in... "

Cecilia Gotherstrom, Swedish expat (New Zealand, Australia, Austria) living in the Netherlands and preparing to repatriate

On a personal note, I can tell you that employing mindfulness and practicing meditation, even at a rudimentary level, have been instrumental in helping to handle the stress and difficulties of the last year. They have also helped immensely in dealing with the guilt I've felt at *not* suffering from depression or anxiety, while a close relative and two dear friends have dealt with the double whammy of both.

FAITH, SPIRITUALITY AND REFLECTION

Each of us has a personal belief system of convictions we hold to be true. Our belief system reflects our values and what has deepest meaning for us. This structure is the fundamental basis for how we celebrate life and humanity, share our truths, express hope, mark pivotal milestones, and deal with tumult and adversity. In this section we will consider how faith, spirituality and forms of reflection can bolster our emotional resilience.

RELIGION, FAITH AND SPIRITUALITY IN EXPATRIATE LIFE

For many of us, our personal belief system is the fundamental basis for celebrating life's joy and beauty, and for dealing with its tumult and sorrow. When I was younger, I used to look up to the starlit sky in amazement at the wonder of tiny Earth in the great expanse of the universe. You cannot gaze at the moon and the stars without feeling connected to all other human life on this planet – past, present and future. For me, it also brings a sense of our being guided by something far bigger than ourselves.

This topic is not without contention. Religion is perceived by some to be a deliberate effort to keep people accepting of their lesser lot in life, or of the status quo – think Karl Marx's 'opium of the people' quote. For others, organized religions, and the clashes between them, have been responsible for extensive violence, conflict and harm over the centuries. We need only read today's headlines to find examples of the failings of certain religious leaders or the institutions themselves, and it is disheartening the damage these entities – and the fallible humans that run them – can inflict.

But for all the consternation, hypocrisy and angst, why do so many still believe? Religion, faith and spirituality – the search for the sacred that is worthy of veneration – have been a source of comfort and hope throughout history. For every daunting tale of greed or thirst for power, we need only look to our own lives and those of others for examples of the good done in the name of religious or spiritual beliefs. Even Karl Marx acknowledged the role of religion in life. What is often overlooked in the passage containing his aforementioned quote is this preceding sentence: '*Religion is the sigh of the oppressed creature, the heart of a heartless world, just as it is the spirit of a spiritless situation.*'

Call it what you will – religion, faith, spirituality, karma or fate – this is your belief structure. It is how many of us make sense of the world and our role in it, of finding meaning and purpose in our existence.

We tend to be introduced to religious belief in a superhuman deity such as God (or deities, plural) by our parents, extended families and communities. At some point we either choose to embrace that religion, accept our faith, or we don't. Perhaps we decide we don't need religious structure in our lives, or we might decide the

> '*Our belief system reflects our values and what has deepest meaning for us. How we celebrate life and humanity, share our truths, express hope, mark pivotal milestones, and deal with tumult and adversity.*'

> 'Your belief structure is how many of us make sense of the world and our role in it, of finding meaning and purpose in our existence.'

faith in which we were raised isn't the right fit, and set out on a personal search for the one that does. Others might feel observing the Golden Rule (treating others as we wish to be treated) is sufficient. Whatever our opinions, our search for meaning in life takes each of us on our own path.

I am fortunate to have a wide group of friends, many of whom are from various religious persuasions. Others embrace spirituality, involving either a belief system with a higher force or being, or simply a set of ethics and conduct under which they live. Several are on an agnostic journey to find the faith or belief system right for them. One or two prefer atheism. For me personally, my faith has instilled strength and a desire not only to live but to thrive, and to do so with purpose and intention. Regardless of our personal choices, we all are in need of emotional resiliency, and many of us choose to incorporate our choices into our efforts to enhance that resiliency.

RESILIENCE IN BELIEF IN SOMETHING BIGGER

"One of the most important things in living in another culture is the basic, fundamental sense of well-being as a person. It's a feeling of self-identity and self-worth – that I am here, I have a right to be here, and I'm valuable as a person. The extent that we have this is the extent to which we are resilient in the things that come our way... I think if you, yourself, are the only source of your own feelings of self-worth and value, you are probably going to be more susceptible to life's ups and downs. I would encourage others to look for that 'something bigger than ourselves' to feed our sense of identity and well-being, and provides a fundamental stability."

Norm Viss, American repat after three decades away (Nigeria, Netherlands)

The will to thrive brings me back to the original point – practicing one's religion, acknowledging one's faith or seeking a spiritual way forward, offer opportunities to handle the challenges of transitions, cross-cultural interaction and continual change with resilience. When we believe in something bigger than ourselves – whether God or Allah or Buddha or some other entity of significance – we gain insight into our place in the world. We understand the situation we are in is temporary, and we have within us the strength to embrace what we find of a positive nature, to alter what needs adjusting, and to accept what cannot be changed. In essence, we choose to *engage, adapt* and *thrive*.

REFLECTION, DISCERNMENT AND PRAYER

While mindfulness and meditation emphasize ongoing, focused awareness without judgment, reflection and discernment employ our senses to analyze some subject, event or thing. Reflection is thought given to a particular issue or set of circumstances. All encourage a calming, restorative approach. Discernment is the ability to grasp something obscure or determine something of importance. Both rely on consideration, analysis and assessing relative value, and can be useful in understanding changes in our given situation, our reaction to those differences, and exploring ways to deal more effectively with how these changes make us feel. Both can also be faith-based or not.

How might we employ reflection and discernment? For example, when encountering cultural differences such as more aggressive (or passive) behavior than we are used to, or where the concept of personal space differs greatly to what we expect, we can take a step back and think about these sorts of interactions, and our emotional and behavioral responses to them. In many ways journaling is the act of getting out on paper what mindfulness, reflection and discernment show us, but it – and writing – can also be done from a place of religious faith if that is your preference.

In identifying positive and negative triggers in our cross-cultural interactions, we can try to maximize the former and minimize the latter. We can feel irritation or discomfort at curt responses or circuitous non-replies, perceived invasions of personal body space, or the rigidity or looseness of certain societal rules. Or we can choose to recognize these for what they are – cultural differences. Rather than feel the sting of embarrassment at stumbling over the language, we can have a chuckle over mispronunciations and get on with expanding our limited vocabulary.

For those who profess faith, practice a particular religion or seek a spiritual path, prayer can play an important role in facing difficult situations and expressing gratitude for positive ones. Prayer can be a heartfelt request for guidance or assistance, or an expression of thanksgiving or appreciation.

'When we believe in something bigger than ourselves we gain insight into our place in the world. We understand the situation we are in is temporary, and we have within us the strength to embrace what we find of a positive nature, to alter what needs adjusting, and to accept what cannot be changed.'

Unlike mindfulness, meditation, reflection or discernment, prayer is action-oriented – you express gratitude or praise, or seek counsel and direction on a particular issue or endeavor. However, as with those other forms of personal awareness and contemplation, prayer can introduce positive changes in our physiological and psychological well-being.

PRAYER, YOGA AND WELL-BEING TO FIGHT CANCER

"One's emotional resilience as an expat is tested when things 'go wrong' in one's personal life. We were living in Cambodia when I was diagnosed with breast cancer. Medical facilities in Phnom Penn were very limited so it was better to undergo surgery, chemotherapy and radiotherapy 'at home' in South Africa, which meant I would be separated from my husband during most of this period... All in all, anxiety was the hardest thing to deal with and I've had to work hard at building my confidence. I relied on prayer throughout this time and I also found yoga poses combined with a focus on well-being extremely helpful."

Nicky Sully, South African expat (Rwanda, Tanzania, Cambodia) now living in the Netherlands

As with reflection and discernment, meditation can – but need not – be faith-based.

FOCUS AND REALITIES

"I do find Bible meditation and prayer helpful to remind me of my focus and realities in life."

Ruth Van Reken, ATCK and Co-founder of Families in Global Transition

Reflection or prayer can be a balm in the midst of stressful times. One expat shares her story of including prayer in preparation for the transition of her children out of the family nest.

PRAYING FOR THE COURAGE TO LET GO

"A few years ago, my daughter was packing to head out on a gap year between undergraduate and grad school. As she was sorting out her new backpack and thinking of warm clothes for Thailand, Malaysia and Singapore, she was telling me that she had applied for permission to work in the outback of Australia. I listened intently. I quietly prayed to God for strength to let her go. One or two members of my ladies Bible study had already starting regaling me with stories of prayers answered when their son or daughter was 'on gap'.

When my son, Mark, headed for his gap year and decided he'd travel through Africa and sleep in a tent, I thought, 'I don't have the courage for this.' My ladies group would just have to permanently place me on the emergency prayer list. 'It's me, oh Lord, standing in the need of prayer' would be my song every day he was away. Mark, on the other hand, would be fine. It was me, Mark's mother, who had to pray for the courage to let go."

Kathleen McAnear Smith, longtime expat (UK)/ part-time repat

In the end, whether you choose to employ prayer, discernment, meditation or mindfulness is an intensely personal decision. I simply offer them to you as possible tools to draw upon in building and maintaining emotional resilience.

HANDLING NEGATIVE THOUGHTS AND FEELINGS

We all go through periods when our emotional and physical energies are low. We have too much going on – often during transitions or difficult situations involving significant change – and it is easy to become weary or run down. This is when doubt can creep in, and we may find ourselves questioning our decisions and second-guessing our actions. I have certainly found this to be the case while dealing with the health and aging issues of my elderly parents and in-laws, coming to grips with my friend's terminal brain cancer, and our relative's treatment and recovery.

Self-doubt and negative self-talk can be demoralizing. As if that weren't enough, they can also create emotional and situational paralysis, keeping us from taking action to reverse

> 'Our thoughts and emotions are not our actions, but to be able to interrupt, address or change them, we need to admit they exist.'

downward trends and/ or institute helpful changes. These negative feelings drain our energy, erode our motivation and confidence, and whittle away our self-esteem.

We must recognize how insidiously destructive these negative thoughts and feelings can be, and take steps to nip them in the bud. First and foremost, we need to acknowledge their existence. Our thoughts and emotions are *not* our actions, but to be able to interrupt, address or change them, we need to admit they exist. That means owning up to thoughts going through our heads in which we berate ourselves ('You've really made a mess of this job search, no one will want to hire you', 'Why did you do *that*?'), or ascribe negative meaning to other people's words or actions ('He wouldn't have said that if he weren't angry with me', 'She must think I'm pathetic because I can't find my way around/ speak the language/ haven't met a soul here').

Once we identify these negative thoughts and feelings, we can begin to examine them in light of the actual situation. Are our perceptions accurate? Is there another possible explanation? Are we allowing our feelings to color our thoughts? Many times the very things we accuse ourselves of doing wrong actually aren't, or aren't a big deal – they may not even register on other people's radar. We assume someone is ignoring us or doesn't like us when they are simply preoccupied by something going on in *their* life. We're convinced no one in our new neighborhood will be interested in meeting us because they are already well established, when the truth might be they'd welcome someone new bringing a friendly attitude and fresh perspective.

By examining negative feelings or thoughts as they arise, we can assess their accuracy. Then we can decide whether we should set them aside as unlikely or unimportant, replace them with more positive alternatives, or determine what, if any, action is warranted. If we want to replace loneliness with friendship, we can seek opportunities to meet new people instead of staying home alone. Rather than give up on our job search, we could resolve to research the local job market for our occupation, update our résumé or CV, contact three companies to request an information interview, or inquire about career coaches specializing in expat clients.

COMMITTING TO A GOAL

"What has helped me the most is being committed to a goal – a healthy, happy marriage, being fulfilled personally and professionally. Recognizing and believing I have the power to control certain aspects of my life and recognizing I have choices about how I live. What didn't work was doing the same thing over and over and complaining about how horrible it was. What worked is constantly experimenting and changing until I found something I could live with."

Tara Agacayak, American expat living in Turkey

When we realize we can ignore or dispel the negative voice in our head, or do something about how we're feeling, we see we *do* have choices. With choice comes the feeling of having some control over our actions. We may not control a situation – or what others say, think or do – but we can control how we act or respond. More importantly, we have the ability to change how we think, which in turn can change how we feel.

'SEE' YOUR WAY THROUGH

Visualization refers to the practice of making mental images of our visual perceptions, and has been used as a relaxation technique for years. For example, envisioning a walk along a pristine, tropical beach can help us de-stress and shed our worries. We could simply think about taking such a walk, but 'seeing' it in our mind's eye is much more effective. (Actually taking that walk is even more so!) The visual image projected in our mind helps calm body *and* mind. Our muscles start to relax, our heart rate and blood pressure decrease, our breathing becomes regulated.

If visualization can reduce stress and help us relax, are we able to use it to change our mood? The answer is a resounding yes. Just as a method actor draws upon something in his past to elicit the same emotion during a performance, we can make ourselves feel a whole range of emotions simply by visualizing scenarios in which those feelings are present. We need only mentally picture the face of a loved one to make ourselves smile. If we're feeling a little down, rather than merely thinking of something happy, such as a circus or a giggling child, we can *see* it in our mind. If we want to feel stronger or tougher, we can imagine a ferocious lion, or a mountaineer about to plant the flag at the summit after an arduous climb. If we wish to project calm, we can envision the smooth surface of a placid body of water.

Whether we are trying to change our feelings or reinforce them, visualization helps. But it can be an even more powerful tool in our emotional resilience arsenal when we go beyond envisioning images to make us feel differently, to using mental visual projections to help *bring about* something we wish to make happen. Instead of culling through our minds for a picture of something we've seen or experienced, we can visualize situations we want to manifest.

How does this work? In her book, *Creative Visualization: Use the Power of Your Imagination to Create What You Want in Your Life*, Shakti Gawain writes of learning to use our creative imagination in a more conscious manner, to create an image of something we want to occur. Focusing on this image and giving it our attention opens us – and our conscious and subconscious mind – to creating the circumstances under which it can happen. In short, you become what you envision. You achieve what you imagine.

Gawain includes several exercises in her book, and recommends entering into a meditative state before projecting an image of the reality you wish to create, as if it already exists. The effect of this is to: *'dissolve barriers to natural harmony and self-realization, allowing everyone to manifest in his or her most positive aspect.'* Gawain asserts creative visualization is the natural result of these basic principles:

- Our physical universe is composed of magnetic energy which attracts similar energy
- We can create something in thought first, then manifest it physically ('form follows idea')
- Whatever we radiate is what we attract, and therefore, create

According to Gawain, all you need for successful creative visualization are desire, belief and willingness to accept what you seek. This emphasis on belief, mental acceptance and receptivity is echoed by Joseph Murphy with his phrase: *'what is impressed in the subconscious is expressed.'* In his book, *The Power of Your Subconscious Mind*, Murphy explains that what we pray for, what we desire – regardless of religious or spiritual orientation – becomes true based on the law of belief: *'when the individual's subconscious mind responds to the mental picture.'*

From a neuroscientific perspective, concentrating on a visual image of our choosing (or writing something down, or speaking it aloud, as we shall see in coming sections) sets in motion an important process. Doing so alerts the part of our brain which acts as the control center for incoming data – the reticular activating system (RAS) – to look for anything related to our envisioned goals or desires. We set up a filter for the RAS to sort through all of the information our brain receives, to find whatever may impact our ability to make our wants reality. The RAS in turn tells our cerebral cortex to pay attention to those important bits amid all other incoming information. We start noticing information that might assist us in achieving our ambitions, and our subconscious and conscious minds work to help us put that new knowledge to work.

> 'Concentrating on a visual image of our choosing, or writing something down, or speaking it aloud alerts part of our brain to look for anything related to our envisioned goals or desires. We start noticing information that might assist us in achieving our ambitions, and our subconscious and conscious minds work to help us put that new knowledge to work.'

How might expats/ cross-culturals utilize visualization? Whether preparing to move countries, learn a foreign language, find activities or work we enjoy, or become more deeply involved in our cultural community, we can imagine visual images of ourselves as if the future has already arrived. We 'see' ourselves settled into a cozy home, with packing boxes, misplaced items and shipping bills of lading a thing of the past. We envision ourselves chatting animatedly with friends in our new language, working at a fulfilling job, or doing things that interest and energize us. We visualize ourselves traveling, exploring, experiencing and learning about the cultures we come from and the one(s) we inhabit. Then we can relax and calmly go about our business, secure in the knowledge our mind is receptive to making these things happen.

'SEEING' FORWARD TO ACHIEVE SUCCESS

"Being an expatriate you're naturally a person in transition. Your worst days can leave you feeling unmoored and alienated. Your best days bring a sense of your agile nature and the qualities that make you unique from the people who surround you and the people back home. Working toward an understanding of what it will take for you to feel your best in your environment I think is extremely worthwhile. Your answers perfectly define you, and the more closely they are incorporated into your business plans the better chance you have of career success abroad.

After five years in Malaysia, 14 in Turkey and now currently in the US, I have made the limbo state of expatriatism (i.e., not belonging to your surroundings but having to navigate them in culturally appropriate ways AND honor the truth of who you are at the same time), a strength instead of a weakness.

With my career disrupted by international relocations and watching the traditional media business being disrupted by digital and social media, my particular modus operandi has evolved into gate jumping. That's a combination of reaction to obstacles in my environments, and a commitment to not be hindered by 'what is'.

Gate jumping can work for expats of all kinds. Here's how I do it – fearlessly operating without borders instead of accepting my off-the-grid, situation-mismatch as a paralyzing disadvantage. Time zones, language barriers, geographical distances, old-school thinking and collapse in my industries of media and entertainment? These things don't stop me. Being an early adopter of Twitter, I use it for continuing education such as virtually attending conferences and entering high level discussions in my topics of interest, to networking and meeting my peers around the world."

Anastasia Ashman
American expat (Italy, Malaysia, Turkey) now repatriated to the US

Ashman employs a form of visualization in making happen what she desires. Referring to her commitment not to be hindered by 'what is', she focuses instead on identifying what she really wants or feels she needs, wherever in the world she happens to be. By believing our answers to these questions – *What is it that I want for my life? What do I truly need?* – and envisioning the kind of life/ work we want, we, too, are receptive to making that occur.

WHAT IS WRITTEN BECOMES REAL

It is a similar process when we decide to put in writing what we wish to occur. When we capture a thought, desire, wish or goal on paper, we are taking a step towards seeing it come to fruition. As with visualization, in writing things down we are employing the power of positive thinking. Our conscious mind acknowledges what to date has remained hidden or unexpressed. Even if we never share what we've written with a single soul, we know that longing exists. We gain clarity on what we desire, register our intention and focus on the outcome we want to experience.

In her book, *Write It Down, Make It Happen: Knowing What You Want and Getting It*, Henriette Anne Klauser explains how recording what we want can help make it come true. She shares many stories of individuals – including celebrities – who, believing in the power of expressing in written form their goals or dreams, have done so and gone on to achieve them.

> 'In addition to being descriptive, journaling might also hold insights into the prescriptive. By offering us a chance to explore what is bothering us (or similarly, what is working) and why, we can note patterns and formulate possible solutions or ways we might deal with things.'

Klauser believes our written desires send a notice to the universe that we're ready to receive, and the universe sends back little signals and messages of coincidence to indicate work is being done to make things happen. As to how this happens, she considers the possibility that positive responses to writing things down may result from: *'energy waves, transmissions, vibrations, whatever, that attract people, solutions, to us. Others call it 'divine intervention'...I, for one, hold a little bit of each of them.'*

We can start by making our own list of goals or describing a desired outcome. Either way, Klauser recommends we silence our inner critic, write quickly, and include everything that comes out, no matter how far-fetched it might seem. After all, the lists that many of her subjects made didn't seem particularly realistic either, yet they achieved their goals nonetheless.

JOURNALING

Many of us keep a personal journal in which we note issues and events in our lives, and our thoughts and feelings and events about them. These may include successes, highlights, hopes, dreams and triumphs as well as problems, fears, concerns and things that haven't worked out. In addition to being descriptive, journaling might also hold insights into the prescriptive. By offering us a chance to explore what is bothering us (or similarly, what is working) and why, we can note patterns and formulate possible solutions or ways we might deal with things.

If we're feeling sad, blue, less than excited about the opportunities present in building a life in a new place, or otherwise stuck in a transitional rut, it helps to remember that we can't address what we don't recognize. Too often we chalk up our ambivalence as being tired, overworked or overwhelmed. It's entirely possible we are any or all of these. Sometimes there is more going on inside, and if we want to change something, we need to understand it. As journaling provides an outlet to capture our thoughts and emotions, it is a helpful tool for detecting trends and discerning potential triggers and/ or usual responses. It also gives us the benefit of hindsight when seeking to understand, disrupt and change our ways.

Laura J. Stephens, a therapist and repatriated Brit, learned the value of journaling when she found herself dealing with depression during her second expatriate experience. In her emotionally honest autobiography, *An Inconvenient Posting: An Expat Wife's Memoir of Lost Identity*, she candidly chronicles culture shock and her surprising downward descent after begrudgingly moving to Houston for her husband's career. Stephens credits journaling as a key aspect in her recovery, as it gave her the time and emotional space to process and integrate the change and loss with which she was dealing. In regularly recording her emotions, perceptions and actions in a personal diary, she learned to observe and acknowledge *what* was going on inside and around her and *how* it felt. This also provided her significant insight into possible reasons *why*.

Stephens explains: *'Throughout the day we have thousands upon thousands of thoughts, most of which come and go in a second. Many of these thoughts will link us to memories, often the same ones being replayed over and over, again and again. The result is we reinterpret how we feel based on repetitious ways of processing. By writing these feelings down we can observe our own thought patterns as they emerge, clearing a path for new ones. Essentially, by grounding our thoughts on paper and thereby observing them, we create ourselves space for alternative ways of thinking... If we know what is wrong we can take the necessary action to make changes in our lives. And if we let go of the past we can more easily give our attention to the present.'*

Mindfulness and self-awareness are crucial, and journaling is a great way to monitor, evaluate and alter thoughts, feelings and behaviors.

BLOGGING AND WRITING

Let me start by saying that blogging is indeed a very specific form of writing, as is journaling. Whereas journaling is self- or inwardly-focused and usually intended for our own eyes only, blogging – shortened from 'web log' – is a more outwardly-focused, written expression of our ideas, thoughts and interests. The Internet is full of millions of instructive blogs on every conceivable subject. Want to learn more about art, politics, business, history, culture, music, cooking, fashion, expat life or learning a new skill such as blogging? The choice is mind-boggling.

For every informative expat blog expounding on the '*Top ten places to live overseas*' or '*How to move abroad*', there are others written by expats trying to make sense of what is happening to and around them in their cross-cultural existence. These blogs tend to be more personal in nature, with the blogger reflecting on experiences, events and emotions in their lives, blurring the line between public and private. It is this latter type of blog that can be similar in both intent and result to journaling, as the blogger shares in an effort to try to work through and make sense of what is going on in their lives. In the process, he or she often finds a larger community of others with similar experiences. Connections are made and suddenly they don't feel quite so confused, alien, alone. Many an expat/ cross-cultural blogger have found their tribe – or at least one of them – online.

Expressing yourself through blogging can be a positive experience, but thought should be given as to what you share and how you say it. Once blogged, it's out there in perpetuity so you'll want to think twice about ranting or sharing sensitive information. Similarly, you owe it to others to respect their privacy. In this next story, one expat shares how he became involved in blogging when his family moved overseas, and how his perspective – and his blogging – changed over time.

SHEDDING UNHELPFUL VIRTUAL BAGGAGE

"It required a sustained effort by my wife over several weeks to persuade me to move. Even my London friends who were originally from New York and California raised their eyebrows, because this wasn't just a move to the USA, it was a move to Florida, USA; somewhere they couldn't identify with at all. Amongst all the playful jibes about old people, alligators, the accent my young children would adopt and the general culture (or lack of it), there was a common insistence I should start a blog. Knowing me and knowing Florida, they expected an almighty culture clash, and they expected it to make entertaining reading.

I duly gave my new blog the tagline, 'Learning to love all things American – including the Americans' and proceeded to give my initial readership what they wanted: stories of apprehension, crossed wires, confirmed stereotypes, logistical nightmares and general mishap. It was great fun, well-received and felt rather therapeutic. Whenever anything went awry, my reaction, and that of those around me, would be 'at least this will make a good blog post!' Even those who never commented online would tell me when I spoke to them how much they loved my blog, and perhaps I should consider writing a book.

Very soon, however, it became more of a constraint than a release. The need to keep the blog fresh made me constantly focus on the negative aspects of my expat experience, or at least nurture a very British perspective on everything, often editing or exaggerating events – essentially for the entertainment of others. Furthermore, as I began to befriend and engage more Floridians online, I had to consider a more complex audience for my posts, and was occasionally embarrassed by the comments made by friends back home that were less than flattering towards my host nation.

It had always been in the back of my mind that my online activity might neatly document a transformation through experience from initial incomprehension and frustration, to a life-affirming understanding and acceptance of my new surroundings, but this proved to be a fantasy. Real life rarely follows the progressive steps of the story arc so universally adhered to by writers of fiction and producers of so-called 'Reality' TV. Sometimes we had to resolve problems and ponder decisions affecting the whole family with no idea how things would turn out. The need to concurrently maintain the voice of my blog, with its associated tweets and Facebook updates, added to the pressure and risked subverting our decision-making process.

Just a few months after arriving in Florida, I consciously changed the nature of my online writing. Blogs tend to attract new readers all the time, but those who had followed it from the start would have noticed my posts became less regular for a period of time and subsequently more about our general experiences as a family both good and bad, referring to our expat status only when relevant. The more observant reader might also have noticed the disappearance of one or two of the earlier posts altogether, along with the second clause of my tagline ('–including the Americans'), which now seemed plain rude. Perhaps this was the point when my blog adopted a weaker narrative or became less entertaining for some, but it also marked the point when I shed some of the unhelpful virtual baggage that I had brought with me from England, giving me more freedom to deal with the real life issues of being an expat in the USA."

Craig Myles
British expat living in the United States

Writing, like storytelling, speaks to deep and powerful desires within us to express ourselves and share experiences. This holds true whether we're writing blog posts, articles, thought pieces, poetry, flash fiction, book reviews, short stories, novellas, novels, non-fiction books. Each has its own form, structure, intent and audience, even if that audience is only the blogger him/ herself. If writing is an interest of yours, exploring other genres can be a natural progression for expressing yourself. I enjoy the creative challenge posed by writing in different genres – fiction and non-fiction alike – and I'm far from alone in that.

SURVIVING THROUGH WRITING

"One of the major things that helped me survive my early years as an expat, adapting to a country that looked like my native California in so many ways, but was anything but, was writing. If not for the Internet, I would not have had the connection to family and friends at home – a major survival mechanism in itself. Those emails turned into website posts, then stories being published in an anthology (Tales from the Expat Harem, 2006). I'm now writing a book about our story of an independent Californian female meeting a tribal Turkish Kurdish male, and our creative efforts to weave cultural differences and similarities into a hybrid life. Our story illuminates the human connections between seemingly disparate worlds by weaving words, fibers and handcrafts into a creative force for bridging cultures.

Being able to pour my feelings of limbo, disillusionment, and frustration into words and not actual rants against my husband and family probably kept me (and them) sane and together, and my family in CA from worrying too much about me since they could read what we were up to."

Catherine Salter Bayar, US expat in Turkey

While many people, like the expat in the previous story, use writing as a means of creative expression, or to make/ maintain connections, some make it the centerpiece of their life's work. Publisher, author, journalist, poet, instructor and serial expat Jo Parfitt has built a portable career – several careers, in fact – around writing. Yet even she shares the personal need to express herself through her writing, and in the process finds a way to feed her resilience.

WHAT MAKES ME RESILIENT

"I know that a few things make me resilient – growing a support team and finding people who buoy me up. I need to get out there and network and to ask. I also know, that for me, I need to find something meaningful to do, based on my passion. That is writing, so when I did that I became happier. Denying who I am makes me vulnerable and unhappy."

Jo Parfitt
English expat (Oman, Norway, Dubai, Brunei) now living in the Netherlands

Many people enjoy writing poetry not only for the aesthetic creations that can result, but also as a method for capturing and making sense of deep-rooted feelings.

ALL AT ONCE

All at once.
'Missing' becomes a state of being, a condition of the heart.
A constant, lingering reminder that reality is now dream.
That while pieces are replaced and repaired, others are torn away and bruised.
That while it may function, it is hardly whole.
A way of life with a cycle of give and take, gain and loss, opportunity and sacrifice.
Time made, and time lost.
Bridges built, and bridges broken.
Tragedy and triumph, serenity and sorrow.
Happiness and heartache.
A heart scattered across the world can never be completely whole.

I guess it's true that you never know what you've got until it's gone.
'Granted' becomes an irrevocable habit.
'Moving on' turns into routine, but never fully leaving it all behind.
Gathering up as much as we can at the end, and carrying it as far as we allow.
Slowly dropping pieces on the way, to make room for the new, but never forgetting the old.

It's the pieces that make up who we are.
Making us from everywhere.
And from nowhere.
All at once.

Cat Foster, American ATCK (Southeast Asia) now living in the US

Whatever form your writing takes – letter, email, Facebook entry, Tweet, blog post, article, poem, story, book – it is meant to be read, even if only by yourself. This reinforces the bond between you and your reader(s).

> *'Writing, like storytelling, speaks to deep and powerful desires within us to express ourselves and share experiences.'*

NEVER UNDERESTIMATE THE POWER OF THE SPOKEN WORD

Communication is the act of sharing or exchanging information. Along with reading, writing and listening, it is a cornerstone to learning. It is an essential element in forging connections with others. The visual, auditory and kinetic cues (e.g., body language, tone, touch) available when speaking with another person or group, coupled with the words themselves, combine to tell us far more than anything we read. That's why a phone call is more personal than an email, and a face-to-face encounter even more so. It's also why we remove ourselves from physical interaction with someone when we're feeling negatively toward them.

Expressing ourselves verbally is also a powerful tool, which bolsters our emotional resilience in several ways. First, there is a social connection we make when conversing with someone. No matter how in-depth or fleeting that connection may be, for those moments in time, we are engaged as one human being to another. Regardless of our individual personalities, we are social animals who need contact with others. When we don't have such attachments, we fail to thrive. We need only think of the critical role of contact in early childhood development, or of the loneliness – and physiological

> *'Expressing ourselves verbally is also a powerful tool, which bolsters our emotional resilience. There is a social connection we make when conversing with someone. When we don't have such attachments, we fail to thrive.'*

and psychological repercussions of isolation – in individuals to realize its importance. That is why advanced societies make the effort to create connections with those who may be isolated (e.g., the elderly, sick or disabled).

> 'When we engage in social behavior, our bodies release oxytocin, a chemical associated with bonding, relationships and love. We feel good about the interaction and about ourselves. The subconscious message is one of validation.'

Second, when we engage in social behavior, our bodies release oxytocin, a chemical associated with bonding, relationships and love. So all those times you've been told to join a group, meet someone for coffee, invite someone over, or 'find a tribe, make an effort'? When we do so, the oxytocin makes us feel good about the interaction and, just as importantly, about ourselves. The subconscious message we receive is one of validation; someone else finds us worthy of time, attention and communication.

Third, conversation is an important mechanism for problem-solving. We discuss negative feelings, fears, insecurities, worries and concerns. We can gain information to help avoid exacerbating the situation further. We can examine what's really bothering us and figure out the underlying reasons why. Then we can consider potential solutions and any changes to be made in thought, word or deed. We can evaluate the alternatives, come up with an intended course of action and take steps to carry it out.

It's certainly possible to do all of this by ourselves, and we often do when dealing with our problems. However, it is often done faster, more effectively and with greater insight when we put heads together. Sometimes we need the added value of experience from someone who knows us – or the situation – well, such as a spouse or partner, close friend or group of friends, or a family member. Other times we benefit from the detached perspective of someone who isn't personally involved (e.g., a trusted colleague or other person whose opinion we respect).

> 'Doing a broader range of logical and creative activities helps ensure we are using various parts of both sides of our brain.'

Finally, don't underestimate the power of the spoken word. Who among us hasn't said aloud – even if only whispered under our breath – something to encourage or cajole ourselves to action? *I can do this. Do your best. Keep going.* We learned earlier that both visualizing and writing down our goals or deepest desires can help bring those things to fruition. Similarly, affirming them aloud can have the same results. Sharing them verbally with others creates a public record to which we are then held accountable. By communicating our intentions orally, we also tell our reticular activating system and cerebral cortex to 'get in the game' and start listening for, and capturing, relevant information that might help us. When I first told my family, close friends, my writing mentor, and ultimately my blog readership that I was writing this book, it helped immeasurably in both ways – through heightened awareness and accountability.

> *'Visualizing and writing down our goals or deepest desires can help bring those things to fruition. Similarly, affirming them aloud can have the same results.'*

CULTIVATING CREATIVITY

Creativity is the making, building or developing something of perceived societal or cultural value to others. Each of us needs an element of creativity in our lives. Even if we don't think of ourselves as particularly creative, or work in a so-called creative field or line of work, we all need to develop new ideas, and employ new ways of thinking or doing things, to stay abreast of current developments or get ahead in our profession. The strict divide between a logical, analytical left side of the brain and an artistic, imaginative right side of the brain isn't as clear-cut as we may have previously been led to believe. There is far more interaction between the two brain spheres, and different forms of creativity come from each. Doing a broader range of logical and creative activities helps ensure we are using various parts of **both** sides of our brain.

MOVE ABROAD, GET MORE CREATIVE

"Speaking from my personal experience, I do feel more creative since moving to Spain. Part of the reason, I think, is the need to communicate in a foreign language. Searching for the right word, trying to find the correct way to ask for something forces my brain to be active, even when it's something simple like buying milk. Of course, sometimes, even today, I can't always come up with the right word or the correct tense, which makes me look for non-verbal ways to communicate – miming, sketching, a combination of the two with a few made-up words thrown in. The end result is I usually get what I want, utilizing parts of my brain that wouldn't have been used otherwise, making the most mundane of actions stimulating.

But more than the language, I'd say the increased creativity has more to do with the freedom of thought and openness that comes with moving to a foreign land. Basic assumptions about life are challenged by new experiences. I've learned there is often no right or wrong way to do things – only different. A walk in the park triggers a whole new thought process when I compare my new life to the one I left. While without the comfortable surroundings of my past, I'm forced to get out and experience life, rather than settle into a daily routine of letting it pass me by while I watch TV or daydream. So by the end of even the most unadventurous day, my mind is full of sights, sounds and smells that it wouldn't have been otherwise, which in turn spurs my creativity inspiring me to write.

So if you're feeling bored, stagnated and uncreative at home, sell your possessions, buy a ticket for a place you've always wanted to go and set a goal to stay for one year. Perhaps, you won't stay forever, but even if that's the case, you'll return a different, more creative person with enough material to paint that picture, sing that song or write that which you've always had in you."

Jeremy Holland
Anglo-American expat now living in the Netherlands after Spain

We've already addressed the creative pursuits of writing, blogging and journaling, and as the previous story exemplifies, traveling/ living across cultures. Now we'll look at additional ways to express ourselves and pursue creative passions.

MUSIC

Many of us sing along to the radio while driving and listen to our favorite music at home. But what about hearing it live, being present while music is created? It's a whole new experience, one that can lift our mood and get the creative juices flowing. Opportunities abound to attend a performance of a musician, singer, band, orchestra, opera, or an open-air concert or outdoor festival. The Dutch revere jazz, so spending a day at the Haarlem Jazz festival was an entertaining experience for Husband and me to bridge our home and current cultures. It needn't be expensive to go to a concert as many schools, universities and houses of worship offer free or low-cost events.

You might also interject music into your life by learning to play an instrument or continuing previous lessons, or by joining a choir or other singing group. Two acquaintances of mine became involved in a local Dutch community choir, a friend sings in her church choir, while another has taken up long-desired piano lessons.

ART

You can stimulate your creative streak by visiting local and national museums, attending a 'museum night' or checking out galleries and exhibit openings where you can meet the artists. If you're more 'hands-on' you can take painting, drawing, sculpting or photography lessons offered by the community or local artists.

When I was at university I lived in a dormitory popular with students of the fine arts. I didn't know that much about art, but over time I became friends with several art students, and began to learn what motivated them to create what they did. Each year the art students would host shows of their art, open to fellow students and the public. Sipping cheap wine, viewing the pieces and hearing them discuss their creative endeavors made art so much more accessible than staring at it statically.

Fast forward many years, and one of the things Husband and I enjoyed about where we lived in the US were the monthly 'art walks' from gallery to gallery in a nearby community. We also loved the annual county art weekends where you could visit, view the work of, and chat with, dozens of local artists. Imagine our delight when we learned our Dutch neighborhood has its own version of a biannual art walk, the *Statenkwartier Kunst Route*. The wine offered is a bit better than in university days, but the fascination remains of seeing artists' creative expressions and having them described in their own words.

CRAFTS AND COLLECTIONS

Perhaps your artistic interest lies in sewing, weaving, knitting, crocheting, scrapbooking, calligraphy, jewelry making, origami or otherwise creating some sort of craft. The next story tells of how the creative efforts of one expat helped build bonds to her community and family.

AN IMPORTANT SURVIVAL TOOL ADAPTING AS A NEW EXPAT IN TURKEY

"Knitting, textiles and handcrafts – having a creative outlet bonded me to local women in our family and beyond, and helped me express myself beyond cultural differences.

They've also created a business for us – our tagline is 'sharing the common language of craft'. A life-long designer, my creativity took off in this new environment so steeped in history, multiple cultures and strong textile traditions, so having always worked in a field that is all about trend, change and innovation was a huge help in going with the flow."

Catherine Salter Bayar, US expat in Turkey

While living abroad, we often collect things to serve as souvenirs, cultural remembrances of our times and travels there. For some these physical reminders might be postcards, posters, pottery, wine corks, bar coasters, menus, matchbooks, figurines, *objects d'art* or, in my case, thimbles.

COLLECTING MEMORIES ALONG THE WAY

"I have started collecting memories in photos and scrapbooks that the kids and I look back on and remember things we have experienced and people we have met. I wish I had started this earlier on our travels."

Helen Maffini, serial expat now living in her eleventh country

As the words of Franklin Delano Roosevelt remind us: *'Happiness lies not in the mere possession of money; it lies in the joy of achievement, in the thrill of creative effort.'* Find a creative effort that interests you, and you'll find a source of happiness. Some creative outlets are also the perfect opportunity to learn a new skill. As you practice and improve, you may find yourself getting into what Mihaly Csikszentmihalyi refers to as 'the flow' (*CHAPTER 7: BRAIN-BODY CONNECTIONS AND POSITIVE PSYCHOLOGY*).

SELF-CARE

Self-care comprises a whole range of actions we can take to enhance our physical and emotional well-being. These include eating healthy foods, getting sufficient sleep,

'The heart of self-care is treating ourselves with compassion, respect and kindness.'

working out, maintaining a proper weight, watching the alcohol, going easy on ourselves when needed, and otherwise taking care of ourselves.

The Importance of Being Kind to Yourself

The heart of self-care is treating ourselves with compassion, respect and kindness. This may mean treating ourselves gently when undergoing transitions or periods of intense change.

Accept to Determine Whether to Control, Change or Do

"I admitted and accepted I was lonely and scared whenever I moved abroad. This was therapeutic. Once I accepted how things were, I was then able to look at what I could control, change, or do. I would ask myself 'What one small thing can I do today that will make me feel a little better?' I would treat myself to a magazine or a fresh cup of tea in a local café. Such simple things can be hugely effective."

Carrie Sanderson
Anglo-Dutch Adult TCK/ CCK living in the Netherlands

Another expat emphasizes the need for being patient with ourselves and our given situation. She, too, has her own short list of little things to relax and de-stress.

Take time for yourself

"Patience has been a key requirement for dealing with day to day frustrations. It is easy to feel overwhelmed and lonely when exiting the home country as no one else goes through the experience with you. It is a tsunami of details at the time of moving. Long walks, deep breaths, and taking time to do something for yourself (e.g., massage) can be helpful. Not to mention the wonders of a glass of wine!"

Laura, American expat living in the UK

As we read earlier, four-time expat Nicky faced the challenge of dealing with breast cancer while in Cambodia. Despite requiring them to be separated for several months, Nicky and her husband decided it was best for her to return to their native South Africa for treatment. During this time, she found herself in need of support as well as self-care.

BE RECEPTIVE TO POSITIVE SUPPORT AND ELIMINATE THE NEGATIVE

"It was a traumatic time especially as my mother had died of cancer the year before my diagnosis. However, I strived to be strong for the sake of my family. My husband was with me when I had to have surgery and for a week thereafter. He kept in daily contact with me when he returned to work in Cambodia. Communicating in this way helped me tremendously. I also planned a visit to Cambodia halfway through my treatment and this proved to be something positive to strive for.

I also learnt to accept and appreciate support from my sons, my sister and my friends. Although I had to live alone for most of this period I rarely felt truly alone as I was receptive to so much positive support. I did find I had to cut out people who made me feel anxious."

Nicky Sully, South African expat (Rwanda, Tanzania, Cambodia) now living in the Netherlands

As Nicky's story indicates, not all people are able to offer positive support during difficult times. Sometimes their own fears, insecurities or insensitivity get the better of them, and they say, do or act in ways that aren't fully supportive. In this case, it's best to remember your first responsibility is to yourself and healing. Taking a break from people who unwittingly interfere with that priority may be warranted.

DEALING WITH LOSS IN A HEALTHY MANNER

"When my house burned down in Tanzania, it was two pillars – emotional resilience and my community – that helped me process and work through the loss, and use that challenge to become a better, more focused person. I had a strong yoga practice and a good network of friends, and had seen strong examples of others moving through grief

in a holistic, healthy way that became my role models. I accepted my feelings, allowed myself to react to the loss deeply in safe environments, and I let myself be where I was without judging or trying to fix things that didn't have clear solutions.

I tend to be a bit impatient, but you can't hurry healing. Our bodies have an innate and immutable wisdom that closes wounds, mends bones, and allows us to grow whole again. Our minds, however, tend to get in the way. I had to trust my own process of healing and recovery, and the more I did so without judging or hurrying, the better I felt."

Elie Calhoun, American ATCK who has lived most of her life in Africa, including Kenya, Egypt, Tanzania, Liberia and Senegal.

Not everyone has the benefit of what Elie refers to as *'strong examples of moving through grief in a holistic, healthy way'*, so her specific examples of self-care after sustaining a difficult loss are instructive. In the end, each of us has to figure out what works best. Sometimes answering the simple question, 'Will this do more harm than good?' is helpful.

HEALTHY DIET AIDS RESILIENCE

Healthy eating means making good food choices. A good diet provides the fuel your body requires – appropriate amounts of high quality calories containing vitamins, minerals, protein, carbohydrates, healthy fats, fiber. Eating well helps keep in balance hormones regulating the body's natural indicators of hunger (ghrelin) and satiation (leptin) to avoid over- or under-eating. It also promotes physical and emotional well-being, helps with our energy level to keep us active, and better able to participate fully in life.

'When my house burned down in Tanzania, it was two pillars – emotional resilience and my community – that helped me process and work through the loss I had to trust my own process of healing and recovery, and the more I did so without judging or hurrying, the better I felt.'

NUTRITION, HEALTHY EATING AND EMOTIONAL RESILIENCE

"The food we eat, the way we nurture ourselves, is the most important of the basic human needs defined by Maslow. This, to most of us, automatic routine, affects everything in our bodies – and don't forget that our brains are a part of our bodies.

I give workshops and seminars, coach individuals, teams, families and companies next to writing articles and blogging about this, but to sum it up for you to build up your emotional resilience:

- *Eat breakfast, always*
- *Keep your blood sugar balanced by eating every three hours*
- *Stay away from the alcohol*
- *If you don't eat fish or seafood approximately five meals per week, do take an Omega 3 supplement*
- *Make at least one mealtime per day 'sacred'; a time when you hang out with family or friends*

The real traditional foods originating from the location you are in have a deep connection to the land, to the traditions, the culture, to the roots of that country. Whether you are there for a short or long posting, you want to feel welcome and rooted, that you can stand with two feet on the ground. This is what eating seasonal foods connected to where we are does to our bodies our nervous systems and our energy."

Cecilia Gotherstrom, Swedish expat (New Zealand, Australia, Austria) now living in the Netherlands and preparing to repatriate

By eating a nutritionally balanced diet, limiting the empty calories of alcohol and junk food, and remaining properly hydrated, we can maintain our bodies – and minds – in a healthy manner. This helps provide the energy we need when dealing with life's difficulties. Author, journalism professor and food activist Michael Pollan summarized healthy eating with the simple phrase: '*Eat food. Mostly plants. Not too much.*'

FITNESS, PHYSICAL ACTIVITY AND PLAY

We know that being active is good for us. Physical activity helps keep our body and mind healthy by strengthening our muscles and cardiovascular system, increasing our stamina, and triggering the release of the euphoria-inducing chemical endorphin. When we exercise, we tend to feel a sense of accomplishment – causing the release of feel-good serotonin. It clears our head, reduces stress, helps us relax and feel refreshed. Exercise can also help us maintain a proper weight, build strong bones and improve the quality of our sleep.

> 'Physical activity helps keep our body and mind healthy by strengthening our muscles and cardiovascular system, increasing our stamina, and triggering the release of the euphoria-inducing chemical endorphin feel-good serotonin. It clears our head, reduces stress, helps us relax and feel refreshed.'

If we select activities we enjoy, or which can be done in the company of others, we can also socialize and have fun while reaping these health benefits.

According to the US Centers for Disease Control, adults need a *minimum* of 150 minutes moderate-intensity aerobic activity, such as brisk walking, or 75 minutes at a vigorous level of intensity such as jogging or running (or a mix of both intensity levels), *in addition to* muscle-strengthening activities involving all major muscles groups, at least two times weekly. Ideally we would be getting twice these amounts. The key is to include activities which enhance our aerobic ability, strength, conditioning, flexibility, stamina, endurance and agility.

EXERCISE GIVES YOU SPACE TO LET THINGS GO

"Exercise, and in particular running, keeps me sane. I make sure I enjoy exercise, whether it's running, a team sport, yoga or an action sport. It has to be fun, otherwise I won't do it. Even a short ten-minute walk around the block or in a park can lift my mood. It gives me space to let things go and to get out of my mind. It strengthens my body and when I 'achieve' a walk, a run, or standing up on a surfboard, I know that if I can do that, I can achieve other things in life, too."

Carrie Sanderson, Anglo-Dutch Adult TCK/ CCK living in the Netherlands

Physical activity is an important part of a multi-pronged approach to enhancing our emotional resiliency. During the toughest times, it isn't always easy to maintain a regular exercise regimen. Still, most of us can squeeze in a half hour for yoga, stretching, simple exercises or a walk.

STAY ACTIVE

"Exercising, being active, being outside, having massages, being with friends, doing something you enjoy – all helped me to build and maintain resilience."

Nicola McCall, British expat/ repat

The great thing about physical activity is that every little bit helps, and it needn't all be done at once. Studies show health rewards exist even when done in increments of as little as ten minutes at a time. In a perfect world we could all spend an hour or more exercising daily, but it isn't, and most of us don't.

However, if we make it a priority we can fit in opportunities throughout our busy days. We can do stretches and isometric exercises before our morning coffee or tea. We can walk whenever possible, and use the stairs rather than an elevator. Go for a walk or a jog before (or after) dinner. Practice yoga alongside a DVD or video online. Take a long bike ride or play a round of golf on the weekend. Play tennis, join a running club or go for a swim. Hit the dance floor or take dancing lessons. Don't stand idly at your child's sports practices, kick the ball while waiting, or do a few laps around the field or pitch. Take the dog for a quick walk in the morning, meet up with friends at the gym to work out or take an exercise class together. Just get moving.

REJUVENATING REST

Sleep is integral to our physical, mental and cognitive health, quality of life and overall well-being. It supports growth and development, enhances learning and problem-solving skills, balances our hormones, and allows our cardiovascular and immune systems to repair and remain healthy:

- **Sleep:** In a pair of articles for the *New York Times*, Personal Health columnist Jane E. Brody highlighted not only the benefits, but also the absolute *necessity* of adequate sleep at every age, and the negative effects of not getting it. Studies indicate continually insufficient sleep has been linked to stress, heart disease, high blood pressure, chronic inflammation, obesity/ being overweight, diabetes, moodiness, and depression. Sleep deprivation can lead to fatigue, mental impairment, poor decision-making, and slower reflex response. It also suppresses the immune system and negatively affects productivity, concentration and memory.

- **Quality as important as quantity:** It is during deep sleep – usually not reached until the sixth hour or later – that our brain takes the information it has learned during the daytime, converts it to long-term memory and files it for future access. New pathways between neurons are developed, making room for this and future information retention and storage.

- **How much is enough:** It depends on the individual, but studies have found the healthiest adults regularly sleep seven to eight hours a night. Another study conducted by the University of California at San Diego, and the American Cancer Society found the highest mortality rates among people who sleep less than four and *more* than eight hours of sleep nightly.

- **Excess sleep isn't good for you:** It leaves you sluggish, listless and, surprisingly, tired. Sleeping too much can be a sign of withdrawing or hiding away. It also keeps you from taking action to improve your situation. Continued oversleeping could also be a warning sign of depression.

So how do improve our chances for having restful, rejuvenating slumber? The good news is there are many simple steps we can take for healthy sleep. Here are several suggestions:

- Ensure you do some physical activity daily. Endorphins will make you feel better, your body will benefit and in turn serve you better, and you'll be naturally tired at the end of the day.

- If you're waking up tired, look at your bedtime and when you need to wake up, and adjust accordingly. It's easy to get caught up in a good book or an interesting show on television, but don't let these pursuits get in the way of relaxing and preparing to sleep. Be consistent.

- At night keep your bedroom dark and on the slightly cool side (i.e., 70°F or lower).

- During the day seek at least half an hour exposure to sunlight as this helps regulate your deep sleep patterns.

- Before you retire, avoid overstimulation by overeating/ drinking, caffeine, alcohol, nicotine. Turn off all electronic devices at least an hour beforehand, as the light from their screens has been found to suppress the release of sleep-inducing melatonin.

- Take a hot bath or shower just before bed.

- While lying in bed, try conducting a mindfulness body scan – sequentially concentrate on each part of your body, noting how it feels and then relaxing it.

- If you are a light sleeper consider incorporating the use of quiet 'white noise' in the background.

- Milk, avocados, bananas, turkey and sunflower seeds all contain another sleep-inducer, tryptophan.

- Try an over-the-counter herbal approach with tea containing valerian, chamomile and lavender (my personal favorite).

- Discuss with your doctor taking low-dose melatonin, or if all else fails, a sleep prescription.

Nothing feels better than a good night sleep, but often we don't get as much as we should. Sometimes we have to make an effort to ensure we get it. As Benjamin Franklin noted: '*Early to bed and early to rise, makes a man healthy, wealthy and wise.*'

Avoid Risky Behaviors

Risky behaviors are those we may turn to in order to numb or shock ourselves into feeling 'alive'. They include alcohol, prescription and recreational drugs, and promiscuous or dangerous behaviors. Overeating shows up here too, as some people turn to favorite foods – often those they recall from childhood or a happier time – to help comfort themselves. When food is being used to block negative feelings such as sadness, loneliness, lack of confidence, low self-esteem or despair, it is essentially being abused. It likely won't help take your mind off those unpleasant feelings for long, it certainly won't address the underlying causes or fix a difficult situation. Similarly there are those who seek to control their intake of food in an unsafe manner, either through severe deprivation (anorexia) or a cycle of binging and purging (bulimia).

It is important to keep an eye not only on ourselves, but our loved ones, too. While these risky behaviors may appear at all ages, they are particularly damaging when present in adolescence or teenage years when our identity development is still evolving.

CHAPTER 13: OPTIMISM

Optimism is generally defined as the tendency to take a more encouraging or positive view. It means being disposed toward hopefulness, looking on the most favorable side or positive interpretation of conditions or events, expecting the best possible outcome. However, in the framework of positive psychology, optimism is broader in that it is active in its orientation and focused on the future. It includes finding meaning, setting goals, taking action, conveying gratitude, maintaining perspective, discovering hope and incorporating humor into our lives. Laughter not only helps us feel physically better, it also makes us more attractive to be around, improving our interactions with others:

- Don't settle for living a life of 'making do' in your current situation. Don't let life pass you by – find meaning in your actions, and make changes as necessary.

- Set goals, no matter how small or seemingly insignificant, and plan ahead to meet them.

- Remind yourself regularly of upcoming activities or events. If you aren't particularly interested in them, but haven't yet identified other activities to take their place, at least give them a chance in the interim.

- Do your best to enjoy situations once involved, especially the opportunity to interact with others. Socialization lifts our spirits and encourages the release of the feel-good chemical oxytocin.

- Savor the enjoyment of scheduling and looking forward to upcoming events and activities.

- Realize there is no one 'right' way. Remain open to finding your way, and be flexible.

- Maintain perspective and realize difficult times do eventually pass. Transitions can be tough, but the only way is through them.

- Don't sit on the sidelines – getting involved helps improve our current situation and future quality of life.

- Participation, movement and interaction can all contribute to becoming involved and integrated.

- Consider the people, events and things for which to be grateful. By conveying gratitude, we feel better about our immediate situation and discover hope. As Cicero noted: *'Gratitude is not only the greatest of virtues, but the parent of all the others.'*

> *'Optimism is generally defined as the tendency to take a more encouraging or positive view. It includes finding meaning, setting goals, taking action, conveying gratitude, maintaining perspective, discovering hope and incorporating humor into our lives.'*

- Incorporate humor in daily life to feel better and improve interactions with others.

IMPORTANCE OF A POSITIVE ATTITUDE

We know through brain-body connections we have the ability to affect our moods by how we act. Just as a negative outlook can set in motion a downward spiral of feelings, thoughts and behavior, maintaining an upbeat demeanor can help reinforce positive emotions and actions. One of the keys to emotional resilience cited most often by expats/ cross-culturals is that of having a positive attitude.

KEEPING EXPECTATIONS WIDE OPEN

"I think my emotional resilience has been quite high because the move and expat experience overall has been a choice and not a necessity. This was a move made because we wanted to and not because we had to, which I think makes a big difference in our outlook on the whole experience. Also, because I have never lived overseas my expectations have been wide open, so not knowing what to expect may have been an advantage. I may have been more resilient because I was excited about and looking forward to this move. There were some minor bumps along the way but I looked at this as part of the adventure."

Rose P., American expat living in the Netherlands

> *'Just as a negative outlook can set in motion a downward spiral of feelings, thoughts and behavior, maintaining an upbeat demeanor can help reinforce positive emotions and actions.'*

Our outlook and how we choose to focus our attention matter. If we look for the good in a situation, we're apt to find it. If we're convinced things will go badly, they probably will.

ATTITUDE IS ALL IN THE PERSPECTIVE

"The thing that keeps me going is a positive attitude. There is much to be said for the phrase 'a glass half full'. It is all in the perspective. You and you alone are responsible for your happiness. It is up to you to convince yourself that the next phase will be possible, and maybe even awesome. Attitude takes you a long way. Happy people enjoy life. Keep focused on the positive, the good, and figure out what you are going to do with the opportunities coming your way. How can I make a difference, be someone who cares, and be happy with the present?"

Martha P. Gonzalez, American expat in Sakhalin, Russia, after the Netherlands

I especially like the phrase 'Happy people enjoy life' and the connection Martha makes between a desired outcome – enjoying life – and how to go about achieving it by staying positive and embracing opportunities to become happy by making a difference. The next story reiterates this theme of being open to opportunities.

ATTITUDE MATTERS

"We have settled in to life here quite well. My husband has found a niche where he can put all of his past experience and expertise to good use at work. I love where I work and the people I have the good fortune to work with.

In dealing with this big adjustment, attitude matters. I view new experiences as an adventure, and I've had so many wonderful adventures since I've been here. At first, just going to the grocery store was an adventure in itself. Getting used to the traffic-flow patterns (or lack thereof) in the grocery stores took some time. Now I'm right there with the rest of 'em.

Another thing that has helped us get integrated quickly is our dear neighbors. They are always right there to help us figure out or sort through whatever we are facing, and always willing to help us with whatever we need. Neither my husband nor I are good at asking for or accepting help. But somehow when we found ourselves in our new environment, we found a way to open ourselves up to others (our neighbors, especially), and we have received a far greater reward – their friendship – than we could have ever anticipated."

Patti Tito, American expat living in the Netherlands

No more is a positive attitude reflected than in the next story. Often when we move from one culture to the next, we tend to focus on what we are losing, who we are leaving behind. Being able to think of each transition as an opportunity to build a brand new life – like reincarnation – is a wonderful gift to give ourselves.

ALMOST LIKE REINCARNATION

"Moving country forces you to rise to the challenge. From an early age I was exposed to change, but it was always positive change because my family made it a constructive experience, using optimistic words, and being excited about the new adventures to come. What some people would consider a stressful life change, I see as a challenge and adventure as I discover a new environment, and make a new life for myself.

It's almost like I have been reincarnated each time I move. I have new challenges, a new social life, new daily habits, and new hobbies. With each of my five moves in 17 years, I have had to remain flexible and positive, with high hopes and expectations to maximize all the opportunities that each move creates. Being optimistic, not being afraid of the risks or worst-case scenarios, but instead thinking how to make it work. Everyone and every place can be appreciated, you just have to spend time looking.

You can do that with anything in life; it's all about positive cognitive thinking and having a hardy personality. It's important though that you are not avoiding the problem, but rather facing it with a smile on your face.

It was the positive triad that got me through – positive thinking, being appreciative, and having a supportive family. A supportive family who knows about and can ingrain positive thinking and problem solving into your second nature has been the key to my being a happy expat."

Rebecca Claudia Zijderveld, Dutch TCK/repat currently living in the Netherlands after Italy, Sweden, Dubai and Singapore

As a TCK, Rebecca clearly sees the importance of her parents having modeled a positive approach to expatriate life. We can choose to focus on the opportunities afforded by it, or we can fixate on the negatives. By her own admission growing up amid her family's upbeat manner, positive thinking, and emphasis on gratitude, has made these attributes part of her own nature. The next story also reinforces the idea of appreciation.

BUILDING OPTIMISM THROUGH GRATITUDE

"Another great way to reflect on what I've achieved and build optimism, is through a gratitude journal in which I note down at the start of the day three or more things I am grateful for. This helps me to greet the day in a positive state of mind."

Carrie Sanderson, Anglo-Dutch Adult TCK/ CCK living in the Netherlands

Identifying and acknowledging what we appreciate and are thankful for encourages us to think, feel and act in a more positive manner. By making ourselves regularly think about those things for which we are grateful, we not only send the message that these things do exist, we also teach ourselves to be more hopeful. There is no 'right' way to do this. Some people like to do this twice daily, others twice weekly. For example, upon waking in the morning consider one or two things you appreciate. Then before falling asleep at night, think of things you did or said to help express gratitude. By writing down these thoughts in a 'gratitude journal' we can see the cumulative, affirming effect of these positive interactions. Gilbert Chesterton captured the importance of an appreciative perspective when he said: *'When it comes to life, the critical thing is whether you take things for granted or you take them with gratitude.'* Doing the latter feels far better and is good for us, too.

MAINTAINING A SENSE OF HUMOR

A sense of humor is an important tool in our emotional resiliency toolbox. Laughter brightens our mood, lifts our spirits and helps us relax by decreasing the levels of the stress hormones cortisol and epinephrine in our system. Since these hormones tend to suppress our immune system, there has been considerable medical research conducted on the positive impact of laughter in helping patients with HIV and cancer. Laughter helps lower blood pressure, improves vascular blood flow, and releases endorphins which can help alleviate discomfort and pain.

We needn't look far to find humor in cross-cultural life. When the first edition of her book, *Forced to Fly: An Anthology of Writing That Will Make You See the Funny Side of Living Abroad*, proved popular, serial expat Jo Parfitt found herself releasing an expanded, second edition last year. Full of humorous stories of mishaps, missteps and miscommunication, *Forced to Fly* is a wonderful reminder of the importance of stepping outside a situation and seeing how comical real life can be. The ability to laugh at ourselves and/ or our circumstances is powerful, even if only after the fact. It allows us to put difficult or uncomfortable events into perspective.

Humor helps build affirmatory emotions and a more positive point of view, while keeping us from feeling 'victimized' by what is just everyday life. While it may not have seemed that amusing to her at the time, we cannot help but chuckle at the thought of Parfitt running out of gas in 100°F heat in the middle of an Omani roundabout, trying to deal with an irritated policeman, late to pick up her son at school, and a trunkful of fresh fish beginning to gently steam. We're not laughing *at* her, and she's now able to laugh *with* us.

Sometimes we have to dig deep to find the humor in certain situations, but in most instances it is there.

Reframing

"One piece of advice I'd offer for making the best of a situation is reframing – quickly looking for and seeing the positive in a situation, and the humour, too. When you present something in a negative light, it is that way; when you see or find positive in it, it is that way."

Nicola McCall, British expat/repat

When reframing a particularly aggravating situation, it may take us a little longer to see the humor. If enough irritations or setbacks occur, they begin to add up and eventually we can't help but notice the aggregate is rather amusing, perhaps even comical. The next story is a good example of choosing to find humor during the tough times.

> 'One piece of advice I'd offer for making the best of a situation is reframing – quickly looking for and seeing the positive in a situation, and the humour, too.'

MENTAL GYMNASTICS AND A SENSE OF HUMOUR

"Wikipedia give a definition of resilience as the ability of a material to absorb energy when it is deformed elastically, and release that energy upon unloading. Yep. I can relate to that. Expat life has certainly deformed me, and I'd be the first to accept that it has done so elastically, since I now have the mental constitution of an industrial rubber tyre. As for releasing the energy, 'Bounce' is my new middle name. (I'd have preferred Beyoncé, but sometimes life takes over regardless). It does take some mental gymnastics to move to a new home in a vastly different country with a completely foreign tongue and utterly alien cultural ways. So where did I lay my hat, I hear you say? Tristan da Cunha? Ittoqqortoormiit? No, Spain, actually.

Although I came from the UK, which is part of Europe (as far as contributions go), to settle in Spain, which is part of Europe (as far as development grants go), the differences to be found were surprisingly huge and immensely trying.

My biggest personal challenge though – and it has challenged me on every level, not least the emotional one – is that of trust. My experience of professionals in the UK was that there were good, there were bad and there were all shades in between. But if you engaged the services of a professional, there was trust. It wasn't necessary to validate his professional status by demanding sight of his qualifications, by checking his affiliation with his professional body, by photocopying these documents and keeping them on file. Here, I came very unstuck.

We bought a large plot of land that boasted both an old house and a large old barn. That is, they may have been present on the land but were non-existent where paperwork was concerned. The notary should have put things right upon the sale of the land to us. As indeed should our solicitor. But each of them gave that same couldn't-care-less shrug and claimed it was somebody else's problem.

So we engaged an architect, recommended by a builder, to make things right so we could actually convert the house into a... house. It's a long story, but it transpired the architect did none of the things he was supposed to do, even though he had assured us all was proceeding swimmingly as the new house was built, and then he promptly disappeared over the horizon when the brown stuff hit the fan.

We were ridiculed by the powers-that-be because we had no copy of the architect's qualifications. What the...? It has taken several years and an enormous fine to get us out of the woods (although not yet fully in the clear – we will have a demolition file open on the house for another ten years). This brings me to what is, in my opinion, one of the most destructive emotions expats suffer when they are out of the comfort zone of the familiar – fear.

I have been to hell and back as a result of this. I was convinced I would be incarcerated, or at the very least deported. I had visions of bulldozers flattening the place with me and mine within. I lived in constant dread of policía patrol cars. Until one fine day my nearest and dearest neighbour sat me down and talked me round. 'They will not demolish your house,' she told me. 'You are one of some 300 built here without licence. If the mayor attempted to pull down all those properties, someone would shoot him, without doubt.'

This made me laugh, for the first time in a long while. And talking about it, engaging with the good people of this village, I heard the same sentiments oft-repeated. Even by the very policía of whom I was so frightened, but who are now on chatting terms when they descend into the valley to keep an eye out for miscreants. Now, I will go so far as to say I am pretty blasé about it all. And yes, the resilience is transferable.

My recent long, hard battle to get a fully licensed and legal business up and running in the barn, although every bit as challenging as were the problems with the house, has been tackled without faltering. I may still rant about the ridiculous processes and demands that have been made of me in order to achieve my goal, but I have hit every one head-on and come through it all with success. So I have engaged – check. I have adapted – check. Now I hope I am about to thrive."

Deborah Fletcher, British expat living in Spain

According to an old Irish proverb: '*A good laugh and a long sleep are the two best cures for anything.*' If we can't find humor in the ridiculous, perhaps a good night's sleep will help. If that doesn't work, we can always look outside our situation for things that make us laugh. Check out stand-up comedy acts on television or online, read an amusing book, watch a funny movie or television show. Get a joke book, practice a few particularly silly ones and try sharing them with friends and family. It doesn't matter how good you are at telling jokes because sometimes the mangling of them is even funnier.

If we want to inject some humor in life, young children can be an absolute gold mine. They're constantly questioning why things are the way they are. They find certain words odd-sounding, and may mix up or mispronounce words. There is so much they don't know, and they're constantly learning new information, new skills and how the world works. Sounds like many of us, just arrived in a new country where everything seems alien and we're trying to find our way.

HONOR YOUR DECISIONS

One way to manifest optimism in our life is remembering why we choose to be where we are. Did we end up in this cross-cultural move for a relationship, or for our or a loved one's job/ career? Whatever the reason, we should honor that commitment by giving it our best effort. Time passes whether we're happy or not, so better to make the most of it. Even if we find ourselves in a place/ situation we truly do not like, we can assist our adjustment – and possibly our acceptance – by taking action. Sometimes all it takes is finding those one or two friends who help make any place better, or at least easier to tolerate. We may end up surprising ourselves and coming to enjoy where we are.

THE IMPORTANCE OF CHOICE

"I think being able to choose whether or not we moved overseas made a big difference in our emotional preparation/ resilience. And also being open to asking questions and reaching out for help is what has helped and continues to help in making a difference."

Rose P.
American expat living in the Netherlands

Viewing something as the result of a choice, rather than an obligation or something over which we have no control, does tend to make us feel more kindly toward a decision. We feel vested in the outcome, and take responsibility for our actions.

REMEMBERING YOUR CHOICE AND WHAT YOU LOVE ABOUT IT

"I enjoy being an expat. My husband and I have recently happily extended our assignment in the Netherlands for another four years, so my son can finish high school here and we can continue to enjoy our expat lifestyle. We have lived outside the US for almost 12 years, first in Australia, then Scotland and now the Netherlands. I can't claim to have loved every minute of our expat experience, but overall it has been a very positive, stimulating and enjoyable time for our family.

Along the way, I've gotten to know a lot of other expats and ex-expats, many who've loved their experience and some who have not. I've often pondered what it is that allows me to be happy in circumstances others struggle with.

Both my husband and I made a positive choice to embark on an overseas assignment. We were interested in seeing new places and 'escaping' our somewhat dull American suburban existence and predictable corporate tracks. So, we both approached expat life with a positive attitude.

There have been times as an expat when I've gotten down either because I was feeling the strain of living in a new or foreign environment, I'd had yet another good friend move on, or because I felt I'd given up the opportunity to have a challenging career. Each time I've had to remind myself I was doing what I'd chosen to do, and I've had to remember what I love about being an expat, and make myself get out there and enjoy the experience."

Sara C., American expat living in the Netherlands after Australia and Scotland

There is no rule that says you have to be deliriously happy about every single aspect of a life choice. Few of us ever are. When times get tough, it does help to remember why we have made the choices we have. In considering our options, we often find we'd make them all over again.

COMMITMENT TO YOUR DECISION HELPS YOU THROUGH

"I moved to the Netherlands more than eight years ago. Although I already had an excellent job before I moved, and had a Dutch partner, the first year was quite tough for me. If I think what made it so difficult was the lack of a support network of family and friends – apart from my boyfriend of course – culture shock and not speaking Dutch.

My first job in the Netherlands required me to travel abroad a lot and I spent almost 50 percent of my time away from home. Because of that, the whole process of 'nesting', finding new friends, etc., took much longer.

I did not speak Dutch to start with and often did not feel 'part of the group'. Although most Dutch people I knew spoke English, and they did speak English to me one-on-one, when in a group, after a few minutes of conversation they would speak Dutch. That was extremely frustrating. One of my main goals was to learn the language as soon as possible. I noticed that being able to understand and make myself understood in Dutch had a huge impact on me feeling at home in the Netherlands.

Within the first year, I made my first 'real' friendships, and sharing my life with these people has made me feel very happy. But it wasn't until I left and returned to the Netherlands, after a couple of months stay in Brazil, that I really considered the Netherlands my home. When I came back I felt immediately – I am at home here. It was a very special moment.

I believe my determination to achieve what I want (i.e., learning the language), being open to new experiences and a belief that I made a right choice by moving have helped me to 'survive'– that and taking responsibility for my own decisions. I also believe it would have been much easier for me if I had been aware it can be difficult in the beginning and what I went through was part of a normal process."

Dorota Klop-Sowinska
Polish expat (Brazil and Mexico) now lives in the Netherlands

Over and over again we hear the same chorus – take responsibility for our decisions, remain open to opportunities and experiences, work through the frustrations, stay positive. Change and transitions aren't easy to deal with, but eventually we get through them, and we often find ourselves in a better place for having weathered them.

THE PAST AS FUTURE

Mindfulness reminds us to live in the present. However, when things aren't going well, we can augment our mindful practice with a review of earlier experiences. By looking to the past to help inform the future we consider what went well, what didn't, and why. We buoy our confidence by building on our successes. We seek to replicate the conditions of what worked for us previously, and we scour our failures to glean lessons learned.

In order for such an assessment to be most effective, it should have the following components:

- **Experience inventory review:** Think back on similar past situations, or ones which might be relevant to the current one. These can be when you were happy, healthy, involved and balanced, or during times you were the exact opposite.

- **Identify your 'best practices':** Reflect on things you did which either contributed to a prior positive situation, or helped you move beyond a more negative one. Also give some thought to behaviors or actions which made things worse; resolve not to repeat them, and consider how you might do things differently in the future.

- **Make an action plan:** Pick two or three of your previous best practices and consider how you can incorporate them into your present situation.

We're more apt to achieve the improvements we seek when our action items follow the 'SMART' format, making them specific, measurable, attainable, realistic and timely. Ideas such as '*I should get more sleep like I used to*' or '*I should get more socially involved like I was in Singapore*' or '*I want to experience more of the local culture as I did in Madrid*' are too vague. In coming up with small, detailed, measurable goals you are able to hold yourself accountable. Better yet, write down your goals *as if they are already achieved*. Read them aloud regularly, and visualize yourself successfully carrying them out. Now your goals might look like this:

> '*I find it so relaxing to get into bed at 10 pm each night and take a few minutes to review my day before turning off the lights by 10:15 pm.*'

'I really look forward to late Sunday afternoons when a small group of people – friends, neighbors, colleagues, or their guests – join me for conversation and a simple meal.

'I feel so much more a part of Toronto now that I identify and engage in at least one cultural activity weekly.'

The following story exemplifies the idea of using the existence of past accomplishments as a springboard for future success. If you've done something before, you have the experience and the confidence to do it again.

ACKNOWLEDGE THE LITTLE ACCOMPLISHMENTS

"I make sure I pat myself on my back for every accomplishment, even little ones; it helps me to reflect on what I have already achieved. I view new challenges with a degree of determination and optimism, knowing I have already managed to overcome other obstacles. I did this recently when I moved back to the Netherlands. I reminded myself I have moved countries before and managed to build my life in those countries. I can do it again, it just takes time."

Carrie Sanderson, Anglo-Dutch Adult TCK/ CCK living in the Netherlands

Another benefit of acknowledging little accomplishments? According to Loretta Graziano Breuning, celebrating a small victory releases dopamine, which makes you feel good. Find something to celebrate every day for 45 days – how long Graziano Breuning says it takes to build new neuron pathways in your brain to make a habit take root – and you'll not only have a daily boost of dopamine, it will be become something you do without thinking. In this manner you learn to be happy with your progress toward a goal, and not simply the accomplishment itself. Breaking down a large project into small, easily doable steps allows us to celebrate our progress. This is why so many of us get a little lift from making a 'to do' list and checking off items as we complete them.

> *'Find something to celebrate every day for 45 days – how long it takes to build new neuron pathways in your brain to make a habit take root – and you'll not only have a daily boost of dopamine, it will be become something you do without thinking.'*

LEARNING ACCEPTANCE

"Acceptance – It doesn't mean you're giving up on things, it just makes it easier to do something different and new. Another tool I use regularly is '4 choices' do you:
- *change the situation*
- *change how you feel about, have expectations of, or behave in the situation*
- *tolerate the situation (find humour, reframe, ignore, etc.)*
- *leave the situation, and the impact of that.*

Another aspect is taking responsibility for yourself and the decisions made, or where you can make the decisions you can and be responsible for the outcomes."

Nicola McCall, British expat/ repat

Shifting our perspective of what acceptance means, considering our 'four choices', and owning our decisions are all good tactics for becoming more comfortable in our present situation. Optimism means we *embrace change* rather than fear it.

BECOMING MORE RESILIENT WITH TIME AND EXPERIENCE

"I am an expat who is now living in my 11th country so we have had plenty of experiences that have gone well and not so well.

With each move I think it becomes easier. You realize there will be a period of adjustment – a period of highs followed by a lower period – you are able to see that things will settle and get better with time. What has gone well is the adjustment of our children with each move. The kids have been very resilient and have benefited enormously from each move.

What has not gone well? Nothing really stands out as a huge mistake. Yes, things have gone wrong but nothing looking back stands out glaringly. Things have been hard at times – it is not easy moving overseas, but I definitely believe it is worthwhile looking back. There is not one move I regret. Every move has given our family great experience and challenges, but the opportunity to learn and try new things.

I think all of us have become more resilient with time and with each move. You realize that when things may seem hard and difficult that is a temporary situation and things will get better. Especially for the kids, I think they can look back and say 'that was hard for me but I overcame it and stuck with it and now I can do it'. One challenge has been to keep up their music and sports with the changes in different places, but they have learned new things, tried new ideas and I think gained overall in their pursuits.

My children are both confident and outgoing and I believe that comes from their experiences overseas. They know how to make friends, how to overcome adversity (e.g., starting a new school and needing to catch up on certain areas or being ahead in other areas) and how to adapt to situations."

Helen Maffini, serial expat now living in her eleventh country

By recognizing current difficulties are temporary and we've overcome hardships before, we can take a more positive attitude of knowing we can do so again. We find it easier to become – or remain – optimistic. We integrate our past into our present to reach the future state we desire.

> *'A tool I use regularly is '4 choices:*
> - *change the situation*
> - *change how you feel about, have expectations of, or behave in the situation*
> - *tolerate the situation (find humour, reframe, ignore, etc.)*
> - *leave the situation'.'*

PART IV:

THE EMOTIONALLY RESILIENT EXPAT

'Twenty years from now you will be more disappointed by the things you didn't do than by the ones you did do. So throw off the bowlines. Sail away from the safe harbor. Catch the trade winds in your sails. Explore. Dream. Discover.'

Recently discovered to be attributed to the mother of H. Jackson Brown, Jr.

STORM'S AFTERMATH

Early on I felt helpless, like an alien thrust into unfamiliar territory, the landscape forbidding and not remotely recognizable. Occasionally I would awaken in the middle of the night, panic rising inside as I immediately remembered the terrible troubles with which we were dealing. I would lie there in the darkness feeling overwhelmed, wondering when or how the healing would come. I learned to breathe deeply, focusing on the rise and fall of my chest, slowly relaxing my body to help calm my mind.

I kept my tears to myself, and spent my days trying to navigate this new terrain. I learned it's not unusual for someone to experience pangs of guilt and shame over the disruption and emotional turmoil resulting from their illness, and the last thing I wanted to do was inadvertently fuel those feelings. Over time the urge to cry lessened, and my eyes stopped welling up whenever I had to discuss what was going on. I came to realize hiding my emotions wasn't setting a healthy example, either. Sometimes crying is a healthy release of emotional and physical tension, like a summer thunderstorm. Lightning strikes, the rain falls, and then you gather yourself together and get on with doing what needs to be done.

The beauty – and yes, there is a raw beauty, even in the darkest of times – of dealing with the worst is the way in which it crystallizes your thoughts on what is truly important. It isn't the things you were doing, or your plans, and it isn't what people might think or say. There is a real clarity that comes with the understanding that *nothing* else matters except helping those we love as they go through difficult times.

And with that understanding comes acceptance that life changes, sometimes not for the better or at least not at once. These are the stuff large life transitions are made of. Each person deals with this differently. For me it has meant some tears shed during quiet moments. We acknowledge the pain of losing others, or seeing loved ones suffering, and it takes a toll. But then we wipe away the tears, take a few deep breaths and renew efforts to help. It becomes a feeling of galvanizing strength with the realization I cannot help anyone if I am a mess myself. With that remit in mind, I would redouble self-care efforts. These included a few minutes of meditation in the mornings, long walks with the dog, increased exercise, practicing mindfulness, keeping meals healthy and nutritious, limiting the wine.

Throughout the past year I continued writing, albeit in a more fractured, haphazard way. Sometimes I could sit and compose a decent draft of an article or short story, and other times the faucet of words was firmly wrenched shut. I've blogged less frequently, unsure of what to write. I haven't wanted to be either falsely upbeat or too much of a downer, yet also cautious about not bursting the bubble of our privacy. Certain projects, including this book, were set aside for months on end. This is life. Sometimes bad things happen, we change course, and do what is needed.

I spent considerable time researching and reading to understand, and occasionally to escape. I took to heart the words of many contributors in their stories and emails, sharing what worked for them in their darkest times. I expressed gratitude. Yes, even in the midst of everything going on, there still were many things for which to be thankful. Confiding in a couple close friends – themselves familiar with the difficulties of dealing with a sudden rough patch of one crisis after another, or of having dealt with their own depression or that of a loved one – gave me additional insight into what this beloved soul was going through, and helped immensely.

As hard as you try, I learned you cannot make someone else get well. You cannot will them to get better. But you can have faith in them. You can soothe and support and be steadfast in your conviction that together you will figure out the way ahead. You can offer hope that the situation will not last forever, and it need not define them. Most of all, you can be there.

With time, attention and – most importantly – love, things do improve. Slowly but surely, the worst of the storm has passed. The sun is once again peeking through the clouds, and for that, I am grateful indeed.

CHAPTER 14: FACTORS™ IN EMOTIONAL RESILIENCE

We've examined expat/ cross-cultural life and identified several issues which can bring about difficulty and pain. We've explored developments in brain-body connections and a number of fields of study, which collectively offer ways to strengthen our emotional resilience and alleviate our suffering. We've taken that information and applied it directly to intercultural challenges, arming ourselves with tools, techniques and tips for living a more resilient life.

So what are we to make of all of this?

We've heard from expats, cross-culturals, TCKs, CCKs, and global nomads, past and present. They've shared their thoughts and experiences about the good, the bad and even the ugly side of life lived across cultures. We've perused key points and insights from books, articles, journals, websites and blog sites. We've digested dozens of stories, suggestions, recommendations and regrets.

What does it all *mean*?

After more than two years living, breathing, wondering, researching, reading, writing, asking, listening, questioning, extracting, simplifying, pondering and trying to put it all together in a cohesive whole, here's what I've come up with:

- **Everyone everywhere needs emotional resilience:** Our very humanity means no life is so gilded, so protected, so effortless, so unaffected that resilience is unnecessary. We all need to be able to adapt to the significant challenges, misfortunes and setbacks life throws our way. We also need to maintain or eventually return to a positive view of ourselves during or after such turmoil.

- **Possessing emotional resilience doesn't protect us from hardship, misfortune, turmoil or strife:** It won't keep us from harm or hurting, but it can improve our ability to deal with and recover from these events.

- **We can maintain, enhance, restore and renew our levels of resiliency:** It may take time, effort, energy, persistence and mindful attention, but it is possible. Moreover, it is crucial we do so.

- **We can practice resilience consciously and conscientiously:** When we practice resiliency in our daily lives, we make it easier to stress less and address the smaller, day-to-day irritations and difficulties which confront us. More importantly, practicing resiliency helps prepare us to acknowledge, confront, and deal with the larger, deeper, more painful events and hardships that will come our way.

- **All life requires transitions and change, and living across cultures exposes us to an overlay of additional emotional challenges:** These transitions can be significant, sustained and continual, and the stages of change take time and may be painful. Issues can include identity, identity development, home, belonging, culture shock, restlessness, rootlessness and more.

- **Transitions and change bring opportunities, challenges, enriching gifts and difficult losses, but above all, they bring growth:** It is up to us whether we choose to embrace this growth as positive or negative. Bad things may happen to us, but that does not mean good cannot come from it. Sometimes the lessons are profound.

- **To strengthen our stores of emotional resilience, we can incorporate FACTORS™ into our lives. FACTORS™ stands for:**
  - Family
  - Awareness
  - Communication
  - Transitions
  - Optimism
  - Rituals
  - Significance/ something bigger than ourselves

Over time I've realized the underlying core of these seven recurring themes helps point the way toward a healthier, more positive, cross-cultural experience. I have captured these themes in the simple mnemonic memory device, **FACTORS™**. I don't offer this to be glib or trite, but rather to help focus on what is most important among all the stories, information, research, concepts, theories and data.

FAMILY

Family is paramount. It doesn't matter whether we were a tight-knit or dysfunctional family when we began our expat/ cross-cultural journey, whether we are single, in a relationship or the parents of two, three or seven children. Everyone is part of a family unit, whether through blood or marriage or friendship. In every case, we are looking to each other for connection, stability, a sense of home and of belonging, community, caring and love. Family members need to know they are cared for, valued and loved.

If the primary relationship within a family suffers, it is likely the relationship between parent and child will suffer too. The sad fact is that just as many non-expat marriages do strain, some expat marriages don't bear the weight of moving, changing, transitioning and crossing cultures. It is even more critical as expat spouses to do our utmost to maintain strong, healthy relationships. If separation and divorce are in the cards, both parties must make every effort to remain a viable, centering presence in the lives of our children. It is *that* important – the stakes are *that* high.

AWARENESS

Awareness of the challenges and opportunities inherent in the expat/ cross-cultural experience is important. At a minimum, it helps to have an understanding of the range of key issues expats face (culture shock, identity, home, belonging and so on). In addition too, an understanding of transitions phases, change model stages and the various tools outlined (resilience, emotional, social and cultural intelligence, intercultural competency, positive psychology, mindfulness and so on), and awareness of the relevance and linkage among them in building emotional resilience.

It is particularly important we are aware of our emotions, and learn to employ self-calming techniques to quiet negative self-beliefs and decrease personal distress when our emotions threaten to overwhelm us. Awareness includes accurately sending and picking up on the signals of ourselves and others, especially if we or someone we care about is disoriented, confused or having difficulty with transitions.

> 'Practicing resiliency helps prepare us to acknowledge, confront, and deal with the larger, deeper, more painful events and hardships that will come our way.'

COMMUNICATION

Maintaining open, ongoing contact is crucial – it must be candid and continuous. Listen, talk, write, share experiences, or just be together. Fostering communication helps maintain and strengthen our familial and friend connections. We then have a better sense of where each member is in terms of identity congruence (integrating all the pieces of who we are), emotional resilience and optimism, in addition to both the expat transition process phases and change model stages, and can act accordingly. Through communication we can employ empathy (the ability to understand and share how others are feeling) and compassion (awareness of the suffering of others coupled with the wish to relieve it).

TRANSITIONS

Transitions are to be respected. The **transition process phases** take us from involvement to leaving, to a transitory state, to entry and finally to re-involvement. As we make this journey, we go through the **stages of change** – denial, anger/ irritation, bargaining, depression, and ultimately acceptance. Pollock and Van Reken's **RAFT** (Reconciliation, Affirmation, Farewells, Think destination, page 228) is a good a place to start to ensure we

> 'Transitions and change bring opportunities, challenges, enriching gifts and difficult losses, but above all, they bring growth.'

'leave well to enter well' whether we are the ones doing the leaving, or are being left behind when others we care about leave. These RAFT actions can help us navigate ourselves, and our family members, through the expat transition process and the change model, with optimism, emotional resilience, emotional/ social/ cultural intelligence, intercultural competency and identity intact.

OPTIMISM

Optimism, and the corresponding emotional resilience, emotional and social intelligence, cultural intelligence, intercultural competence and mindfulness *can* be learned, developed and strengthened. All are important contributors to our sense of identity. They also impact our dealing with the change model and moving through transitions. Optimism is future-oriented, and helps us discover hope, practice gratitude, maintain perspective, visualize improvement and incorporate humor in our daily lives.

RITUALS

Rituals help establish and reaffirm our sense of self (identity), and can be used to boost communication, optimism and emotional resilience. Rituals not only remind us where we came from, they also reflect where we've been along the way, resulting in who we are today. They are a form of shared memories and help to create and maintain bonds. By acknowledging their importance, we honor ourselves and our experiences.

SIGNIFICANCE/ SOMETHING BIGGER THAN OURSELVES

It is my personal opinion that we human beings need – and fare better when we have – belief in a higher being, or that which brings order to our universe. It may be religious faith, spirituality, karma, fate, or simply the gnawing sense we were put on this earth for a purpose. Whatever we choose for our belief system, it helps give our lives structure, meaning and significance, and I believe we benefit from it, individually and collectively. It helps us find our way in life, set goals, take action. It is what keeps us from being self-absorbed and ego-centric. It helps us express gratitude and appreciation, and practice empathy and compassion for ourselves and others.

I profoundly believe all of us – currently living, aspiring to live or having lived cross-culturally – benefit enormously from building our emotional resilience reserves. As I said at the beginning of this book, we start with tiny, focused steps to build emotional resilience through the rich variety of tools and practices available to us.

Now we are wrapping up the essence of what emotional resilience can mean to us and how to cultivate it, I would like to reiterate – if you, a family member or someone you know seems particularly stuck in a transition process phase or change model stage, or are exhibiting signs of depression or helplessness, please *do not hesitate to seek assistance*. As several of the contributors shared in their stories, sometimes sharing their concerns was enough to help turn things around, other times treatment in the form of therapy and/ or medication may be advised. There should be no stigma or shame in working with a therapist, counselor, psychologist, psychiatrist or other health practitioner. Placing the well-being of yourself or your family above all else is a sign of emotional strength, maturity, and ultimately resilience.

CHAPTER 15: CONTINUING THE CONVERSATION

As this book draws to a close, it is only fitting we take stock of the original intent: learn more about and embrace emotional resilience as integral to dealing with the difficulties, challenges and continuous change inherent in expatriate life. We've explored new findings and recent cross-disciplinary developments in the physiological and social sciences that can help us increase our reserves of resilience, especially in tough times. Building on the experiences, insights, research and hard work of many – and sharing the stories of those who came before us – we are in a better position to aid and encourage expats and cross-culturals to live healthier, more positive, emotionally engaged, culturally connected global lives.

I hope this book has fulfilled its purpose by offering you a wide array of tips, recommendations, tested techniques and practical solutions to help enhance emotional resilience in your life, and the lives of those for whom you care. I am indebted to Doug Ota for his suggestion: '*As with any food rich in nutrition, this book is best sampled regularly and digested slowly.*' I hope you will keep it close at hand, refer to it often, and perhaps return to it as needed for fresh insight and perspective. Discuss it, share it, pass it on.

However, please remember this book is not written in a vacuum. It is part of an ongoing dialogue among those who have led mobile, cross-cultural, global lives and wish to share their experiences, observations and insights. It is meant to continue the conversation started long ago, a discussion which keeps evolving and becomes richer with time and testimony.

We expats/ cross-culturals do our best to care for, raise and guide our TCK/ CCK children

'This book is part of an ongoing dialogue among those who have led mobile, cross-cultural, global lives and wish to share their experiences, observations and insights. It is meant to continue the conversation started long ago, a discussion which keeps evolving and becomes richer with time and testimony.'

to adulthood (and beyond), while also staying connected to and supporting our aging parents and relatives. We sometimes have a few wrenches thrown in due to our lack of immediate proximity. We do this while maintaining a (hopefully) healthy family life and juggling work and career aspirations, a coterie of devoted friends, fitness, favored activities, community involvement and personal growth.

We're told to get more sleep. It seems we need it far more than we know. I'm talking good quality sleep which rejuvenates and restores. The kind most of us haven't experienced since childhood when we could zonk out with the best of them. The last time I recall going to bed and sleeping through the night, waking refreshed and raring to go? Somewhere between the university days – late nights writing papers, early morning classes, cramming for tests and partying as if it were pop/ funk star Prince's proverbial 1999 – and the arrival of children.

For more than two years I've been reading and researching the importance of emotional resilience in expat life for this book, and the list of things I *could, should, ought* to be doing to maintain some semblance of emotional and physical well-being is starting to verge on the unhealthy.

Almost, but not quite.

I'm not quibbling with the need to watch what I eat, exercise on a regular basis to drop unwanted pounds and help maintain cardiovascular health, strength, flexibility and endurance. We need to be eating healthy foods with plenty of fresh fruits and vegetables, going easy on meat, alcohol and high-calorie stuff with minimal nutritional value.

We're instructed to remember the multivitamins, fish oil and calcium tablets. Eliminate the carbonated beverages, watch the caffeine, drink green tea, stay hydrated with plenty of pure, clean water.

In addition to those eight hours of restful sleep nightly, we're to excel in our careers with meaningful work which pays the bills and makes a difference, meditate to clarify our minds, read for pleasure, read to gain new knowledge and expand said clarified minds. We're encouraged to unplug from too much time spent online or using various screens (you can insert your own temptations here), spend time with others to fulfill our intrinsic need for interpersonal connections, spend time alone for emotional balance. We're also to address our spiritual needs, fit in volunteer work to build community and help others, retain a sense of gratitude, and on and on.

We're supposed to do all this and somehow remember to throw in a few loads of laundry, walk the dog, keep the fridge and pantry reasonably stocked, vacuum occasionally, dust now and then, brush our teeth at least twice daily and change the cat litter?

Remember, this is the 'must do' list *before* we even add anything related to caring for babies or toddlers, chauffeuring adolescents, ensuring our teens aren't running amok and our young adult children are on track, climbing the corporate/ non-profit/ small business/ government ladder or helping to deal with the latest development in our elderly parents' gradual decline.

If it seems like a lot, that's because it *is*.

Just when we figure how to juggle the various requirements in our daily life, they change and we're often left standing with someone's unmet need lying on the ground. Most often it's one (or more) of our own.

And so it goes.

Let's face it. Life is complicated and messy. Sometimes it's a bit overwhelming. Regardless, I hope you will take the time to relax, draw a deep, meditative breath or two, and assess whether you can honestly say you're doing the following:

- **Engage:** Are you interacting with your physical and cultural surroundings? Are you deeply connected to others, near and far? Are you fully involved in activities and issues that resonate with you? If you answered no to any of these questions, are you considering ways to rectify that?

- **Adapt:** Are you comfortable with the conditions of the life you lead, adjusting to what you are able and accepting what you cannot? Are you able to modify, minimize or resolve any disconnects between the reality in which you exist and the values, beliefs and attitudes that matter to you? Are you mindful in your cross-cultural interactions? Are you enacting the changes necessary to make peace with difficulties and irritations to move beyond mere survival? Are you employing self-care, empathy and compassion?

- **Thrive:** Do you seek out and embrace opportunities for positive change and growth? Are you both comfortable in and energized by your life? What else could you imagine doing to prosper cross-culturally. Are you truly flourishing?

Living an expat, cross-cultural life can be, and is, wonderfully enriching, but it adds its own special challenges which need to be acknowledged and addressed. I hope this book offers you valuable insights, practical advice, helpful suggestions and an appreciation for the amazing opportunities life presents to each and every one of us.

Let's continue the conversation. Above all, I hope you engage, adapt and thrive.

AFTERWORD

While many books don't include an afterword, I cannot imagine doing so with this book. I believe on a matter as subjective and deeply personal as embracing emotional resilience to thrive across countries and cultures, it is not only fitting but also important to end with the broader insights and perspectives of experience. I can think of no one more appropriate to have the last word on the importance of expats/ cross-culturals enhancing their emotional resiliency, than Julia Simens, international counselor, speaker, and author of the acclaimed book, *Emotional Resilience and the Expat Child*.

'Few will have the greatness to bend history, but each of us can work to change a small portion of events, and in the total of all those acts will be written the history of a generation. It is from numberless diverse acts of courage and belief that human history is shaped.'
Robert F. Kennedy

The original premise of this book, even the need for this book, comes from our time in history. Expats are increasingly common in our global world. I am a firm believer that storytelling can be the key to success in developing happy children and happy adults.

When so many of us joined together to support global nomads around the world, it was because this is also our life. Raising children in your home country can be challenging in many ways, but can you imagine raising your child abroad? This was the choice made by many of the voices in Linda Janssen's book. Others talked of their personal growth through the experience. Both were undertaken while continually on the move.

An increasing number of children are being raised in foreign countries, as their parents are sent overseas by their businesses, corporations or government agencies. Some choose to go abroad because they are people who want to see the world. In today's global community, all of us are searching for effective tools to help our children thrive. Giving ourselves the ability to voice our experiences, tell our stories and grow is a very powerful tool.

When you look at the human resources departments of many major corporations around the world, the focus can appear to be only on work permits, government requirements and physical moving. How could such widely held practices continue? When will these organizations/ corporations realize the emotional well-being of their employees is the key factor in a successful career?

A good, working definition of emotional resilience is the ability to 'engage, adapt and thrive'. This is why leaders in the field of expat/ cross-cultural issues – the Useems, Pollock, and Van Reken – voiced the need for global nomads to have support in their transitions, and why Goleman, Seligman and Amen focus on personal growth. This leads to Bryson, Pascoe, and Quick, supporting global nomads in key stages in their life. We can only look forward to more from Petriglieri, Grappo and Janssen. I feel 'we' are so convinced of the need for this support, these views and policies, that we are sure anyone opposing them must be deceived of reality or lack knowledge about personal growth. We are a world which is indeed global and wanting to be resilient, happy, and engaged.

Does the lack of support in global companies lead, inevitably, to a major crisis? Of course not – though it's hardly conducive to a stable workforce or long-term continuation of growth. What inevitably arises from this lack of support is the attempt by the spouses/ partners, utterly convinced of its rectitude, to use all available resources to support their family. This is why we research, blog, tweet, and support other global nomads around the world.

"The rapid changes in the 21st century have left everyone from ambitious first-time entrepreneurs to seasoned business owners facing unique challenges that leave them feeling anxious and uncertain about their own capabilities," says Viki Winterton, global coach and founder of the Expert Insights™ Family of Opportunity magazines, coaching networks and directories, programs and events. Everyone needs to build on his or her own baseline of resiliency. Companies have the need for getting the right employees with the right skillsets in the right places at the right times. And this will continue to grow. But we must also address the ability for personal and family growth.

Janssen reminds us we *can* maintain, enhance, restore and renew our levels of resiliency. It may take time, effort, energy, persistence and mindful attention, but it *is* possible. With mindful self-compassion, we're better able to recognize when we are under stress and confront the issues in our lives. Mindfulness allows us to take a kinder and more sustainable approach to life's challenges. Self-compassion gives us emotional strength and resilience, and also provides us with the support to make necessary changes in our lives and reach our full potential.

We need to use humor, hope and empathy to build up our adult/ child relationships and emphasize respect and dignity for everyone as we move around the world and shape our human history.

Julia L. Simens
Author, *Emotional Resilience and the Expat Child: Practical Tips* and *Storytelling Techniques That Will Strengthen the Global Family*
www.jsimens.com

REFERENCES AND RESOURCES

BOOKS

Amen, Daniel G., MD. *Change Your Brain, Change Your Body: Use Your Brain to Get and Keep the Body You Have Always Wanted*. Random House Digital, Inc., 2010.

Amen, Daniel G., MD. *Change Your Brain, Change Your Life: The Breakthrough Program for Anxiety, Depression, Obsessiveness, Anger and Impulsiveness*. Random House Digital, Inc., 2008.

Anthony, Gerald W., Ph.D. *Cultural Rehydration: A Laymen's Guide to Dealing with Culture Shock*. 2009.

Ashman, Anastasia M. and Jennifer Eaton Gökmen, eds. *Tales from the Expat Harem: Foreign Women in Modern Turkey*. Dogan Kitap Publishing, 4th ed., 2007.

Borysenko, Joan, Ph.D. *It's Not the End of the World: Developing Resilience in Times of Change*. Hay House, Inc., 2009.

Brayer Hess, Melissa and Patricia Linderman. *The Expert Expat: Your Guide to Successful Relocation Abroad*. Nicholas Brealey Publishing, 2007.

Bryson, Debra R. and Charise M. Hoge. *Portable Identity: A Woman's Guide to Maintaining a Sense of Self While Moving Overseas*. Transition Press International, 2003, 2005.

Copeland, Anne P. and Marissa Lombardi. *In Their Own Voice: Intercultural Meaning in Everyday Stories*. The Interchange Institute, 2011.

Costa Eriksson, Simone T. and Ana Serra. *The Mission of Detective Mike: Moving Abroad*. Summertime Publishing, 2010.

Covey, Stephen R. *The Seven Habits of Highly Effective People: Powerful Lessons in Personal Change*. Free Press, 1989.

Csikszentmihalyi, Mihaly. *Flow: The Psychology of Optimal Experience*. HarperCollins, 1990.

Davis, Martha, Ph.D., Elizabeth Robbins Eshelman, MSW., and Matthew McKay, Ph.D. *The Relaxation and Stress Reduction Workbook*. New Harbinger Publications, Inc., 6th ed., 2008.

Elmer, Duane. *Cross-Cultural Connections: Stepping Out and Fitting In Around the World*. InterVarsity Press, 2002.

Frederickson, Barbara, Ph.D. *Positivity: Groundbreaking Resource Reveals How to Embrace the Hidden Strength of Positive Emotions, Overcome Negativity, and Thrive*. Crown Publishers, 2009.

Gamble, Kathleen. *Expat Alien: My Global Adventures*. CreateSpace, 2012.

Gawain, Shakti. *Creative Visualization: Use the Power of Your Imagination to Create What You Want in Your Life*. Revised edition, Nataraj Publishing, 2002.

Gidley, Apple. *Expat Life: Slice by Slice*. Summertime Publishing, 2012.

Goleman, Daniel. *Emotional Intelligence: Why It Can Matter More Than IQ*. Bloomsbury, 1996.

Goleman, Daniel. *Social Intelligence: The New Science of Human Relationships*. Hutchinson, 2006.

Goleman, Daniel. *The Brain and Emotional Intelligence: New Insights*. More Than Sound LLC, 2011.

Goulston, Mark. *Just Listen: Discover the Secret to Getting Through to Absolutely Anyone*. Amacom, 2010.

Graziano Breuning, Loretta, Ph.D. *Meet Your Happy Chemicals: Dopamine, Endorphin, Oxytocin, Serotonin*. System Integrity Press, 2012.

Heinzer, Jeanne A. *Living Your Best Life Abroad: From Surviving to Thriving.* Summertime Publishing, 2009.

Hofsteede, Geert. *Culture's Consequences: Comparing Values, Behaviors, Institutions and Organizations Across Nations.* Sage Publications, Inc., 2nd ed., 2001.

Hofsteede, Gert Jan, Paul B. Pederson and Geert Hofsteede. *Exploring Culture: Exercises, Stories and Synthetic Cultures.* Intercultural Press, Inc., 2002.

Kabat-Zinn, Jon. *Mindfulness for Beginners: Reclaiming the Present Moment and Your Life.* Sounds True, 2011.

Klauser, Henriette Anne, Ph.D. *Write It Down, Make It Happen: Knowing What You Want and Getting It.* Scribner, 2000.

Lanier, Sarah A. *Foreign to Familiar: Understanding Hot- and Cold-Climate Cultures.* McDougal Publishing, 2000.

Lantieri, Linda and Daniel Goleman. *Building Emotional Intelligence.* Sounds True Inc., 2008.

Livermore, David A. *Cultural Intelligence: Improving Your CQ to Engage Our Multicultural World.* Baker Academic, 2009.

Livermore, David A. *Leading With Cultural Intelligence: The New Secret to Success.* Amacom, 2010.

MacPherson, Mary-Anne M., RHN., RNCP., ROHP. *Stress Free For Life NOW!* Health Transformation Publications, 5th ed., 2012.

Maffini, Helen. *Sammy's Next Move.* Summertime, 2011.

Martins, Andrea and Victoria Hepworth. *Expat Women: Confessions – 50 Answers to Your Real Life Questions About Living Abroad.* Expat Women Enterprises Pty Ltd. ATF Expat Women Trust, 2011.

McAnear Smith, Kathleen. *Parents on the Move! Preparing Your Family for a Successful and Creative Relocation.* DestinyImage™ Europe, 2010.

Mycklebust, Maggie. *Fly Away Home*. Summertime Publishing, 2012.

Minirth, Frank, MD. *Choosing Happiness: Even When Life is Hard*. Spire, 3rd ed., 2011.

Murphy, Joseph. *The Power of Your Subconscious Mind*. SoHo Books, 2012.

Neenan, Michael. *Developing Resilience: A Cognitive-Behavioural Approach*. Routledge, 2009.

Ni Bhroin, Niamh. *The Singing Warrior: Finding Happiness After a Past Filled With Pain*. Summertime Publishing, 2011.

Parfitt, Jo, ed. *Forced to Fly: An Anthology of Writings That Will Make You See the Funny Side of Living Abroad*. Summertime Publishing, 2nd ed., 2012.

Parfitt, Jo and Colleen Reichrath-Smith. *A Career in Your Suitcase*. Summertime Publishing, 4th ed., 2013.

Pascoe, Robin. *A Broad Abroad: The Expat Wife's Guide to Living Abroad*. Expatriate Press Limited, 2009.

Pascoe, Robin. *A Moveable Marriage: Relocate Your Relationship Without Breaking It*. Expatriate Press, 2003.

Pascoe, Robin. *Raising Global Nomads: Parenting Abroad in an On-Demand World*. Expatriate Press, 2006.

Pascoe, Robin. *Homeward Bound: A Spouse's Guide to Repatriation*. Expatriate Press, 2000.

Payot Karpathakis, Emmanuelle. *Pixie's New Home*. Summertime Publishing, 2012.

Payot Karpathakis, Emmanuelle. *Pixie's Holidays*. Summertime Publishing, 2013.

Pittman, Dr. Lisa and Diana Smits. *Expat Teens Talk: Peers, Parents and Professionals Offer Support, Advice and Solutions in Response to Expat Life Challenges as Shared by Expat Teens*. Summertime Publishing, 2012.

Pollock, David C. and Ruth E. Van Reken. *Third Culture Kids: Growing Up Among Worlds*. Nicholas Brealey Publishing, 3rd ed. 2009.

Puddicombe, Andy. *How Mindfulness Can Change Your Life in Ten Minutes a Day: A Guided Meditation*. St. Martin's Griffin, 2012.

Quick, Tina L. *The Global Nomad's Guide to University Transition*. Summertime Publishing, 2010.

Reivich, Karen, Ph.D. and Andrew Shatté, Ph.D. *The Resilience Factor: Seven Keys to Finding Your Inner Strength and Overcoming Life's Hurdles*. Broadway Books, 2002.

Sand-Hart, Heidi. *Home Keeps Moving: A Glimpse Into the Extraordinary Life of a Third Culture Kid*. McDougal Publishing, 2010.

Scott, Jack. *Perking the Pansies: Jack and Liam Move to Turkey*. Summertime Publishing, 2011.

Seiden, Othniel J., MD. *The Joy of Volunteering: Working and Surviving in Developing Countries*. Thornton Publishing, 2007.

Seligman, Martin E. P., Ph.D. *Learned Optimism: How to Change Your Mind and Your Life*. Vintage, 2006

Seligman, Martin E. P., Ph.D. *Authentic Happiness: Using the New Positive Psychology to Realize Your Potential for Lasting Fulfillment*. Free Press, 2002.

Seligman, Martin E. P., Ph.D. *Flourish: A Visionary Understanding of Happiness and Well-being*. Free Press, 2011.

Siebert, Al, Ph.D. *The Resiliency Advantage: Master Change, Thrive Under Pressure, and Bounce Back From Setbacks*. Berrett-Koehler Publishers, Inc., 2005.

Silverton, Sarah. *The Mindfulness Breakthrough: The Revolutionary Approach to Dealing with Stress, Anxiety and Depression*. Watkins Publishing, 2012.

Simens, Julia. *Emotional Resilience and the Expat Child: Practical Tips and Storytelling Techniques That Will Strengthen the Global Family*. Summertime Publishing, 2011.

Smith, Carolyn D., ed. *Strangers at Home: Essays on the Effects of Living Overseas and Coming 'Home' to a Strange Land.* Aletheia Publications, 1996.

Stephens, Laura J. *An Inconvenient Posting: An Expat Wife's Memoir of Lost Identity.* Summertime Publishing, 2012.

Storti, Craig. *The Art of Crossing Cultures.* Intercultural Press, 2nd ed., 2007.

Thomas, David C. and Kerr Inkson. *Cultural Intelligence: Living and Working Globally.* Berrett-Koehler Publishers, 2009.

Transler, Catherine. *Turning International: How to Find Happiness and Feel at Home in a New Culture.* De Zandloper Publications, 2012.

Van Reken, Ruth E. *Letters Never Sent: A Global Nomad's Journey From Hurt to Healing.* Summertime Publishing, 4th ed., 2012.

Vines, Carolyn. *Black and (A)broad: Traveling Beyond the Limitations of Identity.* Adelaar Books, 2010.

Westman, Jack C., MD., MS., and Victoria Costello. *The Complete Idiot's Guide to Child and Adolescent Psychology.* Alpha Books, 2011.

Williams, Wendy. *The Globalization of Love.* Originally published Summertime Publishing, 2011.

Zolli, Andrew and Ann Marie Healy. *Resilience: Why Things Bounce Back.* Free Press, 2012.

ARTICLES/ ESSAYS

Bhattacharjee, Yudhijit. *The Benefits of Bilingualism: Why Bilinguals Are Smarter.* New York Times Sunday Review, Mar. 17, 2012.

Brody, Jane E. *At Every Age, Feeling the Effects of Too Little Sleep.* New York Times, Oct. 23, 2007.

Brody, Jane E. *A Good Night's Sleep Isn't a Luxury – It's a Necessity.* New York Times, May 30, 2011.

Chan, Amanda L. *Mindfulness Meditation Benefits: Twenty Reasons Why It's Good for Your Mental and Physical Health.* The Huffington Post online.

Connor, Kathryn M., MD. *Assessment of Resilience in the Aftermath of Trauma.* Journal of Clinical Psychiatry, 2006; 67 (suppl 2): 46-49.

Coutu, Diane L. *How Resilience Works.* Harvard Business Review, May 2002.

Coutu, Diane L. *How Resilience Works: Improvising Your Way Out of Trouble.* Harvard Business School Working Knowledge, Aug. 26, 2002.

Ernst & Young's Globalization Report. *Looking Beyond the Obvious: Globalization and New Opportunities for Growth.* Released Jan. 2013. *update*

Grappo, Rebecca. *Building Resiliency in Global Nomads.* US Foreign Service Journal, December 2008; 76.

Grappo, Rebecca. *Promoting Your Child's Emotional Health.* US Foreign Service Journal, June 2011; 73.

Hofstede, Geert. *Dimensionalizing Cultures: The Hofstede Model in Context.* Online Readings in Psychology and Culture (International Association for Cross-Cultural Psychology), 2(1) Article 8, 2011.

Jha, Alok. *Being Bilingual May Delay Alzheimer's and Boost Brain Power.* The Guardian, Feb. 18, 2011.

Johnson, James P., Lenartowicz T., Apud, S. *Academy of International Business.* Journal of International Business Studies, 2006

Lambiri, Vicki. *TCKs Come of Age.* March, 2005.

McCaig, Norma M. *Growing Up With a World View: Nomad Children Develop Multi-Cultural Skills.* US Foreign Service Journal, September 1994, 32.

Petriglieri, Gianpiero. *Moving Around Without Losing Your Roots.* Harvard Business Review online, Oct. 3, 2012.

Quick, Tina L. *The Four Pearls of Successful University Transition.* Expatarrivals.com.

Schaetti, Barbara. *Phoenix Rising: A Question of Cultural Identity. Strangers at Home: Essays on the Effects of Living Overseas and Coming 'Home' to a Strange Land.* Carolyn D. Smith, ed. Aletheia Publications, 1996. Link to an adapted version of the essay here: http://www.transition-dynamics.com/phoenix.html

WEBSITES

ACCOMPANYING PARTNER CAREER SUPPORT

www.GlobalNiche.net – Seasoned expat professionals in culture, media, psychology and information technology, lead a community helping others combine their experience, talents and interests to discover borderless life/ work solutions.

www.ThrivingAbroad.com – The Thriving Abroad four-part *Decide-to-Thrive* program enables global mobility and talent management professionals to meet the challenge of addressing the needs of their assignees' accompanying partners. They support the expat accompanying partner through the entire relocation experience, from initial decision to creation of a fulfilled life abroad.

CULTURAL INTELLIGENCE/ INTERCULTURAL COMPETENCY

www.culturalq.com – The Cultural Intelligence Center, led by Dr. David Livermore and Dr. Linn van Dyne, is dedicated to improving the understanding of cultural intelligence. Website includes assessment tools, certification, research and information, training and consulting.

www.GoCultureInternational.com – Home of the GoCulture Assessment tool, this website uses intercultural competency assessment and coaching to devise flexible solutions for cultural preparation and support. *'We focus on helping you discover your capabilities and channeling your mobility efforts.'*

EMOTIONAL/ SOCIAL INTELLIGENCE

http://danielgoleman.info – Daniel Goleman's website on emotional, social and ecological intelligence, including a blog, articles, news on developments in the EQ field, and assessments to measure emotional intelligence.

www.emotional-intelligence-education.com – Run by serial expat Helen Maffini, this website explores social emotional learning and wellbeing tools: activities, skills, games, and the latest research to enhance your family's emotional intelligence.

www.talentsmart.com – Website offering free articles, books, tests, information and a newsletter, billing itself as the *'world's #1 provider of emotional intelligence'*.

EXPAT/ CROSS-CULTURALS

http://www.ameriforce.net – AmeriForce Publishing offers publications supporting US military members and families (e.g., Military Families magazine).

www.ExpatArrivals.com – Local information for global expats, including country, city and international school guides, articles and an expat forum.

www.Expatica.com – News and information for the international community of English-speaking expatriates living, working, studying in, and moving to the Netherlands, Belgium, Luxembourg, Germany, France, Spain, Portugal, Switzerland, United Kingdom, South Africa and Moscow.

www.EasyExpat.com – Information for expatriates on overseas moving and relocation abroad, including city guides, expat forums, expat blog network, interviews, classifieds and job listings.

www.ExpatFocus.com – Information and advice for expats moving, living, working and retiring abroad. Learn about jobs, visas, banking, insurance, property, retirement overseas.

www.ExpatWomen.com – Expat community site for expatriate women living overseas. Includes interviews, expat blog directory, success abroad stories and relocation resources.

www.FIGT.org – The Families in Global Transition organization, global leader in cross-cultural education and training to support the entire expat family. FIGT offers information-packed conferences and year-round benefits through its Membership Program and expanding educational website.

www.InterchangeInstitute.org – Dr. Anne P. Copeland's not-for-profit research organization to help smooth intercultural transitions. They conduct research on the process of intercultural transition, produce publications to assist newcomers to the US, design and deliver specialized cross-cultural training workshops, and train and consult professionals in the field.

www.InternationalFamilyTransitions.com – Comprehensive service specializing in helping students who have been living outside their passport countries, successfully manage their transition to college/ university, whether they are returning to their home country or going on to another host country. IFT also provides resources to those who support TCKs and other international students on the receiving end.

MENTAL HEALTH

www.InternationalTherapistDirectory.com – This website provides an increasingly comprehensive online global listing of professional mental health therapists familiar with the TCK and international expatriate experiences.

www.mayoclinic.com/health/depression/MH00103_D – This is the link for the *Depression Self-Assessment* on the Mayo Clinic website, where clinical experts provide current medical information and news on health topics. There is extensive information on depression and anxiety, and you can sign up for a '*Managing Depression*' newsletter.

www.MentalHelp.net – This website exists to promote mental health and wellness education, information and advocacy. Offers resources in self-help, psychology and mental health, and has psychiatrists online around the clock to answers questions.

www.PsychologyToday.com '*Health, help and happiness*' commentary, research and news covering all aspects of human behavior, from the workings of the brain, to relationships, family life, emotion management and mental health.

www.webmd.com/depression/depression-health-check/ – This is the *Depression Health Check* on the WebMD website, a leading source for trustworthy and timely health and medical news and information: '*better information, better health.*'

MINDFULNESS/ MEDITATION

www.FreeMindfulness.org – '*A project in compassionate collaboration.*' Home to a growing collection of free downloads/ exercises for mindfulness-based meditation.

www.helpguide.org/mental/stress_relief_meditation_yoga_relaxation.htm – Learn how to relieve stress and boost your mood with powerful relaxation techniques in this article on HelpGuide.org. '*Expert, Ad-Free Resources Help You Resolve Health Challenges.*'

POSITIVE PSYCHOLOGY

http://www.authentichappiness.sas.upenn.edu/Default.aspx – The website of Dr. Martin Seligman, Director of the University of Pennsylvania's Positive Psychology Center. In addition to articles, resources and information on initiatives in positive psychology and well-being, it contains questionnaires on emotions, engagement, meaning and life satisfaction.

THIRD CULTURE/ CROSS-CULTURAL KIDS

www.DenizenMag.com – An online magazine created by twenty-something Third Culture Kids, to build a thriving community centered on quality content and relevant conversation on TCK topics of interest. It represents the modern global nomad community, complete with attitude, expression and creativity.

www.DrieCulturen.blogspot.nl – Dutch for 'three cultures', this blog written by an adult TCK is: *'All about kids growing up in other cultures: Third Culture Kids, expat kids, refugee kids, immigrant kids.'*

www.expat-kids.com – *'The Insider's Guide to Expatriate Kids'* website providing news and tips for expat parents and children.

www.ExpatKidsClub.com – Child psychologist Kate Berger offers cultural consultancy and mental health coaching for expatriate children and adolescents (i.e., Third Culture Kids), who are challenged with day-to-day issues surrounding life in a non-native country.

www.expatteenstalk.blogspot.com – Psychologist Lisa Pittman and Educational Therapist Diana Smit's blog about issues faced by expat teens in their book of the same name.

www.HomeKeepsMoving.blogspot.com – Heidi Sand-Hart's site continues *'the rambles of a Third Culture Kid'* as she makes her way in the world.

http://ismk.org/ – The International Society of Missionary Kids website seeks to equip, engage and enable missionary families. It includes sections for missionary kids (MKs), adult MK, and MK parents as well as other general information.

www.jsimens.com – Julia Simens' website helping transitioning families worldwide. It includes her articles on early childhood, education, identifying and dealing with emotions, parenting and handling transitions.

www.passionateparenting.nl – Passionate Parenting's specialist services (including seminars, workshops and resources) are designed to benefit expat, international and local parents of children of all ages in The Hague, Netherlands.

CONTRIBUTORS

Tara Agacayak is an American expat in Turkey and co-founder of GlobalNiche.net – www.globalniche.net her third business venture. She promotes creative entrepreneurship of the self – www.taraagacayak.com

Kate Allison is one of the co-founders of *The Displaced Nation*, a website for global voyagers, where she writes the popular fiction serial *Libby's Life*. Visit her at – http://thedisplacednation.com

Antoine has lived in England, Malta, Belgium and now the Czech Republic and considers himself to be British, Maltese, and occasionally, confused. He blogs about this at – http://unexpectedtraveller.wordpress.com

Anastasia Ashman is a 'visionary for the global life we lead' and a Californian with 14 years abroad in three countries. She is co-founder of www.GlobalNiche.net and creator of Expat Harem – www.about.me/anastasia.ashman

Aisha Ashraf is a freelance writer and creator of *Expatlog: Life Without Borders* – a collection of irreverent observations on mental, physical and spiritual journeys from an accidental expat cultural chameleon – http://expatlog.com

David Beckett, author of *Amsterdam...the Essence and Three Minute Presentation: 33 Three Minute Tools to Help You Deliver Outstanding Presentations*, creator of the Best Three Minutes series, digital publisher and iBooks developer – www.theessenceonline.com, and www.best3minutes.com

Liam Brennan is a composer/ musician and long-suffering husband of the author Jack Scott. In 2008 the plucky couple moved to Turkey and the best-selling book, *Perking the Pansies, Jack and Liam Move to Turkey*, was born – www.jackscott.info/liams-music

Tracey Buckenmeyer has worked in humanitarian aid for more than 20 years, with the Peace Corps and the United Nations. Her job gives a unique perspective of the world, which she tries to capture through photography and writing.

Elie Calhoun is an ATCK and American aid worker who's lived most of her life in Africa, including Kenya, Egypt, Tanzania, Liberia and Senegal. She helps expats live healthier, happier lives and writes at – www.expatbackup.com

Carole is a tree-hugging British expat with a bizarre sense of humor, living in Portugal. She struggles with the various problems associated with integrating with the locals, due to cultural and language problems. Fortunately the Portuguese don't seem to mind, although some 'holier than thou' expats are a different matter. She blogs at – http://pigletinportugal.com

Philippe Caron-Audet hails from Quebec City and has been living abroad since the age of 18. He has worked and resided in France, England, Malaysia, Switzerland, Czech Republic and Tunisia. He is a French teacher passionate about discovering new ways and cultures.

Sara Crabtree is an American expat and lives with her family in the Netherlands after stints in Australia and Scotland. Her oldest children are back in the US studying and working. Previously working as a chemical engineer in the energy sector, she now is an active volunteer in her community.

Jane Dean is an Anglo-American expat/ serial immigrant. Her family of TCK/ global nomads have flown and nested across the globe, bringing a new learning curve of global parenting. She is an editor and writer currently living in the Netherlands – www.wordgeyser.com and Twitter @wordgeyser.

Ameena Falchetto is a half English, half Egyptian adult TCK born in Dubai. She's started businesses in the UAE and in the South of France where she is a Marketing Consultant helping entrepreneurs globally – http://ameenafalchetto.com

Deborah Fletcher is a Brit who escaped the greyness of the UK in 2003, fled to beautiful southern Spain, adapted. Wrote a book along the way and collected some ridiculous animals. Not yet dead (as far as she knows). Blogs at – www.bittenbyspain.com

Maria Foley is a Canadian writer and repat who has lived, worked, and raised TCKs in Australia, Singapore, and France (twice). She is the Culture Subject Matter Expert at Global Connection and blogs about expat and repat life at – www.iwasanexpatwife.com

Cat Foster spent 15 years of her childhood in South East Asia before returning to the USA for university. She graduated with a degree in Journalism in hopes of continuing to see the world. You can find her writing portfolio and blogs at – http://catfoster2009.wordpress.com

Kathleen Gamble is an American TCK born and raised overseas who continued the expat life as an adult. Now back in the US she blogs at – www.ExpatAlien.com and writes a weekly column at the Baltimore Post Examiner. Her memoir *Expat Alien* came out of her childhood journals.

Michelle Garrett is a long-term American expat making a life overseas, raising a blended family, herding cats, chasing chickens and attempting the Good Life in England – www.theamericanresident.com

Liv Gaunt is an experienced expat and world traveler who shares her many misadventures (in addition to photos and travel tips) at The World is Waiting – www.theworldswaiting.com

Martha P. Gonzalez is a hereditary expat who lives with her husband in Sakhalin Island, Russia, after having lived six years in the Netherlands with their family. Their two children now attend college back in the US. She blogs at – http://fmfegonz1.blogspot.nl

Cecilia Gotherstrom is a certified Yoga teacher and nutritionist, founder of Ahimsa & Satya Yoga & Nutrition in The Netherlands. Teaches, coaches and writes about Yoga, nutrition and animal communication in English, Swedish and Dutch language markets across all layers of society – www.ahimsa-satya.com, http://yogalifenutrition.wordpress.com

Rebecca Grappo, founder of RNG International Education Consultants, LLC, has given numerous presentations on TCKs in addition to written articles for print publications and online sites. She specializes in individualized student placement for boarding schools and universities. Her website is – www.rnginternational.com

Natasha Gunn is a writer, online journalist and yoga teacher. She has lived and worked in London, Paris, and now Amsterdam, where she lives with her two children – www.makingspace2change.com

Kym Hamer is an Australian businesswoman and writer, living in London and blogging at – www.GiddayFromTheUK.com

Valerie Hamer is a writer, global nomad, coffee addict and author of *Picky, Sticky or Just Plain Icky?* and *A Blind Date Conversation: South Korea* – www.smashwords.com/books/view/137638 and – www.farawayhammerwriting.com

Jeremy Holland is an Anglo-American ATCK who spent his formative years in the

Philippines, Saudi Arabia and England. He is the author of *From Barcelona: Stories Behind the City* – http://books4spain.com/book/detail/from-barcelona-1 about his recent years in Spain. He works for the non-profit WYSE travel confederation – http://www.wysetc.org/ in the Netherlands.

Annie Huang currently lives in Los Angeles, California. Though it's a home, she's already planning her next one. Follow her on twitter @msanniehuang.

Janneke Jellema is a Dutch adult TCK (Zambia, Malawi, Zimbabwe) and medical doctor now living in the Netherlands. She blogs as DrieCulturen (Three Cultures) *'all about children growing up in other cultures'* http://drieculturen.blogspot.com/ and you can follow her on twitter @DrieCulturen.

Dorota Klop-Sowinska Expat and International Career Coach, Founder of www.dosocoaching.com supporting, motivating and empowering internationals to a successful career and life abroad. Author of the *ABC of Expat Woman's Life series*.

Sarah Koblow is a mother, writer, social worker, counselor, teacher, serial expat and successful STAR (Spouse Travelling and Relocating). She currently lives in Doha, Qatar while completing her memoir, PGCE teacher certification and battling with menopause. She blogs at – www.countonlysunnyhours.wordpress.com

Erica Knecht is a Canadian living in Indonesia by way of Japan, China, India, Switzerland and France. She is a mother, professional nomad, freelance writer, blogger and lover of cheese. No surprise then, that she married a Swiss chef. She writes about the culture of parenting at – http://www.expatriababy.com

Matt Krause, American writer and expat, has what can only be described as a deep and discerning love affair with Turkey. Author of several books including *A Tight Wide-open Space*, he recently completed the 1,300 plus mile walk across Turkey, sharing his progress, perceptions and insights along the way and gathering material for new books – http://heathenpilgrim.com

Nicole Le Maire, founder of Human Resources Global Limited and NewToHR draws on her years of experience to assist expatriates and HR professionals. Her consultancy assists small organizations and junior HR professionals in a non-traditional HR way. She has lived in the US and many countries in Europe and the Middle East – www.humanresourcesglobal.com/, www.NewToHR.com

Helen Maffini is a serial expat who has lived in eleven countries with her husband and two daughters. She is passionate about Third Culture Kids and exploring ideas to help these children. She is the author of two books, *Sammy's Next Move*, and *Developing Children's Emotional Intelligence* – www.emotional-intelligence-education.com/ and www.family-travel-scoop.com

Chris Marshall lives in Almerimar with his wife Sands, five cats, two Harley Davidsons and far too often a glass of red wine. He runs the expat website – www.almerimarlife.com and spends as much time as he can helping Sands with their re-homing and transport project for abandoned and rescued cats and dogs in Spain – www.alstrays.com

Nicola McCall, MCIPD, is a Human Resources and Coaching professional now repatriated to the UK, Nicola's way of life has always had an international focus due to her upbringing, career and relationships – www.livelifenowcoaching.com

Sareen McLay lived in Oman and Malaysia before moving to the Netherlands. She has recently been the poet-in-residence for *The Underground* monthly newspaper in The Hague. In addition to taking various writing courses, she is currently working on a book for children.

Raquel L. Miranda writes a family travel blog about US Foreign Service family of five, three being children under seven years of age, sharing three languages, cultural differences and social adjustments daily. Impressions as foreigners, spouses, parents, travelers – www.3rdCultureChildren

Craig Myles is a stay-at-home dad whose family relocated from a market town in the home counties of England to South Florida in 2011. He writes about parenting, travelling, and living as an expat – www.trailinghusband.com and on Twitter as @TrailingHusband.

Niamh Ni Bhroin is an Irish writer living in the Netherlands. She is author of *The Singing Warrior* and blogs at www.thesingingwarrior.com

Rose P. is an American expat living with her husband and two children in The Hague, Netherlands. She works for an international organization.

Jo Parfitt, author, publisher, journalist, speaker, writing mentor and owner of SummertimePublishing.com and ExpatBookshop.com. Her primary website is www.joparfitt.com and Twitter @joparfitt.

Reina Rácz is a Dutch-Hungarian ATCK, writer, illustrator, translator and editor at www.rites.eu currently living in the Netherlands.

Judy Rickatson is a Canadian immigrant/ expat/ repat who has lived in the UK, Azerbaijan, Egypt and the UAE and currently serves as Social Media Manager for Families in Global Transitions. She blogs at – http://www.expatriatelife.wordpress.com/ and tweets as @wifeinasuitcase.

Catherine Salter Bayar is a California native Catherine designer/ writer who designed textiles, clothing and interiors worldwide before moving to Turkey in 1999. Now in Istanbul, she weaves words, fibers and handcrafts into a creative force for bridging cultures – http://www.bazaarbayar.com

Heidi Sand-Hart is an adult Third Culture Kid who grew up in England, India and Norway due to her parent's work. She wrote *Home Keeps Moving* as a tool to help fellow TCKs and bring more exposure to the topic – http://homekeepsmoving.blogspot.com

Carrie Sanderson is a writer and Adult CCK. She blogs about health and well-being at – http://carrie-health-healing.blogspot.com and shares her creativity at – http://carriesanderson.wordpress.com

Ingrid Schippers is a yoga-based personal development counselor, workshop presenter and author of *The Life Makeover Manual, Journey Book* and the *Who Am I* personal development cards – http://www.theportableyogacompany.com/. Together with Scotsman Tom McKerley, she co-authored the genealogy mystery bestseller, *Bloodlines: Touch Not the Cat* –http://www.touchnotthecat.com

Jack Scott, washed-up ex-pretty boy and accidental author of *Perking the Pansies, Jack and Liam Move to Turkey*, a bitter-sweet tragi-comedy recalling the first year of a gay couple in a Muslim land. Look out for the next instalment, *The Sisterhood*, coming out soon – www.jackscott.info and www.perkingthepansies.com

Charalampos Sergios is a Greek expat currently residing in Amsterdam. He is the co-founder of – www.IamExpat.nl and an amateur photographer – www.Photographi.com

Evelyn Simpson, co-author of the *Career Choice and the Accompanying Partner Survey Report*, is a Director of Simpson, Wiles and Associates Ltd. She is the co-creator of Thriving Abroad, a comprehensive support system for accompanying partners designed to facilitate empowered international relocations. Evelyn has lived in six countries on three continents and currently calls Brussels, Belgium home – evelyn@thrivingabroad.com, www.thrivingabroad.com

Nicky Sully is a South African expat language teacher and lives in The Hague, Netherlands with her husband. She has also lived in Tanzania, Rwanda and Cambodia. She has two grown up sons.

The Over-thinking Expat is an American living in the United Arab Emirates, writing about her experiences and observations as an expatriate, a traveler, and a human – http://www.overthinkingexpat.wordpress.com

Patti Tito, an American, became an expat in the Netherlands when her husband accepted a position with an international company. Her background is in the ICT field. One of the things she loves about living in the Netherlands is that town centers are set up for bicyclists and walkers – http://www.linkedin.com/in/pattibtito

Roy Lie A. Tjam is a Caribist, hailing from the Caribbean. He is active in the expat world as an event organizer and information officer. He also reviews books and writes articles. rojax@usa.net.

Heather Van Deest is a writer and editor who has lived in Bangkok, Thailand since 2005.

Norm Viss is an American repat after three decades abroad in Nigeria and the Netherlands. A certified, accredited professional coach and author with BA and Masters degrees in cross-cultural studies and theology, he applies his extensive experience to help others deal with isolation and build community as co-founder of Expat Everyday Support Center – http://expateverydaysupportcenter.com

Russell V. J. Ward has been a British expat for more than a decade. Having lived in Canada by mountains and snow, he now lives in Sydney by the ocean and writes about his search for a different way of life at – www.insearchofalifelessordinary.com. He can be found on Twitter as @russellvjward.

Stephanie Ward is the Marketing Coach for Entrepreneurs. Get her Free Special Report, *7 Steps to Attract More Clients in Less Time* at – www.fireflycoaching.com

Louise Wiles currently lives in Lisbon, Portugal, and is a Director in Simpson, Wiles and Associates Ltd and co-creator of *Thriving Abroad*, a comprehensive support solution for accompanying partners designed to facilitate empowered international relocations. Louise@thrivingabroad.com – www.thrivingabroad.com

Steph Yiu is an ATCK and the founder of an online magazine for Third Culture Kids and Global Nomads – www.DenizenMag.com

Shannon Young, an American writer, has lived in England and now Hong Kong. She's the author of *The Olympics Beat: A Spectator's Memoir of Beijing* – http://shannonyoungwriter.com

Rebecca Claudia Zijderveld, an 18 year-old repatriated TCK who has lived in the Netherlands, Italy, Sweden, Dubai, Singapore and finally back to the Netherlands. She plans to study management in the UK and aspires to work as a marketing manager in an international business.

Susan Zijderveld has moved seven times in 20 years in Australasia, Europe, Asia and the Middle East, with a multinational company. She and her husband have a mixed culture marriage, and both are Adult TCKs, making their children third-generation TCKs.

INDEX

ABOUT THE AUTHOR

Linda Janssen is a writer, speaker, consultant, global adventurer and cultural enthusiast. With a B.A. in International Relations and a Masters in Public and International Affairs, she has spent nearly three decades working in and around the international arena. Passionate about exploring and learning across cultures, she has traveled to more than 30 countries on five continents, and lived in the US, Mexico and the Netherlands. Her website, www.AdventuresinExpatLand.com, contains resources, information and her popular blog on topics of interest in expatriate, cross-cultural life. She is married to an adult Third Culture Kid, the mother of two TCKs, and lives with her family in the Netherlands.

Check out www.theemotionallyresilientexpat.com

For bulk orders at a corporate/ group rate, please email the author at linda@theemotionallyresilientexpat.com

ALSO AVAILABLE FROM SUMMERTIME PUBLISHING:

"An entertaining story, told with wit and insight"
Paul Burston, author, The Gay Divorcee

PERKING
THE PANSIES

Jack and Liam move to Turkey

JACK SCOTT

FOREWORD BY DOUG OTA

EMOTIONAL RESILIENCE
AND THE EXPAT CHILD

Practical tips and storytelling techniques that will strengthen the global family

Julia Simens

The
Global Nomad's Guide
to
UNIVERSITY TRANSITION

Tina L. Quick

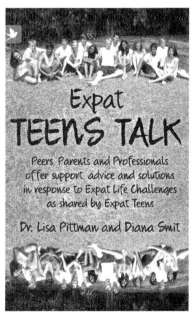

Expat
TEENS TALK

Peers, Parents and Professionals offer support, advice and solutions in response to Expat Life Challenges as shared by Expat Teens

Dr. Lisa Pittman and Diana Smit

357

CPSIA information can be obtained
at www.ICGtesting.com
Printed in the USA
LVOW04s2119200916

505505LV00007B/10/P

9 781909 193338